American Labor and Economic Citizenship

Once viewed as a distinct era characterized by intense bigotry, nostalgia for simpler times, and a revulsion against active government, the 1920s have been rediscovered by historians in recent decades as a time when Herbert Hoover and his allies worked to significantly reform economic policy. In *American Labor and Economic Citizenship*, Mark Hendrickson both augments and amends this view by studying the origins and development of New Era policy expertise and knowledge. Policy-oriented social scientists in government, trade union, academic, and nonprofit agencies showed how methods for achieving stable economic growth through increased productivity could both defang the dreaded business cycle and defuse the pattern of hostile class relations that Gilded Age depressions had helped to set as an American system of industrial relations. Linked by emerging institutions such as the Social Science Research Council, the National Urban League, and the Women's Bureau, social investigators attacked rampant sexual and racial discrimination, often justified by fallacious biological arguments, that denied female and minority workers full economic citizenship in the workplace and the polity. These scholars demonstrated that these practices not only limited productivity and undercut expanded consumption, but also belied the claims for fairness that must buttress policy visions in a democracy.

Mark Hendrickson is an assistant professor of history at the University of California, San Diego.

American Labor and Economic Citizenship

New Capitalism from World War I to the Great Depression

MARK HENDRICKSON
University of California, San Diego

CAMBRIDGE
UNIVERSITY PRESS

University Printing House, Cambridge CB2 8BS, United Kingdom

One Liberty Plaza, 20th Floor, New York, NY 10006, USA

477 Williamstown Road, Port Melbourne, VIC 3207, Australia

314-321, 3rd Floor, Plot 3, Splendor Forum, Jasola District Centre, New Delhi - 110025, India

103 Penang Road, #05-06/07, Visioncrest Commercial, Singapore 238467

Cambridge University Press is part of the University of Cambridge.

It furthers the University's mission by disseminating knowledge in the pursuit of education, learning and research at the highest international levels of excellence.

www.cambridge.org
Information on this title: www.cambridge.org/9781107028609

© Mark Hendrickson 2013

This publication is in copyright. Subject to statutory exception and to the provisions of relevant collective licensing agreements, no reproduction of any part may take place without the written permission of Cambridge University Press.

First published 2013
First paperback edition 2015

A catalogue record for this publication is available from the British Library

Library of Congress Cataloging in Publication data
Hendrickson, Mark, 1971–
American labor and economic citizenship: new capitalism from World War I to the Great
Depression / Mark Hendrickson, University of California, San Diego.
pages cm
Includes bibliographical references and index.
ISBN 978-1-107-02860-9 (hardback)
1. Labor – United States – History – 20th century. 2. Labor policy – United States – History – 20th century. 3. United States – Economic conditions – 1918–1945. 4. United States – Economic policy. 5. Capitalism – United States – History – 20th century. I. Title.
HD8072.H37 2013
331.0973´09042–dc23 2012044076

ISBN 978-1-107-02860-9 Hardback
ISBN 978-1-107-55967-7 Paperback

Cambridge University Press has no responsibility for the persistence or accuracy of URLs for external or third-party internet websites referred to in this publication, and does not guarantee that any content on such websites is, or will remain, accurate or appropriate.

For Mary O. Furner

Contents

List of Illustrations and Table	page ix
Acknowledgments	xi
Abbreviations	xv

	Introduction	1
1.	"Hoovering" in the Twenties: Efficiency, Wages, and Growth in the "New Economic System"	35
	Postwar Labor Unrest and the Arrival of Herbert Hoover	39
	Confronting and Defining Waste in Industry	42
	A Public Concern: The Workday in the Steel Industry	47
	Wages, Hours, and "a Feeling of Partnership"	56
	"This Almost Insatiable Appetite for Goods and Services": The NBER Celebrates the Worker-Consumer	64
	Conclusion	75
2.	Wages and the Public Interest: Economists and the Wage Question in the New Era	78
	Mistakes and Makeovers: Wage and Price Statistics, 1914–1925	82
	Measuring Wages in the Postwar Era	91
	Wages as a Public Concern	94
	Prosperity and Wage Justice: The Post-1922 Real Wage Increase	104
	Conclusion	108
3.	Enlightened Labor? Labor's Share and Economic Stability	111
	The AFL's Search for a New Mission	116
	The Rise of the Labor Research Bureau	119
	More than Just More: A New Wage Policy for Organized Labor	124
	Labor's New Friends	129
	The AFL as a Watchdog for Economic Stability	134

	Open the Books: The LBI's Examination of Profits	139
	"Assuming Responsibility for Service:" The B&O Experiment	141
	Conclusion	151
4.	A New Capitalism?: Interrogating Employers' Efforts to Cultivate a "Feeling of Partnership" in Industry	154
	Interrogating New Capitalism: The RSF Studies	160
	The Filene Department Store and Dutchess Bleachery Investigations	162
	The Rockefeller Plan in the Coal and Steel Industry	171
	Conclusion: A New Capitalism?	178
5.	Gender Research as Labor Activism: The Women's Bureau in the New Era	180
	Empowering Expertise: The Creation of the Women's Bureau	188
	Redefining Women Workers as Breadwinners	194
	Labor Inquiry as Activism through Gendered and Race Knowledge	197
	Advocating Labor Standards Before and After Adkins	204
	Conclusion	213
6.	The New "Negro Problem"	216
	An Intractable Condition	219
	Celebration and Concern: First Steps at Making Sense of the Migration	222
	The Rise and Fall of the Division of Negro Economics	229
	The Red Summer and the Emergence of Charles S. Johnson	239
	Conclusion	246
7.	Promising Problems: Working toward a Reconstructed Understanding of the African American and Mexican Worker	249
	Framing the Postwar Immigration Debate	253
	Reconstructing the Public Perception of the Negro Problem	267
	Considering the Relative Position of the Negro and Mexican Worker	279
	Remaking the Public Image of the Mexican Problem	284
	Conclusion	292
	Conclusion	295
Archival Sources and Abbreviations		307
Index		309

Illustrations and Table

ILLUSTRATIONS

3.1.	"O. K. Choir of Researchers"	*page* 121
3.2.	Baltimore and Ohio Cartoon	149
4.1.	Russell Sage Foundation Cartoon	177

TABLE

5.1.	Were African American Women Underrepresented in WB Reports Relative to their Presence in Industry?	204

Acknowledgments

I have incurred many intellectual, professional, and personal debts during the research and writing of this book. It is a pleasure to have this space to acknowledge those who have contributed to this project. I dedicate the book to Mary Furner, who directed the dissertation on which this book is based. When I measure myself as a scholar, teacher, and mentor, Mary is the standard. As she does with all of her students, I know Mary devoted an incredible amount of time and energy to my development, and for that I am grateful. A career in academia can be a winding one, and Mary has offered friendship, guidance, and encouragement every step of the way.

The University of California, Santa Barbara, provided a stunning setting in which to study history and a wealth of friends and colleagues who contributed to this work and to my appreciation of the craft of history. Alice O'Connor served on the dissertation committee and has provided guidance in many forms and at many times over the years. The same holds true for Nelson Lichtenstein, who provided invaluable insights that improved the dissertation and the book. John Majewski, Elliot Brownlee, Anne Peterson, Maeve Devoy, Randy Bergstrom, Stephen Weatherford, Eileen Boris, Josh Ashenmiller, John Baranski, Jay Carlander, Sarah Case, Carl Harris, David Torres-Rouffe, and Ken Mouré all contributed in important ways to my intellectual development. Richard Sullivan provided friendship, support, intellectual stimulation, and occasional diversions from the hard work of research and writing.

Roland Guyotte, Bert Ahern, Bart Finzel, Don Thompson, and the late Dimitra Giannuli all served as friends, teachers, and mentors in the early years of my intellectual development. Over the past several years, many friends and colleagues have generously offered helpful guidance on various aspects of the book. I am particularly grateful to Ruth Alexander, Michael Bernstein, Christopher Capozzola, Nayan Shah, Natalia Molina, Nancy Kwak, David Gutiérrez, David Roediger, Todd Henry, May Fu, Andrew Morris, and Casey Walsh. Samara Paysse and Laura Holiday provided editorial assistance at various stages in the book's development.

At Cambridge University Press, Eric Crahan and Debbie Gershenowitz provided guidance and helpful advice throughout the process. The comments of two anonymous readers for Cambridge helped me to sharpen my argument and the book's claims. I am grateful to the University of Chicago Press for permission to draw on my chapter "Steering the State: Government, Nongovernmental Organizations, and the Making of Labor Knowledge in the 1920s," published in Doug Guthrie and Elisabeth Clemens, *Politics and Partnerships: Associations and Nonprofit Organizations in American Governance* © 2010 by The University of Chicago, and to Cambridge University Press and the *Journal of Policy History* for permission to draw on my article "Gender Research as Labor Activism: The Women's Bureau in the New Era."

A number of generous fellowships provided perhaps the most precious resource available to historians: time to research and write. In the early stages of the project, the Social Science Research Council (SSRC) dissertation fellowship on philanthropy and the nonprofit sector provided not only a year to work, but also introduced me to an interdisciplinary group of scholars who shaped the project in its early stages. I am particularly grateful to David Hammack and Elisabeth S. Clemens, who provided helpful comments on early drafts of my work at a dissertation workshop in 2002 for SSRC fellows in Montreal and at the SSRC Capstone Conference on Philanthropy and the Nonprofit Sector in Florence. Clemens and Doug Guthrie's comments on early drafts of an article helped shape both the article and the larger book project. Dissertation fellowships from Aspen Institute and the Institute for Labor and Employment provided an additional two glorious academic years to continue working on the dissertation. At University of California, San Diego, a course reduction in my first year, combined with support for travel to a number of archives, allowed me to conduct much of the research and writing that went into Chapter 7 of the book. The Gertrude and Theodore Debs Memorial Fellowship at Indiana State University gave me the opportunity to begin my graduate training. While at Indiana State, I benefited greatly from Richard Schneirov's friendship and guidance. Having Jason Martinek as friend and classmate at Indiana State University made the experience all the more enjoyable and intellectually stimulating.

Conducting research often involves travel, and timely and crucial support came from a number of sources. In the dissertation phase, travel grants from the Rockefeller Archive Center, Smith College, the All-University of California Economic History Group, and the University of California, Santa Barbara, department of history made a number of trips to archives on the East Coast possible. An appointment with the University of California Washington Center in Washington, DC, provided me with the time to complete a significant portion of the research for the book. More recently, travel support from the Hellman Foundation; the University of California, San Diego, Arts and Humanities Initiative; and the University of California, San Diego, department of history allowed me to finish the research for the book.

While in the archives, I benefited from the assistance of archivists and librarians at the National Archives at College Park, Rockefeller Archive Center, Library of Congress, George Meany Archives, Howard University, Catholic University of America, Sophia Smith Collection at Smith College, Department of Labor, Department of Commerce, Bancroft Library, Herbert Hoover Presidential Library, and Wisconsin Historical Society. Librarians at the University of California, Santa Barbara; Colorado State University; and the University of California, San Diego, provided valuable assistance in finding and retrieving any number of important research materials.

Our home, friends, and family have always provided the most consistent source of joy and support. Most of the writing for the book took place at our dining room table, which was convenient for me, but it meant that Juanita shared her home with mountains of documents and a frequently distracted husband. Juanita's support, love, and patience make it easy to imagine a lifetime together. We have moved from one coast to the other more than once and welcomed into our family two wonderful children, Jack and Kate. Jack's anticipated arrival spurred me to finish the first draft of the dissertation; after he arrived, progress slowed, but his birth and Kate's three years later enriched our family beyond any accounting. My parents, Connie and Jerry Hendrickson, taught me the value of hard work, family, and education. Ruth Hendrickson, my sister, has always been one of my biggest supporters and has spearheaded the effort to ensure that I don't take myself too seriously. I am grateful too for the support of our broader extended family, whose contributions and talents run the gamut from introducing me to the work of Herbert Marcuse to the finer points of carbles, cabinet making, and carpentry. When in search of sustained periods of relaxation and reflection, we have always returned to Lake Superior and our many friends in Michigan's copper country. My thanks to all.

Abbreviations

FREQUENTLY CITED JOURNALS AND PERIODICALS

AER	*American Economic Review*
AF	*American Federationist*
AFL:WNS	*American Federation of Labor Weekly News Service*
AHR	*American Historical Review*
ALLR	*American Labor Legislation Review*
FFW	*Facts for Workers*
IMJ	*International Molders' Journal*
JAH	*Journal of American History*
JASA	*Journal of the American Statistical Association*
JEWO	*Journal of Electrical Workers and Operators*
JPE	*Journal of Political Economy*
JPR	*The Journal of Personnel Research*
LA	*Labor Age*
LEJ	*Locomotive Engineers Journal*
MLR	*Monthly Labor Review*
MMJ	*Machinists Monthly Journal*
NCSW	*Proceedings of the National Conference of Social Work*
NR	*New Republic*
NYT	*New York Times*
PSQ	*Political Science Quarterly*
QJE	*Quarterly Journal of Economics*
RC	*Railway Clerk*
UMWJ	*United Mine Workers Journal*

INSTITUTIONS AND ORGANIZATIONS

AFL	American Federation of Labor
BOC	Bureau of the Census
CFIC	Colorado Fuel and Iron Company
DNE	Division of Negro Economics
DOL	Department of Labor
FCA	Filene Co-operative Association
IAM	International Association of Machinists
LSRM	Laura Spellman Rockefeller Memorial
NAACP	National Association for the Advancement of Colored People
NBER	National Bureau of Economic Research
NCSW	National Conference of Social Work
NICB	National Industrial Conference Board
NUL	National Urban League
NWP	National Women's Party
RSF	Russell Sage Foundation
SSRC	Social Science Research Council
USES	United States Employment Services
WB	Women's Bureau
WIS	Women in Industry Service
WTUL	Women's Trade Union League
YMCA	Young Men's Christian Association
YWCA	Young Women's Christian Association

Introduction

Our society today is as fluid as molten iron; it can be run into any mold.
   George Soule, New Republic *Editor*[1]

The war has "cleared the way for a science of ideas in action" that look to "intellectual competency, to competency of inquiry, discussion, reflection and invention organized to take effect in action directing affairs."
   John Dewey[2]

On June 10, 1929, President Herbert Hoover laid the cornerstone to the new Commerce Building in Washington, DC. Hoover placed a time capsule in the cornerstone that included early U.S. patents, Mark Twain's pilot's license, correspondence by George Washington and Thomas Jefferson, and a copy of the recently released survey of the economy, *Recent Economic Changes*. Referring to the study, Hoover collaborator Assistant Secretary of Commerce E. E. Hunt wondered, "What will be thought by those who open the cornerstone as they read of our enthusiasm over 'consumer demand,' bathtubs, radios, automobiles, a plentiful food supply, steam laundries, high wages, scientific management in industry, and growing leisure? Shall we seem wise or only foolish to those who study us with the detachment of years ago?"[3] Hunt's implied

---

[1] Quoted in Daniel T. Rodgers, *Atlantic Crossings: Social Politics in a Progressive Age* (Cambridge: Belknap Press of Harvard University, 1998), 299.

[2] Quoted in Robert B. Westbrook, *John Dewey and American Democracy* (Ithaca: Cornell University Press, 1991), 276.

[3] E. E. Hunt, "Apologia Pro Vita Nostra," File January 1930, 2, Chronological Files of E. E. Hunt, Box 1, Record Group (hereafter RG) 73, National Archives at College Park, MD (hereafter NA).

optimism would pale in a few short months, as would the ability of most Americans to purchase the consumer marvels mentioned. Even so, the period between World War I and the Great Depression needs to be understood as a unique period, incubating innovative and lasting policy paradigms whose relevance to twentieth-century political-economic history has too often been underestimated.

Initially in response to World War I-era unrest, a diverse group of policy makers addressed a range of long-standing and seemingly intractable problems, confident that the 1920s provided a unique moment full of opportunities. A new, fair, and prosperous version of capitalism, a group led by Herbert Hoover came to understand, could be achieved by focusing on steady economic growth and business cycle stability. *American Labor and Economic Citizenship* depicts this vision as something more than the sum of warmed-over paternalism, welfare capitalism, employee representation schemes, and experiments in scientific management. Adherents to this new economic vision redirected their attention from old sources of conflict and social unrest such as the distribution of income and control of the workplace to new possibilities based on a belief in the shared and common interests of capital and labor in increasing productivity, worker purchasing power, and profits. A confluence of economic changes and circumstances gave this new vision relevance and legitimacy, but demographic changes and new forms of advocacy argued for an expanded understanding of which groups should benefit from these changes. The increasing presence of women in the work force during the war and the migration of African American, Mexican, and Mexican American workers to the industrial North provided an opportunity for a group of emerging experts and reformers to challenge assumptions about race, gender, ethnicity, and work, and to lay claim to the benefits of this new economic system for all workers. Along the way, all of these groups – those surrounding Hoover and those interrogating demographic changes – worked to redefine which issues were best settled between private individuals or local interests and which issues were so entwined with the public and national interest as to merit intervention on behalf of the general public.

George Soule and John Dewey nicely capture the sense of a moment when the truly ferocious changes brought on by World War I left society both inchoate and open to change. Ezra Pound's characterization of Western civilization as "botched" was not shared by economic leaders in the United States, who emerged from the war strangely confident in their ability, as Dewey suggests, to use "inquiry, discussion, reflection and invention" to solve even the most pressing, long-standing, and troublesome of public questions. And we should make no mistake about it; the molten state of postwar America emerged from the heat generated in the cauldron of wartime industrial and international conflict. With wild price and wage volatility reminiscent of the Civil War, workers' significant wartime gains in nominal wages were outpaced by rampant inflation that pushed up the cost of living by some 65 percent over the course of the war.[4] At the same time that World War I stimulated demand for U.S. manufactured goods, immigration plummeted from more than 1.2 million in 1914 to an average of just over 230,000 between 1915 and 1919. In industry, draconian employer treatment of labor and falling real wages led to an unprecedented level of unrest, with four thousand four hundred fifty strikes in 1917 alone.[5] Desperate for workers, industry turned to African American, women, and, increasingly, Mexican workers from the Southwest and Mexico. White workers in cities like East St. Louis responded to the reality of a racially integrated workplace with deadly attacks on black workers and neighborhoods. If American leaders had any real questions about the volatility of the situation, they needed only look to the unfolding Russian Revolution for confirmation.

The armistice, if anything, exacerbated violent conflict at home that pitted not only labor against capital but, increasingly, white workers against black. With the end of fighting, the federal government cancelled most of its wartime contracts and withdrew price controls. Initially, workers and employers benefited from high demand for consumer goods at home and an increase in demand for U.S. goods in war-ravaged Europe, but the prosperity was short-lived and followed by a ferocious mix of inflation and then deflation, unemployment, and labor and racial unrest. Just as veterans returned from the front, with some demanding greater democracy in industry, the cancellation of government contracts shrank demand and the job supply.[6] The loss of price controls and pent up consumer

---

[4] Meg Jacobs, *Pocketbook Politics: Economic Citizenship in Twentieth-Century America* (Princeton: Princeton University Press, 2005), 54.

[5] U.S. BOC, *Historical Statistics, Colonial Times to 1970, bicentennial edition* (Washington, DC: GPO, 1974), Series C89. Also cited in Gary M. Walton and Hugh Rockoff, *History of the American Economy* (Mason: South-Western Cenage Learning, 2010), 387, 403.

[6] On World War I-era unrest and its consequences for labor-management relations, see, for example, Sanford Jacoby, *Employing Bureaucracy: Managers, Unions, and the Transformation of Work in American Industry, 1900-1945* (New York: Columbia University Press, 1985), 133-65; Lizabeth Cohen, *Making a New Deal: Industrial Workers in Chicago, 1919-1939* (Cambridge: Cambridge University Press, 1990), 12-52; Nelson Lichtenstein and Howell John Harris, *Industrial Democracy in America: The Ambiguous Promise* (Cambridge: Cambridge University Press, 1993); and Joseph McCartin, *Labor's*

demand, combined with a sluggish conversion to a consumer economy, led prices to rise some 30 percent between November 1918 and June 1920.[7] As employers mercilessly exercised their postwar leverage to cut wages and drive out unions, American workers walked off the job. In 1919 alone, more than 4 million workers participated in thirty-six hundred strikes.[8]

As it had in 1917, searing racial violence broke out in dozens of American cities during the summer of 1919. Amidst the unprecedented movement of black Americans from the South to the urban North and following violent urban race riots, the *New York Times* described a nation in which the "Negro problem" had "entered upon a new and dangerous phase" that is "in some respects the most grave now facing the country."[9] W. E. B. Dubois reflected a reality, not an aspiration, of American life when he wrote in the *Crisis* in the spring of 1919: "*We return. We return from fighting. We return fighting.*"[10] Resistance to white racism was hardly a new development in African American history, but World War I and the Great Migration provided new tools for that resistance. In New York, the African American population grew by 66 percent in the first years of the Great Migration: in Chicago, it grew by 114 percent, in Detroit by 611 percent, and in Cleveland by 308 percent.[11] When white gangs, such as the Irish Colts in Chicago, attacked black neighborhoods, they met fierce resistance, sometimes by highly trained and battle-tested black soldiers recently mustered out of the military.[12] Harlem Renaissance poet Claude McKay spoke for many when he wrote in 1919, "Like men we'll face the murderous, cowardly pack. Pressed to the wall, dying, but fighting back!"[13]

Great War: The Struggle for Industrial Democracy and the Origins of Modern Labor Relations, 1912–1921 (Chapel Hill: University of North Carolina Press, 1997). On how the war altered ideas about citizenship, see Christopher Capozzola, *Uncle Sam Wants You: World War I and the Making of the Modern Citizen* (Oxford: Oxford University Press, 2008).

[7] Jacobs, *Pocketbook Politics*, 66.
[8] Robert H. Zieger, *American Workers, American Unions*, second edition (Baltimore: Johns Hopkins University Press, 1994), 6.
[9] "For Action on Race Riot Peril," *NYT*, October 5, 1919, sec. 10, p. 1.
[10] W. E. B. Du Bois, "Returning Soldiers," *The Crisis* (May 19, 1919): 13–14.
[11] Nell Irvin Painter, *Creating Black Americans: African-American History and Its Meanings, 1619 to the Present* (New York: Oxford University Press, 2007), 191–2.
[12] William M. Tuttle, Jr., *Race Riot: Chicago in the Red Summer of 1919* (Urbana: University of Illinois Press, 1996).
[13] Claude McKay, "If We Must Die," in *Harlem Shadows: The Poems of Claude McKay* (New York: Harcourt, Brace and Co., 1922), 53. Originally published in *Liberator* in 1919.

Such conflicts as these cried out for action grounded in understanding. In what even now seems like a jarring juxtaposition, the unrest that surrounded World War I coincided with the maturing of an American social science increasingly capable of and confident in its ability to address pressing public concerns. By World War I, a tradition of social inquiry that had its roots in the nineteenth-century work of investigators like Carroll Wright had grown up and was moving outside of the state. Coming now from a range of academic, nonprofit, business, and government agencies, a new class of experts on race relations, labor, and economic issues convened in search of solutions to vexing public problems brought to a head by the war. In the process, they worked toward a greater degree of intellectual authority for their visions of society and their role in bringing them about. Classic works by Gianfranco Poggi, Thomas Kuhn, Clifford Geertz, Max Weber, and other scholars of the state, social investigation, and social and political thought have described how, historically, as states grow and mature they increasingly come to rely on reason and ideas to legitimate the use of power and to defend or argue for particular visions of society.[14] Dating back to the Enlightenment, a recognition

[14] My understanding of the importance of knowledge, ideas, expertise, social learning, institutional capacity, and deliberation in the policy-making process is informed by the work of a range of scholars, most important, Jürgen Habermas, *The Structural Transformation of the Public Sphere: An Inquiry into a Category of Bourgeois Society*, translated by Thomas Burger with the assistance of Frederick Lawrence (Cambridge: MIT Press, 1998); Phillip Ethington, "Hypotheses from Habermas: Notes on Reconstructing American Political and Social History, 1890–1920," *Intellectual History Newsletter* 14 (1992): 21–40; Craig Calhoun, ed., *Habermas and the Public Sphere* (Cambridge: MIT Press, 1997); Hugh Heclo, *Modern Social Politics in Britain and Sweden: From Relief to Income Maintenance* (New Haven: Yale University Press, 1974), particularly chapter six, "Social Policy and Political Learning," 284–322; Michael J. Lacey and Mary O. Furner, "Social Investigation, Social Knowledge, and the State: An Introduction," in *The State and Social Investigation in Britain and the United States*, eds. Michael J. Lacey and Mary O. Furner (Cambridge: Cambridge University Press, 1993); Terrance Ball, James Farr, and Russell L. Hanson, eds., *Political Innovation and Conceptual Change* (Cambridge: Cambridge University Press, 1989), particularly Farr's essay, "Understanding Conceptual Change Politically," 24–49; Quentin Skinner, "Some Problems in the Analysis of Political Thought and Action," *Political Theory* 2 (1974): 277–303; Thomas Kuhn, *The Structure of Scientific Revolutions* (Chicago: University of Chicago Press, 1962); Mary O. Furner and Barry Supple, *The State and Economic Knowledge: The American and British Experiences*, eds. Mary O. Furner and Barry Supple; Gabriel Poggi, "The Modern State and the Idea of Progress," in *Progress and Its Discontents*, ed. Gabriel Almond (Berkeley: University of California Press, 1982); Michael J. Lacey and Mary O. Furner eds., *The State and Social Investigation in Britain and the United States* (Cambridge: Cambridge University Press, 1993); Oz Frankel, *States of Inquiry: Social Investigations and Print Culture in Nineteenth-Century Britain and the United States* (Baltimore: Johns Hopkins University Press, 2006); Sara E. Igo, *The Averaged Americans: Surveys,*

of the need for intellectual authority may have weakened in the more partisan decades of the nineteenth century, but, among policy activists, intellectuals, and reformers across racial and class lines, this awareness came surging back along with the wartime and postwar intensification of objective social problems presented by industrialization and the growing capacity of social science expertise to respond to them. Times of upheaval and crisis such as wars and recessions create a demand for solutions, opening opportunities for critical social theorists and policy entrepreneurs who can mobilize knowledge and articulate strategies for recovery and renewal. In addition to fomenting new expertise and strategies, as historian Daniel Rodgers has suggested, such highly fraught times often create political and policy space for solutions already in existence, awaiting a time when they can be fruitfully applied.[15] The World War I-era was just such a time.

Some, of course, thought the right way forward was retreat. Presidential candidate Warren G. Harding's famous but vacuous call for a "return to normalcy" belied the reality of a deeply troubled nation increasingly led by new leaders in industrial and economic thought who had little in the way of a mawkish longing for what had come before. They aimed instead for what they called a new economy or new capitalism. As the following chapters reveal, the need to better understand modern capitalism and to craft a new vision for industrial relations led to the proliferation of new institutions devoted to examining the New Era economy.[16] These efforts extended well beyond academia and more traditional institutions

---

Citizens, and the Making of a Mass Public (Cambridge, MA: Harvard University Press, 2007); Leon Fink, Stephen T. Leonard, and Donald M. Reid, *Intellectuals and Public Life: Between Radicalism and Reform* (Ithaca: Cornell University Press, 1996); and Alice O'Connor, *Social Science for What? Philanthropy and the Social Question in a World Turned Rightside Up* (New York: Russell Sage Foundation, 2007). For a review of the more recent literature, see Mary O. Furner, "Inquiring Minds Want to Know: Social Investigation in History and Theory," *Modern Intellectual History* 6 (2009): 147–70. On state capacity, see the exemplars of the American Political Development School, Theda Skocpol, Peter B. Evans, and Dietrich Rueschmeyer, eds., *Bringing the State Back In* (Cambridge: Cambridge University Press, 1985) and Stephen Skowronek, *Building a New American State: The Expansion of National Administrative Capacities, 1877–1920* (Cambridge: Cambridge University Press, 1982). For an analysis of political learning going on within reform movements that emphasizes the development of interest group politics, see Elisabeth S. Clemens, *The People's Lobby: Organizational Innovation and the Rise of Interest Group Politics in the United States, 1890–1925* (Chicago: University of Chicago Press, 1997).

[15] Rodgers, *Atlantic Crossings.*
[16] Guy Alchon, *The Invisible Hand of Planning: Capitalism, Social Science, and the State in the 1920s* (Princeton: Princeton University Press, 1985).

of inquiry. In the nonprofit sphere, philanthropic organizations such as the Russell Sage Foundation and Twentieth Century Fund considered new efforts to bring democracy into industry, while the National Urban League (NUL) turned its attention to understanding, publicizing, and improving race relations. Leaders in the Laura Spellman Rockefeller Memorial (LSRM) linked the Great Migration to the influx of Mexican workers and probed the meaning of these changes by way of important investigations by Paul Taylor, Mario Gamio, Charles Johnson, and others. In the federal government, bureaus and departments such as the U.S. Public Health Service, Department of Commerce, Bureau of Labor Statistics (BLS), Women's Bureau (WB), and Division of Negro Economics (DNE) examined the economy and workers' place in it from an array of vantage points. Labor unions, too, recognized the importance of research and expertise to advancing the cause of all workers, building up union research bureaus in individual unions, the larger AFL, and outside research organizations supporting organized labor such as the Labor Bureau Incorporated (LBI).

The New Era emphasis on an expanding economy as a "cure for all ills" – to borrow a phrase from historian Robert M. Collins's examination of the politics of growth in the post–World War II era – suggests that we can locate the roots of what Collins has nicely described as the "protean" idea of "economic growthmanship" in the New Era.[17] Hoover and his allies constructed and advocated this New Era vision of a new economy in a manner that was ideologically as well as empirically driven. Proponents stressed that employers and employees shared an interest in increasing production and promoting consumer spending in order to smooth the business cycle. Experts in labor and managerial economics redefined their own understanding of waste in industry to include not merely the costs involved in efforts to maintain "worker control" of the pace and volume of production, but also grievously low wages, employee overwork, inefficient union work rules, and needless labor conflict.

Further, economic growth propelled New Era economic thinkers to replace older struggles that turned on the distribution of income with a new conceptualization of an ever-expanding economy that stressed the potential of employer-employee cooperation to achieve economic stability and both to increase wealth for investors and to raise living standards for workers. Whereas the Populists and Progressives had earlier argued

---

[17] Robert M. Collins, *More: The Politics of Economic Growth in Postwar America* (Oxford: Oxford University Press, 2000), 23 and 234.

for redistribution by way of the income tax and higher wages mandated by labor standards, the Hooverites promoted economic growth, stability, and cooperation as the most effective means of addressing deeply rooted industrial and labor problems. This new thinking amounted to an almost utopian conceptualization of an economy in which fair distribution of income would arise out of persistent economic growth. Such an argument should sound familiar. In his 1958 book, *The Affluent Society*, John Kenneth Galbraith argued, "Production has eliminated the more acute tensions associated with inequality. And it has become evident to conservatives and liberals alike that increasing aggregate output is an alternative to redistribution or even to the reduction of inequality."[18] Hoover and his allies would have concurred with this sentiment. They also shared with their post–World War II counterparts a belief that prosperity required a balance between production and consumption. The debate concerning the best means of generating and maintaining this balance was rooted in the New Era and persisted well into the post–World War II period.

Such an approach to the formation of a new, social science-based political economy for the 1920s can help us to better understand the New Deal and post-New Deal eras. Between the late 1930s and the end of World War II, according to historian Alan Brinkley, various competing visions of policy making gave way to a version of commercial Keynesianism that limited statist efforts to control the business cycle through fiscal and monetary interventions that did not involve extensive federal responsibility for maintaining full employment through planning.[19] An examination of the New Era suggests that policy makers in the 1920s were well on their way to establishing a coherent and consumerist vision of economic policy, one in which the state would play an important role in facilitating economic growth and efficiency. Building on Brinkley's work, historian Kathleen Donohue suggests that not until the 1940s did economic experts square the interests of consuming citizens with those of business.[20] Donohue suggests that labor activists in the 1920s would have been puzzled by calls for "workers of the world to throw off their chains

---

[18] John Kenneth Galbraith, *The Affluent Society: 40th Anniversary Edition* (New York: Houghton Mifflin Company, 1998), 80.
[19] Brinkley identifies four traditions specifically: antimonopoly, planning, associationalism, and radical alternatives. Associationalism does not adequately incorporate the visions under investigation here.
[20] Alan Brinkley, *The End of Reform: New Deal Liberalism in Recession and War* (New York: Vintage Books, 1995); Kathleen Donohue, *Freedom From Want: American Liberalism and the Idea of the Consumer* (Baltimore: Johns Hopkins University Press, 2003).

and usher in a consumer-oriented economy of abundance." Yet the work of the AFL regarding the relationship between consumption and economic stability suggests that the concept of a "consumer-oriented economy of abundance" would not have been much of a mystery to 1920s labor activists in the AFL, or to the many nonaffiliated unions and union activists that embraced the AFL's efforts to work with employers to increase productivity and to ensure that workers received their fair share of these gains.[21]

American Labor and Economic Citizenship argues that New Era wage and business cycle analysis played a key role in the recognition that a fair and stable set of economic relations could be fostered by economic growth and facilitated by what I will describe later as – yes, largely agreeing with historian Ellis Hawley – a voluntary corporatist vision of the state and society, but with a twist. More than encouraging cooperation among like producers to achieve cooperation in reaching greater efficiency, Hoover and his allies actually moved beyond their initial focus on the production side of the "production-consumption" model that took consumers for granted. Indeed, by the latter part of the decade, Hoover and his associates in organizations such as the National Bureau of Economic Research embraced the importance of consumption in what they termed a "production-consumption" conceptualization of a smoothly running economy and society. Further, Brinkley argues for the continuation of a producerist idea that, I argue, had long disappeared. By the New Era, producerism had been entirely replaced by a model that both recognized citizens' identity as consumers far more than as producers and understood the vital importance of consumers in addressing a business cycle that Wesley Mitchell and others were now reinventing as a structural element of unregulated capitalism. Equally important, by moving beyond the group that surrounded Hoover to include the many other sources of labor and economic expertise – among them Labor Bureau Inc., AFL, and economists such as Paul Douglas and Alvin Hansen – contributing to deliberations concerning the labor and economic problems of the decade, historians can now see that the policy discourses in this pivotal decade were more dynamic and included a much broader range of issues than previously suggested.

A number of factors – many ephemeral – persuaded the New Era economic leaders surrounding Hoover that a new consensus, turning on economic growth, had settled what only recently seemed like intractable economic and social problems. Policy makers' apparent success in

[21] Cf. Donahue, *Freedom from Want*, 190.

ushering the economy out of the post–World War I recession and strike wave, with only the lightest touch – at least as they saw it – from the state, bolstered their confidence that they were well on the way to solving the problem of the business cycle. Additionally, between 1914 and 1925, economists had deliberated on what to do about the recent discovery that real wages, rather than steadily climbing, had fallen between the 1890s and 1907 and then again during the war. But by the mid-1920s, newly improved wage and price statistics and measuring techniques confirmed that, since 1922, real wages had reversed their decline, allowing a broad swath of American workers to benefit, if perhaps only modestly, from economic prosperity and historically low levels of unemployment.[22] Mid-decade immigration reforms that tightened the labor market further supported the belief that this uptick in real wages could be sustained. An expansion in consumer credit fortified this apparent prosperity by generating demand and allowing many Americans to take home cars, refrigerators, radios, and other durable goods with only a down payment. As Martha Olney has demonstrated, this durable goods revolution was reflected in consumer debt as a percentage of personal income, which jumped from 4.5 percent to 9 percent between 1918–20 and 1929.[23]

Skyrocketing corporate profits, the emergence of the United States as a creditor nation, and the gradual conversion of production toward consumer goods further confirmed a new consensus that extended well beyond business leaders and Republican politicians. The dramatic decline in labor unrest, falling prices for agricultural goods, and increasing access to secondary education provided still more evidence.[24] Looking back,

[22] See Chapter 2 in this volume on real wages. On unemployment in the 1920s, see Stanley Legerbott, *Manpower in Economic Growth: The American Record since 1800* (New York: McGraw Hill, 1964), who concluded that unemployment had been historically low between 1923 and 1929, at 3.3 percent; Robert M. Coen, "Labor Force and Unemployment in the 1920s and 1930s: A Re-examination Based on Postwar Experience," *The Review Of Economics and Statistics* 55 (1973): 46–55 revised Lebergott's estimate upward to 5.1 percent for the same years. See also Christina D. Romer, "New Estimates of Prewar Gross National Product and Unemployment," *Journal of Economic History* 46 (June 1986): 341–52; Christina D. Romer, "The Great Crash and the Onset of the Great Depression," *QJE* 105 (August 1990): 597–694; Christina D. Romer, "Spurious Volatility in Historical Unemployment Data," *JPE* 94 (February 1986): 1–37; and Sanford Jacoby, *Employing Bureaucracy*, 167–205.
[23] Martha Olney, *Buy Now Pay Later: Advertising, Credit, and Consumer Durables in the 1920s* (Chapel Hill: University of North Carolina Press, 1991). On the experiences of working-class Americans in this period, see Cohen, *Making a New Deal*.
[24] On access to education, see Claudia Goldin and Lawrence F. Katz, *The Race between Education and Technology* (Cambridge: Belknap Press of Harvard University, 2008). On strikes, see Department of Labor, *Fifteenth Annual Report of the Secretary of Labor*

policy makers' optimism concerning the increasing productive capacity of industry seems well founded. Comparing the 1920s to the rest of the twentieth century, economic historian Alexander J. Field has found an annual Total Factor Productivity (TFP) increase of 5.12 percent in manufacturing between 1919 and 1929, far higher than any other period in the twentieth century.[25] In the face of these changes, even the American Federation of Labor embraced cooperation, economic growth, and consumption as political and economic objectives. By producing a body of statistically grounded and sophisticated data sets, organized labor worked hard to establish a place for itself in this new paradigm, even as policy makers such as Hoover, who originally embraced a role for unions, determined that unions had little role to play in a modern, consumer-driven economy.

Unlike recent times when the issue of income inequality has again emerged as a salient issue among political and economic leaders, the New Era emphasis on growth blinded many policy makers and observers to the issue of income inequality, which increased significantly between 1921 and 1929.[26] Rarely over the course of the decade did policy makers

(Washington, DC: GPO, 1927), 51-2. On falling agricultural prices, see Walton and Rockoff, *History of the American Economy*, 404-5. For a recent treatment of the United States as a creditor nation, see Liaquat Ahamed, *Lords of Finance: The Bankers Who Broke the World* (New York: The Penguin Press, 2009). On conversion of the consumer economy, see Michael Bernstein, "Why the Great Depression Was Great: Toward a New Understanding of the Interwar Economic Crisis in the United States," in *The Rise and Fall of the New Deal Order: 1930-1980*, ed. Steve Fraser and Gary Gerstle (Princeton: Princeton University Press, 1989), 34-5; Michael Bernstein, *The Great Depression: Delayed Recovery and Economic Change in America 1929-1939* (Cambridge: Cambridge University Press, 1987).

[25] Alexander J. Field, "Technological Change and U.S. Productivity Growth in the Interwar Years," *Journal of Economic History* 66 (March 2006): 214, 227; Alexander J. Field, *A Great Leap Forward: 1930s Depression and U.S. Economic Growth* (New Haven: Yale University Press, 2011). The next closest growth period in TFP, according to Fields, was 1929-41, which saw an annual TFP growth rate of 2.6 percent. Field attributes the 1920s growth to a reorganization of factories and the increasing use of small electric motors and electricity in consumer goods (i.e., vacuum cleaners, refrigerators, washing machines, radios, toasters, etc.) See also Paul Kendrick, *Productivity Trends in the United States* (Princeton: Princeton University Press, 1961).

[26] On the movement and distribution of wages and income in the New Era, see Charles F. Holt, "Who Benefited from the Prosperity of the 1920s," *Explorations in Economic History* 14 (July 1977): 277-89; Frank Stricker, "Affluence for Whom? – Another Look at Prosperity and the Working Class in the 1920s," *Labor History* 24 (Winter 1983): 17-23; Jeffrey G. Williamson and Peter Lindert, *American Inequality: A Macroeconomic History* (New York: Academic Press, 1980), 77-82, 284; Gene Smiley, "Did Incomes For Most of the Population Fall from 1923 to 1929?" *Journal of Economic History* 43 (March 1983): 209-16; Stanley Kuznets, *Shares of Upper Income Groups in Income and*

examine the issue of income inequality, and when they did, as we will see in Chapter 1, they got it wrong, concluding that income inequality had not increased. Though the decade provided a fertile ground for vibrant and influential debates about wage policy and the trajectory of real wages, the economists and economic policy makers who surrounded Hoover devoted remarkably little attention to comparing the modest rise in real wages with the much larger increase in total national product and business profits. The belief seemed to be that either economic growth had solved or would solve these problems or, as economist A. F. McGoun argued in 1924, "inequality in itself is only an evil when carried so far as to leave the poor short of necessaries for the full development of their efficiency."[27]

The absence of further analysis on this point suggests three possibilities. First, New Era corporate profits (as distinguished from proprietary capitalists' profits of the earlier era) had gained a level of legitimacy among economists and policy makers that had not previously existed. Partly as a result of their acceptance of marginalist economic theory, economists and others accepted very high profits as legitimate rate of return for the value that capital and stockholders added to the production process. This shift had its roots in the well-documented emergence of neoclassical economics at the turn of the century, but post–World War I economic growth – grounded largely in hefty capitalization of new industries – gave it new relevance. Second, economists and policy makers may have paid less attention to growing income inequality because it had become so common. As Simon Kuznets noted in the 1950s, inequality increased over the course of the long Gilded Age and through the 1920s, interrupted only by income compression during World War I. Placed in the context of increasing inequality since the latter part of the nineteenth century, the significant increase we see in the New Era might have been easily passed over.[28]

Savings (New York: NBER, 1953); Elliot Brownlee, *Dynamics of Ascent: A History of the American Economy* (New York: Alfred A. Knopf, 1974), 264–84; and Emmanuel Saez, "Striking It Richer: The Evolution of Top Incomes in the United States (Update with 2007 Estimates)," 5. Accessed at http://elsa.berkeley.edu/%7Esaez/saez-UStopincomes-2007.pdf.

[27] A. F. McGoun, "Inequality and Accumulation," *JPE* 32 (December 1924): 663–4.

[28] Key works on the history of income inequality include Simon Kuznets, "Economic Growth and Income Inequality," *AER* XLV (1955): 1–28; Jeffrey G. Williamson and Peter H. Lindert, *American Inequality: A Macroeconomic History* (New York: Academic Press, 1980); and Claudia Goldin and Robert A. Margo, "The Great Compression: The

Third, this apparent oversight suggests a failure to recognize that concentrating so much income into a small group of earners might stunt demand for the consumer products that American industry could now produce in such growing abundance. As John Maynard Keynes and others would observe a decade later, when hard times hit, wages might be "sticky" but output was not. When demand ebbed late in the New Era, manufactures might hold off on layoffs for a stretch – as Hoover advocated – but when demand failed to recover, layoffs ensued and a vicious cycle of falling demand and employment put the nation on track for the worst economic downturn in its history. The lack of demand did not come as a surprise to everyone, though. As historian Meg Jacobs has described it, a group of New Era "purchasing power progressives" warned, without significant effect, that an insufficient supply of wages created an untenable situation in which aggregate demand would prove insufficient to absorb the growing capacity of industry.[29] Coming at the issue from a quite different perspective, economist Alvin Hansen considered the composition of industry and warned that a failure to shift production away from capital and toward consumer goods would result in an increasingly productive economy with few benefits for workers and consumers.

   Other changes that further undermined this vision often went largely unnoted in the New Era. In an economy increasingly dominated by modern corporations rather than individual proprietors, satisfying New Era stockholders became the chief concern for managers and executives. The Hooverite vision assumed the participation of powerful, farsighted business leaders who would shelve short-term gain in favor of the long-term interests of the enterprise, the economy, and society. As some New Era observers noted, the shift from proprietary to corporate capitalism supplanted the autonomous business owner with managers obligated to serve the interests of anonymous stockholders. In a confidential 1929 memo to Russell Sage Foundation (RSF) executive director John Glenn, RSF research director Mary van Kleeck asked, "What, after all, should be the relation of stockholders to the directing of policy of a company?"[30] Whether in

---

Wage Structure in the United States at Mid-Century," *QJE* CVII (February 1992): 1–34; and Peter Levy and Peter Temin, "Inequality and Institutions in 20th Century America," NBER Working Paper, 2007. See also Barry Bluestone, "The Inequality Express," *American Prospect* 20 (Winter 1995): 82–3.

[29] Jacobs, *Pocketbook Politics*, 53–92.
[30] Mary van Kleeck to John Glenn, January 1, 1929, Folder 1591 File, Study Correspondence, Box 103, Mary van Kleeck Papers, Smith College.

securing workers a fair share of productivity gains or negotiating the rocky terrain of corporate governance, the need to satisfy investors concerned with nothing but the bottom line threatened the much-anticipated harmony of interests between employers and employees. As New Era economic governance ideas took shape, they left unresolved the best means of guaranteeing either fair labor relations or the consumer purchasing power necessary to maintain such a system.

Mainstream unions did not challenge the new paradigm of growth through cooperation toward production efficiencies in a meaningful way, but others did. Advocates for African American, Mexican, Mexican American, and women workers developed a contending body of expertise that worked quite deliberately to challenge the notion that economic growth alone could be counted on to generate a fair and equitable society. As issues such as the length of the workday and the regulation of the business cycle became national concerns that merited public action, this other group of experts and advocates recognized the New Era as an opportunity to use demographic change, along with the broader rethinking of the economy and society, to compel a reexamination of ideas about race, ethnicity, and gender in relation to work and citizenship. Relying on the power of inquiry and investigation to erode long-held beliefs and practices and on a resourceful mobilization of support from the nonprofit, government, and academic sectors, these experts and advocates launched a two-pronged effort. First, they made the case that these workers had taken full advantage of the opportunities opened up by a tight labor market and wartime demand. No longer, they argued, could anyone make a credible case that black and Mexican workers were biologically or culturally predisposed to occupy a subordinate station in the agricultural, railroad, and domestic occupations of the South and Southwest. Nor should anyone give credence to stereotypes of women workers as incidental members of the labor force or of Mexican workers as a special class of laborers destined to return to Mexico. During and after the war, they argued, these groups had demonstrated a desire and ability to rise in occupations traditionally dominated by white men. Second, these experts used inquiry and investigation to make clear that only persistent and active efforts by individuals and groups could maintain the lines that divided Americans on the basis of sex, race, and ethnicity. Americans could only fully realize a fair society and a new economy, they argued, when obstacles premised on outworn ideas about race and gender had been forthrightly addressed.

Experts examining black, women, and Mexican workers contested the theoretical, ideological, and empirical basis of the emerging consensus concerning how the labor market functioned and what role the state should play in shaping the market. In the era of *Adkins*, the Supreme Court had found that the state had little constitutional power to intervene in the contractual relationship between private individuals and entities. Such relationships were best governed, the Supreme Court argued, by market forces and individual decisions regarding how best to value time and labor. Building on a case made by progressives of an earlier generation, advocates for women and racial minorities embraced a more statist formulation of the relationship between the state and the protection of liberties. The Women's Bureau, for instance, argued strenuously for recognition of the importance, ability, and ambition of women workers, while at the same time empirically demonstrating the need for legislation to protect women workers against exploitation linked directly to their status as women. WB leaders evaluated the *Adkins* decision as "nothing short of a calamity to the women workers of this country." Labor standards, the WB argued, were perfectly appropriate for dealing with poor working conditions.[31] Similarly, advocates for black workers demonstrated again and again the ability of these workers to succeed in industry, but at the same time they argued that, given evidence of past and present racial injustice, the federal government needed to pay particular attention to the plight of black workers. Congress and the Supreme Court on different occasions rejected these views. In *Adkins*, the majority found that suffrage and other changes had brought "the ancient inequality of the sexes … almost, if not quite, to the vanishing point."[32] And, regarding black workers, Congress rejected appeals for the continuation of the Division of Negro Economics after the war, in part on the grounds that no similar government body was devoted to considering the conditions of Jewish, Polish, or other groups of workers.[33] Remarkably, changes brought on by emancipation, migration, franchise, or some other factor had, according to the Court and Congress, dissolved long-standing gender and racial

---

[31] "Calls Wage Ruling by Court a 'Calamity,'" *NYT*, April 12, 1923, 11.

[32] Nancy Woloch, *Muller v. Oregon: A Brief History with Documents* (Boston: Bedford/St. Martin's, 1996), 54–5; Alexander Tsesis, *We Shall Overcome: A History of Civil Rights and the Law* (New Haven: Yale University Press, 2008), 196–7.

[33] Congress, House Committee on Appropriations, *Sundry Civil Appropriation Bill, 1921. Part 2: Statement of Mr. George E. Haynes and Mr. Karl F. Phillips*, 66th Cong., 2nd sess., March 20, 1920, 2164.

conflicts. The evidence brought forth by advocates for women and racial minorities suggested otherwise. If the federal government could intervene dramatically in the most private aspects of American life and commerce in order to enforce (however ineptly) the Eighteenth Amendment, they wondered, then why not the Fourteenth and Fifteenth Amendments as well? Couldn't this same government see the wisdom and justice in, at the very least, protecting the most exploited and vulnerable American workers?

These groups also raised questions about the Hooverites' faith in a cooperative vision and economic growth to smooth the relationship between labor and capital. In doing so they described a more nuanced and contingent understanding of the relationship, not just between labor and capital, but among specific groups of workers and employers. Here Hoover's faith in farsighted capitalists and the shared interest of homogenized labor and capital was challenged by a more wary and historically informed analysis. The NUL, for instance, framed the New Era tension between black and white workers historically, describing the institution of slavery as "a form of organization of black labor which succeeded" also "in grinding white labor into the earth." Emancipation, in this telling of the story, had kept white workers "restless and uncomfortable," culminating in the ongoing effort of some trade unions and employers to cooperate in order to bar black workers from certain occupations and workplaces. This effort to maintain cross-class, white racial solidarity, the NUL argued, had been and remained a fool's errand: "There has never been a time when some employers would not yield to the advantage of more work for less wages against the arguments of race."[34] While Hoover argued that economic growth and stability could solve America's social problems, the body of New Era expertise cultivated by the NUL and many others raised another set of key questions and portrayed a society whose problems could not be so easily addressed.

Along the way, these New Era experts and advocates worked to diversify the labor question so that it better represented the experiences, abilities, and aspirations of these new industrial workers. Rooted in concerns about concentrated power reaching back to the early republic, the meaning of the labor question evolved over the course of the late nineteenth and early twentieth centuries. At the core of the labor question, however, we can identify a concern with how to square the democratic promise of the nation with the plainly undemocratic organization of modern

---

[34] "Negro Labor Past and Present," *Opportunity* 5 (May 1927): 126–7.

industry. Certainly, earlier iterations of the labor question had marginalized issues of gender and race. In the New Era, advocates for a more equitable society had come to believe that the demographic change brought on by war and revolution, in combination with talk of using knowledge and expertise to build a new economy, had forced open the door to a new understanding of the labor question that recognized the heterogeneous nature of the work force. For the labor question to be meaningful, they argued, it could no longer exclusively reflect only the narrow interests of highly skilled, male workers. Significantly, this New Era understanding of the labor question embraced by these various groups occurred at a time when the labor question itself had been transformed. As the contest over workers' control of the production process eased, deliberation on the labor question shifted away from older producerist ideals and toward, as historian Rosanne Currarino has described it, "the question of the full participation in social life and calls for the ability to enjoy the full fruits of industrial abundance."[35] The arguments and evidence put forth by advocates for women, black, and Mexican workers aligned nicely with this more recent formulation of the labor question.

These efforts to diversify the labor question and expose the uneven benefits offered by the New Era economy achieved mixed success. Within the Department of Labor, the Women's Bureau grew into an important organization that coordinated federal and state policies and built up an impressive body of knowledge demonstrating the need for legislated labor standards to protect poor workers and families regardless of gender. In doing so, WB advocates of protective legislation for women challenged Hooverite thinking. Though they consistently stressed the progress made by women in industry, their investigations found little evidence to support the notion that economic growth alone could be counted on to distribute income or opportunity fairly.

By contrast, after a promising wartime beginning, the Division of Negro Economics, also located in the Department of Labor, proved susceptible to policy makers' willingness to ignore the condition of black workers, who increasingly worked in low-wage manufacturing jobs in the North, lived in highly segregated urban communities, and faced the constant threat of racial violence. Like the WB, the DNE emerged from a wartime concern with finding industrial workers as men entered the armed forces and immigration from Europe declined. The DNE, however,

---

[35] Rosanne Currarino, *The Labor Question in America: Economic Democracy in the Gilded Age* (Urbana: University of Illinois Press, 2011), 116.

assumed greater importance as the Great Migration continued to take shape. Deeply concerned with the demographic change and violent racial unrest that accompanied the migration, policy makers looked to the DNE for explanations as to the scope of the migration and its significance. In their roles as interpreters and investigators, DNE investigators made clear that the "Negro problem" was a national issue rather than an intractable, regional condition the nation as a whole could largely ignore. Following the war and the elimination of the DNE, labor and race relations experts in organizations such as the NUL sought and gained critical funding from various philanthropies to support their investigations. Though these nonprofit institutions were denied state-sanctioned legitimacy, they kept the "Negro problem" in the public eye and challenged an ideology of black inferiority. Speaking before the SSRC Hanover Conference in the fall of 1928, the Laura Spelman Rockefeller Memorial's Leonard Outhwaite noted in language echoed by many observers during the decade: "The [Negro] problem as a whole was at one time a southern problem; it is now a general national problem" brought about by the Great Migration. "Many of these questions of the ultimate relationship of the two races," Outhwaite presciently noted, "are very far from settled."[36]

A similar trend can be found in the study of the rapidly changing "Mexican problem" that by mid-decade rivaled the "Negro problem" for public attention. In this case, government officials and activists who opposed and advocated migration were deeply invested, politically and economically, in long-established stereotypes concerning the inferiority of people of Mexican descent. As was the case with the "Negro problem," the increased rate of migration of Mexican workers brought the "Mexican problem" into clearer focus and altered the nature of the debate. Early in the decade, policy makers took comfort in their belief in a fundamental difference between the European immigrant and the Mexican migrant. The Mexican, it was understood, came to the United States for short bouts of intense labor in unskilled occupations in the fields and railroads of the Southwest. With no interest in or possibility of upward mobility in the United States, he inevitably returned to his native land. Agricultural interests, in particular, claimed that this exceptional migration stream provided laborers for industry without the burdens of citizenship.

---

[36] Leonard Outhwaite, Statement at the "Social Science Research Council, Hanover Conference, 1928," 210–11, Folder 1894, Box 330, Series 5, SSRC Collection, Rockefeller Archive Center. Outhwaite served as the LSRM's program officer on issues related to race and race relations.

Events soon stretched this depiction to a breaking point. As migration and immigration from Mexico increased as a result of the unrest surrounding the 1910 Mexican Revolution and the tightening of the labor market during World War I in the United States, another group of social scientists and activists took up the cause of the Mexican immigrant and Mexican American worker and turned to inquiry as a means of challenging the migrant worker narrative. In doing so, these activists demonstrated the permanence, skill, and ambition of Mexican immigrants and Mexican Americans in and beyond the Southwest. Lacking established institutions like the DNE and the NUL, this more disparate project brought together leaders in social work, nonprofits, and academia, along with an emerging group of Mexican American activists.

In the heat of the war, it was clear to these activists that the federal government and the public's newfound interest in these issues created an opportunity to use the federal government, unions, and other organizations as an "opening wedge" for drawing attention to and perhaps resolving not just issues of immediate concern, but long-standing racist and sexist ideas deeply woven into the American experience. They quickly came to believe that a more active state and informed public – that is, a state and public made aware of racial and gender injustice and the inaccurate nature of long-held racist and sexist ideas – could ameliorate many of the injustices confronted by women and racial and ethnic minorities in the period.

The results of these efforts were mixed. Particularly for African American industrial workers, during the 1930s the Congress of Industrial Organizations came to recognize – in no small measure as a result of the work by these New Era investigators and advocates – the necessity of opening local and leadership positions to black industrial workers. The importance of this victory and of the significance of New Era efforts to bring it about should not be discounted. As we will see in Chapters 6 and 7, during the New Era, the NUL did everything from cajoling to threatening to shaming organized labor into recognizing the utter necessity of bringing black workers into the House of Labor. Even in the 1930s, victory in this regard was not imminent and concerns remained. In fact, the NUL and National Association for the Advancement of Colored People viewed the Wagner Act with great concern, fearing it would codify existing discriminatory union and business practices. In practice, however, when the Congress of Industrial Organizations (CIO) explicitly reached out to the NUL and black industrial workers in the 1930s and the New Deal protected their right to organize, many African American industrial workers achieved a path to the middle class.

In other areas, deeply entrenched racism and sexism or a willful ignorance of these issues in politics and public policy networks frustrated these expert-reformers' efforts to diversify the labor question. In fact, the larger policy infrastructure skewed disproportionately in the direction of white men, thereby excluding vast numbers of workers in the United States. In terms that could have just as easily applied to racial and ethnic minorities in occupations not protected by New Deal legislation, economist Paul Douglas, who played a central role in the development of economic and social policy in the New Deal, wrote in his influential 1933 study of unemployment insurance:

> There are some, particularly women who wish to be employed for only a few hours per day or per week. Such persons as these are only casual and incidental members of the labor supply and do not need or deserve the same protection as those who are fully dependent upon industry for employment.[37]

Such an understanding of who worked, for what purpose, and under what conditions went dead against the more diverse narrative of American labor and work that advocates for too-often marginalized groups constructed in the New Era. If we define *reform* broadly enough to include inequities of gender and race as well as class, then certainly a number of the key issues described in the following chapters were far from settled. Indeed, integrating race and gender analysis into the New Era narrative makes it difficult to promote the idea that the 1940s were an "end of reform." No one arguing for greater rights and a fairer society for women, African American, Mexican immigrant, or Mexican American workers in the 1940s would have made that case. The failure of policy makers to recognize the experiences of diverse groups of workers when thinking about issues related to work and citizenship had, of course, real consequences. In their work on the post–World War II period, historians Alice Kessler-Harris, Lizabeth Cohen, Ira Katznelson, and others have described how the narrow views of the work force held by policy makers like Douglas bore bitter fruit in the New Deal and post–World War II eras when economic, labor, and social policies provided a range of benefits for white, particularly male, Americans, but far fewer for African Americans, women, and Mexican Americans.[38]

---

[37] Quoted in Alice Kessler-Harris, *In Pursuit of Equity: Women, Men and the Quest for Economic Citizenship in 20th Century America* (Oxford: Oxford University Press, 2001), 97. For a similar sentiment from W. Jett Lauck, another important advocate of labor, see Leon Fink, *Progressive Intellectuals and the Dilemmas of Democratic Commitment* (Cambridge, MA: Harvard University Press, 1997), 219.

[38] For recent statement of these benefits, see Ira Katznelson, *When Affirmative Action Was White: An Untold History of Racial Inequality in Twentieth Century America* (New

Part of the story here has to do with the history and trajectory of institutional spaces where experts on women and racial minorities could cultivate an audience. For instance, during the New Era, the burgeoning, still contested field of social work provided one of the few venues that welcomed expertise on certain groups of disadvantaged workers. In the New Era, social work as a field was sufficiently in play to sustain a tradition that contained multiple trajectories, including one that encompassed social or political economy within its purview. When Charles Johnson, Ernesto Galarza, and Mary van Kleeck appeared before the National Conference of Social Work, as they often did, they clearly argued against separating gender and race issues from larger economic and social concerns. Looking past the New Era, we now recognize the field of social work would come to be dominated by professionals who embraced a narrower explanation for poverty among select groups. As Alice O'Connor, Andrew Morris, and others have demonstrated, this embrace would lead to causal accounts of poverty that jettisoned analysis of structural inequality in favor of cultural, psychological, and behavioral explanations. The notion that race, gender, and economic conflict could be ameliorated by Freudian psychology, family casework, or an analysis of the character of individuals would have gained no traction with the New Era experts described in this book. As social work achieved increasing legitimacy in the 1930s, its leaders largely and tragically left behind the more structural analysis that characterized a significant thread in the New Era analysis of poverty, justice, and inequality.[39]

York: W. W. Norton and Company, 2005); Elizabeth Cohen, *A Consumers' Republic: The Politics of Mass Consumption* (New York: Vintage Books, 2003); and Alice Kessler-Harris, *In Pursuit of Equity*.

[39] On the emergence of social work, see Andrew J. F. Morris, *The Limits of Voluntarism: Charity and Welfare from the New Deal through the Great Society* (Cambridge: Cambridge University Press, 2009); Linda Gordon, *Pitied But Not Entitled: Single Mothers and the History of Welfare* (Cambridge, MA: Harvard University Press, 1994), particularly 67–108; Roy Lubove, *The Professional Altruist: The Emergence of Social Work as a Career, 1880–1930* (Cambridge: Cambridge University Press, 1965); Alice O'Connor, *Poverty Knowledge: Social Science, Social Policy and the Poor in Twentieth-Century U. S. History* (Princeton: Princeton University Press, 2001); Clarke A. Chambers, "Women in the Creation of Social Work," *Social Service Review* 60 (March 1986): 1–33; Robyn Muncy, *Creating a Female Dominion in American Reform: 1890–1935* (Oxford: Oxford University Press, 1991); Ellen Fitzpatrick, *Endless Crusade: Women Social Scientists and Progressive Reform* (New York: Oxford University Press, 1990); John Ehrenreich, *The Altruistic Imagination: A History of Social Work and Social Policy in the United States* (Ithaca: Cornell University Press, 1985); Michael B. Katz, *In the Shadow of the Poorhouse: A Social History of Welfare in America* (New York: Basic Books, 1996); Daniel J. Walkowitz, *Working with Class: Social Workers and the Politics of Middle-Class Identity* (Chapel Hill: University of North Carolina Press, 1999); Elizabeth Agnew, *From*

Exploration of labor experts' process of social learning about women, black, and Mexican workers during this pivotal decade expands our understanding of the efforts of Mexican American and African American social scientists and labor investigators working in state, academic, and nonprofit institutions. In the 1970s and 1980s, an intellectual breakthrough by historians Mary Furner, Thomas Haskell, and Dorothy Ross revealed how Progressive Era academic social scientists constructed their disciplines to separate the reform-oriented amateur social science of decades past from what leading academics of that era saw as the vastly superior, nonpartisan, and professional work of the "objective" scholarship they could provide, where narrowed empirical investigations could ensure scientifically grounded results.[40] More recently, Margaret Rossiter, Rosalind Rosenberg, Mary Jo Deegan, Ellen Fitzpatrick, Helene Silverberg, and Kathryn Kish Sklar have worked to broaden historians' understanding of the social sciences, social inquiry, and the production of social knowledge to include women in and out of the academy who, according to Sklar, derived their "power and influence ... from their ability to maintain their own social science-oriented institutions, conduct their own social science studies, and advance their own social science goals."[41] An examination of

---

Charity to Social Work: Mary E. Richmond and the Creation of an America Profession (Urbana: University of Illinois Press, 2004).

[40] On the rise of social empiricism and the history of the social sciences, see Mary O. Furner, *Advocacy and Objectivity: A Crisis in the Professionalization of American Social Science, 1865–1905* (Lexington: University Press of Kentucky, 1975); Thomas L. Haskell, *The Emergence of Professional Social Science: The American Social Science Association and the Nineteenth-Century Crisis of Authority* (Urbana: University of Illinois Press, 1977); Loren Baritz, *The Servants of Power: A History of the Use of Social Science in American Industry* (Middletown: Wesleyan University Press, 1960); Thomas Bender, *Intellectuals and Public Life: Essays on the Social History of Academic Intellectuals in the United States* (Baltimore: Johns Hopkins University Press, 1993); Marc C. Smith, *Social Science in the Crucible: The American Debate over Objectivity and Purpose, 1918–1941* (Durham: Duke University Press, 1994); William J. Barber, *From New Era to New Deal: Herbert Hoover, the Economists, and American Economic Policy, 1921–1933* (Cambridge: Cambridge University Press, 1985); Furner and Lacey, "Social Investigations, Social Knowledge, and the State: An Introduction"; Ross, *The Origins of American Social Science*; Donald Critchlow, *The Brookings Institution, 1916–1952: Expertise and the Public Interest in a Democratic Society* (Dekalb: Northern Illinois Press, 1985).

[41] Kathryn Kish Sklar, "Hull-House Maps and Papers: Social Science as Women's Work in the 1890s," in Helene Silverberg, ed., *Gender and American Social Science: The Formative Years* (Princeton: Princeton University Press, 1998), 128. Mary Jo Deegan, *Jane Addams and the Men of the Chicago School, 1893–1918* (New Brunswick: Transaction Books, 1988); Ellen Fitzpatrick, *Endless Crusade: Women Social Scientists and Progressive Reform* (New York: Oxford University Press, 1990); William Leach, *True Love and*

New Era work completed in a range of institutional settings contributes to these effort by historians to broaden our understanding of social science and public policy inquiry to include an emerging body of experts on women and racial minorities who built their own social science research institutions through government, academic, and nonprofit organizations. Rather than drawing expertise from a narrow group of economists or policy professionals, these experts derived their authority on economic and social issues from a diverse disciplinary base that included highly trained social workers, economists, sociologists, philanthropists, and government officials. Articulating this newly expansive vision of social science, Hoover assistant E. E. Hunt wrote to Robert Lynd of the SSRC, "those who have occupied high administrative offices with insight and skill are ipso facto social scientists."[42]

The work of these investigators of gender and race was objective in that it was empirically driven and designed to provide an unflinching depiction of labor and race relations in America, but it was also a form of activism. Rather than simple exhortation, the work of these experts can be best understood as a frontal assault on racist and sexist stereotypes central to a larger intellectual infrastructure that justified an ongoing and active process of discrimination against various marginalized groups in American society. In evaluating the work of experts like Charles S. Johnson, Mary van Kleeck, Ernesto Galarza, and others, we have to determine when these investigators were simply crunching data and when they spoke truth to power. I argue that, in these cases, far more of the latter than the former took place during the New Era. They did not, of course, always succeed, but they did make significant strides in demonstrating that the experiences of diverse groups of workers could not be captured within all-encompassing frames; that is to say, policy makers could not make sense of challenges facing women and racial and ethnic minorities by treating them as if they were white males. Their efforts rested almost entirely on their explicit assumption that a more just, democratic, and equitable version of capitalism could only be constructed if policy makers

---

Perfect Union: The Feminist Reform of Sex and Society (New York: Basic Books, 1980); Margaret W. Rossiter, *Woman Scientists in America: Struggles and Strategies to 1940* (Baltimore: Johns Hopkins University Press, 1982); and Rosalind Rosenberg, *Beyond Separate Spheres: Intellectual Roots of Modern Feminism* (New Haven: Yale University Press, 1982).

[42] E. E. Hunt to Robert S. Lynd, January 17, 1930, File Misc. L 1929; Office of the Secretary, Subject Files of Assistant Secretary of Commerce E. E. Hunt, 1921–31, Box 2, RG 40 General Records of the Department of Commerce, NA.

and the public had a clear idea of who labored and under what conditions, as well as how far the various promises embedded in the New Era economy strayed from reality.

More specifically, framing knowledge generation and expertise in this fashion also helps us to better understand the relationship between activism and professionalization in the social sciences during the first decades of the twentieth century. Dorothy Ross's enormously important *The Origins of American Social Science* argues that, by the 1920s, "scientism" had overwhelmed the progressive aspirations of social scientists. Among many other examples, Ross points to the career of sociologist William Fielding Ogburn. After earning his PhD from Columbia, Ogburn taught at Reed College and the University of Washington. During this time, Ogburn worked actively in labor reform circles, but with growing discomfort. He increasingly became concerned, according to Ross, that his activism cast the university in "disfavor" and that he was working on issues about which he had no particular expertise. By the time he became involved in World War I cost of living studies, he later reflected, he had "resolved to give up social action and dedicate myself to science."[43] There is no reason to doubt Ross's characterization of this transition in the professional life of Ogburn or the many others for whom Ogburn's experiences are representative. But the investigations and activism described in the second half of this book suggest the presence of a whole range of social scientists who, unlike Ogburn, saw empiricism as a path rather than an alternative to social action. They believed that careful investigation carried out with a high regard for methods that identified and corrected for value-laden assumptions could expose pernicious fallacies in both expert and popular belief. In doing so, they challenged academia and the American public to rethink issues vital to the nation's future, ranging broadly from the Chicago school paradigm of the ethnic cycle to widely held beliefs concerning the ability and aspirations of women and racial minorities in the United States.

The importance of nonprofit organizations in this effort and to the larger attempt to reshape capitalism in the New Era points to another defining characteristic of the New Era that has echoes in policy making today: the rise of nonprofit organizations designed to gather theoretical and practical knowledge in order to identify possible solutions to public problems. From the Gilded Age through the 1920s, government study

---

[43] Ross, *The American Origins of American Social Science*, see page 393 for Ogburn example, but 390–470 for Ross's analysis of "scientism" in the 1920s.

of economic and labor questions expanded unevenly and episodically in response to the general ambiguity regarding what role government should play in the economy, what role extra-governmental expertise should play in framing policy, and to various political pressures. As a result, after World War I a certain class of highly charged issues – among them fixing the length of the workday, examining the business cycle, determining responsibility for waste in industry, and probing the nature and claims of black workers – was largely spun off by government and taken up by nonprofits.

The results of these collaborations varied. In some cases, as in the effort to consider the length of the workday in the steel industry discussed in the first chapter, engineering and economic experts in nonprofits turned a rights question into an efficiency issue, opening the controversy up to settlement by adoption of "best practices." In this instance, a variety of experts over time created a body of factual knowledge that persuasively argued for the benefits to the corporation, the worker, and the public of the elimination of the twelve-hour day. Thus here, as in other instances during the decade, the nonprofit setting allowed for the avoidance of confrontation, court intervention, and attempts at federal government enforcement of standards that would likely have transgressed the *Lochner* rule. In doing so, they transformed the issue of the workday in the steel industry from a private concern decided between employer and employee to a civic concern settled through inquiry and deliberation by labor experts and policy makers, whose investigations cultivated public support and convinced industry of the efficacy of the shorter workday. The fluid movement of individuals, findings, and ideas among nonprofit, commercial, and government sectors speaks to the need for an understanding of the policy-making process that more clearly integrates the state and nonprofits. Along these same lines, even when issues were spun off from the government to the nonprofit sector, these were not clean breaks. As Ellis Hawley, Guy Alchon, and others have shown, government leaders such as Herbert Hoover often facilitated and legitimized non-state inquiry and used investigations by nonprofit organizations to rally public, labor, and business support for dramatic changes in the organization of industry, without the assertion and expansion of federal government regulatory authority.[44]

[44] Alchon, *The Invisible Hand of Planning*; Ellis W. Hawley, "Herbert Hoover, the Commerce Secretariat, and the Vision of an 'Associative State,' 1921–1928," *JAH* 61 (1974): 116–40; Judith Sealander, *Private Wealth and Public Life: Foundation Philanthropy and Reshaping of America Social Policy from the Progressive Era to the New Deal* (Baltimore:

This new approach to capitalism and managing the economy was reflected in the expansion of the range of economic issues that shifted from the private to the public domain. No one did more in the period than John Dewey to promote the shifting of boundaries between public and private. Throughout his life, but particularly in the 1920s, Dewey searched for the origins and functions of the modern state and redefined its role as a caretaker for public concerns. Dewey claimed that the public included groups and individuals affected by the consequences of policies and agreements negotiated without their involvement or consent.[45] Inspired by renewed interest in pragmatism generally, and in Dewey's conception of the meaning of *public*, my depiction of the New Era aims to help us better understand key shifts in the areas of American life that have been taken as fair game for public policy. Although the Supreme Court rejected most labor standards legislation during the decade, nonlegislative policy domains provided a number of examples of previously private issues shifting from the private to the public domain. For all of the Hooverites' apparent conservativism, they brought with them a clear understanding that there was such a thing as the public good, that it needed looking after, and that society was something more than the aggregate of rights-bearing individuals. Hoover's efforts to address the length of the workday in the steel industry, form trade associations, and use the government to promote efficiency in industry and society were all premised on the belief that the market, left to its own devices, would not inevitably lead to the good society. American individualism, as Hoover said repeatedly, was a "tempered" individualism that privileged the public good over individual gain.[46]

By increasingly relying on and legitimizing the work of a mix of government and nongovernment agencies, Hoover reorganized the basic institutional structure of United States government knowledge gathering. This process has been scrutinized by historians such as Ellis Hawley,

---

Johns Hopkins University Press, 1997); Richard Magat, *Unlikely Partners: Philanthropic Foundations and the Labor Movement* (Ithaca: Cornell University Press, 1999). For a recent assessment of the role of nonprofits in policy and politics see Elisabeth S. Clemens and Doug Guthrie, eds., *Politics and Partnerships: The Role of Voluntary Associations in America's Political Past and Present* (Chicago: University of Chicago Press, 2010).

[45] Dewey defined the "public" to include "all those who are affected by the indirect consequences of transactions to such an extent that it is deemed necessary to have those consequences systematically cared for." John Dewey, *The Public and Its Problems*, 15–16.

[46] Herbert Hoover, *American Individualism* (Garden City: Doubleday, Page & Company, 1922), 9.

whose work makes clear that to understand the development of Hoover's "associational state" in the 1920s we *must* look outside of the state to these nonprofit organizations. Historian Guy Alchon further builds on the associational model by calling attention to the relationship between nonprofits, specifically the National Bureau of Economic Research (NBER), and state policy making in the 1920s. Alchon describes cooperation between the NBER, select philanthropic foundations, and the Department of Commerce as a "three-legged apparatus" designed by Hoover and his associates to "provide a 'middle way' between statist collectivism and laissez-faire individualism." Alchon's work provides historians with the most comprehensive view of 1920s policy making, but he privileges the NBER's work at the expense of numerous other governmental and nongovernmental institutions that had equal or greater impact on economic inquiry and labor policy. Even in areas that were the primary focus of the NBER studies, such as business cycle analysis, the NBER was beaten to the punch by the American Federation of Labor Research Bureau and others who, by mid-decade, had developed an understanding of the business cycle that identified the need for high wages to provide a market for the increasing number of goods produced by industry. In fact, the NBER's emphasis on the cycle of "production-consumption" in its 1929 publication *Recent Economic Changes* echoed the AFL's earlier findings.

To bring this new economy about, Hoover and his allies embraced what I describe as voluntary corporatism, as distinguished from what has been described in the historiography as corporate liberalism and associational liberalism.[47] Pioneering work by Martin Sklar and others

[47] The literature on liberalism is vast and important. The following is only meant to sketch out some of the approaches to understanding the history of liberalism in the United States. On statist liberalism versus corporate liberalism, see in particular Mary O. Furner, "Structure and Virtue in the United States Political Economy," *Journal of Economic Thought* 27 (2005): 13–39; Mary O. Furner, "Knowing Capitalism;" and Mary O. Furner, "The Republican Tradition and the New Liberalism: Social Investigation, State Building, and Social Learning in the Gilded Age," in *The State and Social Investigation in Britain and the United States*, 171–241. On more statist versions of liberalism, in addition to Furner, see, for instance, Douglas C. Rossinow, *Visions of Progress: The Left-Liberal Tradition in America* (Philadelphia: University of Pennsylvania Press, 2008). The most important early work on corporate liberalism can be found in a number of 1960s publications, including Martin Sklar, "The Political Economy of Modern United States Liberalism," *Studies on the Left* 1 (1960): 17–47; James Weinstein, *The Corporate Ideal and the Liberal State: 1900–1918* (Boston: Beacon Press, 1968); Gabriel Kolko, *The Triumph of Conservatism: A Reinterpretation of American History, 1900–1916* (New York: The Free Press, 1963); and Sklar's later work, which recasts corporate liberalism in a number of important respects, Martin J. Sklar, *Corporate Reconstruction of American Capitalism, 1890–1916* (Cambridge: Cambridge University Press, 1988). On

concerning the history of corporate liberalism suggests the triumph of corporate liberalism by World War I, but the vibrant New Era and New Deal debate over how best to reorder the economy along more liberal lines indicates that this debate was far from settled. In fact, we do not see a continuation of corporate liberalism in the New Era, at least as that term has been used by Sklar and, to a lesser degree, Ellis Hawley. From the standpoint of state development theories, voluntary corporatists embraced the belief that business, labor, and the public were to be represented in a system that minimized the need for regulation. Expert inquiry and investigation into public problems, voluntary corporatists believed, would reveal the most efficient and appropriate means of bringing this vision of society to pass. For Sklar, the central aim of corporate liberalism in law, government, and economics was to win the legal affirmation of the consequences of the Great Merger Movement, namely the capacity of dominant firms to suppress "ruinous competition" by way of administered markets that eliminated overproduction and allowed for some measure of price setting. Acting as a ruling class elite, farsighted corporate liberals won strategic allies among professionals and organized labor in a carefully orchestrated crusade to involve the state – preferably minimally – in removing instabilities in the industrial and financial sectors, rectifying class relations that recurrently threatened the ability of U.S. capitalism to reproduce itself, and eliminating left-democratic movements such as Populism and socialism that threatened to create a political regime built upon ideological parties. The Harding, Coolidge, and Hoover administrations, too, encouraged further stabilization efforts and fostered cooperation within industries by way of trade associations and drastically peddled back enforcement of antitrust laws. Their goals were quite different from the aim of those earlier stabilizers who sought to create and find legal protection for measures – such as the Great Merger Movement – to contrive price-level protecting scarcity. Quite the opposite, in fact; instead, they worked to promote widely shared prosperity by way of economic growth, more widely shared plenty, and the management of the business cycle. Ideologically, if not always in practice, voluntary corporatism embraced the notion that labor and capital shared a common interest in achieving these goals. Thus, voluntary corporatists

the associational state, see Ellis Hawley, "Herbert Hoover, the Commerce Secretariat, and the Vision of an 'Associative State,'" *JAH* 61 (1974): 116–40. Also see Brinkley, *End of Reform* and Brian Balogh, *A Government Out of Sight: The Mystery of National Authority in Nineteenth Century America* (New York: Cambridge University Press, 2009).

recognized the centrality of workers as both laborers and consumers, which stands in marked contrast to the relative absence of labor in the corporate liberal analysis.

Not everyone, of course, embraced the voluntary corporatist ideology. Throughout the New Era, we can see abundant evidence of a continued preference in some quarters for a more statist liberalism, as originally described by Mary Furner, which links the more interventionist policies embraced by some Progressive Era and the New Deal policy makers and reformers.[48] The work of the WB, NUL, Mary van Kleeck, Paul Douglas, and John Maurice Clark should be understood as part of a longer statist liberal tradition with deep roots in the late nineteenth century. This group did not share the Hooverites' faith that economic growth could cure all social ills, nor did they see an economy or society so fundamentally altered that the interests of labor and capital had suddenly aligned. Instead, New Era statist liberals argued that, now more than ever, the state must play an active role in protecting American citizens and workers from the increasing power of corporations beholden to anonymous stockholders. Among other things, this group argued that the federal government should enforce the Fourteenth and Fifteenth Amendments and that the Supreme Court should finally reject outworn, laissez-faire ideas embodied in the *Adkins* decision. Protecting the liberal society, they argued, required institutions – among them independent unions, a strong, informed, and capable state, and robust institutions of inquiry – that could identify public problems and mediate the, as they saw it, often divergent concerns of business, individual, rights-bearing citizens, and the nation as a whole. The Great Depression and New Deal surely confirmed this group's suspicions concerning the weaknesses and vulnerabilities woven into important aspects of New Era economic thought, but the persistent belief through much of the twentieth century in the healing power of growth suggests an economic message that resonated well beyond the New Era.

American Labor and Economic Citizenship begins with an analysis of Herbert Hoover's efforts to surround himself with a group of influential employers, engineers, economists, labor leaders, investigators, and policy

---

[48] Furner, "The Republican Tradition and the New Liberalism: Social Investigation, State Building, and Social Learning in the Gilded Age"; Furner, "Knowing Capitalism,"; Furner, "From 'State Interference' to the 'Return of the Market': The Rhetoric of Economic Regulation from the Old Gilded Age to the New," in *Government and Markets: Toward a New Theory of Regulation*, eds. Edward Baleissen and David Moss (Cambridge: Cambridge University Press, 2009), 92–142.

makers. Working in an era defined in many respects by economic growth and unevenly shared but still quite significant prosperity, this group came to see growth and consumption as the means to address labor-capital conflict and business cycle instability. In this New Era conceptualization of the economy, workers became, as Secretary of Labor James J. Davis described it, "the great buying public" who now served as "a stimulant to both consumption and production."[49] Knowledge and expertise regarding industrial conditions, they came to believe, not worker representation in industry or government control of industry, would point the way to more efficient production and a more just economic order. The first chapter examines how Hooverites achieved positions of authority throughout federal government, academic, and nonprofit institutions and used these positions to shape important aspects of the economic policy discourse of the decade. Bolstered by their apparent success in curing the post–World War I recession, this group went about its work of reorganizing the U.S. economic policy with great confidence. As Chapter 1 makes clear, Hooverites' apparent success in managing the economy allowed Hoover and his colleagues to reshape economic policy, but it also blinded them to flaws in their knowledge and conceptualization of the New Era economy.

Chapter 2 argues that as statistical methods for measuring real wages improved, economists developed a new understanding of the social purpose of wages that challenged neoclassical assumptions while grappling with the significance of the emerging consumer-driven economy. Following the war, Wesley C. Mitchell led a group of statisticians and economists who worked to improve the quality of government statistics. As this effort was taking shape, Paul Douglas, Isaac Rubinow, and others engaged in a series of investigations into the trajectory of real wages in the United States. Their initial findings, which described a troubling story of declining real wages from the 1890s to the early years of the twentieth century, led Douglas and John Maurice Clark to argue for greater public intervention in the economy. Continued efforts to make sense of the movement of wages led to yet another jarring discovery: namely, that since World War I, the real wages of workers had risen by some estimates as much as 30 percent. Chapter 2 considers the efforts of economists in and out of government to better understand the history of real wage movement and its significance.

---

[49] James J. Davis, "The Saving and Earning Wage," File 167/830 Wages, Box 183, Entry 1, RG 174 General Records of the Department of Labor, NA.

Chapter 3 examines how, during the New Era, unions struggled to justify their own existence. It took economists until the mid-1920s to recognize the increase in workers' earning power, but by then unions had already begun to grapple with the implications of this historic change. In an economy where workers seemed to be benefiting from the proliferation of consumer goods despite the decline in union power, the AFL largely turned away from confrontation and efforts to maintain control of the work process, redefining itself as a partner in industry and a watchdog for economic instability. Labor experts associated with organized labor developed institutions of labor investigation in union research departments and in pioneering nonprofit research organizations specifically designed to serve as a research arm to organized labor. As the decade unfolded, these experts developed a new theory of wages designed to ensure economic stability and growth. In addition, they experimented with various means of reorganizing labor-management relations so as to secure optimal productivity while maintaining a place for unions in this new economic system.

The historical actors in Chapters 4 through 7 took a more skeptical view of varying aspects of this much-heralded new economy. The wartime goal of spreading democracy abroad inspired workers to demand a greater democratization of industry at home, but it also stimulated some employers to attempt to invigorate and alter long-standing paternalistic traditions, infusing them with a democratic impulse that sought employee consent and cooperation in increasing efficiency and maintaining economic stability. Various groups made competing claims about the success of these efforts. Chapter 4 describes the Russell Sage Foundation's effort to evaluate the strengths and weakness of the most prominent of these plans. The updating of older traditions and experimentation with new organizational structures took place against the backdrop of changes in the structure of business ownership. Chapter 4 explores how the move from proprietary to corporate capitalism posed a possibly intractable problem for these sorts of experiments by fundamentally altering the relationships among stockholders, managers, and employees. Mary van Kleeck and other RSF investigators came to recognize the importance of individual managers in the development of progressive labor relations strategies in the 1920s and looked with great concern on the rise to power of anonymous stockholders.

The last three chapters describe, in part, a research network that emerged among a cadre of experts and institutions concerned with the status of black, Mexican, and women workers. Facing a constant scarcity of resources, they often collaborated to further each other's work. In the government sphere, Mary van Kleeck, who first headed what would become the Women's Bureau, worked with the Division of Negro Economics to advance inquiry into the status of black women. In the nonprofit sphere, the Laura Spellman Rockefeller Memorial recognized the significance of black and Mexican migration into Northern industry and coordinated the funding for some of the most important studies of the era. At times, this group also recognized shared concerns. When Van Kleeck addressed the NUL and spoke of employers who followed "blindly the myths about the incapacity of women and their industrial traits" and the resulting lack of access to better-paying occupations and equal pay for equal work, leaders in the NUL could nod in agreement. "This situation is almost identical with that of Negro workers," they concluded in the pages of the NUL's monthly, *Opportunity*.[50] Yet at other times, a shared status could be of great concern, as when experts gravely pondered the reality that with the ending of mass immigration after World War I, black, Mexican American, and Mexican immigrant workers appeared to be left to compete with against one another for the least skilled and poorest paying occupations.

Chapter 5 demonstrates that during a decade when policy makers celebrated the fruits of economic abundance garnered with only the lightest touch from the state, Women's Bureau leaders and investigators saw gender research as a form of labor activism that would advance the cause of all workers. This chapter describes how the WB worked to replace false conceptions of the woman worker that emphasized women as exclusively temporary entrants into the labor market, with an understanding that stressed the permanence and importance of women workers and of their wages to a modern industrial and increasingly consumer-oriented economy. Though WB leaders would have preferred the use of labor standards to better the conditions under which American workers worked, the New Era political climate often precluded such ambitious efforts. While they never fully abandoned the labor standards approach, the WB also contributed to more voluntaristic methods of improving working conditions, like those described in Chapter 1.

---

[50] "Tradition and Employment" *Opportunity* 2 (March 1924): 67. For similar sentiments expressed in personal correspondence, see T. Arnold Hill [director of NUL's Department of Industrial Relations] to Mary Anderson, July 20, 1926, file "A" 1926–9, Series 4 Industrial Relations Department, 1922–62, box 1, National Urban League Papers, Library of Congress.

Chapter 6 describes the efforts of African Americans and white labor experts and public officials who scrambled to develop institutions to make sense of the early stages of the Great Migration as it dramatically shook up settled – if utterly racist – patterns of work and residence. These efforts challenged received notions of race relations, which had long taken for granted an "ideology of black inferiority" that for generations had provided for many white Americans a serviceable understanding of the intractable nature of the Negro condition in the South. Their inquiry into the condition of black workers in the 1920s occurred in two intertwined phases, beginning with federal and state government World War I-era investigations of migration and racial violence and later moving to the nonprofit sector. During World War I, the federal government showed a keen if ephemeral interest in black workers. During the war, the War Labor Administration established the Division of Negro Economics within the Department of Labor to answer pressing public questions regarding dramatic changes in the black working class and to coordinate the placement of black workers in war industries. Concurrently, state governments established commissions to investigate the wartime and postwar surge in racial violence in cities such as East St. Louis and Chicago. These World War I-era investigations drew heavily from nonprofit organizations, such as the National Urban League, in filling its ranks of investigators. The investigation into the 1919 Chicago race riot serves as useful transition into the issues addressed in the following chapter for two reasons. First, though the governor ordered the investigation, the state did not see fit to provide any funding for it; instead, nonprofit and philanthropic organizations stepped forward with the funding to underwrite the study. As the next chapter demonstrates, when the federal government lost interest in incendiary race questions early in the decade some of these same institutions provided the funding for continued inquiry. Second, the Chicago investigations heralded the arrival of Charles S. Johnson, who became the decade's most important voice for a new understanding of African American workers and citizens.

Chapter 7 continues with many of the themes developed in the preceding two chapters concerning the use of inquiry as a form of activism. As the Great Migration continued after the war, Mexican immigrant and Mexican American workers increasingly joined black workers in agriculture and industry. When the debate over immigration from Europe picked up following World War I, policy makers concerned with the racial violence that boiled over in the nation's major cities struggled to balance the interests of those who wanted to use immigration policy to maintain some form of racial purity, thus excluding Mexicans from lawful entry, with agricultural interests who claimed that they could not survive without Mexican laborers. Much of this discussion demeaned Mexicans and Mexican Americans as either culturally or racially inferior, but, as with the case of African Americans, many voices offered a fuller and more accurate characterization that unblinkingly challenged the dominant racist narrative. The disappearance of the DNE after the war left a gaping hole in policy makers' resources for making sense of issues affecting black workers. This forced innovative experts and advocates of African American workers to construct non-state institutions of labor inquiry with the assistance of nonprofit and philanthropic organizations such as the National Urban League, the Laura Spellman Rockefeller Memorial, and the Carnegie Corporation. Later in the decade, an emerging group of experts on Mexican American and Mexican immigrant workers, including Paul S. Taylor, Ernesto Galarza, and Emory Bogardus, joined Johnson in combining demographic change, philanthropic funding, and inquiry to compel a rethinking on racial groups who were either ignored or marginalized. By drawing attention to variations across industries, workplaces, and regions, these experts demonstrated that segregation, racism, and discrimination were choices made by those with the power to do so, not inevitabilities or conditions.

I

"Hoovering" in the Twenties

Efficiency, Wages, and Growth in the "New Economic System"

> The new capitalism is making profits through cultivating or extending the principles of cooperation. It demands for its own prosperity, that its employees and the buying public shall be prosperous. It even demands the prosperity of its competitors.
> – Edward A. Filene[1]

> Our workers are the great buying public. If they are enriched they are better buyers, and so are a stimulant both to consumption and production. The manufacturer himself is prosperous only as his and all other wage-earning employees themselves are prosperous. The man who pays good wages is only paying himself good dividends. By paying the wages of contentment he has peace in his own industry, and he promotes peace in every other industry.
> – Secretary of Labor James J. Davis[2]

The period between World War I and the onset of the Great Depression witnessed a seismic shift in the way leading labor-relations experts and policy makers viewed the relationship between labor and capital. As the economy stumbled out of World War I, a conflict model of labor relations

---

[1] Edward A. Filene, "The New Capitalism," *Annals of the American Academy of Political and Social Science* 149 (May 1930): 5.

[2] James J. Davis, "The Saving and Earning Wage," Box 183, Entry 1, File 167/830 Wages, RG 174, NA.

The term *Hoovering* comes from a letter from Assistant Secretary of Commerce E. E. Hunt to New York businessman William Morrow. Hunt writes, "If you ever get down to Washington, be sure to let me know, as it will be a great pleasure to see you. I am still 'Hoovering.'" Hunt to Morrow, May 21, 1929, Chronological Files of E. E. Hunt, Box 1, File May 1929, Record Group (hereafter RG) 73, National Archives, (hereafter NA).

prevailed, suggesting that workers and employers had fundamentally different interests that could be best mediated by some system of collective bargaining. Within just a few years, however, economic stability, increasing real wages, and relative labor peace led labor experts from business, organized labor, academia, and nonprofits to converge around a new model that replaced conflict with an emphasis on consumption and growth as the key to widely shared prosperity, economic stability, and labor peace. Contrary to the World War I-era when the federal government, by way of the War Industries Board and other wartime institutions, intervened dramatically in highly contentious employee-employer relations, the New Era's "new economic system," as Herbert Hoover referred to it, emphasized efficiency, cooperation, and the power of voluntary corporatism to solve intractable workplace and economic problems.[3]

Despite its weaknesses, the vision of a new form of capitalism crafted and embraced by Hoover and his allies had lasting significance. Historian David Hart has argued that Hoover's New Era vision became an enduring – albeit not always effective – blueprint for twentieth-century state and society building. According to Hart, Hoover sought a middle ground between "freedom" and "planning" that could preserve republican virtue by promoting "self-government" of industry through trade associations and by using the government to generate information and expertise that would increase economic efficiency.[4] Indeed, Hoover's understanding of governance has had wide appeal at various moments across the twentieth century, but particularly in the post-1970 era when the political climate turned against the use of a regulatory state to deal with market failure. This conception of governance came to be embraced well beyond the usual cast of anti-statist Republicans. In fact, Hoover would have found much to agree with in President William J. Clinton's effort to reinvent the nation's regulatory regime in order to maximize "voluntary compliance by business."[5]

---

[3] Robert H. Zieger, "Herbert Hoover, the Wage-earner, and the 'New Economic System,' 1919–1929," *Business History Review* 51 (Summer 1977): 161–89. On World War I and the state, see Robert D. Cuff, *The War Industries Board: Business-Government Relations during World War I* (Baltimore: Johns Hopkins University Press, 1973) and Valerie Jean Connor, *The National War Labor Board: Stability, Social Justice, and the Voluntary State in World War I* (Chapel Hill: University of North Carolina Press, 1983).

[4] David Hart, "Herbert Hoover's Last Laugh: The Enduring Significance of the 'Associative State' in the United States," *Journal of Policy History* 10 (October 1998): 419–44.

[5] Edward J. Balleisen, "The Prospects for Effective Coregulation in the United States: A Historian's View from the Early Twenty-First Century," in *Government and Markets: Toward a New Theory of Regulation*, eds. Edward J. Balleisen and David A. Moss

It is vitally important to keep in mind that Hoover and his allies' embrace of the voluntary corporatist model for governance did not constitute merely a warmed-over version of nineteenth-century laissez-faire economics or even that mildly abetted by employer paternalism. Like an earlier generation of investors who had bought out Andrew Carnegie in part to stabilize the steel industry, Hoover was keenly aware of the fallibility of markets. In fact, on many occasions New Era policy makers affiliated with Hoover moved aggressively and decisively to shift the line that marked the boundary between public and private issues. This shift was particularly evident in the apparent resolution of long-standing issues related to the workday in the steel industry, which as recently as 1919 had spilled over into deadly conflict between workers and employers. Taken in the early twentieth century as a private concern to be decided between employer and employee, the hours issue was redefined by New Era leaders of industrial thought as a public concern to be settled through inquiry and deliberation by labor experts and policy makers whose investigations cultivated public support and convinced industry of the efficacy of the shorter workday.

Hoover's vision of a new form of capitalism took shape over the course of the decade and drew adherents from leading business, labor, academic, and government institutions. This group, referred to hereafter as "Hooverites," did not constitute a singular ideological category and came from a diverse array of institutions and backgrounds, but in general its members shared Hoover's confidence that issues such as the business cycle, employer-employee conflict, and draconian working conditions in industry could be addressed through thoughtful deliberation by well-informed experts.[6] Rather than conflict, Hooverites argued, knowledge and expertise of industrial conditions would point the way to more efficient production and a more humane economic order. As their understanding of the labor question evolved during the New Era, they came to

---

(New York: Cambridge University Press, 2010), 444; and Christine Parker, *The Open Corporation: Effective Self-Regulation and Democracy* (Cambridge: Cambridge University Press, 2002), 14. See also Daniel T. Rodgers, *The Age of Fracture* (Cambridge: Harvard University Press, 2011).

[6] On Hoover's rise and his allies in World War I and the New Era, see, for instance, Michael Bernstein, *Perilous Progress: Economists and the Public Purpose in Twentieth-Century America* (Princeton: Princeton University Press, 2001), 52–61; Guy Alchon, *The Invisible Hand of Planning: Capitalism, Social Science, and the State in the 1920s* (Princeton: Princeton University Press, 1985); and Ellis W. Hawley, "Herbert Hoover, the Commerce Secretariat, and the Vision of an 'Associative State,' 1921–1928," *JAH* 61 (June 1974): 116–40.

reject claims that workers and employers had different interests, stressing that all classes benefited from increased efficiency, wages, profits, and consumption. Bolstered by its apparent success in curing the post–World War I recession and the ensuing prosperity, this group went about its work of reorganizing U.S. economic policy with a level of confidence that at the time seemed quite warranted.

Working in an era of unprecedented economic growth, Hoover and his allies dominated the economic policy discourse on the federal level and significantly reshaped economic policy, but too often the absence of contrarian voices blinded them to flaws in their knowledge and conceptualization of the New Era economy. In areas such as income distribution and the need for a coercive power (union or state) to maintain adequate wages in an economy that increasingly relied on consumption as an outlet for the increased productive capacity of highly capitalized industries, the Hooverites misread data, failed to ask critical questions, and ignored conclusions that challenged assumptions about the adequacy of the voluntary corporatist state to address the related problems of unemployment, economic instability, increased income inequality, and low wages. In a significant transformation, by the end of the decade Hoover and his many followers had "learned" that independent rule-making unions were largely an obstacle to the efficient reorganization of industry and unnecessary in maintaining labor peace and a high-wage economy. As we will see in Chapter 3, despite its acceptance of much of the new political economy, organized labor worked hard – at times with a more accurate understanding of the strengths and weaknesses of the New Era economy – to carve out a place for itself in this new policy regime.

The Hooverites' ideas about the best means of organizing industry did not emerge fully formed and instead unfolded over the course of the decade. This chapter begins with an examination of the violent labor conflict combined with calls for greater democracy in industry that led President Woodrow Wilson to call for a series of industrial conferences that demonstrated the obvious relevance of a conflict model for understanding labor-capital relations. In congressional testimony, however, Herbert Hoover, while continuing to recognize the contrary interests of workers and capitalists, suggested a dramatic expansion in the public's role in mediating disagreement between the two parties. As Republicans rose to power after the war, the Hooverites continued to construct a New Era vision for the economy. Two reports by a group of efficiency-minded engineers, one on waste in industry and a second on the twelve-hour day, elevated the role of experts in addressing industrial problems while raising questions concerning the necessity and efficacy of collective bargaining. A period of relative labor peace and increasing purchasing power for workers followed the postwar recession. The responsibility for reporting and sorting out the meaning of the rapid economic changes under way fell to the Department of Labor (DOL), which found and described consistent improvement in the conditions and terms under which American workers labored. By decade's end, reports by the National Bureau of Economic Research (NBER) underscored just how far ideas about the organization of industry had shifted since World War I. In the latter years of the decade, a celebration of economic growth, increased consumption, and labor-management cooperation had displaced conflict and workers' drive for industrial democracy as the most vital issues in discussions among leaders in business, labor, and government.

POSTWAR LABOR UNREST AND THE ARRIVAL OF HERBERT HOOVER

As the nation emerged from World War I, observers would have been hard-pressed to find evidence of a convergence of interests between labor and capital. As described in the introduction, the postwar transition away from a wartime economy produced social and economic upheaval reminiscent of the worst years of the late nineteenth century. The most dramatic and highly publicized of these confrontations took place in the steel industry. In October 1919, as three hundred fifty thousand steelworkers walked off the job, the Woodrow Wilson administration convened the first National Industrial Conference, which brought together business, public, and labor leaders to resolve the postwar labor unrest. Though it raised important issues, the conference was doomed by organized labor's insistence on inserting the steel strike into conference deliberations, by U.S. Steel's unwillingness to negotiate with the American Federation of Labor (AFL), and by the federal government's refusal to get involved in settling the strike. Deep disagreement over the competing conceptions of postwar "industrial democracy" underlay the failure of the conference. Organized labor demanded equal footing with business and a corporatist system for governing industry, whereas business leaders sought to expunge unions from labor relations that they considered to be plant and firm concerns, replacing independent unions with shop committees that had no affiliation with outside unions. Continued labor unrest, the failure of the first conference, and a long-standing progressive desire to square the undemocratic tendencies of industry with the democratic ideals of the nation led Wilson to call the Second Industrial Conference in December.

At its core, the final report generated by the Second Industrial Conference adhered to the conflict model of employee-employer relations, which identified opposing interests of employers and workers and recognized the importance of independent unions for worker representation in defense of employees. The report explicitly recognized these divergent economic interests, concluding, "It is idle wholly to deny the existence of conflicting interest between employers and employees."[7] By unambiguously drawing attention to the fact that unions "also indirectly exerted an influence on standards in unorganized trades," the report recognized the significance of an independent union presence in industry to deter exploitation of workers by employers in nonunion as well as union shops.[8]

The Second Industrial Conference announced the arrival of Herbert Hoover as a leading coordinator and thinker in federal government policy making and revealed important aspects of Hoover's evolving understanding of industrial relations. During the war, Hoover had served ably as the director of the Food Service Administration, building a public persona he now cashed in on. Labor historian Melvyn Dubofsky has argued that Hoover in many respects dominated the conference proceedings, using the conference to call for "recognition of trade unions and the institution of routinized collective bargaining."[9] Dubofsky is correct on this to a point, but closer attention to Hoover's testimony before Congress reveals a tension between the prevailing ideas among industrial relations experts concerning the central importance of collective bargaining and Hoover's ideas about resolving conflict between labor and capital.

In May 1920, Hoover testified before the Committee on Education and Labor concerning the work of the Second Industrial Conference. Hoover did little to question the basic idea that employers and employees had distinct and different interests and he clearly acknowledged that in modern industry the old personal relationship between employer and employee had disappeared and some other mechanism needed to take its

---

[7] DOL, "Report of the Industrial Conference Called by the President," in *Annual Report of the Secretary of Labor, 1920* (Washington, DC: GPO, 1920), 240. See also Gary Dean Best, "President Wilson's Second Industrial Conference, 1919-1920," *Labor History* 16 (Fall 1975): 505-20; and Haggai Hurvitz, "Ideology and Industrial Conflict: President Wilson's First Industrial Conference of October 1919," *Labor History* 18 (1977): 509-24.

[8] DOL, "Report of the Industrial Conference Called by the President," 40.

[9] Melvyn Dubofsky, *The State and Labor in Modern America* (Chapel Hill: University of North Carolina Press, 1994), 80.

place. Hoover did not, however, view collective bargaining alone as the best means of resolving industrial conflict; in fact, in many respects his testimony points to the emergence of core tenets of New Era thinking concerning the best means of settling employer-employee disputes.

First, Hoover rejected the idea that the state should play a role as an arbiter of workplace disputes; instead, he argued for the organization of an industrial conference that would rely on a voluntary system mixing negotiation with investigation and publicity to resolve employment conflicts in which the public had an interest. Second, although binding arbitration enforced by the state repelled Hoover, he demonstrated an eagerness to move private matters, previously negotiated between employers and employees, squarely into the public domain. He argued confidently that moving employer-employee conflict into the public domain would clearly reveal which side was right and public pressure would force a fair and just resolution. In terms of process, if the proposed industrial conference – made up of industrial experts and representatives of employee and employer groups – could not unanimously resolve the issue in conflict, rather than arbitration, the matter would be turned over to the public. In the end, Hoover announced, "The whole thing rests on public opinion." When pressed on this issue by the chair of the committee, Senator William S. Kenyon (IA-R), who queried, "And the decrees are enforced by public opinion?" Hoover responded simply, "Entirely."[10] Third, Hoover distinguished between union and employee interests. On matters such as bonuses or profit-sharing programs, Hoover noted that employers had used such policies to undermine the efforts of unions, but he contended that they had "not been used to the detriment of the employee."[11]

Hoover would soon have an opportunity to test his philosophy against some of the most intractable problems in modern industry. As postwar labor disputes and economic instability dissipated, Hoover's attention shifted to addressing waste and inefficiencies in industry through the instrumentality of the voluntary corporatist state. Hoover and his allies began with an assessment of responsibility for waste in industry that culminated in a not-so-innovatively titled but widely cited study, *Waste in Industry*. Though widely quoted segments of the final report attributed the majority of industrial inefficiencies to employers, a closer reading of the report reveals a pointed criticism of trade union policies in the workplace, suggesting increasing ambivalence concerning what role unions should play in the

---

[10] Congress, Senate Committee on Education and Labor, *Industrial Conference Hearings on Report of the Industrial Conference*, 66th Cong., 2nd sess., May 14, 1920, 40.
[11] Ibid., 36.

New Era economy. This should not suggest, however, that Hoover failed to recognize employee grievances. Following the examination of waste in industry, Hoover, now serving as the secretary of commerce in the Harding administration, moved to a pointed attack on one of the nation's largest employers, U.S. Steel, which had turned back worker gains made during World War I to reinstate the twelve-hour day. Though the Hooverites consistently resisted using the coercive power of the state to effect change, they did not hesitate to use the very ideas Hoover had outlined in his earlier congressional testimony – that is, investigation, public pressure, and moral suasion – to shift issues largely deemed private concerns into subjects for public consideration, debate, and, at times, resolution.

CONFRONTING AND DEFINING WASTE IN INDUSTRY

In late 1920, a group of progressive engineers established the American Engineering Council of the Federated American Engineering Societies (FAES) and elected Hoover the organization's first president. As leader of this professional organization, Hoover spoke out on a wide variety of social and economic issues with an authority that surpassed that of other public figures. During the teens and twenties, no occupational or social group saw its status rise as quickly or as high as engineers did. In the years between 1880 and 1920, the engineering profession grew from seven thousand to one hundred thirty-six thousand members.[12] Thorstein Veblen looked hopefully to the revolutionary potential of engineers and described the emergence of a "class consciousness" in this rising group of professionals, who increasingly felt they alone had the tools and skills to resolve the "growing sense of waste and confusion in the management of industry by the financial agents of absentee ownership."[13]

Though he resigned as president when he moved to the Department of Commerce, Hoover remained involved in the FAES and immediately

---

[12] Edwin Layton, "Veblen and the Engineers," *American Quarterly* 14 (Spring 1962): 70.
[13] Thorstein Veblen, *The Engineers and the Price System* (New York: Viking Press, 1934), 71. The literature on the history of engineering and the rise and fall of engineers as agents of reform and planning is vast, but see Alchon, *The Invisible Hand of Planning*, 63–5; Samuel Haber, *Efficiency and Uplift* (Chicago: University of Chicago Press, 1964); Edwin Layton, *The Revolt of the Engineers: Social Responsibility and the American Engineering Profession* (Cleveland: Press of Case Western Reserve, 1971); Daniel Nelson, *A Mental Revolution: Scientific Management Since Taylor* (Columbus: Ohio State University Press, 1992); Daniel Nelson, *Managers and Workers: Origins of the New Factory System in the United States, 1880–1920* (Madison: University of Wisconsin Press, 1975); and Sanford Jacoby, *Employing Bureaucracy: Managers, Unions, and the Transformation of Work in American History, 1900–1945* (New York: Columbia University Press, 1985).

put leading engineers to work in search of a more orderly way of organizing industry.[14] In 1920, Hoover met with the executive council of the AFL in a meeting *The Survey Graphic* heralded as evidence of a "new understanding between trade unionists and engineers." "Labor leaders seem to be arriving at the opinion that the scientific approach of engineers may be very useful in helping them to reach solution of their own problems while engineers appear to think that the goodwill and creative energies of the workers can only be fully elicited by a call to cooperative service," *The Survey Graphic* reported.[15] In January 1921, as the nation endured yet another deep recession, Hoover appointed fifteen engineers to the Committee on Elimination of Waste in Industry (the number would later expand to seventeen). To study the economic and social costs of waste, the committee quickly gathered "such concrete information as might be used to stimulate action and to lay the foundation for other studies."[16] Over the course of five months, fifty engineers completed the fieldwork for the report with an additional thirty engineers and a number of their associates assisting in the completion and publication of the final report. The engineers examined restrictions and waste in seventy-three plants in the building industry, nine in men's ready-made clothing manufacturing, eight in boot and shoe manufacturing, six printing manufacturers, sixteen metal trades, and thirteen textile manufacturers. More than 100 plants provided additional information for the study.

Then and now the conclusions of the final report have been largely misunderstood. When *Waste in Industry* was published, contemporary observers often pointed to the report's identification of poor management as the most significant factor in industrial waste. The organized labor–affiliated Labor Bureau Inc. (LBI) used FAES research on the shoe industry as evidence that "labor's responsibility" for waste "was far smaller than that of management."[17] Representatives of employers took exception to

[14] Hoover to Calvert Townley, March 11, 1921, Box 23, Folder: American Engineering Council, 1921, Commerce Papers, Herbert Hoover Presidential Library (hereafter HHPL). For evidence of continued involvement, see several folders in Box 23, Commerce Papers, HHPL.
[15] "Unionists and Engineers," *Survey Graphic* XLV (November 27, 1920): 324. See also "Hoover's Appeal for Industrial Cooperation," *Survey Graphic* XLV (November 27, 1920): 325.
[16] Federated American Engineering Societies (hereafter FAES), *Waste in Industry* (New York: McGraw-Hill Book Company, 1921), v.
[17] Labor Bureau Inc. (hereafter LBI), "Wage Theories and Arguments: No. 8 Economic Waste," *FFW* 2 (May 1924): 2. See also LBI, "The Building Construction Industry," *FFW* 3 (August 1925): 1–2.

the report's findings. John Dunlop of *Industrial Management* took away much the same conclusion, referring to the report's conclusions as "a manifest injustice."[18] Historians, too, have focused on the nonlabor component of the report's discussion of waste. Historian Robert Zieger emphasized the report's conclusion that "industrial unrest and unemployment were often the products of poor management, intermittent operations, and wasteful manufacturing process."[19] In some respects this is an accurate characterization of FAES's findings. The engineers did conclude that "over 50% of the responsibility for ... waste can be placed at the door of management and less than 25% at the door of labor."[20] Additionally, the engineers at times embraced organized labor. Investigators optimistically described a constitutive moment for labor organizations, which they indicated had the opportunity to "draft for themselves a new bill of rights and responsibilities." According to the report, unions were "now great organizations with such funds and personnel at their disposal as would have seemed fantastic even a quarter a century ago."[21]

A closer reading of the report, however, would have given unions and their supporters ample reason for pause. Within the domain of employee-employer relations, the FAES identified workers' control as the greatest inefficiency and paid almost no attention to employers' abuse or exploitation of workers. Most of the waste attributable to employers could be corrected through employer associations and agreements on standardization, such as an agreement on paper sizes in the printing industry, but when the analysis turned to inefficiencies in the workplace, the focus switched to unions and their rules and customs.

Much of the criticism leveled against unions turned on their use of work and jurisdictional rules to maintain control of the work process at the point of production. According to the FAES, "Unions frequently require three or four skilled employees to perform various operations on a plain job which a single worker could satisfactorily do by himself." For example, union carpenters would not lay bricks and union printers refused to do a compositor's task of changing imprints.[22] In the printing industries, work rules clearly defined acceptable levels of productivity, which,

---

[18] John R. Dunlop to Hunt, July 22, 1921, Box 190, Folder: Elimination of Waste in Industry, 1921–2, Commerce Papers, HHPL.

[19] Robert H. Zieger, *Republicans and Labor, 1919–1929* (Lexington: University of Kentucky Press, 1969), 90; Alchon, *The Invisible Hand of Planning*, 67; Joseph Dorfman, *The Economic Mind in American Civilization* (New York: Viking Press, 1959), 4: 62–3.

[20] FAES, *Waste in Industry*, 9.

[21] Ibid., 27–8.

[22] Ibid., 19.

to the investigators' minds, restricted output by providing a barrier to rewarding more efficient workers. In construction industries, Sanford E. Thompson, a civil and mechanical engineer and a colleague of Frederick W. Taylor, attacked as inefficient a number of long-held union traditions, including union rules that restricted tasks on a work site to specific union workers, mandated a uniform minimum wage for all working in a trade, and enforced union control over the number of apprentices.[23] Hoover and the other investigators condemned unions for their opposition to the introduction of labor-saving machinery and tools. Among painters' unions, the FAES pointed to the refusal of union painters to use a brush wider than four and a half inches for oil paint or to work on sites that utilized spraying machines. Similarly, plumbers' and steamfitters' unions required that "all pipe up to 2 inches shall be cut and threaded on the job."[24]

In industries with a high union density, investigators' analysis of waste in the workplace skewed sharply against unions and failed to recognize organized labor's role as a protector of workers. In an examination of the costs in the construction of concrete buildings, Thompson reported, "Union labor was much less efficient than the non-union labor."[25] Future Harvard economist John H. Williams arrived at similar conclusions in his examination of the highly unionized printing industry: "Waste is notably less in non-union plants because of lack of restrictions enforced by the unions."[26] Additionally, FAES engineers accused unions of working as a protector of poorly trained workers. For instance, Thompson raised questions about the skill level of union workers, suggesting that amidst tight labor markets, unions had "taken in those having little skill or ability, and these still retain their union cards."[27] This attack on unions is particularly revealing as it suggests an inability by investigators to understand how unions might protect workers from some of the more ferocious aspects of the business cycle and employer exploitation. Further, these investigators' accusations expose an outrageous double standard that faulted unions for waste while ignoring employers' willingness to hire untrained workers in tight labor markets, thereby aiming to depress union wage levels.

[23] Ibid., 79–85.
[24] Ibid., 19.
[25] Ibid., 79.
[26] Ibid., 180.
[27] Ibid., 81.

Investigators continued this line of attack on unions when they outlined their own solutions to the problems they had identified. To correct these labor problems in industry, FAES investigators recommended a dramatic renegotiation or elimination of work rules that prevented groups of workers from executing tasks that fell outside their trades. In the printing trades, increased flexibility of workers, what we might now refer to as cross-training, would allow workers to "perform more than one service" for employers.[28] Further, the engineers advocated an expanded ability for employers to reward individual employees for efficient work, thus transforming union work rules designed to protect trades and promote worker solidarity into evidence that such rules depressed individualized pecuniary rewards for work. For instance, in the printing industry, employers, according to the report, lacked the "ability to determine what a worker can or should do," which left the employer "largely in the hands of employees, for he is unable fairly to reward his workers according to their effectiveness."[29]

Given the FAES's indictment of organized labor, unions might have been left wondering what their proper role was in an economy governed by engineers. Effective "industrial relations," according to the FAES, should be concerned with "educating the workman in the science of process, recording his accomplishment and enabling him to become conscious of the relationship of his work to the whole."[30] Rather than opposing efforts to increase efficiency, the FAES advised unions, they could render no service more valuable "than that of studying the needs of the industries in which they earn a livelihood, and allying themselves with the technicians who serve with them to increase production which will inure to the ultimate benefit of all."[31] With respect to the scope of conflict in bargaining, the FAES suggested that unions' proper role was insisting on "reasonable hours and the best pay obtainable."[32] Unions might also cooperate with management in decreasing industrial accidents, improving workplace safety, and assisting in the monitoring of workers' health through periodic physicals.[33]

The FAES's frequent and detailed discussion of employee responsibility for waste and workplace unrest stood in sharp contrast to its

[28] Ibid., 198.
[29] Ibid., 182–4.
[30] Ibid., 27.
[31] Ibid., 28.
[32] Ibid.
[33] Ibid.

investigators' lack of attention to employer treatment of employees as a source of industry waste. In a report on strikes and lockouts, MIT statistician and American Association for Labor Legislation (AALL) member Carroll Warren Doten indicated that strikes were useful as a "direct defense against injustice and oppression and as the only way of compelling the public to give its attention to hidden evils in industrial relations."[34] No other section of the report came anywhere near this level of frankness in analyzing the power difference between employers and employees in the 1920s or in recognizing the need for some mechanism to compel employers to fulfill their part in the New Era labor-management bargain. Investigators were no more specific in their analysis of the means for settling industrial disputes. In an examination of state and federal government mechanisms for adjusting labor disputes, statistician John Koren, who had conducted investigations for the Department of Labor going back to the Wright years, vaguely advised, "One of the urgent measures ... is to acquire the wisdom to create and operate successfully agencies endowed with sufficient power and wisdom to stop the thousands of destructive and needless controversies over labor questions."[35]

A PUBLIC CONCERN: THE WORKDAY IN THE STEEL INDUSTRY

Having attacked one aspect of waste in industry, the FAES joined labor experts in a wide variety of U.S. and European labor bureaus, health departments, and reform organizations that built a body of persuasive expertise demonstrating the inefficiencies in the twelve-hour day. This approach differed from earlier efforts to attack the long workday, such as the *Pittsburgh Survey* where investigators focused less on efficiency and more on the impact of excessive working hours on families.[36] These more recent studies and the reformers who conducted and publicized the results

---

[34] Ibid., 314. "Carroll Warren Doten," in *Who's Who in America*, ed. Albert Nelson Marquis (Chicago: The A. N. Marquis Company, 1928), 664.

[35] FAES, *Waste in Industry*, 317. "John Koren," in *Who's Who in America*, ed. Albert Nelson Marquis (Chicago: The A. N. Marquis Company, 1924), 1886.

[36] On the *Pittsburgh Survey*, see Paul Kellogg, *The Pittsburgh Survey*, 6 vols. (New York: Charities Publication Committee, 1909–14); "The Three Shifts in Steel," *Survey Graphic* XLV (December 11, 1920): 387. See also Maurine W. Greenwald and Margo Anderson, *Pittsburgh Surveyed: Social Science and Social Reform in the Early Twentieth Century* (Pittsburgh: University of Pittsburgh Press, 1996); Alice O'Connor, *Social Science for What?: Philanthropy and the Social Question in a World Turned Rightside Up* (New York: Russell Sage Foundation, 2007); Charles Hill, "Fighting the Twelve-Hour Day in the American Steel Industry," *Labor History* 15 (Winter 1974): 19–35.

successfully shifted the hours issue from a private concern to be settled between employer and employee to a public concern with ramifications for the public good. Such an approach affirmed Hoover's judgment concerning how best to solve even the most deep-seated of problems.

Around World War I, occasional research in the United States on the two-shift versus three-shift system in continuously operating industries gave way to a flood of investigations. In his early 1920s report concerning shift systems, efficiency expert Horace B. Drury noted, "There is an unbelievable lack of knowledge pertaining to the twelve-hour shift."[37] Investigations in the United States and Britain by Ira Stewart, Carroll D. Wright, and Robert Owen in the nineteenth century and, more recently, Margaret Byington, had publicized the relationship between efficiency and hours, but not until the 1920s did a large body of labor experts turn their attention to using expertise and investigation as a way of persuading business, the public, and policy makers of the benefits of the shorter workday.[38] H. M. Vernon's work with Britain's World War I-era Industrial Fatigue Board, Josephine Goldmark's pioneering prewar study, and a number of other investigations in Europe and the United States made the case that output could be maintained with shorter hours through increased worker efficiency.[39]

---

[37] Horace B. Drury, "A General Survey" in Committee On Work-Periods in Continuous-Industry of the Federated American Engineering Societies (author identified hereafter as FAES), *The Twelve Hour Shift in Industry* (New York: E. P. Dutton & Company, 1922), 31. Horace B. Drury, "The Three Shift System in the Steel Industry," *Bulletin of the Taylor Society* (February 1921).

[38] Margaret F. Byington, *Homestead: The Households of a Milltown* (New York: Russell Sage Foundation, 1910), 35, 171–2. For examples of Stewart's work, see Ira Stewart, "A Reduction of Hours an Increase of Wages," in John R. Commons, et al., eds., *A Documentary History of American Industrial Society* (Cleveland: The Arthur H. Clark Company, 1910), 284–301, originally published in *Fincher's Trades' Review*, October 14, 1865. See also Dorothy Douglas, "Ira Stewart on Consumption and Unemployment," *JPE* 40 (August 1921): 532–43. For a description of Wright's work, see "Engineers on Hours," *Survey Graphic* XLV (October 30, 1920): 151.

[39] For example, see Josephine Goldmark, *Fatigue and Efficiency: A Study in Industry* (New York: Charities Publication Committee, 1912); Felix Frankfurter, *The Case for the Shorter Work Day* (New York: National Consumer's League, 1916); H. M. Vernon, *Industrial Fatigue and Efficiency* (New York: E. P. Dutton, 1921); "Fatigue and the Steel Worker," *Survey Graphic* (June 4, 1921): 312; Edgar L. Collis and Major Greenwood, *The Health of the Industrial Worker* (Philadelphia: P. Blakinston's son & co, 1921); Carter Goodrich, *The Miner's Freedom: A Study of the Working Life in a Changing Industry* (New York: Workers Education Bureau of America, 1925); Charles S. Myers, *Industrial Psychology* (New York: The People's Institution Publishing Co., 1925); Federal Council of Churches of Christ in America, *The Twelve Hour Day in the Steel Industry: Its Social Consequences and Practability of Its Abolition* (New York: Federal Council of Churches of Christ in

The roots of these New Era efforts can be traced back to World War I, when labor experts and reformers started to develop bodies of knowledge more clearly demonstrating a link between increased efficiency and shorter shifts. During the summer of 1918, the United States Federal Public Health Service (FPHS), in cooperation with the National Research Council, brought together physiologists, chemists, and labor experts to conduct a two-year study of hours and fatigue that demonstrated the advantages to employers and employees of a shorter workday. Bryn Mawr graduate, National Consumer League research director, pioneer in the study of the relationship between efficiency and productivity, and sister-in-law to Justice Louis D. Brandeis, Josephine Goldmark, joined Mary D. Hopkins in leading the study. The FPHS found a "steady maintenance of output" in the eight-hour day and a declining output in the ten-hour day. Other benefits of an eight-hour day included a decrease in industrial accidents, turnover, work stoppages, and employee restrictions on output. FPHS investigators also examined the efficiency of twelve-hour night shift work and found "a progressive slowing in the rate of production during the night" and an "abrupt fall of output in the last two hours" of the shift.[40]

This growing body of efficiency and labor expertise found a worthy adversary in Judge Elbert H. Gary and U.S. Steel, whose return to the two-shift system following World War I provided a particularly scandalous example of the elimination of wartime gains in labor standards. In the early 1920s, labor and efficiency experts challenged the leaders of U.S. Steel, who insisted that anything less than a twelve-hour day was unworkable in continuous process industries. In 1910, 63 percent of

America, 1923); LBI, "Wage Theories and Arguments: No. 9 – The Worth of the Worker," *FFW* 2 (June 1924), 1; "Twelve Hour Steel Day Must Go, He Says," *NYT*, December 4, 1920, 17; "Billions Lost to Waste," *NYT*, November 23, 1922, 6; "Engineers Oppose Twelve-Hour Work Day," *NYT*, November 19, 1922, 44; "Finds Eight-Hour Day Aids Steel Mills," *NYT*, June 7, 1923, 10; "The Twelve Hour Day," *NYT*, September 20, 1922, 16; "The Eight-Hour Shift in Continuous Industries," *NYT*, June 18, 1923, 12; "Engineers on Hours," *Survey Graphic* XLV (October 30, 1920): 151.

[40] *Annual Report of the Surgeon General of the Public Health Service of the United States* (Washington, DC: GPO, 1919), 41–3; U.S. Public Health Service, "Comparison of an 8-hour plant and a 10-hour plant," *Public Health Bulletin* 106 (Washington, DC, 1920), 26. The Public Health Service conducted other studies that focused more specifically on the chemical effects of industrial fatigue on workers. See "The Physiology of Fatigue," *Public Health Bulletin* 117 (Washington, DC: GPO, 1921); *Annual Report of the Surgeon General of the Public Health Service of the United States* (Washington, DC: GPO, 1920), 37–8; *Annual Report of the Surgeon General of the Public Health Service of the United States* (Washington, DC: GPO, 1921), 32; *Annual Report of the Surgeon General of the Public Health Service of the United States* (Washington, DC: GPO, 1924), 26.

employees in the iron and steel industries worked a twelve-hour day and 29 percent worked seven days a week.[41] Pressure on U.S. Steel to institute the eight-hour day mounted throughout World War I and reached a fever pitch in 1919, when more than three hundred thousand steel workers unsuccessfully went on strike, demanding the eight-hour day, union recognition, and the six-day workweek.

Commerce Secretary Herbert Hoover led the Harding administration's charge for the adoption of the shorter workday by way of voluntary action rather than legislation. In May 1922, Hoover arranged a White House dinner conference at which he came "armed with reports, studies, and statistics to justify the abandonment of the twelve-hour system."[42] Hoover wrote days after the meeting that he hoped the steel industry would "take action which will give the steel industry credit for initiative instead of waiting until they are smashed into by some kind of legislation."[43] While the conference might appear at first blush to have failed, the publicity it aroused does appear to have had some effect on Gary. Following the White House event and after several meetings with Gary, Columbia University political scientist and Hoover ally Samuel McCune Lindsay described for Hoover his sense of the meeting's impact on Gary. "Judge Gary was impressed by the editorial comments," Lindsay wrote in a personal memo to Hoover, "and I think his committee will be likewise more amenable to the pressure of public opinion by reason of the White House Dinner Conference and the comments that have been made upon it."[44] Indeed, in the weeks after the meeting, Gary solicited confidential opinions from leaders at Commonwealth Steel and Electric Alloy Steel Company, both of which had already converted successfully to the eight-hour day and recommended U.S. Steel do the same.[45]

---

[41] BLS, *Report on Conditions of Employment in Iron and Steel Industry in the United States* (Printed as S. Doc. No. 301, 62nd Cong., 2nd sess.); "Calendar of the Twelve-Hour Day in the Steel Industry," *ALLR* 13 (September 1923): 188; FAES, *The Twelve Hour Shift in Industry* (New York: E. P. Dutton & Company, 1922): 224-7.

[42] Zieger, *Republicans and Labor*, 101. Kendrick A. Clements, *The Life Of Herbert Hoover: Imperfect Visionary, 1918-1928* (New York: Palgrave Macmillan, 2010), 219-21.

[43] Herbert Hoover to John V. W. Reynders, May 22, 1922, Box 614, Folder Twelve-Hour Day, 1921-2, Commerce Papers, HHPL.

[44] Samuel McCune Lindsay to Hoover, May 27, 1922, Box 614, Folder: Twelve-Hour Day, 1921-2, Commerce Papers, HHPL

[45] Clarence H. Howard to Herbert Hoover, June 10, 1922; Howard to Gary, June 5, 1922; Hoover to Howard, June 13, 1922; L. J. Campbell to Hoover, June 17, 1922; Campbell to Committee on Elimination of Twelve Hour Day (AISI), June 15, 1922; Hoover to Campbell, June 22, 1922. All in Box 614, Folder Twelve-Hour Day, 1921-2, Commerce Papers, HHPL.

In public, Gary showed little evidence of a willingness to bend. On May 26, at the annual meeting of the American Iron and Steel Institute (AISI), the research and political arm of the steel industry, Gary ordered an investigation into the viability of the eight-hour day in the industry. Within Hooverite circles, this study was viewed from the start as plainly disingenuous, and its conclusions did nothing to dampen this skepticism. When Judge Gary announced the committee's findings, he reported: "the alleged hardships and ill effects of the twelve-hour day had been misrepresented by those unfamiliar with the industry."[46] Further, a tight labor market and a preference on the part of employees for the twelve-hour day made any switch undesirable and unworkable.[47] The AALL reported, correctly, that the AISI's actions "went dead against the facts brought out in many competent, disinterested investigations."[48]

The task of convincing the steel trust and the public that the eight-hour day was possible and profitable fell on a number of labor experts, engineers, and public leaders, who continued to combine publicity and expertise to make their case successfully. With Hoover's strong support, the FAES turned its attention to the workday in the steel industry. The FAES tapped Horace B. Drury to lead the ensuing Cabot Fund-financed investigation. Throughout this period, Drury, a former Ohio State University economist and member of the Industrial Relations Division of the U.S. Shipping Board, used his investigations for the FAES, Cabot Fund, and Taylor Society to establish himself as a leading expert on the shift system. Drury examined the shift system in a range of industries, while Bradley Stoughton was charged with examining the technical aspects of moving to a three-shift system in the steel industry. Stoughton, a metallurgical engineer with a long association with the industry, held a number of business and university posts, including acting head of the department of metallurgy at Columbia University School of Mines, manager of the Bessemer steel department with Benjamin Atha & Company in New Jersey, vice-chairman of the engineering division of the National

---

[46] Howard H. Cook, "The American Iron and Steel Institute," *Army Ordnance: The Journal of the Army Ordnance Association* 4 (September–October 1923): 76.

[47] "The Work Day in Steel," *Survey Graphic* XLVI (April 24, 1921): 101. Sanford E. Thompson to E. E. Hunt, May 19, 1922; Richard S. Emmet to Thompson, May 20, 1922; and Thompson to Emmet, May 22, 1922, Box 614, Folder Twelve Hour Day, 1921-2, Commerce Papers, HHPL.

[48] Frederick W. MacKenzie, "Steel Abandons the Twelve-Hour Day," *ALLR* 13 (September 1923): 181. Charles R. Walker, "The Twelve-Hour Shift," *ALLR* 13 (June 1923): 108–18; and Charles R. Walker, *Steel: The Diary of a Furnace Worker* (Boston: Atlantic Monthly Press, 1922).

Research Council, and secretary of the American Institute of Mining and Metallurgical Engineers. During World War I, he served as a member of the Welding Committee of the Emergency Fleet Corporation.[49]

Together, Drury and Stoughton attacked U.S. Steel's position from several angles and produced a 300-page report entitled *The Twelve Hour Shift in Industry* (1922), which Hoover described in a letter to President Harding as expressing "unanimity of the whole engineering profession in their demonstration that from a technical point of view there is no difficulty with what was obviously necessary from a social point of view."[50] Drury found numerous industries that had successfully and profitably transitioned from a two-shift to a three-shift system. In nonferrous metal industries in the western United States, companies had successfully moved to the three-shift system at the turn of the century, whereas in the East and South, the managers in these industries had made the switch during and shortly after World War I. Drury found considerable evidence to suggest that a move to the three-shift system benefited both workers and employers. Blast furnace managers in three-shift plants "emphatically asserted" that "the higher grade of labor attracted by the shorter hours, the greater care and alertness, better work, and more skillful operation are all reflected in a saving in cost of production."[51] Similarly, in the pig iron and rolling mills surveyed, investigators found that the eight-hour shift increased efficiency and decreased the costs of production.[52] After a survey of the twenty United States steel mills that had made the move to the three-shift day, Drury concluded, "If all the departments in a steel plant were to be changed from two to three shifts, the increase in total cost for the finished rail, bar or sheet could not on the average be more than 3 per cent."[53] Outside of steel production, Drury found that in "practically every major continuous-industry there are plants which have increased the quality of production per man up to as much as 25 per cent" after going to the three-shift system.[54]

---

[49] Stoughton had also served as the chief of the Costs Statistical Division at the American Steel and Wire Company. Bradley Stoughton, "The Iron and Steel Industry," in FAES, *The Twelve Hour Shift in Industry* (New York: E. P. Dutton & Company, 1922), 217; and "Bradley Stoughton," in *Who's Who in America*, ed. Albert Nelson Marquis (Chicago: The A. N. Marquis Company, 1928), 1999.
[50] Zieger, *Republicans and Labor*, 103.
[51] FAES, *The Twelve Hour Shift in Industry*, 18.
[52] Ibid., 18–19.
[53] Horace B. Drury, "The Three-Shift System in the Steel Industry," *AF* 38 (February 1921): 128.
[54] Drury, "A General Survey," in FAES, *Twelve Hour Shift in Industry*, 212–13.

Turning their attention to U.S. Steel specifically, investigators found the company employed seventy thousand workers in the twelve-hour shift, with another eighty thousand steel workers similarly employed in non-U.S. Steel firms. In Drury's contribution to the report, he publicized the move to a three-shift system in a number of plants, such as the American Rolling Mill Company and the Colorado Fuel and Iron Company, as evidence that continuously operating steel mills could function with a three-shift system. Drury noted, "In the overwhelming majority of the plants which have changed from two- to three-shift operation no technical difficulties have been encountered."[55] Regarding the durability of the move by firms to the three-shift system, he noted, "It is very significant that, during the late period of very acute depression, exceedingly few companies, either in the steel industry or in other industries, have seen fit to go back from eight-hour to twelve-hour shifts."[56] Drury and others also dispelled Gary's spurious assertion that the men in the plants preferred the twelve-hour day by pointing to many workers' willingness to take a pay cut in order to achieve a shorter workday.[57]

Bradley Stoughton wrote the third section of the report, which described the costs and benefits of the three-shift system in the iron and steel industry and demonstrated how, with careful planning, the three-shift system would drive down costs. He provided clear evidence and numerous examples of increased efficiencies and decreased waste resulting from the adoption of the eight-hour day. According to Stoughton, the hard physical labor of steel production meant that firms using the twelve-hour shift had to employ additional laborers on each shift in order to allow for periodic breaks, which sometimes amounted to three and a half hours per shift. Additionally, at the end of shifts, foremen in twelve-hour plants recognized that men were simply too tired to work and frequently postponed production until fresh men arrived in the next shift.[58] Three-shift plant managers also testified that they were able to recruit a "better class of labor" and a sufficient supply of appropriately skilled workers.[59] Finally,

[55] Ibid., 210.
[56] Ibid., 55.
[57] Drury, "Three-Shift System in the Steel Industry," 130; see also "Gary and His Twelve-Hour Day," *AF* 30 (August 1923): 638–47.
[58] Stoughton, "The Iron and Steel Industry," 221, 222, 228, 231, 270–2, and 274–6. For a summary of advantages of the three-shift system, see pages 290–3 of the report and L. W. Wallace, "The Twelve-Hour Shift in American Industry," *NCSW* (Chicago: University of Chicago Press, 1920): 142–5.
[59] Stoughton, "The Iron and Steel Industry," 240–1.

Stoughton pointed to the public relations advantages to employing an eight-hour day. During labor disputes, Stoughton advised, "The company which is working its men only eight hours a day enjoys much greater prestige with the public, whose influence in a labor dispute is always important."[60]

Between 1921 and 1923, religious organizations, labor legislation advocates, and even U.S. Steel stockholders joined Hoover and the FAES in investigating and publicizing the demerits of the twelve-hour day. *The Survey Graphic* devoted nearly an entire issue to the report's findings and to undermining Gary and U.S. Steel's case, and the publication was hardly alone.[61] The National Urban League, which as we will see in Chapter 7 had to constantly balance appeals to employers and organized labor, embraced the committee's findings.[62] To Judge Gary's contention that the three-shift system was unworkable in a tight labor market, a report issued by the Federal Council of Churches of Christ in America, the National Catholic Welfare Council, and the Central Conference of American Rabbis responded that the "shortage of labor was not the reason for the failure to abolish the long day two years ago, when there was appalling unemployment, which could have been in large measure relieved in steel manufacturing districts by introducing the three-shift system in the steel industry."[63] An investigation ordered by the stockholders of U.S. Steel added that "a twelve-hour day of labor, followed continuously by any group of men for any considerable number of years means a decrease of the efficiency and lessening of the vigor and virility of such men."[64] In June 1922, the AALL began publishing a series of articles sharply critical of Gary and the steel companies that clung to the twelve-hour day. The AALL reported that at least twenty non-U.S. Steel firms had adopted the eight-hour day.[65] *The Survey*, meanwhile, noted

---

[60] Ibid., 291.
[61] *Survey Graphic* XLV (March 5, 1921).
[62] "The Twelve-Hour Day," *Opportunity* 1 (July 1923), 194.
[63] "Organized Religion Condemns Gary of Inhuman Twelve-Hour Day," *IMJ* 59 (July 1923) 390–1; "Churches Condemn 12-Hour Steel Day," *NYT*, June 6, 1923, 23; "Long Working Hours Condemned by Rabbis," *NYT*, June 29, 1923, 28; and "Again the Twelve Hour Day," *NYT*, June 7, 1923, 18.
[64] "Organized Religion Condemns Gary," *IMJ*, 390; "Engineers Oppose Twelve Hour Day," *NYT*, November 19, 1922, 44.
[65] "Calendar of the Twelve-Hour Day in the Steel Industry," *ALLR* 13 (September 1923): 188; Mackenzie, "Steel Abandons the Twelve-Hour Day," 183; *ALLR* 12 (June 1922): 121. Walker, "The Twelve-Hour Shift," 108–18; and Walker, *Steel: The Diary of a Furnace Worker*.

in its review of U.S. Steel's annual report that the corporation's profits were such that "whatever practical objections there may be to introducing in 1921 the three-shift system, these obstacles were not financial."[66] Solidifying the consensus further, even John D. Rockefeller, Jr. came out publicly for the shorter day in the steel industry.[67]

Expert advice and informed public opinion mattered. On August 2, 1923, the American Iron and Steel Institute reversed its earlier decision and announced it would eliminate the twelve-hour day as soon as possible. The AALL referred to the change as "one of the most remarkable demonstrations in the history of industrial progress of the power of the public to compel the repudiation by employers of indecent working standards."[68] After its introduction, even former opponents expressed surprise at the quality of work and ample supply of labor in the steel works. The *Annalist*, a Washington, DC financial publication, stated, "There is no complaint whatever from the manufacturers of a shortage of available labor.... Curiously enough, the advertisement which the eight-hour day has received in the last month or so has attracted a considerable number of laborers to the mill centers, and the new laborers seem to be of a higher grade than the steel companies ordinarily have been able to attract."[69]

The successful struggle against the twelve-hour day in the steel industry emboldened Hooverites, who moved with increasing confidence against an array of economic problems and awakened the AFL to the power of facts and expertise to persuade the public and employers of the legitimacy of labor's demands. But the victory, combined with Hoover's earlier testimony and the case presented against unions in *Waste in Industry*, raised questions regarding the necessity of unions to defend workers and the public's interests. Though unions and steel workers had struggled after World War I to eliminate the twelve-hour day once and for all, victory came only when a number of labor experts made the inefficiencies,

---

[66] "The U.S. Steel Report," *Survey Graphic* (April 9, 1921): 42.
[67] "Rockefeller Urges Fairness to Labor," *NYT*, November 16, 1923, 1.
[68] Mackenzie, "Steel Abandons the Twelve-Hour Day," 180.
[69] Quoted in "Eight Hour Day 'Surprises' Editor," *AFL: WNS* 13 (September 1923): 1. For a similar sentiment from business observers, see "Steel Plants Aided by Short Work Day," *AFL: WNS* 13 (November 10, 1923): 1; "Steel Trust Accepts 8-Hour Theory," *AFL: WNS* 13 (March 8, 1924): 1; "Its Work What It Costs," *NYT*, February 28, 1924, 18; LBI, "The Five-Day Week," *FFW* 5 (November 1926): 1–2; "Short Day in Steel Mills has Pleased All," *NYT*, August 31, 1924, 28; Other industries concurred that the shorter day worked well; see "Says Short Day Adds Oil," *NYT*, January 31, 1923.

dangers, and injustices of long working hours a public concern. When U.S. Steel eliminated the twelve-hour day in 1923, organized labor was largely on the sidelines cheering the labor experts and officials who had carried the day. The ability to investigate and settle such a complicated and controversial issue increased the confidence of Hooverites, who believed more and more in the power of unbiased investigation and reasoned discourse to solve long-standing labor and economic problems – precisely the approach Hoover had advocated before Congress in May 1920. By the mid-1920s, Bureau of Labor Statistics (BLS) reports fortified this belief by suggesting that workers were earning more money, working less, and striking with much less frequency – all despite the decline in organized labor's strength.

WAGES, HOURS, AND "A FEELING OF PARTNERSHIP"

After the initial flurry of attention in the early 1920s, the problem of industrial conflict receded in importance among Hoover's followers, who came to take the era's relative economic stability as evidence of their effectiveness in addressing the labor question. Prior to the Harding administration, the Department of Labor had been a key site for drawing attention to important issues facing American workers, but during the 1920s, a diminished department appropriation and evidence of increasing wages, decreased hours, and industrial peace transformed the DOL into a mouthpiece for Hooverites, who congratulated themselves for addressing an issue that only years earlier had seemed as intractable as it had been durable. By mid-1925, Secretary of Labor James J. Davis noted a "better, kindlier feeling among men engaged in industry." Davis confidently announced in his 1925 annual report and elsewhere that American workers "generally are enjoying a prosperity far beyond that achieved by any other people at any other period in history. There is a better feeling prevailing among employers and workers – a feeling of partnership, a realization that the success of the one depends on the success of the other."[70]

---

[70] James J. Davis, *Thirteenth Annual Report of the Secretary of Labor* (Washington, DC: GPO, 1925): 137. For similar statements by Davis, see James J. Davis, *Fourteenth Annual Report of the Secretary of Labor* (Washington, DC: GPO, 1926): 145–6; James J. Davis, *Fifteenth Annual Report of the Secretary of Labor* (Washington, DC: GPO, 1927): 137–45, 206–7; James J. Davis, *Sixteenth Annual Report of the Secretary of Labor* (Washington, DC: GPO, 1928): 166–78; James J. Davis, *Seventeenth Annual Report of the Secretary of Labor* (Washington, DC: GPO, 1929): 2–3.

Davis's leadership of the DOL has properly been criticized by labor historians such as Melvyn Dubofsky, who dismissed Davis as "a veritable Babbitt, a typical small-town booster and joiner, proud of his membership in male fraternal orders and clubs too numerous to count."[71] According to Zieger, when Hoover convened the President's Conference on Unemployment, Davis did not attend the initial meeting, indicating that he had several fraternal conventions to attend. Davis originally was to help direct the conference, but "aside from making suggestions for appointments, he deferred almost completely" to Hoover, "his more able colleague," in Zieger's assessment.[72] Davis avoided taking positions on labor issues that would, seemingly, have been of interest to a person in his position. In a memo to Dr. Julies Klein regarding the administration's position on the five-day workweek, a likely bemused E. E. Hunt wrote, "I had supposed that Secretary Davis was an advocate of the five-day week, but on consulting his private secretary in his absences I find that apparently he has made no public statement."[73]

By any standard, Davis was not a strong secretary of labor. He did, however, preside over the department at a time of deep budget cuts (to some, but not all parts of the department), entirely unsympathetic Republican administrations, and rising concern over immigration and migration as the most public labor issue of the day.[74] Unlike his predecessor, William B. Wilson, a former trade unionist who functioned as

---

[71] Dubofsky, *The State and Labor in Modern America*, 87.
[72] Zieger, *Republicans and Labor*, 90–1. For more on the DOL in the 1920s, see John Lombardi, *Labor's Voice in the Cabinet: A History of the Department of Labor from Its Origin in 1921* (New York: Columbia University Press, 1942); William Breen, *Labor Market Politics and the Great War: The Department of Labor, the States, and the First U.S. Employment Service, 1907–1933* (Kent: Kent State University Press, 1997).
[73] Hunt to Klein, October 16, 1930, General Records of the Department of Commerce, Subject Files of Assistant Secretary of Commerce E. E. Hunt, 1921–1930, Box 2, File Memos to Dr. Julius Klein, RG 40, NA.
[74] On Davis, see James J. Davis, *The Iron Puddler: My Life in the Rolling Mills and What Came of It* (Indianapolis: The Bobbs-Merrill Company, 1922); Joseph P. Goldberg and William T. Moye, *The First Hundred Years of the Bureau of Labor Statistics* (Washington, DC: GPO, 1985), 117, 122, 126, 128, 130, 132, and 136; Judson Maclaury, *History of the Department of Labor, 1913–1918* (Washington, DC: U.S. DOL, 1997); Jonathan Grossman, *The Department of Labor* (New York: Praeger, 1973); DOL, *The Anvil and the Plow: A History of the United States Department of Labor, 1913–1963* (Washington, DC: GPO, 1963). Unlike his predecessors and successors, Davis left almost no papers from his term as secretary in the DOL collection at the National Archives. His personal papers are housed at the Library of Congress, but they contain very little concerning his years as secretary of labor.

an advocate for organized labor and workers, Davis devoted most of his energies to the Department of Labor's Bureau of Immigration and Immigration Service (BIIS).[75] As secretary, Davis did defend the department's turf in some cases, as in 1921 when he successfully fended off Hoover's attempt to move the task of gathering cost of living and price data to the Department of Commerce's Census Bureau, but for the most part, he allowed Hoover to set the federal government's agenda for labor and economic analysis.[76] The *United Mine Workers Journal* editorialized in 1922, "There is a Department of Labor which is supposed to deal with labor problems, but the Hoover idea seems to be that no action of any kind must be taken until it is first Hooverized."[77]

Nonetheless, it was more than rhetoric and the service of a pliant secretary that convinced many labor experts and policy makers that the labor question had undergone a fundamental transformation precipitated by widespread economic stability, industrial cooperation, and prosperity. During the 1920s, the BLS under Commissioner Ethelbert Stewart published studies providing further evidence that wages were rising, hours decreasing, and labor unrest diminishing. Unlike Davis, Stewart was no Babbitt-like figure. After holding a number of government, newspaper, and labor positions in Illinois, where he had at one time been blacklisted by a coffin-making company for his political activities, Stewart worked his way up through the ranks of the BLS, providing long and credible service.[78] More than Davis, Stewart, who had developed a close friendship with Henry Demarest Lloyd at the turn of the century, frequently criticized business. In a review of the management of the textile industry for the AFL in 1929, he suggested, "The situation in the textile industry is just as bad or worse than it is in the bituminous coal industry, and the

---

[75] Zieger, *Republicans and Labor*, 84. For a sharp critique of the DOL's role in the enforcement of immigration law, see former Assistant Secretary of Labor Louis Post, *The Deportations Delirium of Nineteen-Twenty: A Personal Narrative of an Historic Official Experience* (Chicago: Charles H. Kerr & Co., 1923); Henry Raymond Mussey, "Louis F. Post – American," *Nation* 110 (June 12, 1920): 792–3. In 1940, the responsibility for the enforcement of immigration laws was transferred to the Department of Justice.

[76] Goldberg and Moye, *The First Hundred Years of the Bureau of Labor Statistics*, 122.

[77] United Mine Workers, "Hoover Again," *UMWJ* 33 (October 15, 1922): 6. Robert W. Bruere, associate editor of *The Survey*, wrote, "As I go over the annual report of the Secretary of Labor, I find nothing of significance except the work on immigration and the carry-over of social service activity in the Women's Bureau and the Children's Bureau." Bruere to E. E. Hunt, February 20, 1926 General Records of the Department of Commerce, Office of the Secretary, Box 16, File: Misc B (1925) -26, RG 40, NA.

[78] Goldberg and Moye, *The First Hundred Years of the Bureau of Labor Statistics*, 115.

problem is in the hands of men no more competent to solve it."[79] At times Davis's commitments to his associates caused tension between himself and Stewart. In June 1929, Davis's assistant, R. H. Horner, sent a memo to Stewart requesting on behalf of the secretary that he find "a place to which Miss McGarvey could be transferred and could be given a promotion." In a response that suggested larger issues separated the two men, Stewart wrote, "The BLS is not an employment agency for the universities and colleges of the United States, and the fact that a person has not a college degree does not interfere with his employment or promotion in this Bureau, and I hope that it may always maintain itself as an exception to the general rule in this regard."[80]

Despite his skepticism of business, Stewart's BLS provided the raw data that pointed to a turn in the economy toward higher wages and a shrinking workweek. Between 1920 and 1929, 62 of the 243 bulletins published by the BLS described improvements in the nominal wages and hours of workers in specific industries.[81] Fifty-two of these bulletins examined wages and hours in unionized industries, including boot and shoe, bituminous and anthracite coal, cotton, woolen and worsted, slaughtering and meatpacking, iron and steel, lumber, hosiery and underwear, foundries and machinery, and men's clothing. As a result of budget cuts, the BLS gathered wage and hour data for these groups of workers every other year, as opposed to every year, which had previously been BLS practice. These studies also provided important data on nominal wage differentials between men and women, though they did not describe wage differentials among racial groups. As discussed in the next chapter, the failure of the BLS to integrate a cost of living and real wage analysis into its investigations compromised their quality, but the raw data made

---

[79] Goldberg and Moye, *The First Hundred Years of the Bureau of Labor Statistics*, 120; Ethelbert Stewart, "Present Situation in Textiles," *AF* (June 1929): 690. For other examples of Stewart's defense of labor, see Ethelbert Stewart, "The Wastage of Men," *MLR* (July 1924); Chester Destler, "A Coffin Worker and the Labor Problem," *Labor History* (Summer 1971): 409–16.

[80] R. H. Horner to Stewart, June 20, 1929; and the commissioner of labor statistics to the secretary of labor, June 21, 1929. Both correspondence in Records of the BLS, Correspondence of the Commissioner with the Secretary of Labor and units of the Labor Department, 1925–1935, Box 1, Entry 33, RG 257, NA.

[81] Other topics frequently addressed in BLS bulletins in the 1920s, with the number of bulletins devoted to them in parentheses, included accidents and workplace dangers (28), prices (22), labor laws and legislation (17), conferences of government labor officials (13), and workmen's compensation (7). The categories are my own and based on an examination of all BLS bulletins for the period.

it easy for policy makers to surmise wage gains by workers, particularly after 1922.

BLS investigations found noticeable improvements in industries and occupations once the bastion of low wages and long hours. In the iron and steel industries, the BLS tracked a sudden decrease in average full-time hours per week after 1923 and an increase in wages, particularly during the war and following the industry's recovery from the postwar downturn. In an examination of conditions between 1913 and 1926, the BLS concluded, "The long working hours in force in most of the departments in 1913 have been materially shortened and earnings, both per hour and per week, have increased greatly."[82] The BLS attributed the decrease in hours to the industry's move to the eight-hour day beginning in late 1923. A survey of ten departments revealed that between 1913 and 1922 average weekly hours declined slightly from 66.1 to 63.2, but the significant drop came after U.S. Steel started to eliminate the twelve-hour day and the seven-day workweek in August 1923. Between 1922 and 1926, the average weekly hours worked by steel workers fell dramatically from 63.2 to 54.4 hours per week.[83] Though the BLS did not calculate real wages in its surveys, its analysis of nominal wages suggested generally higher wages for iron and steel workers. Nominal weekly earnings for iron and steel workers in the ten departments surveyed increased from $18.89 in 1913 to $34.41 in 1926.[84]

As observers and officials pored over this data, they sensed something more significant than a shift in hours and wages under way. The

---

[82] BLS, "Wages and Hours of Labor in the Iron and Steel Industry: 1907 to 1926," *Bulletin* 442 (Washington, DC: GPO, 1927), 4.

[83] Ibid., 3.

[84] Departments surveyed included blast furnace, Bessmer converters, open-hearth furnaces, puddling mills, blooming mills, plant mills, standard rail mills, bar mills, sheet mills, and tin-plate mills. The BLS investigations included data for select years going back to at least 1910 for all departments, except standard rail mills. BLS, "Wages and Hours of Labor in the Iron and Steel Industry," 1; DOL, *Annual Report of the Secretary of Labor* (Washington, DC: GPO, 1927), 47–8; also see the following BLS bulletins: "Wages and Hours of Labor in the Iron and Steel Industry: 1907 to 1920," *Bulletin* 305 (Washington, DC: GPO, 1922); "Wages and Hours of Labor in the Iron and Steel Industry: 1907 to 1922," *Bulletin* 353 (Washington, DC: GPO, 1924); "Wages and Hours of Labor in the Iron and Steel Industry: 1907 to 1924," *Bulletin* 381 (Washington, DC: GPO, 1925). For a summary of data on wages and hours between 1913 and 1926, see "Average Hours and Earnings in the Iron and Steel Industry: 1913 to 1926," *MLR* 24 (May 1927): 164–5; "Trend of Wages, 1907–1920," *MLR* 13 (December 1921): 81–9. For a summary of data concerning the decline of the twelve-hour day and the seven-day workweek, see BLS, "Hours of Labor and the 7-Day Work Week in the Iron and Steel Industry," *MLR* 30 (June 1930): 182–7; BLS, "Wages and Hours of Labor in the Iron and Steel Industry," *Bulletin* 513 (Washington, DC: GPO, 1930).

antagonistic relationship between labor and capital, they believed, was being eroded by a new "feeling of partnership" in industry. Advocates and identifiers of this "new feeling" found welcome confirmation in BLS statistics on labor unrest. Since 1916, the BLS tracked the number and size of strikes and lockouts by studying newspapers, journals, and periodicals and data provided by the DOL Conciliation Service. The BLS began collecting these data at a time of well-publicized labor unrest. Between 1916 and 1920, workers struck more than twenty-four hundred times per year, with an average of nearly 2 million workers striking annually. After 1923, the number of workers involved in labor disputes plummeted. In 1926, the BLS reported, "The number of disputes in which the number of persons involved was reported was only 783, with 329,592 workers affected, or a smaller number than in any other year since the beginning of the bureau's reports in 1916."[85]

Further making the case for this new sentiment in industry, the BLS learned that nominal increases in wages and shorter hours occurred for both male and female workers. Though the BLS found occupational segregation and wage disparity in industries employing men and women workers, its reports emphasized the wage and hour gains made by both men and women. In the boot and shoe industry, the BLS investigated wages and hours in 91 to 157 establishments per year between 1914 and 1928. These investigations accounted for between 45,460 and 60,692 workers, or roughly one-quarter of employees working in the industry.[86] The aggregate of all employees in the industry saw their full-time workweek fall steadily from 54.7 hours in 1914 to 49.1 in 1928. During this same period, weekly earnings rose from $13.26 to $26.02.[87] Though gender disparity continued, the BLS reported that both men and women

---

[85] DOL, *Fifteenth Annual Report of the Secretary of Labor* (Washington, DC: GPO, 1927), 51–2.

[86] The percentage of employees and firms represented in the study is difficult to approximate. But for 1928, the study included 157 establishments employing 48,658 employees. According to the United States Census, a total of 206,992 wage earners reportedly worked in the boot and shoe industry, suggesting that one-quarter of workers in the industry were represented in the BLS study. BLS, "Wages and Hours of Labor in the Boot and Shoe Industry, 1910 to 1928," *Bulletin* 498 (Washington, DC: GPO, 1929), 38; BLS, "Wages and Hours of Labor in the Boot and Shoe Industry: 1907 to 1920," *Bulletin* 278 (Washington, DC: GPO, 1921); BLS, "Wages and Hours of Labor in the Boot and Shoe Industry: 1907 to 1922," *Bulletin* 324 (Washington, DC: GPO, 1923); BLS, Wages and Hours of Labor in the Boot and Shoe Industry," *Bulletin* 374 (Washington DC: GPO, 1925); BLS, "Wages and Hours of Labor in the Boot and Shoe Industry: 1907 to 1926," *Bulletin* 450 (Washington, DC: GPO, 1927).

[87] BLS, "Wages and Hours of Labor in the Boot and Shoe Industry: 1910 to 1928," *Bulletin* 498 (Washington, DC: GPO, 1929), 3.

benefited from these trends. While men's weekly earnings rose from $12.29 per week in 1914 to $25.14 in 1928, women's weekly wages increased at a slightly slower rate, from $9.05 to $17.76 for the same period. Both men and women workers saw a similar decrease in the workweek, with men's average hours falling from 55 to 49 per week and women's falling from 54.3 to 49.2 between 1914 and 1928.[88] The BLS arrived at a similar conclusion in its analysis of earnings and hours in the hosiery and underwear industries, where the workweek decreased 7.6 percent between 1913 and 1928 and weekly earnings rose 188 percent between 1910 and 1928. The workweek for men and women in these two industries was roughly the same, with men averaging 52.4 hours per week in 1928 and women averaging 51.9 hours. The wage disparity was greater in the hosiery industry than in the boot and shoe industry. In 1928, men's average full-time earnings per week rose to $37.94, whereas women workers earned on average only $18.68.[89]

While Davis, Hoover, and others called attention to evidence of prosperity, an alternative reading of BLS statistics would have provided reason for greater skepticism of this much-heralded economic ascent. For instance, greater attention to the relative position of union and nonunion wages would have undermined the marginalization of organized labor in the Hooverites' vision for the New Era economy. In fact, BLS data clearly demonstrated that union workers' gains in hours and wages kept them well ahead of nonunion occupations and workers. A 240-page 1928 BLS study of 863,922 unionized workers in eleven occupations found that 81.5 percent of union workers "have a week of 44 hour or less."[90]

[88] Ibid., 17. Wages and hours showed improvement, but a 1930 BLS study revealed employment stability remained a problem in the industry; BLS, "Stability of Employment in the Leather and Boot and Shoe Industries," *MLR* 30 (March 1929): 43–5.

[89] The wage differential was less pronounced in the lower-paying underwear industry, where, in 1928, men earned $22.92 per week to women's $16.38. BLS, "Wages and Hours of Labor in the Hosiery and Underwear Industries: 1907 to 1928," *Bulletin* 504 (Washington, DC: GPO, 1929), 2–13; BLS, "Wages and Hours of Labor in the Hosiery and Underwear Industry: 1922," *Bulletin* 328 (Washington, DC: GPO, 1923); BLS, "Wages and Hours of Labor in the Hosiery and Underwear Industry: 1907 to 1924," *Bulletin* 376 (Washington, DC: GPO, 1925); BLS, "Wages and Hours of Labor in the Hosiery and Underwear Industry: 1907–1926," *Bulletin* 452 (Washington, DC: GPO, 1927). For similar findings in other industries, see BLS, "Wages and Hours of Labor in the Men's Clothing Industry: 1911–1928" *Bulletin* 503 (Washington, DC: GPO, 1929), 2; BLS, "Wages and Hours of Labor in Cotton-Goods Manufacturing: 1910 to 1928," *Bulletin* 492 (Washington, DC: GPO, 1929); BLS, "Wages and Hours of Labor in Woolen and Worsted Goods Manufacturing: 1910 to 1928" *Bulletin* 487 (Washington, DC: GPO, 1929).

[90] BLS, "Union Scales of Wages and Hours of Labor," *Bulletin* 482 (Washington, DC: GPO, 1929), 2.

The average full-time workweek for all trades was 44.9 hours per week; chauffeurs, teamsters, and drivers pulled the average up by working an average of 54.8 hours, nearly eight hours more per week than any other group of unionized workers. Between 1913 and 1928, unionized workers' workweek declined by 8.1 percent, while their wages increased 2.4 times.[91] Though these workers had achieved steady improvements in hours and wages since 1907, the most significant gains took place during World War I and after 1922.[92]

Similarly, a close examination of BLS data on the steel industry would have taken some of the sheen off of the widely publicized victory by labor experts in the still union-free industry. For some steel workers, the reduction in hours proved remarkably ephemeral. In six of ten occupational groups in the steel industry, the need to keep works operating continuously or nearly continuously with a smaller labor pool forced an increase in the number of employees who worked seven days a week. In 1914, 53 percent of steel employees in the blast furnace department worked seven days a week. By 1922, that number had fallen to 29 percent, but by 1926 it increased to 49 percent. Similarly, in blooming, standard rail, and plate mills, a higher percentage of employees worked a seven-day week in 1924 than in any other year on record.[93]

Further, while BLS wage and hour data provided Hoover and Davis with ample reason to celebrate the decade's prosperity, these same data sets examined more critically would have raised other important concerns. BLS and Women's Bureau investigations clearly showed that women sought and gained work in numbers that debunked "pin-money" theories of employment. The consistency of the wage disparity and occupational segregation should have raised concerns about the opportunities for the fastest growing demographic group in the nation's work force and about why it was growing so fast. Hooverites might have also paid attention to organized labor's success in pushing up wages and hours in unionized and nonunionized workplaces. As discussed in Chapter 4, Russell Sage Foundation (RSF) reports describing wage setting in the Colorado Fuel and Iron Company, which tied the wages of its nonunion workforce directly to the rate set by the United Mine Workers in eastern mines, provided ample evidence of organized labor's indirect influence on wages in nonunion fields and plants. Also, BLS data clearly showed that union workers' wages and hours improved at a more rapid rate than those of

---

[91] Ibid., 14.
[92] Ibid., 14–15; "Union Wage Rates in 1928," *MLR* 27 (November 1928): 10–18.
[93] BLS, "Union Scales of Wages and Hours of Labor," 10.

nonunion workers. As organized labor's presence in industry declined, one of the few coercive mechanisms for maintaining the high-wage economy eroded.

This sort of analysis did not get much traction in the New Era. Rather than focus on these potential problems, the Hooverites devoted most of their attention to celebrating the post-1922 economic achievements and developing mechanisms to maintain economic growth, stability, and prosperity. The NBER emerged as the main site for this celebration.

"THIS ALMOST INSATIABLE APPETITE FOR GOODS AND SERVICES": THE NBER CELEBRATES THE WORKER-CONSUMER

The NBER conducted the most widely cited economic investigations of the period. Edwin E. Gay, founding dean of the Harvard Business School, and Wesley Mitchell, an economist trained at the University of Chicago, led the push for the NBER's establishment and set its early agenda. During World War I, Mitchell and Gay were among a number of economists who served in the federal government and found the government's economic expertise sorely wanting. Reflecting on the origins of the NBER, Mitchell wrote, the NBER "was organized the year after the war closed ... by a group of economists, most of whom had shared in the wartime mobilization and learned from hard experience how inadequate was their equipment for dealing with the problems put up to them. They wanted to increase knowledge of the sort the war had demanded, for they believed that it would be valuable also in peace."[94] Organized partially in response to postwar demand for a more empirical approach to the study of social problems, the NBER described itself as a part of a need for "exact and impartial determinations of facts bearing on economic, social, and industrial problems."[95] Toward that end, the NBER worked for a

---

[94] Quoted in Robert Cuff, "War Mobilization, Institutional Learning, and State Building in the United States, 1917–1941," in *The State and Social Investigation in Britain and the United States*, eds. Mary O. Furner and Barry Supple (Cambridge: Cambridge University Press, 1993), 398; Originally Wesley Mitchell, *Economic Research and the Needs of the Times*, NBER, Twenty-fourth Annual Report, April 1944, 11.

[95] NBER, *Recent Economic Changes in the United States* (New York: McGraw-Hill, 1929), 1: xxxv. On the NBER, see Alchon, *The Invisible Hand of Planning*, 52–76; Ellis W. Hawley, "Economic Inquiry and the State in New Era America: Antistatist Corporatism and Positive Statism in Uneasy Coexistence," in *The State and Economic Knowledge: The American and British Experiences*, eds. Mary O. Furner and Barry Supple (Cambridge: Cambridge University Press, 1990), 287–324; Dorothy Ross, *The Origins of American Social Science* (Cambridge: Cambridge University Press, 1991), 325, 397–8, 413; Yuval Yonay, *The Struggle Over the Soul of Economics: Institutionalists and Neoclassical*

better understanding of what it deemed pressing social and economic issues related to national income, wages, and the business cycle. To build an objective image, however, NBER leaders explicitly rejected any role in policy making or policy advocacy.

Given how central the NBER and Mitchell were to 1920s policy considerations, it is worth noting that Hoover would have preferred to have Mitchell in Washington and working by his side at Commerce. Shortly after taking office, he made an impassioned appeal to Mitchell to join him, specifically offering him a position as an "economic advisor to the entire Department." Hoover nearly begged: "I feel that you are the one man in the country who could adequately take care of this job and I sincerely hope you can see your way clear to let us have your services for a year." After taking some time to consider the offer and citing "obligations both of a professional and personal sort" that bond him to New York, Mitchell declined. But he praised Hoover's effort "to utilize whatever help economics can render to government," which seems "to me one of the most promising developments of our time."[96]

Though NBER leaders took pains to gather input from an impressive range of institutions and to cultivate a public image of impartiality, most of its leaders leaned in the direction of a Hooverian understanding of the social and economic problems faced by the nation. Among the organizations that would nominate NBER leaders were the AFL, Chamber of Commerce, American Bar Association, American Economic Association, and the National Conference Board. Despite the diversity of leadership, the NBER's analysis embraced core voluntary corporatist assumptions, including modest state intervention, microeconomic solutions to the business cycle, and the recent emergence of a convergence of employer and employee interests.

Not surprising then, the NBER quickly found an ally in Secretary Hoover, who was just then organizing a conference to examine the causes of postwar unemployment and economic instability. According to historian Michael Bernstein, Mitchell and Gay "persuaded Hoover to engage the NBER as the empirical arm of the conferences inquiry."[97] Hoover's cultivation and exploitation of issue networks among foundations, academics, nonprofits, government, business, and labor organizations,

---

Economists in America Between the Wars (Princeton: Princeton University Press, 1998), 51–3, 140–3; Bernstein, *Perilous Progress*, particularly 40–8.
[96] Hoover to Mitchell, July 29, 1921, and Mitchell to Hoover, August 3, 1921, Box 416, Folder "Mitchell, Wesley C., 1921–1927 & undated," Commerce Papers, HHPL.
[97] Bernstein, *Perilous Progress*, 43.

combined with the commerce secretary's intimate involvement with the production and presentation of the investigations, helped place the NBER economic reports at the center of New Era policy discussion. In describing Hoover's role in implementing the recommendations of NBER investigations, Hoover's assistant secretary of commerce, E. E. Hunt, wrote to the Laura Spelman Rockefeller Memorial's (LSRM) Beardsley Ruml, "I doubt if the results would have received more than passing attention from those who are responsible for policy-making if it had not been that Mr. Hoover set up a committee … and made public the results with all the supporting weight of the Department of Commerce and the prestige of the President's Conference on Unemployment."[98]

Initially, NBER leaders struggled to raise money without unduly compromising the NBER's objectivity or reputation. For instance, the Carnegie Corporation and later the LSRM provided the financial backing for the NBER's investigations, which caused concern among NBER organizers such as N. I. Stone, the general manager of Hickey-Freeman Company, who wrote to NBER president M. C. Rorty regarding "the propriety of receiving contributions from Mr. Rockefeller." "I can see the possible criticism that might be raised by people on the outside of the Bureau in casting doubt upon the impartiality of the Bureau's investigations," he lamented. Stone suggested that the NBER solicit "even moderate subscriptions" from labor organizations such as the AFL and the International Ladies' Garment Workers Union that are "now in the habit of engaging trained economists to represent their cases."[99] George Soule, who also sat on the board of directors, conveyed concerns over the perceived impact of Rockefeller money on the NBER given the "traditional hostility to Mr. Rockefeller's benefactors on the part of labor organizations." Soule wrote frankly, "In spite of Mr. Rockefeller's good intentions, the fact is patent to all that many of his most important properties pursue an antiunion policy, and this serves to keep the traditional hostility alive."[100] The AFL's John Frey, who served as vice-president of the bureau and a labor representative on the board of directors, stood at the center of efforts to resolve concern over funding from Rockefeller. By the fall of 1922, Frey was convinced that, if Rockefeller was "willing

---

[98] Hunt to Ruml, December 12, 1923, LSRM Collection, Series 3, Box 86, Folder 902 PCU, 1923–7, Rockefeller Archive Center, Tarrytown, New York (hereafter RAC).

[99] N. I. Stone to M. C. Rorty, October 23, 1922, Rockefeller Foundation Collection, Series Economic Reform, Box 18, Folder 143 NBER, RG 2, RAC.

[100] Soule to Rorty, October 18, 1922, Rockefeller Foundation Collection, Series Economic Reform, Box 18, Folder 143 NBER, RG 2, RAC.

to make a liberal donation ... without any strings attached," the NBER "would be justified in receiving the donation."[101]

Unfortunately for organized labor, NBER investigations cemented unions' position as a marginal player, while celebrating high worker wages, economic stability, and unprecedented levels of consumption. The NBER reports reflected a growing sense of confidence among policy makers regarding the direction of the U.S. economy and a belief that accurate data and modest government intervention could correct problems such as unemployment and low wages. Until the 1929 publication of *Recent Economic Changes*, where it appeared that the labor question had been answered, NBER reports on labor confined themselves to a narrow range of labor concerns, including the accuracy of data on unemployment, the size of organized labor, and the size and distribution of the nation's income. These early investigations were important in summarizing and publicizing BLS data and helping to develop new measurement tools that better assessed the condition of labor, but in general they did not provide any new insights into the labor question. By design, the NBER often tried to avoid taking positions on controversial issues. In the foreword to Leo Wolman's report on the growth of trade unions, Wesley Mitchell recognized that unions affect "both the size and the distribution of the national income," but he stated that NBER investigators had no opinion "about the promise or the danger to American life from the growth of trade unions."[102]

[101] Frey to Rorty, October 23, 1922; Rorty to Frey, November 3, 1922; Frayne [general organizer, AFL] to Rorty, November 3, 1922; Rorty to Stone, October 27, 1922; Rorty to Frayne, October 27, 1922; and Rorty to Beardsley Ruml, November 4, 1922. All letters in Rockefeller Foundation Collection, Series Economic Reform, Box 18, Folder 143 NBER, RG 2, RAC. There appears to be more to the relationship between the Rockefellers and the AFL (particularly Gompers) than meets the eye. Various philanthropic leaders and business interests funded the completion of Gompers's memoirs, including John D. Rockefeller, Jr., Edward A. Filene, Owen Young, and Julius Rosenwald, each of whom donated $1,000 to the effort. See Frey to John D. Rockefeller, Jr., March 11, 1922. After Gompers's death, Rockefeller, Jr. wrote by hand a letter expressing his condolences to Mrs. Gompers. See Rockefeller to Mrs. Gompers, December 16, 1924. More strange, in February 1930, Mrs. Gompers wrote directly to Rockefeller begging for work. She wrote in part, "I thought perhaps you might know of something or other that I could do. I am sure that I am capable of something worth while if given a chance.... For the past year my Father has really been supporting me, but now he is ill and only has months to live at most, so that I must have some means to live." Gertrude Gleaves Gompers (Mrs. Samuel Gompers) to Rockefeller, February 26, 1930. All letters mentioned previously discussing the Gompers-Rockefeller relationship are located in Rockefeller Foundation Collection, Series Economic Interest, Box 13, Folder 97 Samuel Gompers and AFL, RG 2, RAC.

[102] Mitchell, "Foreword," in Leo Wolman, *Growth of American Trade Unions, 1880–1923* (New York: National Bureau of Economic Research), 6.

Early NBER studies continued a trend among Hooverites of marginalizing the importance and utility of organized labor in resolving public problems. In the first major work by the Hoover-NBER alliance, *Business Cycles and Unemployment* (1923), reports by John Andrews and Leo Wolman pointed to the inability of workers' organizations to provide unemployment benefits for even their own members and instead advocated various forms of unemployment insurance. According to the secretary of the AALL, John B. Andrews, "trade unions through their out-of-work benefits have provided … for only a small minority even of their own unemployed members."[103] Local unions sometimes offered out-of-work benefits to members, but only six national unions provided such membership benefits. Increasingly, unions listed the suspension of membership dues during periods of unemployment as an out-of-work benefit, and when robust benefits were offered, they put tremendous strain on union finances. Andries Meyer, the president of the Diamond Workers, indicated, "It is impossible, in the long run, for a trade union to maintain an adequate system of unemployment benefits."[104] Andrews added that poor union administration of funds, or outright corruption, further undermined the viability of union unemployment benefits.[105]

In *Business Cycles and Unemployment* and other NBER reports published during the early 1920s, investigators paid keen attention to the role business leaders and individual industries did and should play in the New Era economy. Leo Wolman's 160-page report on unions would seem to have provided an opportunity for the NBER to give similar treatment to unions; instead, Wolman stuck to a purely statistical analysis of the growth, character, and demographics of the labor movement between 1897 and 1923. Mitchell's introduction hinted at an understanding of unions' larger role, claiming that the "trade union movement affects productivity and affects wages – that is, it affects both the size and the distribution of income." In the body of the report, however, Wolman provided few insights into the function of unions in the New Era economy. This is somewhat surprising given Wolman's background. In 1914, he completed his PhD at Johns Hopkins, where he studied with George Barnett and Jacob Hollander. In addition to his work with the NBER, Wolman served as the director of research for the Amalgamated Clothing

---

[103] John B. Andrews, "Trade Union Out-Of-Work Benefits," 300 and Leo Wolman, "Unemployment Insurance," 303 and 340–1. Both in President's Conference on Unemployment, *Business Cycles and Unemployment*, 304 and 340–1.
[104] Andrews, "Trade Union Out-Of-Work Benefits," 297.
[105] Ibid., 298–300.

Workers of America.[106] Despite his background, Wolman's report was neither insightful nor innovative. In fact, as recently as 1922, Barnett, his former advisor, had published articles with similar conclusions detailing the growth of trade unions between 1897 and 1922.[107]

With the publication of *Recent Economic Changes* (*REC*) in 1929, the NBER finally integrated workers into its evolving conception of the New Era economy and anointed the newly discovered linkages between economic stability, high wages, increased productivity, and constantly increasing consumer demand. In proposing the *REC* project, Mitchell conveyed the optimism of the time, writing to Hunt, "Ordinarily people propose to investigate matters which have gone awry. The present proposal is to find out why matters have gone so well."[108] Prior to its publication, Hunt expressed considerable excitement regarding the importance of the report, writing to Beardsley Ruml of the LSRM, "I have never been engaged in any undertaking which seemed more stimulating or promising than this."[109]

All of this culminated in the belief, on prominent display in *REC*, that New Era economic changes and policies had birthed a new system of labor relations in which employers rewarded the cooperative spirit of workers with higher wages meant to spur consumption. According to the NBER investigators who contributed to *REC*, improvements in wages, hours, and consumer demand and increased stability of prices combined to create a new era of shared employee-employer interest in U.S. industrial relations. In *Business Cycles and Unemployment* (1923), investigators had only once and very briefly – in a report by Brown economist William A. Berridge – mentioned the link between workers' spending and economic stability.[110] By 1929, however, the Committee on *REC* explained that consumption, underwritten by high wages, was the dominant characteristic of the period and the means to achieve industrial

---

[106] Dorfman, *The Economic Mind in American Civilization*, 5: 520–1.
[107] George Barnett, "Growth of Labor Organization in the United States, 1897–1914," *QJE* 30 (August 1916): 780–95; George Barnett, "The Present Position of American Trade Unionism," *Paper and Proceedings of the Thirty-Fourth Meeting of the American Economics Association* 12 (March 1922): 44–55.
[108] Mitchell to Hunt, October 24, 1927; also see Hoover to Dr. F. P. Keppel, October 26, 1927; Hoover to Col. Arthur Woods [president of LSRM], all in LSRM Collection, Series 3, Box 86, Folder 902 PCU 1923–7, RAC.
[109] Hunt to Ruml, December 15, 1928; see also Hunt to George E. Vincent [president of the Rockefeller Foundation], LSRM Collection, Series 3, Box 86, Folder 903 PCU 1928–30, RAC.
[110] William A. Berridge, "What Present Statistics of Employment Show," in *Business Cycles and Unemployment*, 64.

peace and prosperity. It repeatedly stressed the importance of an increased rate of "production-consumption" and high wages, which the committee described as the "fundamental development" of the period. Writing separately, Hunt wrote that *REC* had lifted "consumption to first place in our national economy."[111] The report itself pointed to unnamed "leaders of industrial thought" who after the war recognized that high wartime wages, accumulated savings, and pent-up consumer demand "poured into the channels of commerce." These industrial leaders "began consciously to propound the principle of high wages and low costs as a policy of enlightened industrial practice."[112] The result was a process of making "dormant demands effective"; "it is this degree of economic activity, this almost insatiable appetite for goods and services, this abounding production of all things which almost any man can want, which is so striking a characteristic of the period covered in the survey."[113]

Increased productivity attributed to cooperation and improved production methods allowed for the satisfaction of these "dormant demands." In his analysis of productivity, efficiency, safety, and technology, mechanical engineer L. P. Alford claimed that a "turning point in the more economical utilization of production factors seems to have taken place about 1919–20."[114] Using government and National Industrial Conference Board data, Alford calculated a productivity increase (defined here as the power per wage earner) of nearly 31 percent between 1919 and 1925, which rivaled an overall increase of 47 percent for the years between 1899 and 1919.[115] Willard L. Thorp's analysis of the scale of production relative to the number of wage earners between 1914 and 1927 described a 12 percent increase in the average number of wage earners per establishment but a 141 percent increase in the value of the products produced per establishment.[116] In surveying the rapidly improving railroad industry, William J. Cunningham noted a 17 percent increase in output per man hour between 1920 and 1926, which he attributed to better

---

[111] E. E. Hunt, "Apologia Pro Vita Nostra," President's Organization for Unemployment Relief, Chronological Files of E. E. Hunt, Box 1, File January 1930, 4, RG 73, NA.

[112] "Report of the Committee" in NBER, *Recent Economic Changes in the United States* (New York: McGraw-Hill, 1929), 1: xiv.

[113] Ibid., xv.

[114] L. P. Alford, "Technical Changes in Manufacturing Industries," in NBER, *Recent Economic Changes in the United States* (New York: McGraw-Hill, 1929), 1: 166.

[115] Ibid., 104.

[116] Willard L. Thorp, "The Changing Structure of Industry," in NBER, *Recent Economic Changes in the United States* (New York: McGraw-Hill, 1929), 1: 167.

equipment, more adequate facilities, and "improvement in morale and degree of employee co-operation."[117]

REC reports were quick to emphasize that workers/consumers – it was getting harder and harder to tell the difference – had benefited from increased productivity through increases in nominal and real wages. Leo Wolman and Frederick C. Mills reported on the trajectory of real wages. Wolman, largely summarizing parts of BLS studies, cited the general increase in union and nonunion workers' nominal wages from 1913 to 1926. Though his index was weighted toward building and printing trades at the expense of manufacturing industries, Wolman noted, "The striking feature ... of all union rates, is the slight decline in rates during the severe depression of 1920 to 1922 and the decided upward movement since 1922."[118] In his analysis of the workweek and stabilization of employment since World War I, Wolman described the general trend downward in the number of hours considered "full time" and a dramatic decrease in layoffs.[119]

The celebration of the era's prosperity continued in the REC's analysis of real wages. Building on Paul Douglas's work measuring real wages addressed in the next chapter, Frederick C. Mills described a long period of negligible real wage increases prior to 1922, after which real wages began to increase. Mills reported that though nominal wages increased at a nice clip between 1896 and 1913, the "purchasing power, or real wages" of workers were "not so impressive." "For all workers, the gain" over the preceding twenty years "was at a rate of one-half of 1 per cent each year, representing a slow but sustained improvement in well-being," he wrote, but one in which workers' earnings "barely kept ahead of living costs."[120] In the postwar years, workers' real and nominal wages increased at a greater rate. Mills's research on wages and prices for the period between 1922 and 1927 revealed "a gain in the purchasing power of wages in general at a rate of 2.1 per cent a year."[121] Mills concluded that the "postwar gain in the purchasing power of labor has been at an appreciably higher

---

[117] William J. Cunningham, "Part 1. Railways," in NBER, *Recent Economic Changes in the United States* (New York: McGraw-Hill, 1929), 1: 285.

[118] Leo Wolman, "Labor," in NBER, *Recent Economic Changes in the United States* (New York: McGraw-Hill, 1929), 2: 436.

[119] Ibid., 445, 464–5.

[120] Frederick C. Mills, "Price Movements and Related Industrial Changes," in NBER, *Recent Economic Changes in the United States* (New York: McGraw-Hill, 1929), 2: 626.

[121] Ibid., 633.

rate than it was between 1896 and 1913."[122] This important increase in real wages paled when compared to the rise in business profits. According to Mills, "Profits of industrial corporations increased, between 1923 and 1927, at an average rate of 9 per cent a year."[123] Mills did appear alarmed with this potential imbalance, remarking with apparent approval that the slight decline in wholesale prices in combination with increasing wages, profits, and productivity marked this period as one with "few precedents in prewar experience."[124]

The NBER's work on income distribution provided further, if entirely spurious, evidence supporting Hooverites' vision of New Era economics. Unfortunately, despite progress in calculating national income distribution and inequality by the NBER's Willford King, the *REC* grossly misinterpreted the state of wealth and income inequality that occurred as business profits outpaced worker wages between the end of World War I and 1929. Economist and *REC* investigator Morris A. Copeland provided a sobering assessment of the changes in the national income and its distribution that pointed to regions and industries struggling during the decade. But Copeland found no evidence of increased inequality. According to Copeland, "The available evidence certainly does not tend to confirm the theory some have advanced that the distribution of income was more nearly equal during the war, and has since tended in the direction of increasing inequality."[125] In his 1930 NBER report, *The National Income and its Purchasing Power*, King concurred, concluding, "there is practically no tendency toward the putting of more income into the hands of the extremely opulent sections of the community."[126] This amounted to a dire misreading of economic data. In fact, contrary to this assertion, more recent economic analysis by economists Jeffrey G. Williamson and Peter H. Lindert has shown that the "theory advanced by some," of narrowing inequality during the war and increasing inequality during the rest of the decade, was correct.[127]

[122] Ibid., 634.
[123] Ibid., 654.
[124] Ibid., 603.
[125] Melvin T. Copeland in NBER, *Recent Economic Changes in the United States* (New York: McGraw-Hill, 1929), 2: 836 and 838.
[126] Willford I. King, *The National Income and Its Purchasing Power* (New York: National Bureau of Economic Research, Inc., 1930), 180.
[127] Jeffrey G. Williamson and Peter H. Lindert, *American Inequality: A Macroeconomic History* (New York: Academic Press, 1964), 77. Also see L. Soltow, *Patterns of Withholding in Wisconsin in 1850* (Madison: University of Wisconsin Press, 1971), 14, 135–9.

In *REC*, NBER investigators spent considerably more time discussing industrial relations than they had in other reports, but their analysis reads more like a celebration of conventional wisdom than a rigorous inquiry. The *REC* studies, by focusing on managerial practices and organized labor's efforts to contribute to increases in production, described a new cooperative spirit in industry. In the introduction to the report, the NBER's Edwin E. Gay surmised that the source of "the friendly working spirit in American labor-relations" could be found in employers' interest in workers' representation schemes and the "new labor-union policy" that "recognizes not the identity but the mutuality of interest between the two parties to the labor contract."[128] Mitchell closed the report with similar praise, concluding that perhaps no change in the report was more important than the change in the AFL and other unions' "economic theories." Unions recognized the "relations between productivity and wages," Mitchell concluded, and worked with "vigor" to implement plans that increased efficiency in industry in a manner that "must startle those who have believed that trade unions are brakes upon economic progress."[129]

In general, the individual reports supported Gay's assessment. Wolman stressed the newly compliant nature of unions willing to accommodate management's interest in increasing efficiency and, in some cases, to do the actual work of disciplining and managing unionized workers. Celebrating in particular plans implemented by the Baltimore and Ohio Railroad and the Amalgamated Clothing Workers, Wolman contrasted this new industrial relations theory with workers' abandonment of World War I-era "experiments in workers' control."[130] This new labor policy had come at a cost, particularly to skilled workers who jealously protected workplace autonomy and control over the training of skilled apprentices, but readers of the report had to look beyond Wolman's analysis of labor to find any discussion of this negative side. Dexter S. Kimball of the American Engineering Council described (and seemed to celebrate) a "continuing tendency for the handicrafts to disappear in favor of the factory process."[131] In the highly unionized construction industry, the Department of Commerce's John Gries noted that the problem of a decreased number of skilled workers had been successfully resolved by

---

[128] Edwin E. Gay, "Introduction" in NBER, *Recent Economic Changes in the United States* (New York: McGraw-Hill, 1929), 1: 3, 5–6.
[129] Wesley Mitchell, "A Review," in NBER, *Recent Economic Changes in the United States* (New York: McGraw-Hill, 1929), 2: 863–4.
[130] Wolman, "Labor," 482–3.
[131] Kimball, in *Recent Economic Changes*, 94.

the "infiltration of workers who have commenced work as journeymen on rougher types of work and gradually acquired experience and skill without formal apprenticeship or instruction."[132]

As if to punctuate still again how far and how decisively removed late 1920s ideas about the American workplace were from the dark days of the post–World War I era, progressive managers who contributed to *REC* described a new system of labor relations in which employers rewarded the cooperative spirit of workers with higher wages meant to spur consumption. Henry Dennison, a progressive business leader, saw 1921 as a pivotal point when employers had undergone a change in their outlook on issues such as wages and unemployment.[133] On wages, Dennison saw a shift from the belief that "every cent paid as increased wages must come from the investor's return" to an approach recognizing that wages that increased with productivity would result in a "consequent increase in purchasing power," which "results not only in higher standards of living and better states of health but also in increases in the quantities and varieties of goods which can be sold."[134] Dennison tracked a change of opinion in employer and trade magazines. He noted that, in 1921, more than 300 articles had been published that provided employers with guidance in cutting wages and estimations regarding how far they would fall; by 1922, these articles had been replaced by pieces describing "wage incentives." As evidence of this trend Dennison cited trade and business periodicals, such as a 1923 article appearing in the *Paper Trade Journal* that announced, "It is becoming a sign of poor management and a mark of disgrace to pay low wages."[135] With respect to the problem of unemployment and unsteady employment, Dennison found that one-half of the 500 individuals surveyed had made "definite measures ... in moderating the severities of seasonal irregularities." Dennison wondered about the durability of the system in the face of a downturn: "The high wage doctrine by 1926 had gained its present standing. Nevertheless, no one can say whether its foothold is as yet strong enough to stand the strains of a long depression." Nonetheless, at the time of the report's publication, Dennison confidently wrote, "There are as yet no signs of its [the high wage doctrine] weakening."[136]

---

[132] John Gries, "Construction," in NBER, *Recent Economic Changes in the United States* (New York: McGraw-Hill, 1929), 1: 252.
[133] Henry Dennison, "Management," in NBER, *Recent Economic Changes in the United States* (New York: McGraw-Hill, 1929), 2: 544.
[134] Ibid., 523.
[135] Ibid., 524
[136] Ibid., 524, 545.

CONCLUSION

The belief that capitalism in the United States had moved beyond older concerns preoccupied with control and conflict and into a new era of increasing wages, profits, consumption, and a durable labor peace permeated the Hooverites' New Era economic discussions. Their effective postwar strategies for managing the economy had, they believed, ushered in a new form of capitalism that answered the labor question by replacing long-standing concerns centered on the problematic relationship between economic concentration and democracy with a new vision of a highly productive and expanding consumer-driven economy. Rather than taking the consumer for granted, the Hooverites came to see consumption and economic growth as the key to resolving a wide range of social and economic problems that reached back to the emergence of industrial capitalism. Though there were pronounced weaknesses in this understanding, the Hooverites went a long way toward centering consumption and the political economy of growth in our understanding of the business cycle and what constituted an effective economic system. This was no small change. Indeed, leisure and consumption had always been good for the wealthy, but prior to the 1920s working-class leisure activities had less positive connotations, often associated with drinking, gambling, and clannish ethnic activities. By the end of the 1920s, Hooverites associated worker consumption and leisure underwritten by high wages with economic stability and with a recognition by workers and employers that they shared a common interest in efficient production for consumption.[137] Citing approvingly the work of Hoover and Secretary of Labor Davis, the *Philadelphia Daily News* editorialized, "The payment of high wages in return for efficiency in production is and must be the rock upon which is built the prosperity of this city, of this state, of the entire country."[138]

---

[137] On changing social attitudes toward consumption, see Kathleen G. Donahue, *Freedom From Want: American Liberalism and the Idea of the Consumer* (Baltimore: Johns Hopkins University Press, 2003); Kathy Peis, *Cheap Amusements: Working Women and Leisure in Turn of the Century New York* (Philadelphia: Temple University Press, 1986); Roy Rosenzweig, *Eight Hours for What We Will* (Cambridge: Cambridge University Press, 1983); Daniel Horowitz, *The Morality of Spending: Attitudes Toward the Consumer Society in America* (Baltimore: Johns Hopkins University Press, 1985); Richard Wrightman Fox and T. J. Jackson Lears, eds., *The Culture of Consumption: Critical Essays in American History, 1880–1980* (New York: Pantheon Books, 1983); Lawrence B. Glickman, ed., *Consumer Society in American History* (Ithaca: Cornell University Press, 1999).

[138] "Secretary Davis Urges High Wages," *Philadelphia Daily News*, May 8, 1929. Article located in President's Organization for Unemployment Relief, Chronological Files of E. E. Hunt, Box 1, File: May 1929, RG 73, NA.

Supporters of the Hooverite vision came from a wide variety of institutions, including organized labor. As we will see in Chapter 3, this vision appealed to a significant number of leaders who led unions rocked back on their heels by postwar economic instability and employers' successful efforts to turn back gains made by membership during the war. In many respects, the AFL's strategy for the 1920s reflected acceptance of the new deal Hoover offered compliant unions. As late as September 8, 1930, the AFL and NBER's John Frey submitted to Hunt an article he wrote for publication in the *Magazine of Wall Street* regarding the AFL wage policy. In the note accompanying the article, Frey wrote, "While it does not contain any new thoughts on the subject, it does express a trade union point of view which is thoroughly in accord with President Hoover's wage policy."[139] Indeed, the push for a "social wage," as the AFL referred to it, that would guarantee workers a share in productivity increases in the pursuit of economic stability, squared perfectly with much of what Hoover and his allies were writing about, particularly by the end of the decade. Unions' precise role in maintaining the high-wage economy Hooverites advocated, however, remained vague, if one existed at all. As reports by the FAES, BLS, and NBER suggested, workers' wages increased, hours decreased, and a consumer economy began to emerge, apparently without the aid of union bargaining power, which fell dramatically even as workers' purchasing power increased.

Which brings us to the significance of agreements negotiated in the public sphere but without the coercive power of the state or unions. The failure to develop coercive mechanisms to maintain this high-wage and high-consumption economy tempts us to think of the New Era as a continuation of the more laissez-faire nineteenth-century policy regime, but a closer look at the Hooverites' vision suggests an evolution in issues deemed worthy of public, and in particular federal government, intervention. While Hoover never came to embrace statist labor standards, he and his allies did differ from conservatives who clung to a "liberty of contract" understanding of labor-capital relations that suggested there was no place for public intervention in negotiations between employers and employees concerning terms of employment. As Hoover's testimony before Congress early in the decade anticipated, the Hooverites worked, often successfully, to move any number of issues – among them the length of the workday

---

[139] Frey to Hunt, September 8, 1930, General Records of the Department of Commerce, Office of the Secretary, Subject Files of Assistant Secretary of Commerce E. E. Hunt, 1921–1931 Box 1, File Misc. F, RG 40, NA.

in steel, waste in industry, and the necessity of high wages – into the public domain. In doing so, they made clear that these were now matters of public concern. If they were naïve in their confidence in the efficacy of "voluntary compliance by business," they were hardly unique. Despite the drumbeat praising the importance of the American consumer in our own time, there is little beyond the "voluntary compliance by business" to ensure the real wages earned by the American worker will keep pace with increases in productivity or provide the means to maintain the purchasing power of the past.

Nonetheless, the Hooverites' faith in the ability of well-informed business leaders complemented by public opinion to ensure the adoption of decisions in the best interest of society appeared to be borne out in many aspects of 1920s labor relations. The perceived acceptance of the "high-wage doctrine" as a means for increasing the standard of living for workers, maintaining economic stability, and providing a dependable consumer outlet for goods suggested in fact a new conception of capitalism that shifted the focus of production from capital goods to consumer.[140] Amongst economists in academia, however, this celebration was tempered by recent discoveries that undermined economists' faith in the quality of government statistics, raised questions concerning the ability of the market to fairly determine wage rates, and led to deep concerns about the composition of New Era capitalism itself.

---

[140] Historians such as Martin Sklar have identified this as the start of the disaccumulation phase of the economy. See Martin J. Sklar, *The Corporate Reconstruction of American Capitalism, 1890–1916* (New York: Cambridge University Press, 1988).

2

Wages and the Public Interest

Economists and the Wage Question in the New Era

Between World War I and the onset of the Great Depression, the debate over the movement of real wages assumed unprecedented importance among policy makers and economists. The stakes in this inquiry were enormous. If real wages moved inexorably upward, then the often violent conflict between workers and employers reaching back to the 1870s could be viewed as an unfortunate consequence of dramatic economic innovation. Nonetheless, the nation could move forward confidently, knowing that over time the economic fortunes of workers had improved and labor peace would likely soon follow. If real wages could be shown to have decreased in recent decades, however, the outlook for workers and the likelihood of labor peace dimmed considerably, as did the persuasiveness of arguments for leaving the determination of wages to market forces and private negotiations between employers and employees.

The World War I and New Era debate over the trajectory of real wages included a number of compelling twists and turns brought on by new discoveries and improved data collection and manipulation. Between the 1890s and 1914, economists, policy makers and other consumers of government labor statistics worked under the assumption that, despite hardships, the real wages of U.S. workers had increased since the late nineteenth century. By World War I, however, the expertise on the wage question coalesced around a more troubling scenario. In 1914, economist Isaac Rubinow published a groundbreaking study that revealed that, rather than rising, workers' real wages had fallen since the 1890s. Economists and government officials, most notably Paul Douglas and Wesley Mitchell, followed up Rubinow's discovery with a flurry of inquiries into the veracity of his claims and the adequacy of government statistics that had failed in many respects to provide a clear picture of the changes in workers' wages. The mobilization of industry for wartime production and rampant inflation only heightened attention to these issues as labor unrest and an increasingly assertive federal government struggled to maintain labor peace, in part through the setting of workers' wages in accordance to changes in the cost of living. Economic and social instability after the war ensured continued focus on the wage question and wage policy. In this phase, economists such as Paul Douglas and John Maurice Clark undermined the belief in efficiency and fairness of long-standing policies that left the determination of wages up to the private sphere where freedom of contract reigned.

The focus shifted yet again at mid-decade, when economists made another shocking discovery anticipated by many union leaders and associates of Herbert Hoover, namely that real wages since the war had increased by as much as 30 percent. The phenomenon of rising real wages combined with dramatic increases in productivity forced labor experts and economists to rethink wages, wage policy, and the role of wages in an increasingly consumer-driven economy. By the late 1920s, wage investigations by economists, unions, government, and nonprofit organizations suggested that the significant real wage gains had been built into the New Era economic system, casting doubt on the need for unions and coordinated wage policies to protect U.S. workers.

While there was much to celebrate in this era, some economists and wage experts saw worrying signs on the horizon. In the latter part of the decade, University of Minnesota economist and future New Dealer Alvin Hansen, an early skeptic of Douglas's grim assessment of falling real wages, emerged as a leading authority on the movement of real wages. Rather than look to statist wage policy solutions to solve the problem of low-wage workers, Hansen advocated a quickening of the recomposition of production from producer (capital) toward consumer goods. The steady rise of real wages that 1920s economists detected could only lead to higher standards of living and economic stability, according to Hansen, if business would produce goods workers could consume. Hansen's important work on the structure of the economy could have served as a warning to the many economists and policy makers who assumed that higher productivity and less waste would automatically lead to a more prosperous and stable economic system. As we will see in Chapter 3, Hansen was joined in raising these concerns, though from a very different perspective, by wage experts in newly emerging research institutions contained within and supporting organized labor.

In many respects, Hansen's concerns were borne out by the Great Depression. In fact, though they worked separately, Hansen and union economic experts were groping toward a secular stagnation theory of the economy. During the Great Depression, Hansen became associated with the idea of secular stagnation, which rejected the belief, largely accepted, by economists and policy makers that depressions and recessions were a departure from the norm. By the late 1930s, Hansen joined John M. Keynes in arguing that the American economy in the Great Depression had moved into a new era in which economic stagnation *was* the norm, save for a dramatic and sustained increase in public spending and aggregate demand. As these next two chapters demonstrate, despite the New Era's deserved reputation as a period of prosperity, many economic experts focusing on different aspects of the labor question uncovered deep structural economic problems and proposed innovative policies that would gain traction in the New Deal.

To assess the significance of these changes, it is useful to look back to the earlier era when economists and government officials mistakenly believed that workers' wages had risen. The period between the 1870s and the merger movement at the turn of the century witnessed three related and relevant economic changes that influenced economic thought, specifically, the fierce contest between workers and employers, the emergence of modern corporate capitalism, and the development of marginalist economics. Historian James Livingston has described the emergence of a late nineteenth-century social movement led by investors and capitalists to legitimize business profits and control work at the point of production. Between 1870 and the 1890s, while capitalists made larger and larger capital investments, workers and unions maintained significant control over work processes and fought business leaders to a standstill, thus limiting the rate of return on capital investment (i.e., profit) and retarding economic growth. By the end of the 1890s, business leaders and investors started to implement a strategy to overcome this "social impasse" by surmounting worker and union resistance to mechanization and management's authority and prerogative, while at the same time consolidating and integrating firms to minimize competition and stabilize prices. As the struggle for control of the shop room floor ebbed, marginalist economic theory rose in academia, having the effect of justifying the place of corporate profit in a modern economic system.[1] In *Distribution of Wealth*

---

[1] James Livingston, "The Social Analysis of Economic History and Theory: Conjectures on Late Nineteenth-Century American Development," *AHR* 92 (February 1987): 69–95.

(1899), pioneering marginal economist John Bates Clark argued that, under perfectly competitive conditions, each factor of production would be rewarded based on the value that factor added to the production process. In rejecting Henry George's attacks on rent and Karl Marx's analysis of exploitation, Clark contended that the distribution of rewards based on marginal productivity was ethical and that the public interest would be largely protected by actual or potential competition. For skeptics, data confirming rising real wages eased concerns over John Bates Clark's linkage of marginal productivity and fairness.

Rubinow's work scuttled many of these assumptions and led a new generation of economists to renew their focus on how best to measure wage fluctuations and whether the state should play a more active role in wage determination. The most obvious and familiar challenge to marginalists' assumptions came from J. B. Clark's former student at Carleton College, Thorstein Veblen, but equally significant challenges came from other corners as well. Innovative economists such as Paul Douglas, John Maurice Clark, Wesley Mitchell, and Alvin Hansen applied new methods for creating longitudinal data sets that contributed in new ways to the civic, academic, and policy discourses about distribution of income and the need for greater protection for American workers. John Bates Clark's son, John Maurice Clark, wrote persuasively about the need to consider labor's cost a fixed cost and for the public to assume a more assertive role in controlling business in the public interest. Douglas, who continued Rubinow's work on the trajectory of real wages, provided concrete policy recommendations for the younger Clark's analysis of workers' plight and became a strong advocate of a variety of statist policy solutions to the low-wage problem, including wage floors and social insurance programs that assumed a highly patriarchical vision of the American household. Laboring steadily at Columbia University and the National Bureau of Economic Research (NBER), Mitchell, whose leading role in directing NBER studies has been well documented, made what ultimately counted as a more important

---

Livingston's analysis of corporate reorganization as a social movement built upon that of Martin Sklar; see particularly Martin Sklar, *The Corporate Reconstruction of American Capitalism, 1890–1916: The Market, the Law, and Politics* (Cambridge: Cambridge University Press, 1988). Livingston extended the theme further to include a cultural dimension in James Livingston, *Pragmatism and the Political Economy of Cultural Revolution, 1850–1940* (Chapel Hill: University of North Carolina Press, 1994). On the struggle for control of the shop room floor, see, for instance, David Montgomery, *Workers: Control in America* (New York: Cambridge University Press, 1979); David Montgomery, *The Fall of the House of Labor: The Workplace, the State and American Labor Activism, 1865–1925* (New York: Cambridge University Press, 1987).

contribution to economic and labor knowledge by assisting Bureau of Labor Statistics (BLS) commissioner Royal Meeker and fellow economist Irving Fischer in the reorganization of BLS index numbers to more accurately represent shifts in wage and price levels.[2] As the decade progressed, economists and government officials came armed with more accurate tools for measuring shifts in wages and a clearer sense that pocketbook issues, such as wages and prices, were very much a public concern.

MISTAKES AND MAKEOVERS: WAGE AND PRICE STATISTICS, 1914–1925

As the nation struggled with World War I-era economic disruptions, government, business, reform, labor, and academic leaders turned to the BLS in a desperate effort to better understand the movement of prices and wages. They found a poorly funded bureau employing antiquated statistical methods and a paucity of data concerning these critical economic issues. These deficiencies became more acute during and after the war as employers, workers, and policy makers wrestled with wild fluctuations in wages, profits, and prices. After a period of fierce criticism and innovation, a revamped BLS emerged in the early 1920s as an organization better suited to making sense of economic fluctuations affecting the nation's workers. In his presidential address before the Eighteenth Annual Meeting of the American Statistical Association in 1918, Wesley Mitchell noted, "No year has brought such stirring changes in American statistics as the year now closing." According to Mitchell, World War I not only "forced the rapid expansion of the scope of federal statistics and the creation of new statistical agencies"; it "led to the use of statistics, not only as a record of what had happened, but also as a critical factor in planning what should be done."[3]

---

[2] In this chapter, I focus largely on the issue of wages, but there is a vast literature on the struggle between institutional and neoclassical economics in this period; see, for example, Malcolm Rutherford, *The Institutionalist Movement in American Economics, 1918–1947: Science and Social Control* (Cambridge: Cambridge University Press, 2011); Malcolm Rutherford, "Understanding Institutional Economics: 1918–1929," *Journal of the History of Economic Thought* 22 (September 2000): 277–308; Geoffrey Hodgson, *The Evolution of Institutional Economics: Agency, Structure, and Darwinism in American Institutionalism* (London: Routledge, 2004); Geoffrey Hodgson, *How Economics Forgot History: The Problem of Historical Specificity in Social Science* (New York: Routledge, 2001); and Yuval P. Yonay, *The Struggle Over the Soul of Economics: Institutionalist and Neoclassical Economists in America Between the Wars* (Princeton: Princeton University Press, 1998).

[3] Wesley Mitchell, "Statistics in Government," *Publications of the American Statistical Association* 16 (March 1919): 223. During the 1920s, prominent economists wrote a

The work of the BLS came under significant fire even before the United States entered the war. Between the 1890s and 1914, economists, policy makers and other consumers of government labor statistics worked under the assumption that, despite hardships, U.S. workers' standard of living moved inexorably upward. The BLS shouldered much of the responsibility for justifying what many political and business leaders surely wanted to believe. In the early 1890s, the BLS under Commissioner Carroll Wright had directed investigations into the movement of wages and prices, which found that workers' wages had increased at a much greater clip than prices. A belief that the Census Bureau should gather basic price and wage data, a reallocation of resources within the BLS to the *Report on the Condition of Woman and Child Wage-Earners*, and an interest in examining labor issues of more immediate concern led Wright to abandon the collection of wage and price data during the 1890s.[4] Revisiting the wage question in 1903, the BLS confirmed that, since the 1890s, worker earnings had far outstripped prices and the purchasing power of workers' hourly wage had increased by more than 5 percent.[5] The lack of consistent data continued in 1907 when budget pressures and a congressional demand for a new major study on women and children workers forced the BLS to abandon its tracking of wages and prices.[6] Nonetheless, the BLS's periodic studies allowed most observers to conclude that real wages had consistently risen. In a bit of an overstatement that exaggerated slightly the level of acceptance of the BLS's conclusions, economist Isaac Rubinow wrote, "Scarcely any American elementary or popular book on economics published during this period

---

number of texts examining the use and construction of index numbers. Wesley Mitchell, *The Making and Using of Index Numbers* (Washington, DC: GPO, 1938); Irving Fisher, *The Making of Index Numbers: A Study of Their Varieties, Tests, and Reliability* (Boston: Houghton Mifflin, 1922); Warren M. Persons, *The Construction of Index Numbers* (Boston: Houghton Mifflin, 1928); Willford I. King, *Index Numbers Elucidated* (New York: Longmans, Green and Co., 1930).

[4] Mary O. Furner, "Knowing Capitalism: Public Investigation and the Labor Question in the Long Progressive Era," in *The State and Economic Knowledge: The American and British Experiences*, eds. Mary O. Furner and Barry Supple (Cambridge: Cambridge University Press, 1991), 246–68; James Leiby, *Carroll Wright and Labor Reform: The Origin of Labor Statistics* (Cambridge: Harvard University Press, 1960), 122; Eric Rauchway, "The High Cost of Living in Progressives' Economy," *JAH* 88 (December 2001): 898–924; and Senate Committee on Finance, "Retail Prices and Wages," *Senate Report* 986, 42nd Cong., 1st sess., 4 vols. (1893); and Senate Committee on Finance, *Wholesale Prices, Wages, and Transportation, Senate Report* 1394, 52nd Cong., 2nd sess. (1893).

[5] BLS, "Wages and Cost of Living," *Bulletin* 53 (Washington, DC: GPO, 1904).

[6] Furner, "Knowing Capitalism," 246–68; Rauchway, "The High Cost of Living in Progressives' Economy," 898–924.

failed to quote these [BLS] figures as evidence of the continued progress of the wage worker."[7]

In the teens, economists' examination of the movement of real wages punctured the BLS's celebration of rising real wages. In a 1914 article for the *American Economic Review*, Rubinow, who earned his PhD in economics at Columbia and became the foremost advocate of social insurance, reworked the BLS's own statistics to show an actual decline in real wages between 1890 and 1907. By demonstrating that, despite workers' increased productivity, "a much smaller share of the value reaches the wage worker now than it did twenty or thirty years ago," Rubinow uncovered an unseemly contradiction in American economic development in the period.[8] He found that the purchasing power of wages had been highest at the end of the nineteenth century as a result of downward pressure on prices, but between 1907 and 1912 it had fallen a grim 12.7 percent.[9] Overall, he concluded, despite significant increases in worker productivity, the "purchasing power of wages in 1913 are not much higher than they were in 1870." Surveying industrial unrest that could in part be explained by the downward movement of workers' purchasing power, Rubinow lamented the relative powerlessness of workers, whose "strenuous efforts" to push up wages through agitation crumbled in the face of frequently rising prices and the "violent growth of profits."[10]

Economists who continued to study the trajectory of real wages during World War I refined but largely confirmed Rubinow's findings. Yale sociologist Henry Pratt Fairchild and Columbia University's F. W. Jones proposed alternative methods of calculating the cost of living that modified and at times tempered Rubinow's general findings but did not undermine his basic conclusions. In their work, they disaggregated segments of the working class and reconfigured workers' household budgets in order to better understand how wage and price changes had affected different groups of workers. Fairchild developed an index that considered the

---

[7] I. M. Rubinow, "The Recent Trend in Real Wages," *AER* 4 (December 1914): 793–817. Some economists did in fact raise questions concerning BLS data. See, for example, Henry L. Moore, "The Variability of Wages," 22 (March 1907): 61–73 and Davis R. Dewey, *Employees and Wages* (U.S. Census Office: Washington, DC: 1903). For a somewhat surprising defense of the BLS, see Wesley Mitchell, "The Trustworthiness of the Bureau of Labor's Index Number of Wages," *QJE* 25 (May 1911): 613–20.
[8] Rubinow, "The Recent Trend in Real Wages," 817.
[9] Ibid., 799 and 812. For more on inaccuracies in BLS data, see Furner, "Knowing Capitalism," 254–5 and Rauchway, "The High Cost of Living in Progressives' Economy," 900–5.
[10] Rubinow, "The Recent Trend in Real Wages," 813.

household budgets of unskilled wage earners in 1890 and 1908, giving particular attention to the cost of rent in a non-home-owning family's budget. He found that, after covering the most basic costs, a family of five headed by an unskilled worker would have had 15.4 percent of its income remaining in 1890 but only 14 percent in 1908. According to Fairchild, "One thing seems safe to say – that the foregoing data *disprove* the right of anybody to assert with serene confidence that the standard of living of the American common laborer has improved in the past thirty years." "The burden of proof is laid on the optimists, to bring forward some positive verification of their assumptions," he concluded.[11] Jones critically examined and then modified Rubinow's food basket to show that workers' conditions were not as gloomy as Rubinow contended. Using 100 as a base, Jones found that workers' weekly real wages had fallen from an index number of 98.9 in 1890 to 88.4 in 1912. Jones conceded, however, "The doctrine so popular in certain quarters that while the rich have grown rapidly richer in recent years the poor have also steadily risen in the scale of economic welfare, has no foundation in fact."[12]

Recognition of problems with the quality of government statistics generally, and particularly those that concerned labor, continued to percolate after Rubinow published his initial findings in 1914. At a 1915 joint session of the American Statistical Association and American Economic Association, a powerful group of economists and government officials, including E. Dana Durand, Royal Meeker, and Wesley Mitchell derided the quality of government statistics and recommended assistance and oversight from nongovernment statisticians. BLS commissioner Royal Meeker described "a S. O. S. call for help" he had sent out to economists begging for assistance in reorganizing labor statistics.[13] Mitchell, one of the few economists to respond to Meeker's call, railed against the government's price and wage data, charging there was "much that is not clear, and not a little that is patently misleading or flatly wrong."[14] Meeker went so far as to suggest that, given incongruous and incomplete data sets, it was impossible to determine the movement of real wage levels before 1911.[15] In a 1917 paper presented at the American Economic

---

[11] Henry Pratt Fairchild, "The Standard of Living – Up or Down," *AER* 6 (March 1916): 24–5. Italics in original.
[12] F. W. Jones, "Real Wages in Recent Years," *AER* 7 (June 1917): 329–30.
[13] Walter F. Wilcox et al., "The Statistical Work of the United States Government," *AER* 5, Suppl. (March 1915): 174.
[14] Ibid., 182.
[15] Ibid., 173.

Association's annual meeting, Willford I. King, a future member of the NBER and former John R. Commons student at the University of Wisconsin, noted a lack of progress in the coordination and presentation of economic data. According to King, despite wage data collection by the BLS, Census Bureau, and state government labor statistics agencies, "It is most difficult to find any continuous records of the wages of miners, farm hands, clerks, domestic servants and other very numerous and important classes of workers." Further, a lack of consistency in data-gathering practices over time made an "accurate comparison" in data across time "manifestly impossible."[16]

Though World War I would reveal continued inadequacies in government statistics and spur the most dramatic improvements in the BLS's accounting of changes in wages and prices, even before U.S. entry into the war Meeker significantly changed how statistics related to the calculation of real wages were manipulated on three fronts. First, he turned to Mitchell and Fischer, who recommended a move to the use of a chain index in accounting for changes in prices. This meant that rather than having a single base period for prices – it had been 1890–1900 – the BLS would calculate changes in prices from one year to the next, making it easier to account for the relative change in prices.[17] Second, Meeker embraced Mitchell's recommendation that wholesale price data be weighted to account for the relative importance of the good to the overall index.[18] Third, the BLS started down a path that would eventually lead it to dramatically expand the breadth of its wage data. In the mid-teens, the BLS collected wage data in select mass production consumer goods industries (cotton, cotton-finishing hosiery, boots and shoes) and some service and manufacturing industries (building and repairing steam railroad cars and lumber).[19] By 1925, BLS surveys had

[16] Willford I. King, "Desirable Additions to Statistical Data on Wealth and Income," *AER* 7, Suppl. (March 1917): 159.

[17] Joseph P. Goldberg and William T. Moye, *The First Hundred Years of the Bureau of Labor Statistics* (Washington, DC: GPO, 1985), 92. For more on Mitchell's importance, see Samuel Weiss, "The Development of Index Numbers in the BLS," *MLR* 78 (January 1955): 20–5. For Fisher's involvement in the early stages, see Goldberg and Moye, *The First Hundred Years of the Bureau of Labor Statistics*, 102; Frank Julian Warne, H. B. Woolston, I. M. Rubinow, Theresa S. McMahon, W. L. Whittlesey, Scott Nearing, and N. I. Stone, "Public Regulation of Wages," *AER* 5, Suppl. (March 1915): 278–99.

[18] Goldberg and Moye, *The First Hundred Years of the Bureau of Labor Statistics*, 92.

[19] BLS, "Wages and Regularity of Employment and Standardization of Piece Rates in the Dress and Waist Industry of New York City," *Bulletin* 146 (Washington, DC: GPO, 1914); BLS, "Wages and Regularity of Employment in the Cloak, Suit, and Skirt Industry," *Bulletin* 147 (Washington, DC: GPO, 1914); BLS, "Wages and Hours of Labor

expanded dramatically to include "4,336 establishments in 53 industries, with 2,891,724 workers."[20]

These Meeker-led changes culminated in the BLS's publication of Mitchell's *The Making and Using of Index Numbers*, perhaps the most important and accessible statistical text of the period and one that gained added relevance given the price volatility that followed World War I. This study laid out the need for better and more standardized data sets that tracked economic activity and explained the basics of building, weighting, and evaluating index numbers, all in a manner understandable to noneconomists and statisticians.[21] Mitchell's work won high and enduring praise from many corners. In 1955, the seventieth anniversary issue of the *Monthly Labor Review* referred to the study as a clear enunciation of "a role for index numbers which has influenced the Bureau to this day."[22] British economist F. Y. Edgeworth, who along with Alfred Marshall produced pioneering work in the weighting of index numbers, referred to Mitchell's study as "a singularly comprehensive and lucid treatise on this species of measurement."[23] Not everyone would embrace Mitchell's more

---

in the Clothing and Cigar Industries, 1911–1913," *Bulletin* 161 (Washington, DC: GPO, 1914); BLS, "Wages and Hours of Labor in the Building and Repairing of Steam Railroad Cars, 1907 to 1913," *Bulletin* 163 (Washington, DC: GPO, 1914); BLS, "Wages and Hours of Labor in the Cotton, Woolen, and Silk Industries, 1907–1914," *Bulletin* 190 (Washington, DC: GPO, 1916); BLS, "Wages and Hours of Labor in the Lumber, Millwork, and Furniture Industries," *Bulletin* 225 (Washington, DC: GPO, 1915).

[20] Joseph Dorfman, *The Economic Mind in American Civilization* (New York: Viking Press, 1959), 4: 203.

[21] A flurry of books and articles by economists describing the merits of index numbers and the art of constructing an index to answer particular questions followed Mitchell's BLS publication. Inflationary pressures made wholesale and retail price levels a top concern for these studies. See, for example, Fisher, *The Making of Index Numbers*; W. Randolph Burgess, "Index Numbers of the Wages of Common Labor," *JASA* 18 (March 1922): 101–3; George Barnett, "Index Numbers of the Total Cost of Living," *QJE* 35 (February 1921): 240–63; and William A. Berridge, Emma A. Winslow, and Richard A. Flynn, *Purchasing Power of the Consumer: A Statistical Index* (Chicago: A. W. Shaw, Co., 1925). Fisher's study was part of a series of important studies funded by the Pollack Foundation for Economic Research in the 1920s, including Paul Douglas, *Real Wages in the United States, 1890–1926*, William A. Berridge, *Cycles of Unemployment in the Unites States*, and Maurice B. Hexter, *Social Consequences of Business Cycles*.

[22] Weiss, "The Development of Index Numbers in the BLS," 22.

[23] For further praise for the Mitchell-BLS publication, see Frederick R. Macaulay, "Review," *AER* 6 (March 1916): 203–9 and P. G. Wright, "The New Index Numbers of the United States Bureau of Labor Statistics," *QJE* 30 (August 1916): 796–804. Mitchell's study was published in a number of forms by the BLS. It was originally published in 1915 as part of BLS *Bulletin* 173. It was revised in 1921 to incorporate dramatic wartime price changes and published as *Bulletin* 284. Edgeworth's comments refer to the 1915 version of the report. F. Y. Edgeworth, "The Doctrine of Index-Numbers According to Wesley Mitchell,

inductive approach to economics and his emphasis on the need for more and better data. As the interwar period unfolded, Mitchell's institutionalism, particularly his privileging of empiricism over theory, would increasingly pit him against neoclassical economists who derided Mitchell's approach as "measurement without theory."[24]

Despite these gradual improvements, as the nation entered World War I frustration with the poor quality of government statistics continued, leading Mitchell to lament that the war "revealed defects of the federal machinery for collecting statistics with startling suddenness."[25] To fill the void in labor statistics in a highly inflationary economic environment, some nongovernmental organizations experimented with gathering their own data and used it to determine wages. For instance, the Bankers' Trust Co. of New York City appointed a committee of its employees to investigate the cost of living, finding a 21 percent increase in the cost of living. As a result of the study, the company increased the wages of workers who made less than twenty-five hundred dollars annually by between 14.7 and 21 percent.[26] In the burgeoning nonprofit sphere, the newly established National Industrial Conference Board (NICB) gathered its own statistics and published a study of cost of living in the World War I-era that rivaled statistics gathered by the BLS.

Policy makers' inadequate knowledge of changes in the cost of living and wages came to a head first in the wartime shipbuilding industry, where the Shipbuilding Labor Adjustment Board (SLAB) struggled to maintain labor peace and increase production in the nation's shipyards. Rather than coalesce around a common goal of winning the war,

---

Economic Journal 28 (June 1918): 176–7. On Edgeworth's importance, see Mitchell, *The Making and Use of Index Numbers*, 7–8; Wesley Mitchell, *The Making and Using of Index Numbers* (New York: Augustus M. Kelley, 1965; reprint BLS, *Bulletin* 284 Washington, DC: GPO, 1921), iii.

[24] Philip Mirowski, "The Measurement without Theory Controversy: Defeating Rival Research Programs by Accusing Them of Naïve Empiricism," *Economies et Sociétés: Serie Oeconomia* 23 (1989), 109–31; Michael Bernstein, *Perilous Progress: Economists and Public Purpose in Twentieth-Century America* (Princeton: Princeton University Press, 2001), 44–8.

[25] Guy Alchon, *The Invisible Hand of Planning: Capitalism, Social Science, and the State in the 1920s* (Princeton: Princeton University Press, 1985), 26; Mitchell, "Statistics in Government," 224. On the politics concerning inflation during the war, see Meg Jacobs, *Pocketbook Politics: Economic Citizenship in Twentieth-Century America* (Princeton: Princeton University Press, 2005), 54–66.

[26] On this and similar efforts, see Irving Fisher, "Adjusting Wages to the Cost of Living," *MLR* 7 (November 1918): 1–5. See also BLS, "Cost of Living in Relation to Wage Adjustments," *MLR* 10 (January 1920): 148–52; Taylor Society, *Bulletin of the Taylor Society* (October 1919): 29–46.

in the first six months of 1917 the nation's workplaces showed signs of unraveling in often violent confrontation between employers and workers. In all, workers walked off the job more than twenty-three hundred times by June 1917, an increase of more than 300 strikes over the same period in the previous year. The problem was particularly acute in the shipbuilding industry, where labor instability on both coasts slowed the effort to build a "bridge of ships" to Europe. In order to ramp up production for urgently needed vessels, Congress created the Emergency Fleet Corporation (EFC) of the U.S. Shipping Board, which took control of shipbuilding works. To stem unrest in the industry, the EFC reached out to the American Federation of Labor's Metal Trades Department, which led in turn to the creation of SLAB – a tripartite board made up of representatives from labor, the public, and government – that resolved conflict in the industry.[27] In order to set wages in a period of wildly fluctuating prices, SLAB at times cobbled together local, state, and federal data on price and wages to set wartime wages. For instance, in determining a new wage scale for workers in Pacific Coast shipyards, SLAB relied on a combination of federal, state, and municipal reports.[28]

SLAB's work in World War I evolved into the Consumer Price Index (CPI), which remains one of the most important indexes in the construction of economic policy. Indeed, the continuous price and wage statistics developed by the BLS in this period were dramatic improvements over the decennial census and occasional reports on wages, prices, unemployment, and business activity that labor experts had previously relied on. The BLS had monitored some wholesale and retail prices, but not until World War I did it develop continuous index numbers for the entire cost of living, including prices for food, clothing, rent, fuel, light, furniture, furnishings, and sundries. During the early months of 1917, the cost of

[27] Since the EFC was a government body taking control of privately owned shipyards completing work contracted by the government, SLAB did not include a representative from business or the shipbuilders. The absence of a representative from the shipbuilders was lamented by members of SLAB, including SLAB secretary Henry R. Seager, who was also a professor of political economy at Columbia University. See Henry R. Seager, "Effects of Present Methods of Future Wage Adjustments," *Proceedings of the Academy of Political Science in the City of New York* 8 (February 1919): 113. To the extent that this was a problem, the National War Labor Board, which had many of the same functions as SLAB but in a wider range of industries, remedied it by including representatives of business, labor, and the public.
[28] Louis B. Wehle, "Labor Problems in the United States During the War" *QJE* 32 (February 1918): 342. Thomas A. Stapleford, *The Cost of Living in America: A Political History of Economic Statistics, 1880–2000* (Cambridge: Cambridge University Press, 2009), 78–92.

living index (later renamed the CPI) included data from only fourteen shipbuilding cities, but by December, the BLS expanded its coverage to thirty-two cities.[29]

The period between 1914 and the end of hostilities witnessed a dramatic improvement in the quality of government statistics, but some still had lingering doubts. In fact, the demand for more accurate price and wage data and the potential consequences of the BLS's substandard work prior to World War I can be seen in the competition it faced from the NICB, which seemed to be working to supplant the BLS's role as the authoritative source for economic statistics. During and after the war, the BLS and the NICB quarreled openly in statistical and government journals and conferences over which institution could produce the best cost of living index. Founded in 1916 to serve as a research arm for business, the NICB gained prominence for its ambitious range of investigations of price, trade, wage, and industrial issues. Although there was not a tremendous disparity between the conclusions of BLS and NICB studies, the debate revealed important differences in the methods of gathering data and organizing reports. Both indexes relied on BLS data for calculating the price of food, but the NICB conducted its own surveys to gather data on prices for clothing, rent, fuel, light, and sundries. The NICB gathered price and cost of living data by way of a questionnaire distributed to member and nonmember businesses. With the exception of fuel and light prices, where the BLS did rely on a questionnaire sent to coal and wood dealers and gas and electric companies, the BLS dispatched agents to businesses to gather information on consumer prices. In an informative article that detailed the differences in BLS and NICB data, the BLS's Elma B. Carr concluded, "The methods employed by the United States Bureau of Labor Statistics ... are far superior to those of the National Industrial Conference Board."[30] In a comparable piece, Paul Douglas noted correctly the smaller sample size, thinner geographic distribution, and less reliable data-gathering method of the NICB study, concluding that the BLS index

---

[29] George Barnett, "A Critique of Cost-Of-Living Studies," *Quarterly Publication of the American Statistical Association* 17 (September 1921): 904; Elma B. Carr, "Cost of Living Statistics of the U.S. Bureau of Labor Statistics and the National Industrial Conference Board," *JASA* 19 (December 1924): 484–507. Until 1925, the BLS gathered cost of living data on a quarterly basis, but beginning in May budget constraints forced the BLS to conduct these surveys on a semiannual basis. Moye and Goldberg, *The First Hundred Years of the BLS*, 122–4.

[30] Carr, "Cost of Living Statistics of the U.S. Bureau of Labor Statistics and the National Industrial Conference Board," 507.

was "preferable."[31] In response to such criticism, Margaret Loomis Stecker of the research staff of the NICB suggested that Douglas failed to consider carefully the quality of NICB studies; she complained of "much misuse and misinterpretation not only of the data presented by the Board, but also of the data with which the Board's work is compared." Virgil Jordan (NICB) and George Barnett (Johns Hopkins) stepped into the debate as agents of compromise who could recognize strengths in each index. In a response to Carr's article, Jordan tipped his hat to the BLS and suggested that the two indexes were "different in scope and character but similar enough in their general results to serve as a valuable check on each other and to justify confidence in both."[32]

MEASURING WAGES IN THE POSTWAR ERA

After World War I, employers attacked workers and organized labor for using the war to drive up real wages; meanwhile economists struggled to determine the impact of the end of hostilities and the upsurge of labor unrest on wages and prices. To bring Rubinow's data up to date and provide an economic analysis that addressed the complaints of employers, Paul Douglas and Francis Lamberson constructed indexes of wages and prices between 1912 and 1918 that revealed continued downward pressure on workers' purchasing power stemming from the failure of wages to keep up with rampant gold standard inflation. At the end of the war, Douglas and Lamberson reported, "The purchasing power of the established week's work ... was from 20 to 30 per cent less than in the nineties and from 10 to 20 per cent less than in 1915." They concluded, "American labor as a whole, therefore, cannot legitimately be charged with having profiteered during the war. Rather, like Alice in Wonderland, it was compelled to run faster in order to stay in the same place."[33]

[31] Paul Douglas, "The Movement of Real Wages and Its Economic Significance," *AER* 16, Suppl. (March 1926): 22; See also Labor Bureau Inc., "Wage Theories and Arguments: No.2 – Changes in the Cost of Living," *FFW* 2 (November 1923): 7; Joseph Kunz, "An Anti-Labor Sample: The 'Johnny-On-the-Spot' NICB and Its Fine Line of 'Facts,'" *LA* 7 (April 1923): 6–8.

[32] Margaret Loomis Stecker, "Wage Studies of the National Industrial Conference Board: A Reply," *JASA* 18 (June 1922): 258. Douglas responded by reiterating his argument in Paul Douglas, "A Rejoinder," *JASA* 18 (June 1922): 258. Virgil Jordan, "The Cost of Living Indices of the N.I.C.B. and the B. of L. S.," *JASA* 20 (June 1925): 253; Barnett, "A Critique of Cost-Of-Living Studies," 904–9. For a similar depiction of this debate, see Stapleford, *The Cost of Living in America*, 120–9.

[33] Paul Douglas and Frances Lamberson, "The Movement of Real Wages, 1890–1918," *AER* 11 (September 1921): 425–6.

In the New Era, Douglas established himself as a leading expert on the wage question and an advocate of social reform. Douglas was born in Salem, Massachusetts in 1892, but grew up on a Maine farm. He took an active interest in labor issues as an undergraduate at Bowdoin College, where he worked with William B. Catlin. Douglas earned his PhD at Columbia and took classes at Harvard, where he studied the theory of value and distribution with Frank W. Taussig. While completing his dissertation, Douglas worked as an arbiter of labor disputes for the Industrial Relations Section of the Emergency Fleet Corporation and taught at the University of Illinois, Reed College, and the University of Washington. In 1920, shortly before completing his dissertation, Douglas started teaching at the University of Chicago and maintained that affiliation until 1948, when he won election to the United States Senate.[34]

Moving now into an analysis of real wages in the postwar years, economist William M. Persons – who had served on the wartime Committee on the Purchasing Power of Money in Relation to the War – largely confirmed Douglas and Lamberson's conclusion that workers could hardly be cast as wild beneficiaries of war-era price and wage instability. Using 1913 as a base year (base year valued at 100), and with the help of BLS data, Persons determined that the cost of living rose from 177 in June 1919 to 217 in June 1920, before returning to 177 by September 1921. To calculate wages, Persons relied exclusively on full-time union wage rates, which did not provide a completely accurate picture given the likelihood of greater fluctuations in nonunion work and the likelihood that not all union workers found full-time employment. According to Persons, hourly wage rates rose continuously, if not consistently, from 155 in May 1919 to 199 in June 1920 to 205 by May 1921. In light of the economic instability of the period, Persons speculated that at the time of publication it was "probable ... that [wage] rates have declined" and that "non-union rates have declined more than union rates," which led him to conclude that "real wage rates are probably at about their 1913 level."[35]

---

[34] On Douglas, see Dorfman, *The Economic Mind in American Civilization* (New York: Viking Press, 1959), 5: 526–7 and Roger Biles, *Crusading Liberal: Paul Douglas of Illinois* (DeKalb: Northern Illinois University, 2002).

[35] Warren M. Persons, "The Crisis in 1920 in the United States: A Quantitative Survey," *AER* 12 (March 1922): 9–10. Alvin Hansen reported a dramatic rise in wholesale prices prior to the war without a corresponding increase in union wages. As with Persons's findings, Hansen noted a narrowing of the difference in price and wage indexes after the early 1920s. Alvin Hansen, "The Outlook for Wages and Employment," *AER* 13, Suppl. (March 1923): 27–44; Alvin Hansen, "The Buying Power of Labor During the War," *JASA* 18 (March 1922): 56–66.

Also in the early 1920s, University of Minnesota and future New Deal economist Alvin Hansen emerged as an important observer and expert on wages and the cost of living and as a critic of Douglas's work on real wages.[36] Hansen grew up on a farm in South Dakota, the son of immigrant Danes. His interest in industrial relations took him to the University of Wisconsin, where he earned a PhD in economics in 1918. In 1919, after working as an assistant instructor and an instructor at Wisconsin and Brown respectively, Hansen took a position at the University of Minnesota, where he specialized in industrial relations.

In 1922 and 1923, Hansen produced two articles that examined the movement of wages, prices, and purchasing power during the war and immediate postwar years and concluded that Douglas and Lamberson had been too pessimistic in their assessment of real wages, particularly in the years surrounding World War I. Hansen questioned the veracity of Lamberson and Douglas's assertion that real wages for workers fell between 1916 and 1918. Instead, Hansen contended, "The per capita buying power of the wage-earning class during the years 1916–1918 appears ... to have been on the average 8.5 percent above the normal per capita buying power of labor in pre-war days."[37] Hansen provided a twofold explanation for this discrepancy. First, he criticized Lamberson and Douglas's use of wage rates as an accurate measure of worker income. Hansen correctly pointed out that such a measure failed to take into account "overtime and over-time bonuses, full employment for those regularly working, and the employment of members of the family not normally working."[38] When wage rates were low relative to prices, employers would be encouraged to increase the number of hours for current workers and hire others as well, Hansen believed. This could result in an increase in household or individual income, even if (or perhaps because) the wage *rate* remained static.[39]

---

[36] Dorfman, *The Economic Mind in American Civilization*, 5: 546–7; Theodore Rosenof, *Economics in the Long Run* (Chapel Hill: University of North Carolina Press, 1997), particularly 44–76; Alan Brinkley, *The End of Reform: New Deal Liberalism in Recession and War* (New York: Vintage Books, 1996), 129–35; William J. Barber, *From New Era to New Deal: Herbert Hoover, the Economists, and American Economic Policy, 1921–1933* (Cambridge: Cambridge University Press, 1985); and William J. Barber, *Designs Within Disorder: Franklin D. Roosevelt, the Economists, and the Shaping of American Economic Policy, 1933–1935* (Cambridge: Cambridge University Press, 1996).

[37] Hansen, "The Buying Power of Labor During the War," 65.

[38] Ibid.

[39] Ibid., 66; and Hansen, "The Outlook for Wages and Employment," 27–32. For a response to Hansen, see Wesley Mitchell and Mary van Kleeck, "The Outlook for 1923 – Discussion," *AER* 13, Suppl. (March 1923): 45–9.

Second, Hansen criticized Douglas and Lamberson's reliance on union wage scales as representative of workers' wages, asserting there "can be little doubt that union wage scales lagged considerably behind the actual wage rates paid generally."[40] This was a more complicated and in some ways interesting observation that anticipated aspects of Irving Fischer's *Money Illusion* (1928) and Keynes's later observations concerning the "stickiness" of nominal wages. Like Keynes, Hansen understood workers' wages to be sticky on the way down; a fact particularly true for unionized workers who had more power to resist wage reductions. The wages of "common laborers," Hansen argued, were more responsive to economic conditions, leaving this group vulnerable to wage cuts in downturns. In more prosperous or perhaps inflationary times, however, these same common laborers saw their wages increase at a quicker pace than unionized workers, who, perhaps, had to wait for the next round of contract negotiations.[41] Thus the choice of union wage rates, versus those of "common laborers," skewed the data and exaggerated the downward pressure on real wages and the purchasing power of workers during the war period.[42]

WAGES AS A PUBLIC CONCERN

Despite Hansen's criticism, Lamberson, Douglas, and Rubinow's findings stirred a discussion among economists that undermined core tenets of marginal productivity theory, beginning a process that would eventually help push wage policy from a private matter to a public concern. Tying wage adjustments to the cost of living had been a product of World War I policy decisions; yet, prior to the war, Rubinow's discouraging findings had already reignited wage policy debates among economists. At a stimulating 1915 American Economic Association (AEA) meeting, Rubinow had joined other presenters in attempting to provide an economic, moral, and legal foundation to justify minimum wage legislation. Citing his own work on wages, Rubinow suggested that since the 1890s, despite "frantic efforts by labor to gain some advance," a history of "wage fluctuations for the last two decades leaves one disheartened." Rubinow acknowledged ruefully that "wage statistics alone may not convince the constitutional lawyer of the propriety of minimum wage legislation." Even so,

---

[40] Hansen, "The Buying Power of Labor During the War," 65.
[41] Hansen, "The Outlook for Wages and Employment," in particular 39–40 and 44.
[42] In *Real Wages in the United States*, Douglas would end up agreeing with Hansen on this point. See Douglas, *Real Wages in the United States*, vii.

he contended, "It is therefore the duty of the economist and social student to point out that ... minimum wage legislation ... is but a logical sequence of all protective labor and social legislation."[43] Also at the session, Glendower Evans campaigned for wage regulation by summarizing the work of the Massachusetts Minimum Wage Commission. As the Women's Bureau would in the New Era, Evans argued for labor standards protecting women workers on the basis that they faced exploitive conditions in the labor force brought on by their status as women. Attacking the idea that they were temporary entrants in the labor force, Evans said simply, "The vast majority of wage earning women work because they must. And the vast majority earn wages far below the requirements of a decent living."[44] The presence of these two presentations in the same panel proved prescient. During the 1920s, economists studying real wages and experts on women workers were the primary advocates for a strong and statist wage policy to lift the wages of the working poor.

World War I wage policy experiments, improvements in the quality of cost of living data, and the recognition of declining real wages opened the door to a hotly contested wage policy discourse that contemplated the use of cost of living data to adjust wages, create a wage floor, and distribute income. Helen Fisher Hohman of the University of Chicago observed, "the widespread adoption of the cost-of-living principle for" determining wages "is a product of the war." Columbia economist William Fielding Ogburn added, "The standard of living as a factor in setting wages came to be of considerable importance during the war when prices were rising."[45] In a 500-page BLS study describing the uses of the cost of living adjustments in adjusting wages, Elma B. Carr wrote that, prior to World War I, cost of living data was not "sufficiently comprehensive to be used effectively," but that during the war "more satisfactory figures on the cost of living were made available, and they became the controlling factors

---

[43] Warne, Woolston, Rubinow, McMahon, Whittlesey, Nearing, and Stone, "Public Regulation of Wages," 287–9.
[44] Glendower Evans, "The Social Aspects of the Public Regulation of Wages," *AER* 5, Suppl. (March 1915): 276. At the 1915 AER conference, H. B. Woolston, Theresa McMahon, W. L. Whittlesey, and N. I. Stone also endorsed some type of minimum wage. Warne, Woolston, Rubinow, McMahon, Whittlesey, Nearing, and Stone, "Public Regulation of Wages," 281–6.
[45] Helen Fisher Hohman, "The Use of Cost-Of-Living Figures in Wage Adjustments," *JPE* 34 (August 1926): 525. William Fielding Ogburn, "The Standard-of-Living Factor in Wages," *AER* 13, Suppl. (March 1923): 118; see also Barnett, "Index Numbers of the Total Cost of Living," 241. For examples of companies that tied wages to estimated changes in the cost of living, see Fisher, "Adjusting Wages to the Cost of Living," 1–5.

in wage determinations not only in the United States but in foreign countries."[46] Douglas used wartime rationing as a tool to justify the development of wage policies that provided a more equitable distribution of income based, at least in part, on basic household needs. Douglas reasoned, "No one would have proposed as a basis for rationing that the unmarried worker needed as much sugar or flour as his fellow employee who was a father of a family."[47]

These potential uses of statistics did not receive the support of employers and unions, who joined together to condemn the continued use of cost of living data to determine wages in peacetime. Organized labor, wary of any mechanism that limited its ability to get more from employers and concerned that such policies might undermine perceived postwar wage advances, condemned the policy proposal at its national convention in 1921. The AFL Executive Council reported, "The practice of fixing wages solely on a basis of the cost of living is a violation of the whole philosophy of progress and civilization and, furthermore, is a violation of sound economic theory and is utterly without logic or scientific support of any kind."[48] Employers' groups and some economists rejected any suggestion that business and labor might use cost of living studies to adjust wages. While expressing confidence in its ability to index and describe price changes, the NICB's Virgil Jordan insisted that "cost of living figures have no necessary pertinency to the adjustment of wages, and that they are at best no more than a general guide to the course of a certain arbitrary group of retail prices."[49] Economist Asher Achinstein attacked any sort of wage determination based on cost of living data as unworkable, given regional and intraregional cost of living variations. Achinstein questioned the entire endeavor, suggesting that all cost of living studies were based on the "*subjective judgments*" of investigators. "The margin

---

[46] Elma B. Carr, "The Use of Cost-of-Living Figures in Wage Adjustments," *Bulletin* 369 (Washington, DC: GPO, 1925), 1. For similar observations, see Margaret Loomis Stecker, "Family Budgets and Wages," *AER* 11 (September 1921): 465. Jessica B. Peixotto, "Family Budgets," *AER* 17, Suppl. (March 1927): 132–40. For an analysis of economists in wartime service, see Bernstein, *Perilous Progress*, 36–8.

[47] Paul Douglas, "Family Allowances and Clearing Funds in France," *QJE* 38 (February 1924): 251. For a similar point, but concerning the family allowances in France, see J. H. Richardson, "The Family Allowance System," *The Economic Journal* 34 (September 1924): 373.

[48] *The American Pressman* (August 1921): 22; Francis H. Bird, "The Cost of Living as a Factor in Recent Wage Adjustments in the Book and Job Branch of the Chicago Printing Industry," *AER* 11 (December 1921): 622. Samuel Gompers, "Progress in Research," *AF* XXVIII (December 1921): 1009.

[49] Jordan, "The Cost of Living Indices of the N.I.C.B. and of the B. of L. S.," 250.

of error in selection of samples of budgets and prices in different localities largely accounts for the variations shown by the figures that have been and are now being published," he insisted.[50]

Though employers and unions rejected rigid cost of living formulas for determining wages, Douglas and John Maurice Clark continued to work to move the issue of wage determination into the public domain, rather than leaving it simply a term of employment worked out between individual workers and employers. Focusing on the issue of costs, Clark argued boldly for the extension of economists' conceptualization of overhead costs to include workers and then made the case that the public needed to exert some control over modern business. Douglas, implicitly embracing Clark's thinking, advocated the idea of a social minimum and looked abroad for successful examples of wage policies that guaranteed all citizens a basic standard of living.

From his dissertation completed in 1910 at Columbia through the 1920s, Clark focused on understanding the ambiguity in accounting for costs and its significance for understanding modern industry.[51] Not surprising given his father's pioneering role in marginalist economics and steadfast concern with what constituted an ethical society, Clark worked to sharpen economists' understanding of costs and, like his father, brought to the study of economics a clear sense that economists should be concerned with fairness as much as with profits and efficiency. As the younger Clark argued in his dissertation, "The doctrine of free competition has an ethical principle at the bottom of it, but it can be perverted; and if this happens, justice must be restored if possible by some force other than that of private self-interest."[52]

During the 1920s, Clark wrote and spoke frequently concerning modern society's effort to grapple with the proper role of the public in preserving the well-being of individuals in a modern, corporation-dominated economy. His most important work in this area addressed the question

---

[50] Asher Achinstein, "Can Budget and Cost-of-Living Studies Be Used As Aids in Determining a Differential Wage?" *JASA* 29 (March 1929): 39. Emphasis in original. Other observers noted that cost of living wage adjustments worked during times of inflation when prices rose, but did not work in deflationary periods when workers resisted a decrease in their wages; Fisher Hohman, "The Use of Cost-of-Living Figures in Wage Adjustments," 525–9. See also "The American Standard," *NYT* (October 29, 1929): 12. Also cited in Goldberg and Moye, 105.

[51] Laurence Shute, *John Maurice Clark: A Social Economics of the Twenty-First Century* (New York: St. Martin's Press, 1997), 133.

[52] John Maurice Clark, "Standards of Reasonableness in Local Freight Discriminations" (PhD diss., Columbia University, 1910), 15.

of overhead costs in relation to the experience of workers. In *Studies in the Economics of Overhead Costs* (1923), Clark provided an institutional rationale for Douglas's advocacy of alternative mechanisms of determining wages and social welfare programs. Clark linked overhead costs and labor through an analysis of unused capacity and made the case for recalculating the cost of labor to include times when workers were unable to find work. As early as 1920, Clark argued before the AEA that "the laborer's health and working capacity ... must be borne by someone, whether the laborer works or not."[53] Clark, whose words at the 1920 AEA meeting were met with an ovation and who continued to link labor and overhead costs throughout the decade, came to outline two areas where costs absorbed by workers should be considered overhead costs.[54] First, in the case of specialized training, if a worker gained training in an occupation, that training had to be used in that occupation and the investment made in such training could not be withdrawn and applied to a different occupation. As a result, "Wherever a laborer has invested time and money in specialized training, the result is, in a certain sense, fixed capital which is useful in one occupation and in no other, and which must earn whatever return it can, because the investment cannot be withdrawn and moved into some other line of business."[55] Second, workers had basic needs that must be met if they were to sustain themselves. When those needs were not met, the performance of the worker suffered and society had to take on the costs of lost productivity or unused capacities. "From this vantage point," according to Clark, "it appears that a large part of the cost originally counted as wages represents an overhead cost which the laborer is responsible for covering."[56] Thus, given the realities of a modern industrial economy, Clark argued, labor should be considered a "constant cost" rather than a cost that varies with production, as it was presently viewed.[57]

Having made the case for a broader understanding of labor's costs, Clark went on to examine the many inadequacies endemic in modern industries' methods of covering these costs. The realities of a modern economy, for Clark, included the need for unemployment. Rather than

---

[53] Cited in Dorothy Ross, *The Origins of American Social Science* (New York: Cambridge University Press, 1991), 414.
[54] On ovation, see ibid.
[55] John Maurice Clark, *Studies in the Economics of Overhead Costs* (Chicago: University of Chicago Press, 1923), 15.
[56] Ibid., 16.
[57] Ibid., 355–66.

argue whether there should or should not be unemployment, economists would be better served by examining how much unemployment was necessary. In making his case, Clark rejected what he considered an overly simplistic Marxist contention that a permanent unemployed class was necessary to push wages down to subsistence level and instead made a much more nuanced argument. Clark's justification of unemployment, which at some level he thought inevitable, turned on nine points, ranging from the need for workers to have the opportunity to look for the right place of employment to the need for employers to have an adequate pool of employees from which to choose.[58] The specific justifications, however, are less important than the larger significance of Clark's argument. Clark turned his attention to unemployment created by the business cycle and suggested that responsibility for this sort of unemployment rested with industry and that industry, not unemployed workers, should bear a "major part of the burden."[59] Clark concluded that the wage contract was no longer an adequate method of calculating the costs of labor; instead, he advocated a remodeling in the calculation of the cost of labor that included the whole costs incurred by workers.

Underlying Clark's description of overhead costs and his understanding of who should bear the costs of unemployment was a rejection of the Supreme Court, specifically Justice Sutherland's "heart of the contract" argument, which contended that labor standards undermined the ability of employees to freely bargain the terms under which they would work. Sometimes specifically mentioning the *Adkins* decision, Clark attacked the freedom of contract doctrine by drawing attention to the complexity of such contracts in modern society and by attacking the fairness of a system governed by "unregulated competition." Like the National Consumers' League and other advocates of labor standards to be addressed more specifically in Chapter 5, Clark argued that the nature and organization of a modern economy, where corporate employers' power vastly outpaced that of workers, had rendered the "freedom of contract" argument anachronistic. As Clark noted, many issues, such as those related to the construction of workplaces (i.e., plants with dangerous working conditions), fell under what he termed "conditions of labor" that were not open to bargaining. An individual in search of work, after all, could not realistically bargain for a position with U.S. Steel, but only under the provision

---

[58] Ibid., 366–70.
[59] Ibid., 370. To track Clark's thinking on this issue in the early 1920s, see John Maurice Clark, "Some Social Aspects: An Application of Overhead Cost to Social Accounting, with Special Reference to the Business Cycle," *AER* 13, Suppl. (March 1923): 50–9.

that the works be rebuilt to minimize dangerous working conditions. In *Social Control of Business* (1926), Clark went further in justifying a role for public intervention into what had otherwise been private concerns. Here Clark continued to draw attention to the problems generated by modern industry, but now he gave closer scrutiny to the potential of public policies to ameliorate these problems. Reflecting on what he termed "community life," Clark argued that in an entirely individualistic system "innumerable things" were left undone and neglected that could not be addressed through the system of "transactions of free exchange alone."[60]

Clark defended the idea of a social minimum or a minimum wage in the New Era, but he did not specify how such a system might be established. Douglas, however, took up the task and looked abroad for ideas and methods of reorganizing the wage system to serve workers and their families more equitably – particularly male workers, who he assumed headed households.[61] Douglas came to support a two-pronged policy approach of a minimum wage and a per-child family allowance that used family size as one means of determining wages. This analysis and advocacy for family allowances fairly burst upon the scene. In a 1926 review of Douglas's *Wages and the Family*, George Barnett wrote, "Ten years ago the practice of differentiating wages according to family needs was almost unknown." By 1926, however, "millions of employees in France, Belgium, Holland and Germany" were "working under some form of the family allowance system."[62]

To drum up support for wage policy reforms, Douglas drew attention to policy proposals in Australia and Europe and proposed some variation on these plans for the United States. Most of these plans proposed that employers contribute to a central fund that would be distributed to employees based on family size. In New South Wales, the Maintenance of Children Bill of 1919 proposed a board of trade to determine the minimum wage paid to men and women workers. In addition to determining a base wage, the board would determine a sum adequate to support every child in the household.[63] To prevent a preference for single and childless

---

[60] John Maurice Clark, *Social Control of Business* (Chicago: University of Chicago Press, 1926), xiv.
[61] Paul Douglas, "Wage Regulation and Children's Maintenance in Australia," *QJE* 37 (August 1923): 653–4; Paul Douglas, "The Amount and Nature of the Allowances Under a Family-Allowance System," *JPE* 33 (February 1925): 45–59; Dorothy Douglas, "American Minimum Wage Laws at Work," *AER* 9 (December 1919): 701–38.
[62] George Barnett, "Douglas's Wages and the Family," *QJE* 40 (August 1926): 699.
[63] Douglas, "Wage Regulation and Children's Maintenance in Australia," 653–4. Colin Forster, "Unemployment and Minimum Wages in Australia, 1900–1930," *The Journal of*

workers, employers made a monthly per-employee contribution to a central fund from which household payments were made.[64]

Looking to Europe, Douglas found both statist and non-statist means of supporting working families. In many European countries, wage policy changes materialized out of wartime economic crises and often involved industry-wide cooperation to spread the costs among employers. During the war, the French government initially provided a per-child allowance for government employees. In private industry, French employers contributed to a central fund to share the burden of child allowances. Douglas reported that this system originated in the steel industry after a manager in the Joya works investigated the living conditions of employees and requested that the owner fund an allowance system for its workers with children under the age of thirteen. After instituting the plan, the company brought the problem to the regional Metal Trades Employers Association, which adopted a plan that by May 1918 had created a central fund that allowed employers to share the burden of the allowance.[65] By 1920, groups of firms – organized along industry and regional lines – established at least fifty-two funds across a wide variety of industries, some covering as many as seventy thousand workers.[66] According to Douglas, approximately 20 percent of wage and salary earners worked under some form of the family allowance system.[67] The granting of allowances did not come without restrictions that at least suggested a larger concern with social control. Douglas reported that in Strasburg and the lower Rhine, funds explicitly declared, "It [the allowance] may be withdrawn from anyone who puts it to bad uses, or if those assisted are naturally careless."[68]

To implement what would amount to a dramatic overhaul in the purpose and distribution of wages required the construction of state

---

Economic History 45 (June 1985): 383–8; Francis G. Castles, *The Comparative History of Public Policies* (Oxford: Polity Press, 1989); Gosta Epsing-Andersen, *The Three Worlds of Welfare Capitalism* (Princeton: Princeton University Press, 1990).

[64] Douglas, "Wage Regulation and Children's Maintenance in Australia," 655.

[65] Susan Pedersen, *Family, Dependence, and the Origins of the Welfare State, 1914–1945* (Cambridge: Cambridge University Press, 1993), 227–8.

[66] Douglas, "Family Allowance and Clearing Funds in France," 256–9; Also see Pedersen, *Family, Dependence, and the Origins of the Welfare State*, 79–133, 224–85; Seth Koven and Sonya Michel, "Womanly Duties: Maternalist Politics and the Origins of Welfare States in France, Germany, Great Britain and the United States, 1880–1920," *AHR* 95 (October 1990): 1076–108; Douglas Ashford, *The Emergence of Welfare States* (Stoke-on-Trent: Trentham, 1988); John S. Ambler, ed., *The French Welfare State: Surviving Social and Ideological Change* (New York: New York University Press, 1991).

[67] Douglas, "Family Allowance and Clearing Funds in France," 260.

[68] Ibid., 266.

institutional capacity that might support a greatly expanded social welfare system.[69] As Douglas recognized, the lack of an institutional infrastructure made implementing such an ambitious social welfare system more difficult in the United States. In reviewing Joseph L. Cohen's proposal for a consolidation of social insurance programs with a family allowance in Britain, Douglas noted, "The chief advantage which Mr. Cohen claims for such a plan is its 'administrative convenience'; but this, of course, would be lacking in any country such as ours, which has not a well developed system of social insurance."[70]

Clark and Douglas met stiff resistance in their efforts to move the determination of wages into the public domain and to consider more statist mechanisms to protect individual workers and the public interest. For many British and American economists, regardless of the trajectory of real wages, the idea of a family allowance or minimum wage clouded the distinction between charity and wages and undercut the marginal productivity theory of wages, which stressed the fairness in paying workers for the "actual value of the work performed."[71] British economist D. H. MacGregor rejected tying the family allowance to any conception of wages and appealed to the need for distinguishing between earnings, social insurance, and poor relief. For MacGregor and other economists, the family allowance was simply a tax on all employees for choices made by individual workers. A person would not choose to be sick, widowed, or unemployed, but individuals, MacGregor and others contended, did choose to become parents. The former included situations that might

---

[69] Barnett noted Douglas's interest in various wage policies emerged from his concerns over the distribution of income in the United States. Barnett, "Douglas's Wages and the Family," 699–707.

[70] Paul Douglas, "Review," AER 16 (September 1926): 524.

[71] Paul Brissenden, "Review," AER 17 (June 1927): 336. D. H. MacGregor, "Family Allowances," *The Economic Journal* 36 (March 1926): 2; J. D. Cox, Jr., *The Economic Basis of Wages* (New York: Ronald, 1926); Nora Milnes, *The Economics of Wages and Labour* (London: P. S. King, 1926). Milnes suggested, "wages must be based upon the actual value of the work performed, and that all suggestions for calculating them in any other way are bound to defeat their own ends." In a review of Milnes's work, Columbia economist Paul Brissenden suggested that such a policy "does well enough as a negative, abstract proposition, but one may be permitted, perhaps, to question the feasibility of ascertaining the 'actual value of the work performed.'" Brissenden, "Review," 336. Such arguments found fertile ground in England and the United States, where policy makers feared family wage subsidies could lead to an increased birthrate in poor families. The situation was quite different in France and Australia, where policy makers considered family wage proposals a salve for the problem of a declining population. Pedersen, *Family, Dependence, and the Origins of the Welfare State: Britain and France*; A. B. Piddington, *The Next Step: A Basic Family Income* (London: Macmillan and Co., 1921).

merit public assistance, but the later was a choice for which the individual appropriately bore responsibility.[72]

Many of his fellow U.S. economists attacked Douglas's wage policy proposals as best suited for moments of economic crisis when the need for emergency relief was acute, a condition they did not feel existed for employers or low-wage workers in the United States. Johns Hopkins statistician and political economist George Barnett saw merit in the "very moderate payments" introduced in postwar France and Germany, where workers struggled to deal with postwar economic upheaval, but he held that these "exceptional and temporary situations" should not be "a guide to the ordinary conditions of economic life."[73] Although Barnett conceded that increasing the standard of living for poor workers would decrease the birthrate, he cautioned that Douglas's proposal to tie income to the number of children could lead to the opposite effect.[74] Rather than redistributing income, Barnett favored a more even distribution of income over a worker's lifetime to check wasteful spending habits. To this end, he proposed young workers contribute to a social insurance program during their early working years to be drawn upon later when they had families.[75] Still others suggested that it was the responsibility of industry to pay its employees a living wage. Former BLS commissioner and professor at Carleton College Royal Meeker insisted that "industry on the whole was able to pay a living wage" and that the family wage system was a subsidy to low-paying industries by workers.[76] By mid-decade, the debate over the desirability of wage policies to lift up workers came to a standstill, but new discoveries were about to raise questions about the need for such policies in a New Era economy that now appeared to have unlimited potential for growth.

[72] D. H. MacGregor, "Family Allowances," *The Economic Journal* 36 (March 1926): 7–10. For further criticism of family allowances by British economists, see Alexander Gray, *Family Endowment: A Critical Analysis* (London: Ernest Benn, Ltd., 1927); and O. Vlasto, "Family Allowances and the Skilled Worker," *The Economic Journal* 36 (December 1926): 577.

[73] Barnett, "Douglas's Wages and the Family," 705–6.

[74] Ibid., 703. For a similarly skeptical view of family allowances and Douglas's work, see Lettice Fisher, "Wages and the Family," *The Economic Journal* 35 (December 1925): 598–601.

[75] Barnett, "Douglas's Wages and the Family," 706–7. For more on this debate, see Paul Douglas, "Some Objections to the Family Wage System Considered," *JPE* 32 (December 1924): 696; and Ethelbert Stewart, "A Family Wage-Rate vs. A Family Social Endowment Fund," *Social Forces* 6 (September 1927): 120–5.

[76] Jessica B. Peixotto, "Family Budgets: Round Table Conferences," *AER* 17, Suppl. (March 1927): 136.

PROSPERITY AND WAGE JUSTICE: THE POST-1922
REAL WAGE INCREASE

In 1925 and 1926, Hansen and Douglas produced important articles grappling with the importance of real wage change in the larger transformation of the U.S. economy. The innovative use of additional data sets by Hansen and Douglas allowed them to build on Rubinow, Jones, Fairchild, Lamberson, and Douglas's earlier work tracing the movement of real wages since the 1890s, but with a clearer sense of the impact of economic change on various groups of workers. At the 1926 AEA meeting, a session billed as a joint meeting of the AEA, the American Statistical Association, and the American Association for Labor Legislation, focused on the issue of real wages and featured papers by Hansen, Douglas, and Alvin Johnson of the *New Republic*, with Samuel A. Lewisohn as chair. Hansen and Johnson presented papers focused on the utility of knowledge trends concerning real wages as policy and quantitative tools, but the real star of the session was Douglas, who unveiled a new analysis of real wages since the 1890s that stressed workers' recent gains in real earnings.[77]

Douglas found a dramatic increase in workers' postwar real earnings, a fact he attributed mainly to increased production but also to declines in food and agricultural prices and immigration. Using the average annual real earnings of workers between 1890 and 1899 as a base (base equaling 100), Douglas found relatively stable earnings for all workers between 1890 and 1907. Between 1907 and 1920, real earnings fluctuated between a low of 101 in 1911 and a high of 112 in 1913. The real shift occurred after the war when real earnings began a steady increase, peaking at 128 in 1924, the last year in Douglas's analysis. Nearly all groups of workers benefited from these dramatic real wage gains. Workers in manufacturing saw an increase of 28 percent in their real annual earnings over the 1890s base, and transportation workers saw an increase of 22 percent. For all workers considered, the average increase was 27 percent, almost all of which came after 1914. In addition, Douglas acknowledged a number of factors increasing the standard of living for workers that would not be accounted for in monetary earnings, including the decreased size of working-class families, increased number of household members in the work force, decreased number of hours in the working day, and

[77] Douglas, "The Movement of Real Wages and Its Economic Significance," 24, 38. Douglas was aware of the problem of not including unemployment, and in other articles he had worked to develop a method for calculating the impact of unemployment on real wages. Paul Douglas, "Wages and Hours of Labor in 1919," *JPE* 29 (January 1921): 78–80.

increased amount of services provided by government and philanthropic organizations.[78]

A year earlier, Hansen had joined Douglas in revealing the postwar increase in real wages, but with a number of insightful twists. First, Hansen embraced aspects of marginal productivity theory and explicitly rejected Soule, the LBI, and organized labor's claims (discussed in Chapter 3) that labor's share should increase at the same rate as overall productivity. As manufacturing became more capital intensive and per capita productivity increased, Hansen argued, "wages could not increase *proportionally* or there would be nothing with which to pay interest."

It is of course clear that, the more round-about or capitalistic the process of production becomes, the smaller of necessity must be the *share* of the total product going to labor. When an increase in production is due to a greater use of capital, real wages must of necessity lag behind the increase in production.[79]

Second, Hansen observed a steady increase in real wages since 1820 and a "phenomenal rise in real wages" since 1919, as high as "25 to 30 per cent of the pre-war level."[80] Hansen accounted for these changes with attention to, among other factors, the relative price of various inputs, the decline in immigration, the movement of prices, and the "stickiness" of wages. More important, Hansen's analysis added a keen understanding of the dramatic economic changes under way and a warning to economists and policy makers who focused too closely on distribution of income

---

[78] Douglas, "The Movement of Real Wages and Its Economic Significance," 38–41. For similar findings, but with a focus on unskilled workers, see Whitney Coombs, *Wages of Unskilled Labor in Manufacturing Industries in the United States, 1890–1924* (New York: Columbia University Press, 1926). For a focus on increasing comforts of professional workers, see Chase Goding Woodhouse, "The Standard of Living at the Professional Level, 1816-1817 and 1926-27" *JPE* 37 (October 1929): 552–72; Paul Douglas, "Wages" *The American Journal of Sociology* 36 (May 1929): 1021–9. For the best work on 1920s household budgets of different social and economic groups, see University of California, Berkeley professor Jessica B. Peixotto's work, including her "How Workers Spend a Living Wage: A Study of the Incomes and Expenditures of Eighty-Two Typographers' Families in San Francisco," in *University of California Publications in Economics* (Berkeley: University of California Press, 1929); Jessica B. Peixotto, *Getting and Spending at the Professional Standard of Living: A Study of the Costs of Living an Academic Life* (New York: Macmillan Co., 1927); Jessica B. Peixotto, "Family Budgets and University Faculty Members," *Science* 68 (November 23, 1928); Jessica B. Peixotto et al., "Quality and Cost Estimate of the Standard of Living of the Professional Class," in *University of California Publications in Economics* (Berkeley: University of California Press, 1928).

[79] Emphasis in original. Alvin H Hansen, "Factors Affecting the Trend of Real Wages." *AER* 15 (March 1925): 36.

[80] Ibid., 42.

and productivity at the expense of an analysis of the changes, or more important, the lack of changes, in the type of goods produced. Hansen warned that improvements in wages would only be of value to workers if business increased the production of goods workers wanted *and* that were within their budget. According to Hansen:

Increased productivity may ... be expected to increase the real wages of the working class only on condition that this increased production comes within the field of the working man's budget. If improvements result in lower cost and increased production of goods not purchased by workingmen, the real incomes of other classes are increased, but there may be no gain for wage-earners.... Hence, if the question is one in which labor is interested as producer only and not as consumer, he may quite conceivably gain nothing from increased physical productivity.[81]

Here, Hansen anticipated problems in the Hooverites, Douglas, and other labor experts' assumption that increased productivity would or should automatically lead to a higher standard of living for workers; in fact, a failure of business to shift productive capacity from capital to consumable goods could lead to an overproduction of the former and an underproduction of the latter, and, as Hansen suggested, no net gain to workers' standard of living.[82] Such warnings, of course, were not heeded.

Back at the 1926 AEA meeting, Douglas tempered economists and policy makers' celebration of increasing real wages by pointing to persistent unemployment, which even in the most prosperous years of the 1920s inched upward; but he also described dramatic changes in worker behavior and labor institutions as a result of a rise in workers' affluence and hinted, like Hoover, at the diminishing importance of unions as agents of economic change. In what appears to have been a shift from his earlier position that trade unions were vitally needed to maintain wages, the decline in union membership did not seem to concern Douglas, who attributed increased worker earnings to productivity gains rather than worker agitation. "It is difficult ... to ascribe any large share of the economic gains which labor has made to the union movement. The evidence indicates that increases have been about as rapid in

[81] Ibid., 37–8.
[82] Economic historian Michael Bernstein makes a somewhat similar point in explaining the duration of the Great Depression. See Michael Bernstein, "Why the Great Depression Was Great: Toward a New Understanding of the Interwar Economic Crisis in the United States," in *The Rise and Fall of the New Deal Order: 1930–1980*, eds. Steve Fraser and Gary Gerstle (Princeton: Princeton University Press, 1989), 34–5; Michael Bernstein, *The Great Depression: Delayed Recovery and Economic Change in America 1929–1939* (Cambridge: Cambridge University Press, 1987).

unorganized industries as in the organized trades."[83] Prominent defenders of organized labor George Soule and David McCabe objected to Douglas's new analysis of the role of unions. Yet, as the earlier analysis of Hoover and his allies suggests, Douglas was hardly alone in questioning the continued relevance and need for trade unions to protect the interests of workers. In 1926, Soule's objection to Douglas was particularly important because he pointed to the labor movement's influence on nonunion employers, a phenomenon many labor experts and policy makers surrounding Hoover failed to grasp. "We must remember that employers were warned that attempts to reduce wages too drastically would instigate organizing campaigns," Soule contended. "It is therefore difficult to say that the potential power of the unions had no effect on the non-union employers' policy and consequently on the movement of real wages in non-union industries."[84]

Part of the confusion over unions' role turned on the impact of prosperity, which appeared to many observers at the time to facilitate a necessarily transformed role for trade unions. Previously, unions and workers struggled to oppose employer exploitation; however, as a result of wage increases and prosperity, Douglas believed organized labor in the 1920s had "become a business enterprise to secure a larger share of the products of industry for workers who are already above the subsistence living." Douglas, adopting language reminiscent of Simon Patten, portrayed this change in organized labor's tactics as part of a move from a "pain to a pleasure economy."[85] Citing the establishment of labor banks and trade union life insurance, Douglas suggested a new "type of competition between employers and trade-unions is ... developing; namely, a struggle for the economic surplus of the workers and for the savings that are being accumulated by them."[86] According to Douglas, growth of savings accounts, life insurance, and stock purchases fortified workers' savings. It was likely, he believed, "The wage-earners have certainly not spent all of their increased

---

[83] Douglas, "The Movement of Real Wages and Its Economic Significance," 46; Douglas, *Real Wages in the United States*, 564. Also see S. S. Garrett, "Wages and the Collective Wage Bargain," *AER*, 18 (December 1928): 670–83.

[84] George Soule, David A. McCabe, Magnus W. Alexander, Paul Brissenden, "The Movement of Real Wages – Discussion," *AER* 16, Suppl. (March 1926): 59–70.

[85] Douglas, "The Movement of Real Wages and Its Economic Significance," 47–8.

[86] Ibid., 48. On organized labor's foray into banking, real estate, and insurance, see Benjamin Stolberg, "The New Unionism: (With Special Reference to Trade Union Capitalism)" *The Modern Quarterly* 3 (September–December 1926): 292–300 and Thomas Nixon Carver, *The Present Economic Revolution in the United States* (Boston: Little, Brown, and Company, 1926).

earnings but that they have saved a considerable proportion of them and have thus acquired more of stake in the property of the country."[87]

In the last years of the decade, the rise in real wages muffled wage policy debates. A survey of leading sociology and economic journals reveals few articles advocating statist policies to push up workers' wages, except occasional articles on means of protecting women workers.[88] Instead, economists, labor organizations, and policy makers increasingly turned to the elimination of waste in industry and increased productivity to solve the low-wage problem.[89] Douglas was one of the few economists to propose that, in this period of relative prosperity, policy makers should utilize statist solutions to raise the standard of living for society's poorest workers, thus establishing a social role for wages that transcended the wage bargain. In discussing the possibility of providing all unskilled workers with a wage to support a family of five, Douglas noted that "the recent increase in productivity which we have witnessed in this country during the last few years, has ... made even this much more possible than it was a few years ago."[90]

CONCLUSION

In some respects, the debate over wages in this period is notable and significant as much for what it lacked as for what it included. The New Era provided a fertile ground for a vibrant wage policy discourse and an insightful debate over the trajectory of real wages that would later support more statist wage policies. But economists devoted remarkably little attention to comparing the modest but important rise in real wages with the much larger increase in business profits. The absence of analysis on this point suggests, as noted in the introduction, that corporate profits (as distinguished from proprietary capitalists' profits) had by the New Era gained a level of legitimacy among economists that did not exist in the early years leading up to corporate capitalism's emergence. In the late nineteenth century, as James Livingston and others have described it, the worn out labor theory of value was being replaced by marginalist

[87] Douglas, "The Movement of Real Wages and Its Economic Significance," 47.
[88] See 1926–9 editions of *AER*, *QJE*, *Social Forces*, and *American Journal of Sociology*.
[89] For a particularly strident attack on this position, see Paul Douglas, "Review of *The Economics of Wages and Labour* by Nora Milnes," *PSQ* 42 (September 1927): 477–9.
[90] Paul Douglas, "Review of *A Study of the Minimum Wage* by J. H. Richardson," *JPE* 36 (February 1928): 172.

economics and its conceptualization of value that placed its creation at the moment of exchange, rather than in the process of production.[91] To fully discredit the labor theory of value and to break the employer-employee stalemate that in the 1870s through the early 1890s had prevented business owners from garnering what they felt was their rightful claim to profits, employers had to first displace skilled workers' control of work at the point of production. When, at the turn of the century, companies consolidated and integrated to create the modern corporation and management increasingly took control of the workplace, marginalist economists stepped forward with a conceptualization of the modern U.S. economy and its distribution of income "that attributed to capitalists positive service in production," which in turn justified capital's claim to a significant share of the income generated by economic growth.[92] The absence of attention to capital's "wages" in the wage discourse of the 1920s suggests the degree to which profits came to be accepted as legitimate, but the extraordinary disparity between workers' gains in the period and capital's gains, along with Hansen's insights concerning the need to expand production of consumables, might have provided a warning to policy makers rapidly embracing worker consumption as the most important variable in maintaining economic stability.

As prices fell and wages rose, the debate over the proper role of the state and employers in determining and regulating wages remained unresolved. If the Supreme Court clung to "freedom of contract" as a means of overruling minimum wage legislation, economists such as Douglas and Clark in the early 1920s helped to set the foundation for an understanding of wages that recognized that they performed a public as well as an economic function. As we will see in Chapters 3 and 5, economists and Hooverites were hardly alone in arguing for a public-ization of wage issues. Agreement on importance, however, did not translate into a consensus on policies. With employers and unions opposed to any wage legislation, economists and labor reformers aligned with organizations like the Women's Bureau of the Department of Labor were lonely voices building the case for an array of statist wage-labor standards and

---

[91] Livingston, "The Social Analysis of Economic History," 69–95.
[92] Ibid., 92. See also Kathleen G. Donohue, *Freedom From Want: American Liberalism and the Idea of the Consumer* (Baltimore: Johns Hopkins University Press, 2003), 65–9; Furner, *Advocacy and Objectivity: A Crisis in the Professionalization of American Social Science, 1865–1905* (Lexington: University Press of Kentucky, 1975), 186–91; and Michael A. Bernstein, "American Economists and the 'Marginalist Revolution': Notes on the Intellectual and Social Context of Professionalization," *Journal of Historical Sociology* 16 (March 2003): 135–80.

social welfare measures that became mainstays of many New Deal and post-New Deal labor, poverty, and social policies. Differences, too, arose among advocates for more statist wage policies. While Douglas championed the need for labor standards and a family wage, he also clung to a masculine understanding of economic citizenship and argued that women were not part of the "real labor supply."[93] The Women's Bureau, as we shall see in Chapter 5, rejected Douglas's hoary conception of gender in the workplace, arguing strenuously for the integration of issues facing women workers into the larger labor question.

While select economists and labor reformers made the case for protective legislation, organized labor struggled to defend its relevance in an increasingly consumer-based economy and in the face of successive administrations that proved ambivalent at best toward an understanding of the economy that recognized the importance of unions as a factor in a healthy distribution of income. Faced with dramatic shifts in the economy and the proliferation of government and nongovernmental organizations devoted to investigating labor and economic questions, organized labor made dramatic steps to expand its own institutions of inquiry. In the process, organized labor recast itself as an advocate and a tool promoting economic stability and growth that would benefit all segments of the population.

---

[93] Alice Kessler Harris, *In Pursuit of Equity: Women, Men, and the Quest for Economic Citizenship in Twentieth Century America* (New York: Oxford University Press, 2001), 97. On gender and the early years of the AEA, see Bernstein, *Perilous Progress*, 26–7.

3

Enlightened Labor?

Labor's Share and Economic Stability

> Unions have found the labor expert of great aid in overthrowing the "facts" of the employers – and in winning the fight for better conditions.
> – *Labor Age*[1]

> Deteriorating social position – that is, declining purchasing power of the mass of the wage earners in relation to the national product – brings about industrial instability which will develop into industrial crisis.
> – "Organized Labor's Modern Wage Policy" (1927)

During the 1920s, unions struggled to justify their own existence. In an economy in which workers seemed to benefit from the proliferation of consumer goods, access to consumer credit, and rising real wages despite the decline in union power, the American Federation of Labor (AFL) redefined itself as a partner in industry and a watchdog for economic instability. Labor experts associated with organized labor developed institutions of labor investigation in union research departments and in pioneering nonprofit research organizations specifically designed to serve as a research arm to organized labor. As the decade unfolded, these labor experts developed a new theory of wages, worked out new tools to monitor changes in workers' share of production, and put into place new experiments in labor-management relations.

By the end of the decade, organized labor had backed away from efforts to restrict output and other measures the Hooverites had come to understand as wasteful. Instead, unions adopted a new paradigm in labor relations that embedded workers in a consumer society and provided

---

[1] "What the Unions Are Doing on Fact-Finding," *LA* 7 (April 1923): 3.

justification for unions as vigilant protectors of the public's interest and a vital contributor to economic stability. As part of the AFL's larger shift in emphasis from redistribution of national income toward reaping gains from efficient production in a growing economy, labor experts in or closely associated with unions constructed a theory of wages that tied increases in worker earnings to the increased productivity of industry. This approach nicely complemented organized labor's emphasis on the potential of industrial cooperation to advance the interests of workers, the public, and business. In doing so, organized labor added its voice to the New Era debate concerning the sources of economic growth since the 1890s and the best means of ensuring economic stability.

While everyone agreed that productivity had increased dramatically, there was no agreement on how to measure productivity gains, who or what was responsible, for how much, or who should benefit. The key questions of the decade and the various positions taken were presented at a 1928 meeting of the New York chapter of the American Statistical Association. R. P. Faulkner of the National Industrial Conference Board (NICB) suggested that better equipment and organization of industry accounted for productivity gains since 1897. Thus, according to Faulkner, it would be reasonable for labor's share of productivity gains to diminish. Faulkner found, however, that labor's share remained constant and that "the wage earner has shared fully in the recent progress of industry." Labor economist Leo Wolman arrived at the opposite conclusion by comparing wages paid with value added in manufacturing. Wolman found that the ratio of wages to value had fallen dramatically between 1921 and 1925. Economist Sumner Slichter attributed productivity gains to both management and labor efficiency and to greater concentration of industry. Pointing to the need to consider exchange value, Paul Douglas drew attention to the need to replace physical output with the exchange value of the product produced in calculating productivity changes. Economist Henry Dennison added that calculations of productivity should use hours worked rather than the number of workers employed, but John R. Commons indicated that the "most important part of the story" was the number of persons left unemployed by productivity increases.[2]

---

[2] L. W. "Wage Rates and Per Capita Productivity," *JASA* 23 (June 1928): 180–1. The Cobb-Douglas production function upgraded economists and statisticians' ability to describe the impact of changes in wages on the elasticity of demand for labor and the contributions of capital and labor to production; see Charles W. Cobb and Paul Douglas, "A Theory of Production," *AER* 18, Suppl. (March 1928): 139–65; John Maurice Clark, "Inductive Evidence on Marginal Productivity," *AER* 18 (September 1928):

The lack of agreement concerning the reasons for growth at the New York meeting suggests that there was an opening for organized labor to shape policy makers' understanding of one of the most important economic issues of the decade. Indeed, in an era when organized labor's importance came into question, economic experts in and associated with unions proved remarkably adroit at synthesizing disparate aspects of New Era economic thought and fascinatingly prescient in anticipating core tenets of post–World War II economic policy. Rather than making public appeals for a just wage, the labor experts discussed in this chapter refined notions of fairness and in doing so anticipated the tasks of national income accounting that would, after 1946, fall to the Council of Economic Advisors (CEA). Bridging New Era concerns with the business cycle and the postwar preoccupation with economic growth, these labor activists aimed to carve out a role for organized labor as an advocate for increasing production, maximizing purchasing power, and minimizing economic instability. Like John Maurice Clark and Paul Douglas, union labor experts undermined the marginal productivity theory of wages and general distribution taking hold in neoclassical economics. They rejected the marginalist case that, absent "frictions," the market would fairly distribute the nation's growing income based on each unit's marginal productivity. To prevent economic stagnation and decline, these labor experts argued, required that workers obtain a *growing* share of the nation's income.

Organized labor and its allies, however, also embraced aspects of the Hooverites' claims that moderating the business cycle could in part be brought about through increased cooperation and efficiency in industry, which would raise productivity, wages, and profits. Rather than remain passive observers, union leaders worked to carve out a central role for their organizations in this new vision of capitalism. Toward that end, labor leaders joined employers and a burgeoning class of labor experts in

---

449–67. For more on the general productivity discussion, see P. Sargant Florence, "The Measurement of Labor Productivity," *Quarterly Publication of the American Statistical Association* 17 (September 1920): 289–304; George Soule, "The Productivity Factor in Wage Determinations," *The AER: Supplement, Papers and Proceedings of the Thirty-Fifth Annual Meeting of the American Economic Association* (March 1923): 129–40; Sam Lewisohn, "Wage Policies and National Productivity," *PSQ* 39 (March 1924): 97–105; S. J. Coon, "Collective Bargaining and Productivity," *AER* 19 (September 1929): 419–27; Ewan Clague, "Productivity and Wages in the United States," *AF* 34 (March 1927): 285–96. On management's right to a share of productivity, see Willis Wissler [instructor at Ohio State University], "Managers and Workers," *AF* 34 (December 1927): 1462–9.

nonprofit institutions to build new ways of organizing the relationships among workers, unions, employers, and capital.

From this deliberation, organized labor emerged with a wage theory that placed workers' wages at the center of some of the most vexing economic problems of the era. The AFL introduced its new wage theory at a time when the radical business strategies of Henry Ford and other Fordists gained traction in the United States and Europe. Ford combined innovation in the production process that dramatically increased efficiency with a new conception of workers as consumers of the products they produced. The ideas in Fordism and the AFL's wage policy suggest an emerging consensus, or a mental "revolution" as Daniel Rodgers has characterized it, among some labor and industrial thinkers that pointed to the potential of high wages paid to well-disciplined workers to stabilize the economy and erode the antagonistic relationship between labor and capital reaching back to the labor wars of the late nineteenth century.[3]

Chapter 3 begins with an overview of the difficulties workers' organizations faced in the 1920s and their response. Increasingly, organized labor looked to the power of research, inquiry, and investigation to confront an uninterested public, a skeptical federal government, and hostile business interests. No doubt, organized labor came to embrace inquiry in part due to the apparent failure of a more confrontational approach to maintain important gains made by unions during World War I. In the context of the industrial unrest during and after World War I, militant antiunion forces bent on turning back labor's wartime gains reacted in ways that were quite familiar, such as the National Association of Manufacturers' (NAM) Open Shop campaign and Attorney General Palmer's red-baiting of organized labor and reformers. From the perspective of unions, these attacks did not signal a new chapter in labor-capital relations; organized labor was long familiar with such attacks and had to do little to accommodate itself, ideologically or tactically, to such an environment.

The terrain on which organized labor operated, however, did change dramatically as the 1920s unfolded. Improvements in wages and the apparently sincere – if often inadequate – effort by a range of experts and investigators to move beyond a more conflict-based understanding of the "labor problem" constituted a transitional moment in the history of labor-capital relations in U.S. history. Further, the methods employed by Hooverites and others to smooth the business cycle and the relationship

---

[3] Daniel Rodgers, *Atlantic Crossings: Social Politics in a Progressive Age* (Cambridge: Cambridge University Press, 1998), 371–2, 374.

between labor and capital suggested that the arena in which class conflict would go on had shifted to a more discursive one, where one must be armed with knowledge. To construct a body of expertise that served organized labor's interests, unions and friends of unions created international, national, and local research bureaus of their own. Two of the most important of these labor research institutions were the AFL Research Bureau and the Labor Bureau Inc. (LBI). With concern over the direction of real wages spreading to include a wide group of labor experts, the AFL and LBI proposed an understanding of wages that stressed workers' roles as consumers rather than producers. The AFL constructed statistical tools that allowed its experts to monitor wages and production and to notify policy makers when workers' ability to consume (i.e., wages) did not keep up with production. Organized labor's concern with production and economic stability occurred in the context of a larger ideological shift within the AFL and other unions, which increasingly portrayed themselves as partners in industry, rather than employers' adversary. This can be seen not only in the AFL's new wage policies, but also in actual efforts to reconstruct unions' role on the shop room floor, as in the Baltimore and Ohio Railroad experiment described later in this chapter. Many observers correctly described this shift to fostering economic growth as a turn in organized labor's interest away from earlier concerns characterized as an exclusive interest in distribution and control. But to describe the AFL as only concerned with increasing the size of the economic "pie" diminishes the grander vision held by many labor leaders who came to see themselves and their institutions as the solution to the problem of the business cycle, and thus as linchpins of social and economic stability.

In his analysis of New Era policy making, Guy Alchon describes Hoover's political philosophy, Wesley Mitchell's social science agenda, and foundation support for social science research as the three most important factors shaping "the counter-cyclical machinery that developed in the early 1920s."[4] These were indeed important factors, but Alchon's narrow focus on these groups ignores important planning discourses outside the nexus of the Hooverites and the National Bureau of Economic Research (NBER). This chapter's analysis of efforts by the AFL and labor experts to promote a closer match between the wages of workers and the supply of goods as a cure to the business cycle provides an opportunity to expand the scope of 1920s business cycle analysis to include organized

---

[4] Guy Alchon, *The Invisible Hand of Planning: Capitalism, Social Science, and the State in the 1920s* (Princeton: Princeton University Press, 1985), 72.

labor. While Hoover focused on providing information to employers, organized labor and its associates, more than any other group, correctly identified consumer spending as a potential source of economic stability. By the mid-1920s, organized labor and its allies had warned the public and policy makers that rapacious business profiteering, combined with continued failure to increase wages in accord with rising production in order to guarantee markets for goods, would lead to overproduction and economic disaster.[5] Though the AFL consistently rejected statist intervention during the New Era, union leaders' prescient understanding of the need for stabilization in consumption evolved into more statist solutions in New Deal labor policies, such as the Wagner Act, Fair Labor Standards Act, and Social Security Act.[6]

THE AFL'S SEARCH FOR A NEW MISSION

If organized labor, in particular the AFL, appeared confused and even weak during the decade, it was with very good reason. During the 1920s, unions faced dramatic changes in the political, social, and economic order. More than in previous generations, observers noted that the labor movement was experiencing a brain and talent drain as the most capable workers were promoted to management positions or younger workers chose work in rapidly expanding white-collar and other nonunion occupations.[7] By 1930, more than 30 percent of civilian workers found employment in office, sales, or professional occupations.[8] Economists Sumner Slichter and Alvin Hansen drew attention to the relative decline in the percentage of the work force employed in industrial, wage-earning occupations. In 1870, there were 2.56 industrial workers for every individual

---

[5] Meg Jacobs also points to the importance of the New Era "underconsumption" argument and its impact on New Deal policies in Meg Jacobs, *Pocketbook Politics: Economic Citizenship in Twentieth-Century America* (Princeton: Princeton University Press, 2005), 53–175. For an analysis that tracks labor's "consumerist turn" back to the mid-nineteenth century, see Lawrence B. Glickman, *A Living Wage: American Workers and the Making of Consumer Society* (Ithaca: Cornell University Press, 1997).

[6] Alan Brinkley, *The End of Reform: New Deal Liberalism in Recession and War* (New York: Vintage Books, 1995).

[7] For more on expanded occupational opportunities and upward mobility, see Olivier Zunz, *Making America Corporate: 1870–1920* (Chicago: University of Chicago Press, 1990); Alfred D. Chandler, *Scale and Scope: The Dynamics of Industrial Capitalism* (Cambridge: Cambridge University Press, 1990); Clark Davis, *Company Men: White-Collar Life and Corporate Culture in Los Angeles, 1892–1941* (Baltimore: Johns Hopkins University Press: 2001).

[8] Davis, *Company Men*, 3.

engaged in positions classified as proprietors, officials, professional men, and lower-salaried employees. By 1920, that number had fallen to 1.78. Slichter noted, "As perfected personnel practice improves the ability of employers to pick out from their forces men of talent for managerial positions, the labor movement is likely to suffer even more acutely for want of able leaders."[9] As new career and consumer opportunities opened up to a wider breadth of workers, observers noted that unions saw a decline in their social function and prestige. Portions of Robert and Helen Lynd's *Middletown* and editorials in progressive periodicals read like obituaries for the labor movement. The Lynds observed, "The social function of the union has disappeared in this day of movies and the automobile." Even strong unions like the molders had to "compel attendance at [their] meetings." The Lynds noted that as workers chose other forms of association with their friends and neighbors, community leaders in the press and pulpit increasingly ignored or demeaned the importance of organized labor. A Muncie union leader reported, "The Ford car has done an awful lot of harm to the unions here and everywhere else. As long as men have enough money to buy a second-hand Ford and tires and gasoline, they'll be out on the road and paying no attention to union meetings."[10] The *New Republic* lamented the passing of organized labor as a "social movement ... with regenerative and revolutionary tendencies" and the emergence of a type of unionism that "must now be regarded as an old established institution with a limited field, a camp-follower of organized capitalism."[11] A. J. Muste of Brookwood Labor College piled on, lamenting that AFL policies and tactics were "inadequate to meet the challenge of the new capitalism."[12]

Dramatic changes in the political terrain during and after the war further complicated organized labor's understanding of its place in the political economy. Confident employers and a diffident state quickly dashed workers and unions' hopes for a reconstruction of American industry after the war. During World War I, the federal government had inserted itself

[9] Sumner Slichter, "The Worker in Modern Economic Society," *JPE* 24 (February 1926): 119–20.
[10] Robert S. Lynd and Helen Merrell Lynd, *Middletown: A Study in American Culture* (New York: Harcourt Brace and Company, 1929; reprint New York: Harcourt Brace and Company, 1957), 78 and 254, fn 6. For further discussion of the impact of the automobile on 1920s community and culture, see ibid., 251–63. For more context on the Lynds' observations, see Kathleen G. Donahue, *Freedom from Want: American Liberalism and the Idea of the Consumer* (Baltimore: Johns Hopkins University Press, 2003), 170–3.
[11] "A Motionless Labor Movement," *NR* LI (June 1, 1927): 31.
[12] A. J. Muste, "Organize to Fight A.F. of L. 'Lethargy'" *NYT*, May 26, 1929, 20.

into employer-employee relations, often in favor of labor, to guarantee industrial peace and continued production. After the war, employers sabotaged efforts such as the National Industrial Conferences that attempted to reconstruct industry along more democratic lines or to establish a corporatist structure for governing industry. The return of business-friendly Republican administrations to the White House temporarily sealed off any hopes for a prolabor, statist turn in labor relations. On the shop room floor, brutal postwar defeats in the steel and railroad industries merely capped off a troubling era that featured attacks on labor's left wing in the Palmer Raids and a frontal assault on unions through the National Association of Manufacturers' Open Shop campaign.

While little was new on that front, unions did confront greater uncertainty when it came to union wage theories and policies. To strengthen demands for wage increases in the immediate postwar years, labor advocates pointed to Isaac Rubinow and other economists' discovery that, despite dramatic increases in productivity, real wages had declined since 1890. For instance, a report by the LBI's George Soule presented at the annual meeting of the American Association for Labor Legislation (AALL) argued against employers' assertions that increased productivity automatically led to increased wages. "While per capita production increased with great rapidity from 1899 to 1919, the purchasing power of wages actually declined," he contended.[13] For some, tying wages to the cost of living seemed reasonable. During the war, many employers voluntarily joined the National War Labor Board (NWLB) and Shipping Board in using new cost of living data to determine wages. In general, unions expressed little dissent from this wartime policy. After the war, however, as wages appeared to outpace prices in some union occupations, employers turned the cost of living argument back on organized labor, working now to cut wages. Always skeptical of state intervention in labor relations and now questioning the limitations explicit in tying wage gains to inflation, organized labor came out of the war searching for a new wage policy that squared with postwar economic realities.

The move of the steel industry from the twelve-hour to eight-hour day provided evidence to many labor leaders of the potential of solid research to sway business and government leaders and the public. Rather than relying on the power of strikes or boycotts – important tools, no doubt – in the 1920s, the AFL and other unions took an active interest in crafting a knowledge base and forming strategic alliances with

---

[13] LBI, "Does Hard Work Bring More Pay," *FFW* 1 (January 1923): 1.

research organizations and experts who would help unions make better sense of the dramatic economic changes under way and to build arguments for better working and living conditions for the nation's workers. Though the AFL would never admit to the possibility of reasoning with an employer as recalcitrant as Judge Elbert H. Gary, especially so close to the disastrous 1919 steel strike, the successful postwar struggle against the twelve-hour day in the steel industry awakened the AFL to the power of facts and expertise to convince employers and the public of the legitimacy of labor's demands on a narrow group of issues. By 1925, labor experts turned their attention to understanding and promoting a new conception of wages that sought to solve public problems they believed had been caused in part by a lack of good information.

THE RISE OF THE LABOR RESEARCH BUREAU

To better understand the postwar shifts in the economic terrain and to compensate for the withdrawal of the state from aggressive labor investigation, unions in the 1920s established a dizzying array of research bureaus and knowledge-generating institutions. A *Journal of Electrical Workers and Operators* (*JEWO*) editorial suggested, "It is unthinkable that any modern organization will undertake to do business without ... an intelligence office whose function is to study, investigate, [and] inquire."[14] Within organized labor, individual unions such as the Amalgamated Clothing Workers, International Brotherhood of Electrical Workers, Brotherhood of Maintenance of Way Employees, International Typographical Union, and International Ladies' Garment Workers Union formed their own research departments, as did the more closely affiliated allied craft departments, such as the Railway Employee Department, which established a joint bureau of research in Chicago.[15] Surveying the

[14] "I.B.E.W. Research," *JEWO* 26 (September 1928): 462.
[15] For a sample of the support for increasing the research capacity of unions in the 1920s, see "Research Paves New Way to Reign of Reason," *JEWO* 26 (August 1927): 412; "Research Plan of Brotherhood Adopted Rapidly," *JEWO* 29 (December 1930): 680; "Work of the Statistical Bureau Begun" *Supplement to the Typographical Journal: Proceedings of the 68th Session of the International Typographical Union*, Atlanta, Georgia (August 13–18, 1923): 25; E. L. Oliver, "Whadda' You Mean – A Research Department?" *RC* 27 (September 1928): 413–14; "Industrial Research By Organized Labor," *MLR* 27 (November 1928): 4–9; Florence Thorne, "Facts Workers Need," *JPR* 3 (July 1924): 77–80; George Soule, "Why 'Big Six' Won," *LA* 11 (January 1922): 1–3; William H. Johnston, "Facts Beat the Enemy: Value of Expert in the Industrial Fight," *LA* 7 (April 1923): 1–3; Stuart Chase, "Labor + The Technician – The Stockholder," *LA* 7(April 1923): 9–11; Prince Hopkins, "Out of the Trap: Knowledge Necessary for the

situation in Europe, the LBI and Russell Sage Foundation's Ben Selekman noted a "wide-spread and simultaneous incorporation of research into the program of European labor" that "warrants the conclusion that fact-finding represents a new but undoubtedly permanent development in union administration."[16] Labor colleges such as Brookwood Labor College and nonprofits such as the LBI complemented organized labor's efforts to gather expertise about the economic life of union members and workers. Though these new labor experts focused on a variety of issues, much of their work sought to further the public, unions, and policy makers' understanding of the nature of wages in a modern industrial economy and the role the state, unions, business, and the public should play in their determination.

Among the many labor research bureaus to emerge in the decade, the LBI and the AFL Research Bureau produced the most widely cited and influential studies on worker wages and economic stability. Through the 1920s, Florence C. Thorne, longtime secretary to Samuel Gompers and his successor, William Green, served as director of the AFL Research Bureau. Born in Hannibal, Missouri in 1877, Thorne attended Oberlin College in 1897 and 1898 before taking teaching jobs in Georgia and her hometown. In 1909, Thorne entered the University of Chicago Graduate School and began work on a thesis concerning the AFL. While conducting her research, she met Samuel Gompers. By 1912, Thorne had left the University of Chicago to serve as the assistant editor of the *American Federationist* (the monthly publication of the AFL). Though Gompers held the post of editor, Thorne assumed most of the editorial duties and became one of Gompers's closest confidants, eventually helping him to write his memoir.[17] Historian Philip Taft wrote of Thorne, "Although she always kept herself in the background, she played an important and vital role in the presentation of the ideas and policies of the A. F. of L."[18]

Workers' Freedom," *LA* 7 (April 1923): 21–3; Esther Lowell, "Research – For What?" *LA* 12 (March 1928): 8–10; Fannia M. Cohn, "Facts to Light the Way," *LA* 12 (June 1928): 17–19; Albert Theodore Helbing, *The Departments of the American Federation of Labor* (Baltimore: Johns Hopkins University Press, 1931); Morris Llewellyn Cooke, "Organized Labor and Research," *AF* (August 1927); 951–5; "The Labor Bureau," *Survey Graphic* (July 16, 1921): 523–4; "Research The Key," *AF* 34 (August 1927): 913; and several articles in *JEWO* (September 1928).

[16] Ben Selekman, "Research in European Trade Unions," *AF* 35 (October 1928): 1220.
[17] Gary Fink, *Biographical Dictionary of American Labor* (Westport: Greenwood Press, 1974), 548–9.
[18] Philip Taft, *The A. F. of L. From the Death of Gompers to the Merger* (New York: Harper and Brothers, 1959), xi.

Enlightened Labor?

ILLUSTRATION 3.1. "O.K. Choir of Researchers." 1923 cartoon appearing in *Labor Age* suggesting the need for labor organizations to build research institutions to confront employers' research organizations. Caption below reads, " If Labor's research agencies, and *Labor Age*, would join this chorus there would be such sweet harmony." See *Labor Age* 7 (April 1923): 14.

AFL documents and the personal papers of union leaders leave the precise origins of the AFL Research Bureau vague, but by the mid-1920s it published and reported frequently concerning unemployment in the trades and wage rates for union and nonunion industries. In his public pronouncements on wages, President Green drew his data and ideas directly from the work of the bureau and its two chief investigators, Jürgen Kuczynski and Marguerite Steinfeld, who authored most reports by the AFL Research Bureau.[19]

Similar to the NICB's function as a research arm for business, LBI founders aimed to provide a research arm for organized labor that complemented AFL-type union research bureaus. LBI leaders envisioned a role for the organization as "an auxiliary to the labor movement ... to put the weapons of facts and figures in the hands of union representatives to use in the service of the rank and file."[20] Alfred L. Bernheim, Evans Clark, David Saposs, and George Soule founded the nonprofit organization on May 1, 1920 in New York, with Stuart Chase and Otto S. Beyer joining the organization a short time later.[21] Though Saposs would leave LBI to join the faculty of Brookwood Labor College in the fall of 1922, Clark, Bernheim, Soule, Chase, and Beyer remained active participants in the LBI throughout the 1920s. They accepted as clients only organizations working in the interest of labor, but they reserved the right to work with employers if a joint agreement could be fashioned between workers and employers. In its first three years of existence, the LBI

---

[19] For an interesting portrait of Steinfeld and Kuczynski, see Marc Linder, *Labor Statistics and Class Struggle* (New York: International Publishers, 1994), 13–26.

[20] LBI, *The Labor Bureau, Inc.: Annual Report, 1921* (New York: The Labor Bureau, Inc. 1921), 2. The LBI was not alone in its research mission. The *Labor Press Directory* lists eleven "Workers' Education and Research" periodicals and bulletins published in 1925. Eight of them began publication after 1919. Solon De Leon and Nathan Fine, *American Labor Press Directory* (New York: Rand School of Social Science, 1925), 13–14. On the changing role of intellectuals in the labor movement, see Benjamin Stolberg, "The New Unionism: (With Special Reference to Trade Union Capitalism)," *The Modern Quarterly* 3 (September–December 1926): 297.

[21] For more on the founding of the LBI and its purpose, see *The Labor Bureau, Inc. An Account of the First Years Work* (New York: The Labor Bureau, Inc., 1921); Louis F. Budenz, "Servants of the Labor Movement," *LA* 7 (April 1923): 4–5; George Soule, *The Intellectual and the Labor Movement* (New York: League for Industrial Democracy, 1923); George Soule, "Work of the Labor Bureau, Inc.," *JPR* 3 (July 1924): 81–9; and Jacobs, *Pocketbook Politics*, 75–6. For more on Chase and his work in the 1920s, see Robert B. Westbrook, "Tribune of the Technostructure: The Popular Economics of Stuart Chase," *American Quarterly* 32 (Autumn 1980): 387–408. On Beyer, see David M. Vrooman, *Daniel Willard and Progressive Management on the Baltimore and Ohio Railroad* (Columbus: Ohio State University Press, 1991), particularly chapters 2 and 3.

served some 212 international, national, local, and district unions, and by 1923 it had established offices in New York City, Chicago, Boston, and San Francisco.[22] Unions asked the LBI to investigate or determine "statistics dealing with comparative wages, with the cost of living, with standards of living, and with all the things which ordinarily come into arbitrations." Throughout the 1920s, labor papers credited LBI reports as key to victories in contract negotiations, government hearings, and public debates. Organizations that ranged from the Consumers' League to the Uniformed Fireman's Association of New York utilized briefs written and researched by the LBI in support of wage and hour legislation. For example, Soule testified as a representative of "the public" and an economic expert before the New Hampshire legislature when it deliberated on the need for a forty-eight-hour law for women.[23] Over time, unions requested that the LBI engage in more ambitious and theoretical work. For instance, the LBI constructed a means of negotiating wages for International Association of Machinists members employed in navy and arsenal works that tied real wage increases to the increase in national productivity over a period of years.[24] By 1923, the International Typographical Union and the Brotherhood of Railway Clerks had hired the LBI to assist in the establishment of permanent research departments within their own union structures.[25]

Along with serving unions through unpublished background research, the LBI published a monthly bulletin, *Facts For Workers*, which many unions used liberally to supplement their own journals, pamphlets, and other publications. The "Terms of Subscription," as printed in each issue of *Facts For Workers*, described the publication as "issued primarily for republication in trade union journals and labor papers." Union periodicals frequently used these articles without acknowledging that the LBI produced them. The LBI usually divided its coverage in *Facts For Workers* between "Special Features" and "Monthly Summaries." Starting in 1923, its first full year of publication, the "Monthly Summary" included a general review of the economic conditions concerning labor for the month;

[22] LBI, *Annual Report, 1923* (New York: The Labor Bureau, Inc., 1923), 2–3.
[23] See Soule to Felix Frankfurter, February 24, 1925, Container 103, File Soule, George 1921–30, Felix Frankfurter Papers, Manuscript Division, Library of Congress, Washington, DC (hereafter LOC).
[24] Soule, "The Work of the Labor Bureau Inc.," 81–9. For a description of a proposed LBI plan to organize textile workers in Philadelphia, see LBI to Thomas F. McMahon (president of the United Textile Workers), 1922, Box 1, File 1922, David Saposs Papers, Wisconsin State Historical Society, Madison, Wisconsin (hereafter WSHS).
[25] "What the Unions are Doing on Fact-Finding," 3.

an analysis of the cost of living, wages, or the job market; a review of profits, sales, and finance in industry; and a brief summary of industrial conditions in select industries, usually including automobiles, paper and printing, building construction, coal, iron and steel, and textiles. The "Special Features" for each month incorporated an ambitious range of topics and investigations. These included a summary of the results of an intensive and widely cited investigation for the Pullman porters in 1927, a twelve-part series on wage theories and arguments, a nineteen-part series on basic industries, and a five-part series on the increased standard of living throughout the population.

MORE THAN JUST MORE: A NEW WAGE POLICY FOR ORGANIZED LABOR

Although the Women's Bureau and Paul Douglas led the way in proposing statist solutions to the wage problem, they were not alone in their efforts to make wage determination a public concern. After the decline of postwar reconstruction hopes, a group of labor experts worked toward a new understanding of wages. The AFL did not invite the state into the bargaining process, as Douglas and the WB had recommended, but it did stress that wage determination must be understood as an act with public implications (i.e., for economic stability) well beyond the individual employees and employers.[26]

In the context of postwar labor unrest, inflation, and continued declines in real wages, it was not clear what tack unions should take in advocating wage increases. With the exception of economists and public officials who adhered to the market principle of wage determination, most observers expressed confusion regarding the best determinants of wages. In his analysis of wages and the business cycle, economist Herbert Feis noted, "It is plain that ... we move almost blindly in our settlement of the wage question.... The condition of the labor market, the temper and bargaining spirit of the workers, and the length of existing wage contracts determine the course of events, and not intelligent prevision."[27] Even Hoover and his closest allies wondered about the basis for wage adjustments. When

---

[26] On rejection of the living wage, see "Former Wage Concepts Rejected; Labor Wants More than 'Living,'" *AFL:WNS* 15 (January 16, 1926): 1; "Living Wage Theory is Rejected; High Output Must Benefit Labor," *AFL:WNS* 15 (August 28, 1926): 1.

[27] Herbert Feis, "The Consuming Power of Labor and Business Fluctuations," *AER* 16, Suppl. (March 1926): 80; Herbert Feis, "A New Wage Policy for Labor?" *Survey Graphic* 15 (January 1926): 498.

Enlightened Labor? 125

the Social Science Research Council (SSRC) was founded, Hoover's closest assistant, E. E. Hunt, requested that the SSRC take up among its initial research questions the "Basis of Settlement in Wage Adjustment."[28] In *Facts for Workers*, the LBI prefaced its twelve-part series on wages by suggesting, "There have been many neat little theories to account for the course of wages; each in turn has been given up or changed, as more was learned about the subject."[29] By 1922, the *Typographical Journal* – the monthly publication of the International Typographical Union (ITU) that included a monthly section on wage scale increases in the printing trade – addressed the question "Are Wages Too High?" on page one.[30] The ITU's negative answer to the question would surprise few readers of the journal, but the debate itself highlights the confusion surrounding the wage question in the 1920s and the impact of employers' – who had insisted unions used the war inappropriately to drive up wages – arguments on the postwar labor discourse.[31]

In 1922, the AFL convention ordered a study conducted of "the principles that properly underlie wage determination," which appears to have been an effort to get a handle on the wage issue and retrieve some control over the wage policy discourse.[32] By 1925, the study evolved into the AFL's most important statement on wages to date.[33] At the October 1925

---

[28] The SSRC recognized the importance of the question but opted not to pursue it. See "Minutes of the Social Science Research Council, February 24, 1923–September 3, 1926," Series 9, Box 349, Folder 2077, page 42, SSRC Papers, RAC.

[29] LBI, "Wage Theories and Arguments: No. 1 – Introduction," *FFW* 2 (October 1923): 1–2.

[30] ITU, "Are Wages Too High?" *The Typographical Union* LX (May 1922): 625–6; Basil Manly, "Are Wages Too High?" *IMJ* LVIII (May 1922): 223–7; Basil Manly, "Are Wages Too High?" *IMJ* 58 (June 1922): 291–6; United Mine Workers, "Why Should Employers Think of Slowing Down Business and Reducing Wages in This Present Period of Reconstruction?" *UMWJ* 30 (January 1, 1919): 4.

[31] By August 1923, the ITU joined the ranks of a growing number of unions by establishing a statistical bureau to "properly equip committees of local unions in negotiation of wage scales and assist them where arbitration is undertaken." See *Supplement to the Typographical Journal: Proceedings of the 68th Session of the ITU, Atlanta, August 13–18, 1923* (November 1924): 24–5; United Mine Workers, "Why Would Employers Think of Slowing Down Business," 4; Mary van Kleeck, "Modern Industry and Society," *AF* 33 (June 1926): 699.

[32] Matthew Woll, "Labor Seeking Light on Wages," *IMJ* LVIII (March 1922): 114; "Wages," *AF* 29 (January 1922): 68. Also see Matthew Woll, "Wage Theories," *IMJ* LVII (May 1921): 267; John P. Frey, "A Sound Basis for Wages," *IMJ* LXII (January 1926): 1–6; "Is the Federation's New Wage Principle Sound?" *LEJ* 59 (December 1925): 910; and Fannia M. Cohn, "Increased Productivity – For Whom," *LA* 12 (April 1928): 3–5.

[33] For evidence of an early commitment to high wages as a means of stabilizing the economy, see AFL, "Labor's High-Wage Theory First Met Usual Ridicule," *AFL:WNS* 18 (October 6, 1928): 1.

Atlantic City convention, the AFL adopted a new wage resolution that, as historian Meg Jacobs has described it, "justified high wages as essential to sustaining macroeconomic demand."[34] In advocating what it referred to as "higher social wages," the AFL distinguished this "third phase" of its wage struggle from statist solutions to the low-wage problem and its own former "nominal" and "real" conceptualizations of wages. According to the AFL, in the first phase of its understanding of wages, unions had simply asked for "more" or higher wages, but recognition of increasing prices forced unions to rethink their justification for wage adjustments. AFL wage policy literature did not specify a date for this change; however, the general downward pressure on prices between 1870 and 1896 that resulted from cutthroat competition between firms and from monetary deflation seems a likely period when prices would not have been a major concern for unions.[35] At the turn of the century, business integration and consolidation and the rise of corporate capitalism, combined with workers' loss of control of production to managers, allowed businesses to set prices and wages with a level of autonomy that did not exist in the nineteenth century. These changes, combined with gold standard inflation and the expansion of the money supply, pushed up prices, causing the purchasing power of workers' wages to stagnate or to decline. The combination of these turn-of-the-century changes likely led organized labor to think increasingly of wages in relation to the price of goods. This cost of living conception of wages – the AFL termed this the second phase of the evolution of its wage policy – fell out of favor among workers and unions in the early 1920s, when employers used price deflation to demand wage cuts and workers recognized dramatic increases in the productive power of industry.[36]

The third or "social wage" phase emerged in the 1920s, when organized labor discovered an increase in productivity without proportionate increases in workers' consuming power. To maintain "labor's share," the AFL proposed a calculation of wages largely divorced from price changes and based instead on the economy's growing wealth and productivity. Importantly, the AFL attributed increased productivity to workers and not to increased mechanization or the reorganization of industry by capital and management, which might have justified employers and investors

---

[34] Jacobs, *Pocketbook Politics*, 82.
[35] AFL, "Organized Labor's Modern Wage Policy," 14.
[36] LBI, "Wage Theories and Arguments: No. 2 – Changes in the Cost of Living," *FFW* 2 (November 1923): 6; AFL, "Organized Labor's Modern Wage Policy," 7.

receiving a greater share of the national income. Adjusting wages to the cost of living, according to the AFL, protected workers against the ravages of inflation, but it did not protect the "social position of the wage earner in relation to other consumers."[37] To solve this problem, the AFL recommended that wages be adjusted so they would maintain workers' purchasing power relative to other groups' claims on the national income. As friendly critics of the AFL wage policy correctly pointed out, it was not immediately clear what mechanism or index would be used to make these adjustments. In a *Facts For Workers* article, the LBI wondered if productivity would be measured on the basis of the whole population, output per worker, or number of hours worked, and if wage adjustments should be made on an industry, firm, or economy-wide basis. More significant, the LBI also questioned how to determine a just "social wage" in light of the need for capital investment. "How much can social wages grow at any given time without harmfully limiting the amount of industrial income which should be devoted to new capital equipment – that is, to the new factories and machinery which make greater productivity possible?" the LBI wondered.[38]

As important as the policy, however, was the AFL's skillful casting of its new wage theory as something greater than just an effort to get more for workers. Perhaps inspired by economists and policy makers' increasing concern with the business cycle, the AFL moved beyond mere concerns with production and distribution, explicitly linking the social position and purchasing power of wage earners to social and economic stability. According to the AFL, "If the share of Labor in the value of the product declines, Labor's purchasing power over the product produced by manufacturers declines, Labor can buy comparatively fewer commodities and a business depression may develop."[39]

---

[37] AFL, "Organized Labor's Modern Wage Policy," 17; and Jürgen Kuczynski and Marguerite Steinfeld, "Wages in Manufacturing Industries, 1899 to 1927," *AF* 35 (July 1928): 830–5.

[38] LBI, "Labor's Share in Production," *FFW* 6 (October 1927): 1–2. "The Workers' Share in Production" and "Economists on Wages Theories" both appear in *Survey Graphic* (March 11, 1922): 927–9.

[39] AFL, "An Index of Labor's Share in Production and Consumption," *AF* (April 1928): 489–90; also see AFL, "The Five Day Week," *AF* (November 1926): 1299; Frey, "A Sound Basis for Wages," 3; and Jürgen Kuczynski and Marguerite Steinfeld, "Wages in the Pig Iron Industry," *AF* 34 (May 1927): 559. Marc Linder argues that Kuczynski served as "President Green's Marxist Ventriloquist" and that the federation's wage policy was a successful effort by Kuczynski, who he describes as a German Marxist, to smuggle Marx's ideas about exploitation into the AFL. See Linder, *Labor Statistics and Class Struggle*, 13–25.

The AFL's emphasis on the relationship between economic stability and high wages dramatically widened the appeal of its new wage theory. The AFL wage policy received considerable support, not only from labor organizations and social reformers, but also from business leaders who recognized the economic and social benefits of increasing worker purchasing power by way of high wages and efficient mass production. The *Locomotive Engineers Journal* cheered the burial of the phrase "a fair day's wage for a fair day's pay" as an "ambiguous phrase devoid of economic content," while the *Machinists Monthly* commended the AFL for its "courageous" effort to "formulate a principle of wages."[40] A growing group of supporters of high wages in the academy and business, including Columbia economist Sumner Slichter, Yale economist Irving Fisher, and "amateur" economists William Trufant Foster and Waddill Catchings, as well as LBI founder George Soule, pointed to the potential of wages to stabilize an economy that, after decades of persistent instability, showed the potential of evolving into a stable, high-wage economy that relied on consumer markets to maintain commodity demand.[41] Employers, including General Electric president Gerard Swope, Baltimore and Ohio Railroad president Daniel Willard, and Owen D. Young, spoke publicly about the social and civic importance of higher wages and the fact that higher wages did not automatically mean higher costs.[42] The Federal Reserve, too, provided an implicit endorsement of AFL policy, acknowledging the importance of consumer power and high wages to maintain demand for the ever increasing supply of consumer goods. According to the Board, "A national income larger than in 1922, arising both out of increased earnings of factory workers and larger proceeds from the

---

[40] "Is the Federation's New Wage Principle Sound?" *LEJ* (December 1925): 910; Charles L. Reed, "Labor's New Wage Policy," *MMJ* 38 (February 1926): 60, 95. See also "High Wage Economy," *JEWO* 25 (June 1926): 266; "A New Wage Policy," *MMJ* 40 (January 1928): 37; Elsie Gluck, "The Significance of Labor's Wage Statement," *AF* 34 (February 1927): 214–20. For a more cautious endorsement of the AFL wage plan, see LBI, "Labor's Share in Production," 1–2.

[41] For evidence of support from business and academia, see "Labor's High-Wage Theory is Gaining Friends," *AFL:WNS* 15 (September 26, 1926): 1; Irving Fisher, "Labor and Scientific Management," *AF* 34 (June 1927): 694–9; Edward Berman, "Labor and Production," *AF* 33 (August 1926): 964–9.

[42] "Mr. Swope Sees the Light," *AF* 31 (July 1924): 573; "Wages," *AF*, 1301; Willard to E. E. Hunt, January 26, 1929, General Records of the Commerce Office of the Secretary, Subject Files of Asst. Secretary of Commerce Edward Eyre Hunt, 1921–1931, Box 1, File Federal Employment Stabilization Board, RG 40, National Archives at College Park, College Park, MA (hereafter NA).

sale of farm products, furnished the buying power to absorb the year's increased output of goods."[43]

LABOR'S NEW FRIENDS

Since Samuel Gompers famously portrayed intellectuals as barnacles on the labor movement, the relationship between organized labor and sympathetic public intellectuals had often been troubled. The story of Brookwood Labor College in the 1920s would seem to suggest little had changed. In the early 1920s, Brookwood emerged as a site where intellectuals, labor leaders, and workers could learn from each other and construct a new understanding of industrial relations. Despite an early honeymoon period and significant union funding, by 1928 the AFL executive council red-baited Brookwood faculty and withdrew its support, while urging all other unions to do the same.[44] AFL problems with the politics of Brookwood faculty were compounded by a certain arrogance of college leaders that union leaders had, rightly or wrongly, come to expect from left-leaning intellectuals. In an article describing new approaches to organizing workers, Brookwood director A. J. Muste described the "psychology of American workers" as "mentally sick, twisted, tied up." According to Muste, workers "need to be psychoanalyzed ... need to have their thoughts and feelings laid bare before their own eyes. They know too many things that are not so, they are living a dream world, not a real world, in a world of fears, illusions, fairies and bogey men."[45] Union leaders unlikely saw things in quite this same light.

---

[43] "Trade Unions' Fight for High Wages is Patriotic Effort," *AFL: WNS* 13 (January 5, 1924): 1. Also see "High Wages Turn Wheels of Industry," *AFL: WNS* 13 (January 12, 1924): 1.

[44] "Astounding Action of A. F. of L. Against Brookwood," *LA* (October 1928): 23; A. J. Muste, "Mother Throws out the Baby," *LA* (October 1928): 20–2; "Brookwood Carries On," *LA* (November 1928): 3; "The Case Against Brookwood," *LA* (May 1929): 4.

[45] A. J. Muste, "Education and the Unorganized," *LA* 12 (April 1928): 9. See also Richard Altenbaugh, *Education for Struggle: The American Labor Colleges in the 1920s and 1930s* (Philadelphia: Temple University Press, 1990); Jo Ann Robinson, *Abraham Went Out* (Philadelphia: Temple University Press, 1981). Particularly in the early 1920s, Thorne appears to have had a close professional relationship with David Saposs and his wife, Bertha Saposs. During their time at Brookwood, Thorne employed David and Bertha Saposs (though Ms. Saposs appears to have done most of the work) to conduct a survey of published literature on trade unionism for the AFL. See Thorne to Bertha Saposs, September 14, 1923; Thorne to David Saposs, October 12, 1923; David Saposs to Thorne, October 24, 1923; Thorne to David Saposs, October 26, 1923; David J. Saposs Papers, Box 1, File 1923, WSHS.

Even so, the often reactionary and frequently indiscriminate red-baiting politics of the AFL during the 1920s masked a willingness of union leaders to work openly with a number of sympathetic intellectuals and experts. AFL leaders such as John P. Frey found willing allies in the likes of Waddill Catchings, William T. Foster, and the LBI's George Soule. Catchings, a graduate of Harvard Law, occupied a number of important posts at Sloss-Sheffield Steel Company and Goldman, Sachs, and Co. During World War I, he served on the secretary of labor's advisory committee, where he played a pivotal role in persuading steel industry executives to support the Wilson administration's business and labor policies. In 1920, he formed the Pollak Foundation for Economic Research to examine the means by which "industry may be organized and the products of industry distributed to yield the people generally the largest possible satisfaction."[46] Foster, a Harvard graduate and president of Reed College, headed the Pollak Foundation and helped Catchings to articulate his ideas.

The AFL's John P. Frey, who brought the full weight of the AFL with him, joined with Foster, Catchings, and the LBI to advocate new labor and business practices. Born in Mankato, Minnesota in 1871, Frey exemplified the social mobility available to ambitious, articulate, and talented trade unionists in the early part of the twentieth century. Before leaving the International Molders Union (IMU) in 1927 to become the secretary treasurer of the AFL's Metal Trades Department, Frey served as vice-president of the IMU, editor of the *International Molder's Journal* – an important trade union journal with a circulation upward of thirty-five thousand – and secretary of the Committee on Resolution at AFL Conventions.[47] A close confidant of Gompers, Frey traveled in a wide range of union and nonunion circles. In the teens, he wrote favorable, if somewhat vague, articles describing the work of Robert F. Hoxie and the relationship between labor and scientific management, which previewed elements of the AFL's cooperative posture in the 1920s.[48] He frequently occupied positions in nonunion institutions, including a lectureship at the

---

[46] Cited in Joseph Dorfman, *The Economic Mind in American Civilization* (New York: The Viking Press, 1959), 4: 340.
[47] Circulation data from *American Labor Press Directory* (New York: Rand School of Social Science, 1925), 4.
[48] John P. Frey, "The Relationship of Scientific Management to Labor," *JPE* 21 (May 1913): 400–11; John P. Frey, "Robert F. Hoxie: Investigator and Interpreter," *JPE* 24 (November 1916): 884–93. Frey's papers contain numerous lengthy and thoughtful letters from Gompers discussing Frey's career in the labor movement. See John P. Frey Papers, Box 10, File Gompers, Samuel, Correspondence, 1908–1924, LOC.

University of Chicago, NBER, and membership at the prestigious Cosmos Club of Washington, DC, which he joined in 1929 with the endorsement of a wide variety of business, labor, government, and academic leaders.[49]

By the mid-1920s, Foster, Catchings, and Frey, with Soule providing additional public support, formed an effective alliance that bolstered their collective position within economic policy and labor reform circles. AFL unions, congressional committees, business groups, future New Dealers, and other labor experts read and listened closely to Foster and Catchings' innovative work describing the relationship between economic stability, monetary policy, and rising wages.[50] Their work received significant attention and reviews by prominent economists, statisticians, political scientists, and sociologists, including Frank Knight, John Maurice Clark, and R. G. Hawtry.[51] Some of the excitement surrounding their work derived from the authors' offer of a five-thousand-dollar reward for the best criticism of *Profit*. Contenders submitted their reviews to the Pollak Foundation where former AEA presidents Wesley Mitchell and Allyn A. Young evaluated them. Working together, Foster and Catchings challenged orthodox wage theory, rejecting the idea that wages should be determined by some automatic equilibrating tendency in the market. Economists who embraced marginal productivity theory of wage determination going back to John Bates Clark argued that the only necessary intervention in the market would be to remove frictions such as monopoly, but the AFL and its allies dismissed as foolishness the idea that unrestrained markets would naturally move toward a fair distribution of income. They asserted instead that economic stagnation and decline

---

[49] On Frey, see "John P. Frey, Late Editor," *IMJ* 63 (October 1927): 607; Fink, *Biographical Dictionary of American Labor*, 237–8. I established the relationship between Frey, Foster, and Catchings through a reading of their correspondence during the 1920s. See John P. Frey Papers, Box 9, File: Foster, William Trufant, Pollak Foundation for Economic Research, LOC. Some letters endorsing Frey's candidacy for the Cosmo's Club are in this collection. Others can be found in various Department of Labor and Department of Commerce National collections at NA.

[50] Dorfman, *The Economic Mind in American Civilization*, 4: 343; Brinkley, *The End of Reform*, 75–7; Alan H. Gleason, "Foster and Catchings: A Reappraisal," *JPE* 67 (April 1959): 156–72; Jacobs, *Purchasing Power*, 82–6; and Barber, *From New Era to New Deal*, 54–8.

[51] Reviews of Foster and Catchings' work appeared in *JPE, PSQ, AER, American Journal of Sociology, Social Forces*, and *JASA*. Catchings appeared with Frey, Feis, and Berridge on a roundtable conference at the 1926 American Economic Association meeting. See "The Consuming Power of Labor and Business Fluctuation," *Papers and Proceedings of the Thirty-Eighth Annual Meeting of the American Economic Association* 16 (March 1926): 78–88.

could only be prevented by policies mandating that workers receive a growing share of production.

In March 1923, at the American Economic Association annual meeting, Soule offered just such an alternative to the marginalist approach to wage determination. Soule's analysis incorporated a discussion of wages and productivity into the larger economic debate concerning economic stability and the business cycle. Soule drew on data from economists Walter W. Stewart and Edmund E. Day to illustrate the steady increase in productivity since 1900, and a range of state and federal sources to arrive at an index for money and real wages. Soule, in part updating Rubinow's earlier assessment of inert wages and gains in productivity, found that, while productivity had increased more than 30 percent between 1889 and 1919, real wages, based on an index of food prices, were stagnant. Soule concluded: "Even taking into consideration the recent rise in real wages, due chiefly to the more rapid drop of prices than of wage rates since 1920, we have only a 5 per cent increase in the per-capita purchasing power of factory wages to compare with a 30 or 40 per cent increase in per-capita production in the last twenty-five years."[52] To ensure a more equitable distribution of increased productivity, Soule appealed to "those engaged in making wage determinations" and suggested that "Average real wages must be increased at least in direct relation to a smoothed index of national per-capita production."[53] Soule, who along with other LBI leaders had friendly relations with leading Hooverites for much of the 1920s, relayed these published findings to E. E. Hunt, but apparently without significant effect.[54]

While the Hooverites overlooked or ignored Soule's analysis, Catchings and Foster took Soule's "smoothing" process one step further, popularizing an understanding of the flow of wages in relation to the flow of goods. In *Money* (1923), *Profits* (1925), and a flurry of articles, Foster and Catchings promoted an understanding of money velocity that

[52] Soule, "The Productivity Factor in Wage Determinations," 135.
[53] Ibid., 140. Also cited in Dorfman, *The Economic Mind in American Civilization*, 4: 66.
[54] George Soule to E. E. Hunt, January 2, 1925; and George Soule to E. E. Hunt, December 20, 1924, General Records of the Department of Commerce, Office of the Secretary, Subject Files of the Assistant Secretary of Commerce E. E. Hunt, 1921–31, Box 1, File Labor Distribution of Wealth,. On the nature of the relationships among Soule, Stuart Chase, and other LBI leaders, see in addition a series of letters between Chase and Hunt in Box 16, File: Misc. C (1925)-26; and Box 18, File: Misc Correspondence S 1927. All of the above in RG 40, NA. Soule and Hunt had a falling out over an article Soule wrote on Hoover for the *NR* in late 1927. See correspondence between Hunt, Soule, and Herbert Croly in same file.

suggested that wages could be the vehicle to stabilize and grow the economy. Though oversaving and insufficient consumer credit were part of the problem, according to Foster and Catchings, the chief obstacle to continued economic growth, stability, and prosperity was insufficient wages. In an economy that produced more and more goods, falling or stable wages spelled disaster. Foster and Catchings suggested that business had to reinvest profits continually to keep money circulating, thus preventing oversaving – what they often referred to as the "dilemma of thrift." The two economists also urged policy makers to pay close attention to wages in order to ensure enough money remained in the hands of consumers so consumers could purchase the bounty of consumer goods.

Just months after the AFL adopted its new wage policy, *Profits* hit the shelves. Union periodicals gave front-page coverage to the book, often publishing long excerpts and extensive corroborative articles from Frey and others.[55] In a January 1926 *American Federationist* article republished in a number of other trade journals, Foster and Catchings summarized their critique of American underproduction and underconsumption. The underproduction portion of their analysis pointed to unemployment and the underutilization of capital as evidence that "merely moving wages up at the same rate as the cost of living gets them [workers] nowhere."[56] The AFL and Foster and Catchings used this argument as a means of rejecting living wage reforms advocated by economist Paul Douglas and other reformers who tried to utilize federal and state laws to ensure a wage floor for the nation's lowest paid workers. Foster and Catchings cited the AFL's position – that "the practice of fixing wages *solely* on a basis of the cost of living is a violation of sound economy, and is utterly without logic or scientific support of any kind" – in dismissing living wage advocates.[57] Instead, Foster and Catchings identified underconsumption as "the chief cause of our troubles."[58] More specifically, they insisted that

---

[55] At a 1925 AEA session discussing labor and the business cycle, Frey seemed to be previewing the arguments his friends Foster and Catchings would make concerning wages in *Profits*, which also appeared in 1925. Frey identified inadequate wages as the cause of business cycles, pointing out that "man's increasing powers to produce have greatly exceeded man's power to purchase." Frey's remarks were reprinted in "Real Wages Must Be Increased," *IMJ* 62 (June 1926): 338.

[56] William Trufant Foster and Waddill Catchings, "More Pay and Less Work – Is this a Futile Aim?" *AF* 33 (January 1926): 38. Excerpts and quotes from their books were widely cited in trade union journals. For example, see "High Wages the Basis for Prosperity," *LEJ* (March 1926): 169.

[57] Foster and Trufant, "More Pay and Less Work," 38. Emphasis in original.

[58] Ibid., 36.

"The greatest economic need ... is a flow of money to consumers which, after providing for savings, is always approximately equal to the flow of finished goods." Foster and Catchings lamented savings, describing it as a "dilemma of thrift" that took money out of circulation and led to a "deficiency in consumer buying."[59] AFL leaders took it upon themselves to develop the statistical tools to make this policy proposal a reality.

THE AFL AS A WATCHDOG FOR ECONOMIC STABILITY

The notion of dramatic increases in productivity in the 1920s seems normal, if notable, to observers today, but at the time the "discovery" of striking increases in the production of goods, particularly consumer goods, came as a surprise to many labor experts. The LBI synthesized Census of Manufacturers and Federal Reserve reports to publicize a 9 percent increase in productivity and a 3 percent decrease in the number of employees in manufacturing positions between 1919 and 1923.[60] To understand the scope and ramifications of increased productivity, the AFL quickly built up a formidable research bureau that devoted most of its energies to constructing an index determining "labor's share" of the production process. Acting in this capacity, the AFL fashioned itself as a watchdog of economic instability. If the purchasing power of workers fell behind the productive power of industry, labor would sound the alarm. According to the AFL, "The construction of the index, now, permits us to watch the share of Labor, to watch Labor's purchasing power, so that, if Labor's share should decline from month to month, we are enabled to warn industry and the public before it is too late."[61] While the AFL monitored production, the LBI scrutinized business periodicals, government reports, and company financial reports in order to determine the movement of business profits. In doing so, the LBI was one of the few institutions in the 1920s to explicitly question why profits could rise so dramatically and wages so moderately.

As part of the dramatic effort to recast itself as a protector of not only workers but the public as well, beginning in 1925, AFL experts

---

[59] Ibid., 43. For an analysis of the Great Depression that builds on these labor experts' assessment of the relationship between consumer demand and economic stability, see Theodore Rosenof, *Economics in the Long Run: New Deal Theorists and Their Legacies, 1933–1993* (Chapel Hill: University of North Carolina Press, 1997), 41–3.
[60] "Where Have They Gone?" *FFW* 3 No. 7 (April 1925): 1.
[61] "An Index of Labor's Share of Production and Consumption," *AF* 35 (April 1928): 489–90; "The Five Day Week, " *AF* 33 (November 1926): 1299; "Labor, the Consumer," *AF* (November 1926): 1299.

and statisticians constructed a pair of monthly indices designed to measure changes in the "social wage" or "labor's share" of the national economy.[62] Jürgen Kuczynski, assisted by Marguerite Steinfeld, cobbled together often incongruent Bureau of Labor Statistics, Census Bureau, AFL, and National Industrial Conference Board wage data to develop what they described as a "conclusive survey of wage developments."[63] By the mid-1920s, two groups of continuous studies emerged from the AFL Research Department.

First, in October 1927, the AFL began publishing the results of the first data set describing the movement of labor's share of the nation's economic production. AFL experts attempted to determine the percentage of production awarded to labor through wages, in an effort to "make it possible for everybody to watch the development of Labor's share."[64] The AFL championed these broad economic indexes as economic barometers and published them monthly in the *American Federationist*. The AFL proposed, "If the share of Labor in the value of the product of industry declines, Labor's purchasing power over the product produced by manufacturers declines, Labor can buy comparatively fewer commodities and a business depression may develop."[65] The first index was designed to measure labor's share of the income received by the industry. A second index, similar to a modern cost of living index but including only food and clothing, measured the purchasing power of workers' wages. Combined, the indexes suggested that, since 1922, labor's share of production and consumption had increased; yet the increases were highly volatile and in need of stabilization.[66]

---

[62] "Labor's Share of Production Shown by Index, First Time," *AFL:WNS* 17 (September 24, 1927): 1.

[63] For more on Kuczynski and Steinfeld's methodology, see Jürgen Kuczynski and Marguerite Steinfeld, *Wages and Labor's Share* (Washington, DC: AFL, 1927), 7–12.

[64] "An Index of Labor's Share in Production and in Consumption," *AF* 35 (October 1927): 1231.

[65] "An Index of Labor's Share in Production and in Consumption," *AF* 35 (April 1928): 489. For a description of how AFL researchers constructed this index see "Economic Statistics," *AF* 35 (March 1928). There were a number of other efforts to hone the measurement of purchasing power in this period. The J. Walter Thompson Company offered a prize for essays that measured changes in purchasing power for different groups and communities. The winners were published in William A. Berridge, Emma A. Winslow, and Richard A. Flinn, *The Purchasing Power of the Consumer: A Statistical Index* (Chicago: A. W. Shaw Co., 1925).

[66] In another study, Kuczynski compared "prosperity" years for workers and producers to show the degree to which wage cuts contributed to economic decline. See Jürgen Kuczynski, "Wages and the Business Cycle," *AF* 34 (September 1927): 1095–9.

The broad index approximated the movement of labor's share economy-wide, but to understand better the status of labor's share in particular industries, the AFL developed a second, more precise and detailed set of indexes. In October 1927, Kuczynski began publishing a series of studies describing wages in industries employing more than thirty thousand wage earners as well as highly unionized industries with fewer workers.[67] These more concise and focused studies included an estimate of the number of employees working in an industry in a given year, the total wages paid to these employees, and the total value of products produced in each industry minus the cost of materials (otherwise known as the value added in manufacturing). Using 1904 as a baseline, AFL statisticians provided a clear picture of the value of goods produced in an industry and proposed a method that would determine the share of production that would need to go to labor in order to provide a market for the goods produced. Following this general picture of the industry's development over the previous twenty years, the studies moved to a much more specific analysis of occupations within the industry. For instance, a study of the lumber industry included an analysis of wages and production in timber products, planing mills, and wooden boxes.

The "labor's share" industry studies demonstrated extreme wage volatility, a disturbing lack of standardization in wage determination across industries relative to productivity between 1904 and 1925, and a dramatic and dangerous decline in labor's share of production increases since 1921. The first of these studies considered wages in the pig iron industry and culminated in an analysis of the relationship between wages and the business cycle. Kuczynski found that wage and price volatility in the pig iron industry led to "fantastic" fluctuations in the share of the industry's total product going to individual workers, and that only in 1921 did workers receive a share of the industry's production equal to the prewar level.[68] In the rubber industry, an AFL inquiry described dramatic fluctuation in labor's share, which rocketed from a baseline index number of 100 in 1909 to 134.9 in 1923, with only a minor setback in 1914, and then plummeted between 1923 and 1925 to 120.3. In spite of gains, particularly when compared with other industries over a similar period,

---

[67] For a description of the studies, see Jürgen Kuczynski, "Labor's Share in Manufacturing Industries," *AF* 34 (October 1927): 1233. This set of studies evolved into a more lengthy and detailed set of studies by Kuczynski beginning with "Philadelphia Typographical Union Number Two: A Wage Study," *AF* 35 (February 1928): 204–13.

[68] Kuczynski and Steinfeld, "Wages in the Pig Iron Industry," 560–1.

the AFL found the lack of stability in the rubber industry disturbing and warned, "Stabilization is utterly necessary."[69]

Other surveyed industries experienced similar declines in labor's share during the first decades of the twentieth century. In a study of the lumber industry, Kuczynski found significant fluctuation in labor's share after 1904. Though he observed a "rather favorable" trend in workers' share of productivity gains, even here he saw reason for alarm. Between 1921 and 1925, labor's share decreased markedly as productivity increased without corresponding increases in worker wages.[70] The AFL found a similar trend in food production, where labor's share declined by more than 20 percent between 1921 and 1925, to a sub-1904 level.[71] Surveying the transportation industries, the AFL found that in 1919 labor's share briefly regained its 1904 level before falling significantly between 1919 and 1925.[72] In some industries, however, labor's share had declined consistently since 1904. For instance, in industries manufacturing stone, clay, and glass products, labor's share declined almost 20 percent from a baseline index number of 100 in 1904 to 81.2 percent in 1925.[73] Similarly, the AFL observed a downward trend in labor's share after 1921 in textiles, iron, steel, paper, printing, chemicals, and allied products.[74]

The AFL was not alone in this work or the concerns it raised. The LBI conducted a set of studies that, although more focused on the general state of specific industries producing consumer goods, arrived at similar conclusions regarding the relationship between wages, productivity, and consumption. LBI studies focused more on the overproduction side of the equation, but, like the AFL, the LBI recommended increased wages to absorb surplus consumer goods. For instance, in the first of a series of articles on "basic industries," LBI experts employed government data and their own investigations and found a 25 percent reduction between 1916 and 1923 in the "time necessary to make a given number of shoes." Even

---

[69] Kuczynski, "Labor's Share in Manufacturing Industries," 1367.
[70] Ibid., 1239.
[71] "Employment in Manufacturing Industries" and Kuczynski, "Labor's Share in Manufacturing Industries," *AF* 34 (December 1927): 1497–504.
[72] "An Index of Labor's Share in Production and in Consumption," *AF* 34 (November 1927): 1361–7.
[73] "Labor's Share in Manufacturing Industries," *AF* 34 (December 1927): 1504–10.
[74] For reports on these industries, see "Labor's Share in Manufacturing Industries," *AF* 35 (March 1928): 329–39; "Labor's Share in Manufacturing Industries," *AF* 35 (June 1928): 66–79; "Labor's Share in Manufacturing Industries," *AF* 35 (February 1928): 214–28.

taking exports into account, this advanced productive capacity yielded enough shoes to "provide a little over 3 pairs of shoes a year to each, man, woman, and child in the country." As did the AFL reports, the LBI suggested, "If average wages were higher, the excess capacity of the shoe industry might be called upon and unemployment reduced."[75] Economist Walter W. Stewart, too, alluded to the need to coordinate production and consumption at a 1922 AEA discussion of the business cycle. According to Stewart, "The uncontrolled and competitive management of production and the free competitive determination of price now lead to consequences quite as disastrous. Buying power depends upon both price and output, and the collapse of either – at the farm or in the factory – causes a breakdown in the exchange of goods. A proper organization of that vast system of markets and prices which stands between and connects the farm and the factory would cause the products from these two sources to mutually and continuously support one another."[76]

The automobile industry and the relatively high wages paid by employers such as Henry Ford made it an obvious candidate for AFL and LBI consideration. The LBI noted that between 1895 and 1924 the industry expanded from an annual production of four cars to an industry value of $3,168,588,146, which made its value "greater than the wholesale value of the annual production of any other single industry."[77] In 1927, Margaret Scattergood, assistant to Director of Research Florence Thorne at the AFL, provided a detailed analysis of wages in the automobile industry. As in other industries, Scattergood found a declining social wage or labor's share between 1922 and 1925. Scattergood found that although nominal wages had increased dramatically and real wages a little, the "social wage" had declined.[78] The LBI warned of the potential of automobile production to outpace consumers' ability to purchase. Given workers' stagnant to only moderately increasing purchasing power, the LBI added, "It is clear that the industry cannot go on expanding at anything like the recent rate."[79]

As the capacity of the research bureau expanded, AFL experts broadened their investigations to include fluctuations in the buying power

[75] LBI, "The Boot and Shoe Industry," *FFW* 3 (May 1925): 1–2. Statistics from BLS, "Time and Labor Costs in Manufacturing 100 Pairs of Shoes," *Bulletin* 360 (Washington, DC: GPO, 1923).
[76] Walter W. Stewart, "Controlling Business Cycles – Discussion," *AER* 12, Suppl. (March 1922): 42.
[77] LBI, "The Automobile Industry," *FFW* 3 (July 1925): 1.
[78] Margaret Scattergood, "Wages in the Automobile Industry," *AF* (July 1927): 818.
[79] LBI, "The Automobile Industry," 1.

among skilled, unskilled, and nonunionized workers. Occasional topical reports by Kuczynski, Steinfeld, and Scattergood revealed the effect of wage fluctuations and disparity on various industries' low-paid workers. In an investigation that detailed the impact of wage rate instability on skilled and unskilled workers in the pig iron industry, Steinfeld and Kuczynski found that, "The fluctuations in the case of unskilled workers are in the average about 10 per cent higher than in the case of the skilled workers."[80] A detailed 1928 AFL report on all wage workers that combined government and LBI data on wages and a minimum family budget between 1899 and 1927 suggested, "It is no exaggeration to say that about three-fourths of the population of the United States have not the possibility to live a family life of health and decency."[81] Kuczynski and Steinfeld also examined the comparative impact of wage fluctuation on skilled and unskilled workers and found that the buying power of unskilled workers fluctuated at a 10 percent higher rate than the wages of skilled workers; they warned that such fluctuations could lead to social unrest among the largely unorganized unskilled working class.[82]

OPEN THE BOOKS: THE LBI'S EXAMINATION OF PROFITS

The LBI fortified the AFL's research with a close analysis of industry profits that suggested that capital's gains in the decade far outpaced those of workers. While other labor expertise-generating organizations, including the BLS and most economists, appear to have decoupled wages from profits in their analysis of the labor question and national economic concerns, the LBI kept these two issues together and at the center of its analysis of the 1920s economy. As a result of the paucity of analysis from other economic and labor institutions, the LBI's research on company payments of dividends and profits proved more important than its work on wages and productivity. From the fall of 1922 until early 1927, the LBI's *Facts for Workers* published a monthly report detailing the almost constant movement upward of profits and of the payment of stock dividends. The LBI complemented these monthly reports with occasional articles throughout the decade that

---

[80] Jürgen Kuczynski and Marguerite Steinfeld, "Fluctuations of Wages of Skilled and Unskilled Workers," *AF* 34 (July 1927): 800. As noted in Chapter 2, Alvin Hansen arrived at a similar conclusion when he interrogated Douglas's work on real wages. See Alvin Hansen, "The Buying Power of Labor during the War," *JASA* 18 (March 1922): 56–66.
[81] Kuczynski and Steinfeld, "Wages in Manufacturing Industries, 1899 to 1927," 701.
[82] Kuczynski and Steinfeld, "Fluctuations of Wages in Skilled and Unskilled Workers," 797.

compared wages and profits in particular industries and that summarized annual reports that frequently outlined the year's movement of wages and profits. For example, in February 1923, the LBI reported that interest and dividend payments by companies had increased from $361,925,000 in January 1922 to $459,510,000 in January 1923, a dramatic 27 percent increase that vastly outpaced real wage gains. Nominal wages for workers in New York had increased between 2.6 percent and 5.9 percent, but, when the LBI calculated changes in the cost of living, the wage increases disappeared or became losses in worker purchasing power.[83]

When employers negotiating with unions claimed they did not have the resources to increase or maintain wages, the LBI flew into action, examining earnings reports and other evidence that demonstrated that wages could be increased without endangering the company. In cases where poor business practices or the overdevelopment of an industry meant that increased wages would, in fact, run the company out of business, the LBI counseled that such businesses had no place in a modern industrial economy.[84] The LBI grappled with the role of profits in a corporate economy and how unions should handle corporate leaders' and capitalists' demands for a greater return on their substantial capital investments. LBI experts did not deny that corporations had a right to profit; in fact, they encouraged unions to take advantage of this opportunity to define legitimate profits. "No basic standard has ever been worked out in most industries, and the field is free for any argument unions may devise," the LBI advised. The LBI counseled that profits should be large enough to pay a "customary dividend on the capital stock and also to add something to the surplus account."[85] Although it had no problem legitimizing the need for profit and dividends, the LBI warned unions that they needed to look closely at overhead and depreciation costs claimed by employers who might try to use accounting gimmicks to hide surpluses.[86]

[83] LBI, "Review of the Month," *FFW* 1 (February 1923): 2. Similar articles appeared throughout the decade in *FFW*. For a sample, see monthly reports "Profits and Sales" and articles including LBI, "Dividing Up Earnings," *FFW* 1 (March 1923): 2; LBI, "Big Profits in 1923," *FFW* 2 (November 1923): 1; LBI, "Profits Up – Wages Down," *FFW* 2 (June 1924): 2; LBI, "Slaughtering and Meatpacking," *FFW* 4 (November 1925): 1–2; LBI, "Iron and Steel," *FFW* 4 (May 1926): 1–2; LBI, "Profits in 1928," *FFW* 6 (May 1928): 2–3.

[84] LBI, "Wage Theories and Arguments: No. 6 – Financial Condition of Industry," *FFW* 2 (March 1924): 2.

[85] Ibid., 1.

[86] LBI, "Wage Theories and Arguments: No. 6," 1–2; LBI, "How to Read a Balance Sheet," *FFW* 1 (May 1923): 2–3; and LBI, "How to Read a Profit and Loss Statement," *FFW* 1 (June 1923): 1–3.

LBI labor experts, in a move that anticipated Walter Reuther's demand to General Motors, pushed businesses to open their books so that workers and the public might better assess the ability of companies to increase worker pay.[87] In representing the Press Assistants' Union No. 23, the LBI convinced an arbitrator that in order to evaluate the "economic condition of the industry," a phrase in the contract, the LBI had to have access to the company's finances. An LBI and a company accountant negotiated a system that allowed access to the books. Together these two accountants submitted a report to the arbitrator, with separate interpretations of the numbers.[88] In another case, the LBI was retained during a strike by two unions (United Textile Workers and Amalgamated Textile Workers) and the employers in order that it might "make a thorough study of the wages and living costs of the workers and of the financial condition of the leading textile mills." The LBI found that the company's wage cuts were not dictated by economic necessity, and the unions won the strike.[89]

"ASSUMING RESPONSIBILITY FOR SERVICE": THE B&O EXPERIMENT

In addition to identifying and advocating a role for unions in smoothing the business cycle and determining wages, organized labor and its supporters also worked toward the identification of a role for unions in the day-to-day management of industry. A number of plans emerged from these efforts, but the Baltimore and Ohio Railroad Company (B&O) and the railroad unions adopted the most widely publicized and successful of these plans. By 1926, the "B&O plan" had been extended to twenty-two thousand Baltimore and Ohio railroad employees and adopted by non-Baltimore and Ohio railroads with a total of three hundred thousand employees. Organized labor welcomed the opportunity to work with employers and cooperate in this innovative labor-management agreement.[90] AFL president William Green wrote glowingly of the

---

[87] Nelson Lichtenstein, *The Most Dangerous Man in Detroit: Walther Reuther and the Fate of American Labor* (New York: Basic Books, 1995), 220–47.
[88] LBI, *Annual Report: 1921* (New York: LBI, 1921), 5–6.
[89] LBI, *Annual Report: 1922* (New York: LBI, 1922), 6–7.
[90] Otto S. Beyer, "Three Years of the 'B. and O. Plan'" (August 4, 1926), 298–300; "Baltimore Plan of Shop-Craft Settlement," *The Journal of the Switchmen's Union of North America* XXIV (November 1922): 344–6; Soule, "Work of the Labor Bureau, Inc." 84–9; Thorne, "Facts Workers Need," 80; Otto S. Beyer, "The Shop Crafts Move On," *LA* 8 (March 1924): 1–4; Samuel Gompers, "Cooperative Effort Succeeds," *AF* 31 (July 1924): 574; "The Road to Industrial Democracy," *AF* 31 (July 1924): 484. Otto S. Beyer, "How as Well as What," *AF* 33 (August 1926): 938; "President Willard Addresses Editors," *RC* 26

opportunity and responsibility for "wage earners to participate in the development of constructive management policies and the elimination of waste in industry."[91] Along with promoting labor peace, the B&O plan explicitly worked to unleash workers' knowledge of the production process in pursuit of greater efficiency.[92]

The idea of worker collaboration with employers was, of course, not new. In fact, we can see some similarities between the B&O plan and the building trades, which on the eve of World War I made up more than 21 percent of all union workers. In the building trades, a highly localized system of cooperation between highly skilled construction workers and small employers emerged around the turn of the century.[93] Several differences separate the early building trades model from what emerged in the New Era. The first is the size of the employer: the types of experiments in labor-management cooperation that emerged in the New Era were better suited to large employers who had the resources to develop the administrative infrastructure that made these experiments possible.[94] Second, Willard and the management at the B&O demonstrated a willingness to integrate organized labor into new management strategies, but building contractors and employers in places like San Francisco were having none

(April 1927): 130–1; Elva M. Taylor, "Employee Representation on American Railroads," *AF* 33 (November 1926): 1357–65; Otto S. Beyer, *Railroad Union-Management Cooperation* (Washington, DC: AFL, 1925). For a cautious endorsement of the plan, see "B&O Labor-Management Plan Shows Progress," *LEJ* 60 (February 1926): 117. On the B&O plan more generally, see Vrooman, *Daniel Willard and Progressive Management on the Baltimore and Ohio Railroad* and David Montgomery, *Fall of the House of Labor: The Workplace, the State and American Labor Activism, 1865–1925* (New York: Cambridge University Press, 1987), 422–4.

[91] Green to Beyer, April 25, 1925, Box 113, Folder: Correspondence: 1925, Otto S. Beyer Papers, LOC; William Green to B. M Jewell [president of Railway Employees Department], July 16, 1925, AFL-CIO Railway Employees Department Records, 1916–1968, General Cooperation File 1925, 1926, George Meany Memorial Archives.

[92] On the ability of skilled workers to maintain control, see Daniel Nelson, "Scientific Management and the Workplace, 1920–1935," in Sanford Jacoby, ed., *Masters to Managers: Historical and Comparative Perspectives on American Employers* (New York: Columbia University Press, 1991), 74–89.

[93] On building trades, see, for instance, Michael Kazin, *Barons of Labor: The San Francisco Building Trades and Union Power in the Progressive Era* (Urbana: University of Illinois Press, 1989); Grace Palladino, *Skilled Hands, Strong Spirits: A Century of Building Trades History* (Ithaca: Cornell University Press, 2005); and Montgomery, *Fall of the House of Labor*, 293–302. On the percent of union workers in building trades, see Leo Wolman, *Ebb and Flow in Trade Unionism* (New York: NBER, 1936), 20; and Kazin, *Barons of Labor*, 9.

[94] In San Francisco, the number of contractors fluctuated significantly, but it remained a highly decentralized industry. In 1896, according to Michael Kazin, 879 contractors worked in San Francisco; that number fell to 815 in 1922 and fluctuated from a height of 1,113 in 1910 to a low of 766 in 1920. Kazin, *Barons of Labor*, 295.

of that. As Michael Kazin has argued, construction employers may have adopted the language of "economic stability in the public interest," but rather than seeing a legitimate place for unions, these employers by the early 1920s blamed unions for restrictions on output, "wages set without regard for individual merit, and jurisdictional boundaries which hampered efficiency." Though they may have come to see the need to take on more responsibility for the welfare of their workers, "strong unions," employers in the construction industry came to believe, "made harmonious labor relations impossible."[95]

By implementing an industrial-relations plan that devolved control of production to joint worker-manager determination, Otto S. Beyer, William Johnston, and Daniel Willard created one of the most resilient, widely cited, and successful industrial-relations plans of the 1920s. Beyer constructed the plan while serving as a captain in the U.S. Army during World War I. During the war, Beyer directed the technical training segment of the Ordnance Department at Rock Island and implemented an industrial-relations scheme employing cooperative labor-management committees that reviewed "working conditions, production methods, and piecework rates."[96] Trained as an engineer at Stevens Institute of Technology, Beyer worked in the iron and steel industry and in the mechanical department of the Erie Railroad. His first experience as a manager came in 1913 when he moved to Horton, Kansas as the general foreman of heavy repairs in a railroad locomotive shop. In 1916, Beyer was hired to direct the locomotive testing laboratory at the University of Illinois.[97] During World War I, Beyer became increasingly interested in problems of industrial relations. By the end of the war, he was a full-fledged industrial-relations expert, often serving the heavily unionized railroad industry.[98] By the mid-1920s, Beyer worked as an industrial-relations consultant, a technical advisor for the AFL's Railway Employees Department, and a leader in LBI.

Beyer was joined by William H. Johnston, the controversial president of the International Association of Machinists (IAM), whose tenure

---

[95] Michael Kazin, *Barons of Labor*, 252, 255.
[96] Vrooman, *Daniel Willard and Progressive Management on the Baltimore and Ohio Railroad*, 41; "O. S. Beyer, Jr.," *LEJ* 59 (October 1925): 751; William L. Chenery, "Arsenal Employees' Organization" *Survey Graphic* (May 8, 1920): 205-7.
[97] "Editorials," *Survey Graphic* (January 1924): 353; Chenery, "Arsenal Employees' Organization," 205-7; Vrooman, *Daniel Willard and Progressive Management on the Baltimore and Ohio Railroad*, 40-2.
[98] McCartin, *Labor's Great War*, 211-12.

exemplified labor activists' optimism for a dramatic reorganization of the economy prior to World War I and bitter disappointment following the war. A socialist in his early career, Johnston had led a large contingent of union members who opposed cooperative efforts between the IAM and the National Civic Federation (NCF). In 1911, Johnston was elected president of the IAM and the union passed a referendum forbidding IAM members from joining the NCF. The 1911 election of Johnston as president deeply divided IAM membership and alienated Samuel Gompers and the AFL leadership.[99] The IAM made significant gains in membership during World War I when the federal government took control of the railroads. Following the war, Johnston and the IAM were among the strongest supporters of efforts to bring a version of the Plumb Plan, a labor-led movement in England to nationalize the railroads, to the United States. In the United States, the postwar strike wave, open shop movement, and anticommunist hysteria exacerbated internal tension within the IAM, and Johnston moved to shore up his position by "clamp[ing] down on his rivals in 1919."[100] When Johnston and Beyer met in July 1922 in a meeting organized by Justice Louis Brandeis and an official in the Department of Commerce, it was clear that control of the railroads would remain in the hands of private industry and that employers had beaten organized railroad workers in the 1922 Shopmen's strike.[101]

After some debate, Beyer and Johnston approached Daniel Willard with a proposal to reshape labor relations at the B&O Railroad. Willard grew up in North Hartland, Vermont, the son of a successful farmer and devout Methodist. After a short and unsatisfying attempt at agricultural education at the Massachusetts State Agricultural College in Amherst, Willard started his career in the railroad industry on the track gang with the Vermont Central. He moved steadily up the railroad industry ladder, working as a fireman and later as an engineer, during which time he joined the Brotherhood of Locomotive Engineers. In 1883, his career was temporarily sidetracked when he was laid off by the Lake Shore and Michigan Southern and forced to take a lower position (construction train brakeman) with the Soo Line in Minneapolis. Willard successfully

---

[99] Montgomery, *Fall of the House of Labor*, 290–1; Mark Perlman, *The Machinists: A New Study in American Unionism* (Cambridge: Cambridge University Press, 1961).
[100] McCartin, *Labor's Great War*, 206.
[101] Perlman, *The Machinists*, 56–73. On the Shopmen's Strike, see Dubofsky, *The State and Labor in Modern America*, (Chapel Hill: University of North Carolina Press, 1994), 91–7 and Colin J. Davis, "Bitter Conflict: The 1922 Shopmen's Strike," *Labor History* 33 (Fall 1992): 433–55. On Beyer and Johnston, see also McCartin, *Labor's Great War*.

worked in a number of different jobs with the Soo Line and was eventually promoted to trainmaster in 1890. Willard came to the attention of Frederick D. Underwood, general manager of the Soo Line, who took Willard under his wing. In 1903, James J. Hill offered Willard a fifty thousand dollar salary and a one hundred thousand dollar bonus in exchange for his services as vice-president of the Chicago, Burlington, and Quincy Railroad. From there, Willard was offered the presidency of the B&O Railroad.[102] During a 1927 address before the editors of railroad labor journals, Willard was asked if he would still join a union. He replied, "Yes. If I were an engineer I would join the union of my craft. The workers have as much right to organize as employers, and their organizations benefit them."[103]

Willard, Beyer, and Johnston worked together to overcome ethnic divisions in the railroad's labor force, low morale, and deep distrust between management and workers. Willard chose the Glenwood shop in Pittsburgh as a test site to implement the scheme. Beyer and Johnston were not optimistic about the possibilities for success. According to Beyer, after the 1922 railroad strike "production ... quality of work, morale had sunk to extremely low levels" in the thirteen-hundred-man shop. Additionally, the mixing of returning strikers with strikebreakers compounded preexisting tensions among different ethnic groups. B&O historian David M. Vrooman suggests, "The local union organization spent nearly all of its time and effort trying to settle grievances and to resolve disputes between its own members." Reflecting some years later on the decision, Willard said he believed Glenwood to be "the worst shop," but "if it worked there it would be pretty apt to work any place else."[104] B. M. Jewell, president of the Railway Employees Department of the AFL, noted, "There was undoubtedly less production and higher labor costs in this shop than in any other shop on the B&O, and probably on any other railroad in the United States."[105]

The system designed by Beyer and installed with the support of Johnston and Willard legitimized independent unions in the corporate

---

[102] Vrooman, *Daniel Willard and Progressive Management on the Baltimore and Ohio Railroad*, 1–12.
[103] "President Willard Addresses Editors," 131; "Cooperation with Railroad Officials," *LEJ* 61 (April 1927): 1.
[104] Vrooman, *Daniel Willard and Progressive Management on the Baltimore and Ohio Railroad*, 49.
[105] Gilbert E. Hyatt, "O. S. Beyer – Labor's Consulting Engineer," *RC* 24 (September 1925): 351.

governance structure with the aim of increasing employee-management communication and industrial efficiency and promoting cooperation. Within the first two years of its implementation, the plan yielded dramatic improvements in the quality and maintenance of tools, the supply of stock and material, and the organization of the shop. After an initial survey of employer-employee relations, Beyer scheduled union-management conferences to meet every other week.[106] After a period devoted to clearing up "prevailing misunderstandings between management and men," the shop-level meetings turned their attention to problems in the production process. Worker representatives were invited to present suggestions for improving working conditions and workplace efficiency. These conferences generated an impressive nine thousand ninety recommendations – "at least one constructive proposal ... for every two men employed," according to Beyer – for changes in working conditions, tools, job standards, scheduling, and quality control; only 8 percent "were dropped because they were considered impractical."[107]

Employment stabilization and union recognition were the most important benefits of industrial cooperation for unions and workers, but they were not the only ones. To stabilize employment in slow times, the company agreed to discontinue its practices of contracting out repair work and locomotive modernization. Within four months, the B&O began to modernize some 600 locomotives. The company also expanded its production in brake shoe manufacturing, rolling mills, and car truck manufacturing – work that otherwise would have been contracted out to other firms – as a means of steadying work and maintaining wages. By 1926, B&O employees of all classes increased the average number of days they worked per year by twelve and gained a wage increase Beyer estimated to average two-and-a-quarter cents per hour.[108]

---

[106] By 1925, B&O labor and management had held sixteen hundred and nine meetings. Otto S. Beyer, "Railroad Union-Management Cooperation," *Union Management Cooperation* (Washington, DC: AFL, 1925), 17.

[107] Ibid.; Taylor, "Employee Representation on American Railroads," 1357–65.

[108] Beyer, "Three Years of the 'B. and O. Plan,'" 299. For other defenses of the B&O plan, see Louis Silverstein, "Left Wing and Dual Unionism" *Justice* (April 16, 1926): 5; "The Road to Industrial Democracy," *AF* 31 (July 1924): 481–5; "B&O Employees Get Wage Increase," *The RC* 26 (June 1927): 217. There was some dissent on this issue. Using Interstate Commerce Commission data, *LEJ* contended, "Union management cooperation does not necessarily afford greater stability of employment." Indeed, although it would be difficult to quantify, general improvement in the economy likely accounted for some of the employment stability. "Does B&O Plan Stabilize Employment?" *LEJ* 66 (June 1927): 449.

The AFL pointed with pride to the B&O experiment as a model for cooperative labor relations and stressed the ability of unions to provide the institutional capacity to assist in the management of an efficient and disciplined work force. In a labor relations climate where unions were constantly under attack from aggressive employers, the B&O plan demonstrated to the public the possibility of labor accord between reasonable employers and unions and organized labor's ability and willingness to work with employers to increase efficiency, profits, and consumption. In defending the plan in the pages of the Amalgamated Clothing Workers (ACW) journal, ACW research director Leo Wolman described the plan as "a simple device" that allowed unions to assume "administrative responsibilities."[109] Indeed, the plan did provide worker representatives with the opportunity and obligation to discipline obstinate workers. According to Vrooman, union committeemen could and frequently did request "transfers of recalcitrant coworkers to less desirable jobs around the shop."[110] Sometimes the unions' willingness to think like hard-driving managers appeared a bit absurd, as in the case when the union agreed that a Railroad Labor Board ruling that mandated a paid twenty-minute lunch for second and third shifts would be enforced only "under certain special conditions."[111]

Despite these caveats, observers noted that the involvement of workers in the management of industry expanded workers' visions of their importance to the shop and company. They saw something more than platitude in Willard's assessment that active involvement in the plan gave every employee "an enlightened and enlarged view of his own worth and importance as part of the great organization known as the Baltimore & Ohio Railroad."[112] The *Railway Clerk*, the monthly publication of the Brotherhood of Railway and Steamship Clerks, editorialized:

The "state of mind" of the employes is impressed upon one wherever one comes in contact with B&O employes. Their loyalty to the company, their manifest desire to please its patrons, their eagerness to contribute in every way possible to the success of the company is reminiscent of the old days.... In those days every

---

[109] Leo Wolman, "The New Unionism – What Is It?" *The Advance* 10 (December 3, 1926): 9.
[110] Vrooman, *Daniel Willard and Progressive Management on the Baltimore and Ohio Railroad*, 52.
[111] Otto S. Beyer, "B&O Engine 1003," *Survey Graphic* (January 1, 2004): 315. This apparent concession must be considered in the context of the Railroad Labor Board's inability to enforce any of its antiemployer rulings.
[112] Vrooman, *Daniel Willard and Progressive Management on the Baltimore and Ohio Railroad*, 55.

railroader worked for "the best damn railroad in the country." That expression is still popular among B&O employes.[113]

The economic benefits to the company were a source of pride to Willard and the labor movement, which framed the increased profitability of the B&O as affirmation of the benefits of unionization and cooperation. The *JEWO* contrasted the profitability and stability of the B&O with the performance of the Pennsylvania Railroad, which was led by W. W. Atterbury, a champion of the open shop movement. The *Journal* reported:

> Railroad men and financial experts everywhere are commenting on the fact that the Baltimore and Ohio stands out from most of the roads of the country, not merely in improved financial condition, but also in the improved condition of its equipment and service.[114]

After the introduction of the plan, management benefited from fewer grievances, less labor turnover, increased quality of work, greater efficiency, and less absenteeism.[115] Shortly after the start of the program, the B&O resumed the payment of a 5 percent dividend on common stock and announced a significant decrease in its operating ratio (percent of expenses taken out of revenues), both accomplished at a time when the railroad was expanding and other railroads, notably the Pennsylvania, experienced trends in the other direction. Additionally, B&O reliability and productivity increased relative to its competitors and its own previous record.[116]

The B&O plan was not without its detractors, particularly from organized labor's left flank, which had a visceral reaction to worker-management

---

[113] "President Willard Address Editors," *RC* 26 (April 1927): 130.
[114] "A Proof of Union Efficiency," *JEWO* 23 (December 1923): 9. The B&O remained profitable throughout the 1920s. See "B & O Plan Boosts Profits," *LEJ* 63 (February 1929): 101.
[115] Beyer, "B & O Engine 1003," 315.
[116] Beyer and other B&O advocates made numerous favorable comparisons between the railroad and its competitors. Ibid., 316–17. For a more thorough discussion of the increased profitability and efficiency of the B&O, see Taylor, "Employee Representation on American Railroads," 1362; "Cooperation of Trade-Unions with Employers," *MLR* 27 (October 1924): 4–8; LBI, "What Did Anti-Unionism Gain on the Railroads," *FFW* 4 (February 1926): 1; LBI, "Railroad Autocrats Pay the Piper," *FFW* 1 (March 1923): 2; LBI, "Railroad Repair Policy," *FFW* 2 (May 1924): 1; Ottos S. Beyer, "Labor's Contribution to the Scientific Organization of Industry," *AF* 35 (January 1928): 32–35; and LBI, "A Proof of Union Efficiency," *FFW* 2 (November 1923): 1–3; and Sumner Slichter, "Competitive Exchange as a Method of Interesting Workmen in Output and Costs," *Papers and Proceedings of the Thirty-Seventh Annual Meeting of the American Economic Association* (March 1925): 100.

ILLUSTRATION 3.2. Baltimore and Ohio cartoon from the December 1923 *Journal of Electrical Workers and Operators* depicting the benefits of the B&O plan to the company. Atterbury, the figure depicted on the left, was the fiercely antiunion head of the Pennsylvania Railroad. Image courtesy of the International Brotherhood of Electrical Workers Museum.

cooperation, which they understood as a product of class collaboration. The *Labor Herald* routinely attacked the "great treachery" of the B&O plan and "those that thrust it down our throats."[117] The *Daily Worker* damned the plan as a company union aligned with open shop principles and designed to commodify workers. A few lodges in the deeply divided IAM took particular exception to Johnston and union leaders, whom they portrayed as willing to sell out workers in order to preserve their leadership positions in the wake of disastrous postwar strikes. At the seventeenth convention of the IAM in 1924, Seattle Lodge #79 argued, "By the victimization of its most active members, the union will be, and is being used to forward class collaboration, which is sure to result in more damnably intolerable conditions." Winnipeg Lodge #122 described the plan as a "sugar coated pill, which contained within itself the elements for the destruction of all the principles for which the organization had stood and fought in the past." The Winnipeg lodge went on to suggest that B&O-style agreements undercut the principle of class struggle embraced formally by the IAM in its constitution.[118] Even the largely sympathetic *Locomotive Engineers Journal* wondered about the plan: "Just how one person can compel another to 'cooperate' with him is somewhat of a mystery."[119] E. J. Lever, a leader in labor education in Philadelphia and district representative for the Philadelphia Lodges of the IAM, found strengths in the plan but recognized that unions had been "compelled to lean this way, because of our inherent weakness and inability to lick our open shop adversaries in open combat."[120]

[117] "B. and O. Plan to be attacked," *MMJ* 36 (August 1924): 366–7. For a similar debate concerning the Mitten-Mahon Agreement, see W. Jett Lauck, "Mitten-Mahon Agreement" and J. M. Budish, "At the Parting of the Ways," *LA* 12 (September 1928): 2–6; J. M. Budish, "A Suicidal Policy," *LA* 7 (October 1923): 15–19.

[118] IAM, *Proceedings of the 17th Convention of the International Association of Machinists*, (Washington DC: IAM, 1924), 233–41; David M. Schneider, *The Workers' (Communist) Party and American Trade Unions* (Baltimore: Johns Hopkins University Press, 1928).

[119] Harvey O'Connor, "Railroaders at Brookwood," *LEJ* 60 (September 1926): 712; "B&O Shopmen's System Spreads," *LEJ* 58 (February 1924): 113; Stolberg, "The New Unionism," 299.

[120] E. J. Lever, "Continue the Militant Program" *LA* 8 (March 1924): 6; "Emil John Lever," *Who's Who in Labor* (New York: The Dryden Press, 1946), 208. As a member of the Philadelphia IAM, Lever would have had firsthand experience confronting the open shop employer offensive. After World War I, metal trades employers formed a national association that led the fight against unions. For more on the employer offensive in Philadelphia, see Howell Harris, *Bloodless Victories: the Rise and Fall of the Open Shop in the Philadelphia Metal Trades, 1890–1940* (Cambridge: Cambridge University Press, 2000). For general criticism of the labor movement strategy in the period, see "A Motionless Labor Movement," 30–2; and Stolberg, "The New Unionism," 292–300.

Despite the union's post-strike weakness and accusations of class collaboration, labor experts in unions and in business declared that the B&O experiment worked for employers, employees, and unions. In exchange for a significant employer effort to stabilize employment and wages, B&O employees actively worked to improve the quality of the railroad. In return for workers assuming the goals of management (i.e., efficiency and productivity), B&O managers appeared willing to embrace unionized workers. In fact, Beyer went so far as to suggest that workers at the B&O shop acquired a "distinct and useful position in the administrative machinery of the shop ... on par in many respects with the shop supervision."[121] Even leftist labor leaders such as Norman Thomas conceded the plan had been "responsible for greatly improved morale and for more efficient standards of production."[122]

CONCLUSION

During the New Era, the Hooverites largely set the industrial relations and economic policy agenda. The general rightward tilt in the political environment, combined with postwar strike losses, left organized labor dramatically weakened and unwilling or unable to challenge this agenda. Instead, unions and their supporters worked to find a role for organized labor in addressing problems such as the business cycle, waste in industry, and labor-management conflict on the shop room floor. In doing so, organized labor created new institutions that might persuade employers and policy makers that wages needed to be increased in proportion to productivity increases and that unions should play an important role in monitoring and maintaining these wages in their own, but also the public, interest.

The AFL thought its numerous reports on wages would enable organized labor to "warn industry and the public" of a declining labor's share "before it is too late."[123] Labor investigators found no solace in industries where real wages may have stabilized or increased between 1904 and 1925, if these gains had been outpaced by productivity increases. In describing the pig iron industry, Kuczynski acknowledged that "real wages were increasing, no doubt." Even so, "It is not enough that the workman can buy today more commodities than yesterday." What matters is that

---

[121] Beyer, "B & O Engine 1003," 312.
[122] Norman Thomas, "Democracy for Industry," *LEJ* 61 (March 1927): 183.
[123] "An Index of Labor's Share in Production and in Consumption," *AF* 35 (April 1928): 490.

"his share in the national product ought to be kept at the same level."[124] Rather than limiting themselves to demanding "more" for unionized workers, the AFL now pursued a policy it hoped would give union leaders a powerful hand, not only in bargaining for workers, but with a more equal role with business and the state in managing the economy.

In doing so, many labor leaders accepted the basic idea that labor and capital could work out an accord based on Hoover's vision of a new capitalism that featured efficient production and workplace cooperation as the path to increased wages, profits, consumption, production, and economic stability. In 1929, labor expert and John L. Lewis confidant W. Jett Lauck confidently announced a truce between organized labor and employers. According to Lauck:

> The net result [of new wage theories and policies] has been that the employer, realizing that the continuing profitableness of industry is dependent upon an expansion of purchasing power, has willingly accepted and declared that there may be indeterminate wage increases as long as costs [of production] are not increasing and the proper margin of profit is maintained. Organized labor has also given its adherence to this point of view and pledged its cooperation in bringing about the desired end as long as it receives its proper reward.[125]

Though the mechanisms to coerce employers to increase wages and to determine what constituted a "proper margin of profit" and "proper reward" were never fully developed, Lauck and other labor experts were prescient in their understanding of the relationship between consumption and economic growth and stability. In the summer of 1930, as the Great Depression was just taking hold, even Hunt seemed to acknowledge the wisdom of this approach and the possibility that he and Hoover may have overlooked key details. As he cast about for explanations for the downturn, he wrote to economist and Department of Commerce official Dana Durand, "Ever since the depression of 1920–21 and partly as a result of the work of Foster and Catchings there has been great interest in the problem of the buyer's strike, or what amounts to the same thing, curtailed purchasing power." Hunt inquired, "Have you any information which indicates that the present depression is different in some fundamental particular from that of previous depressions?"[126]

---

[124] Kuczynski and Steinfeld, "Wages in the Pig Iron Industry," 560–1. Compare to Donahue, *Freedom from Want*, 190.

[125] W. Jett Lauck, *The New Industrial Revolution and Wages* (New York: Funk and Wagnalls, 1929), 222–3.

[126] General Records of the Department of Commerce, Stack Area 70, row 4, Compartment 20–1, Shelf 5, Office of the Secretary, Subject Files of Asst. Secretary of Commerce E. E. Hunt, 1921–1931, Box 1, File: Misc Dana Durand, RG 40, NA.

The New Era work of Lauck, Hansen, the AFL, the LBI, and others provided a ready-made answer to that question. It should come as no surprise, then, that Lauck and other labor experts from the 1920s would go on to play a key role in constructing strong industrial unions and federal policies supporting a post–World War II economic system that relied heavily on worker consumption as a means of maintaining economic stability.[127] In 1946, Congress passed into law the Employment Act, which created the Council of Economic Advisors (CEA) and charged it "to promote employment, production, and purchasing power." During the New Era, organized labor and its allies sought just such a role for themselves and, in doing so, worked to focus the wage debate on the critical role wages played in stabilizing a highly productive and increasingly consumer-driven economy.

---

[127] For more on the impact of the underconsumption argument on the New Deal and post-New Deal policies, see Jacobs, *Purchasing Power*.

4

A New Capitalism?

Interrogating Employers' Efforts to Cultivate a "Feeling of Partnership" in Industry

> Perhaps one of the most striking developments of the new capitalism have been the changes in the structure of industry. Of these changes the growing separation between ownership and control is of great importance.
> – Harry W. Laidler

> So long as this tendency toward concentration of great wealth exists, there can hardly be any new capitalism.
> – Mary van Kleeck

In part because of their great faith in the wisdom of business leaders whom they believed would administer labor-capital relations in an efficient and fair manner, and in part due to willful ignorance, the Hooverites took for granted that the new version of capitalism provided a framework for melting away class conflict in the American workplace. The B&O experiment seemed to confirm that, given the changes in the economy, labor-capital relations could now, in fact, be worked out to a remarkable degree. But others saw more problematic developments in the organization of industry and in the concentration of economic power that undermined the widely heralded "feeling of partnership in industry," championed by the secretary of labor and many others.[1]

In a 1928 letter in response to French writer M. Just Haristoy, who himself was writing a book on industrial relations experiments in the United States, Mary van Kleeck of the Russell Sage Foundation (RSF) expressed deep skepticism about the whole notion of a "new capitalism."

---

[1] James J. Davis, *Thirteenth Annual Report of the Secretary of Labor* (Washington, DC: GPO, 1925), 136–7.

Haristoy had asked Van Kleeck a two-pronged question: first, what the advantages and disadvantages were to employees and employers of increased participation in stock ownership plans, and second, "whether there is actually a new capitalism and what its future might be." To the first, Van Kleeck gave sound investment advice concerning the dangers of tying one's savings, earnings, and investments to one's workplace – if the company failed, one would lose all three. Combining the questions, Van Kleeck noted that one of the arguments for employee stock ownership was that it would lead to a "diffusion of control which is the essence of the so-called new capitalism." She was dubious about the prospect that placing a modest percentage of a company's stock in the hands of employees could fundamentally alter the nature of capitalism. Van Kleeck asked, "Can there be new capitalism unless there be coupled with employe [sic] stock ownership some representation of the employes in the direction and management of industry?" and concluded firmly: "So long as this tendency toward concentration of great wealth exists, there can hardly be any new capitalism."[2]

Van Kleeck framed her response to Haristoy's query much too modestly, writing that his questions were ones that "I have in my own mind," but not based on "first hand knowledge."[3] In fact, by late 1928, when she responded to Haristoy, no one was better equipped to answer these powerful questions. Van Kleeck came to the study of labor relations with a broad background in political economy that allowed her to understand, more clearly than her peers, the importance of grounding analysis of public problems in a larger understanding of industrial conditions and economic change. In 1904, Van Kleeck had completed her A.B. at Smith College, where she took a number of economics courses and became involved in the industrial work of the YWCA and the Smith College Association for Christian Work. Between graduation and 1909, Van Kleeck worked in New York City as an investigator for a number of reform organizations, including the New York Child Labor Committee and the Consumers' League and Alliance Employment Bureau. During this period, she held a

---

[2] Mary van Kleeck to M. Just Haristoy, November 12, 1928, Box 52, Folder 849, Emp. Rep. General Correspondence, Mary van Kleeck Papers, Sophia Smith Collection, Smith College, Northampton, Massachusetts (hereafter MVK Papers). On employee stock ownership in the period, see Thomas Nixon Carver, *The Present Economic Revolution in the United States* (Boston: Little, Brown, and Company, 1926), especially chapter four. Carver frequently drew attention to the idea of an increasing "diffusion of ownership."

[3] Mary van Kleeck to M. Just Haristoy. For Haristoy's observations, see M. Just Haristoy, *L'Epargne de Travailleurs* (Paris: Marcel Giard, 1932).

College Settlements Association and Smith College Alumnae Association Joint Fellowship that funded her research and allowed her to begin her graduate work in social economy at Columbia, where she studied with economist Henry R. Seager, a longtime defender of organized labor and advocate of public policies to protect workers and retirees. In 1908, Van Kleeck began her long association with the RSF while working on an RSF-funded study of women workers. A year later, the RSF established and Van Kleeck led a Committee in Women's Work. By 1914, she concluded, "distress and poverty among women workers are but phases of" larger "industrial and social conditions." Within two years, she had persuaded the RSF to broaden her department's work to include investigations of all areas of work, renaming it the Division of Industrial Studies.[4] After her World War I service as director of the Woman-In-Industry Service (addressed in greater detail in Chapter 5), Van Kleeck returned to the RSF, where she mounted investigations into New Era labor-capital relations and assisted in the reorganization of government labor statistics after the war. During her World War I service, Van Kleeck worked actively with African American leaders to ensure that black women's experiences were reflected in Department of Labor (DOL) reports. Once she returned to the RSF, she led efforts by the Social Science Research Council (SSRC), National Urban League (NUL), and others to diversify the labor question so that it more accurately reflected the experiences of women and African American workers.

In a period of uncertainty about how to make sense of the proliferation of industrial relations schemes employers promoted as heralding a new phase in American capitalism, labor experts developed a knowledge base on which the public could gauge the success of these programs. Coming from the perspective of expert observers assessing the potential

---

[4] Guy Alchon, "Mary Van Kleeck and Scientific Management," in Daniel Nelson, ed., *A Mental Revolution: Scientific Management since Taylor* (Columbus: Ohio State University Press, 1992), 105. On Van Kleeck, see also John Thomas McGuire, "Continuing an Alternative View of Public Administration: Mary van Kleeck and Industrial Citizenship, 1918–1927," *Administration and Society* 43 (2011): 66–86; Guy Alchon, "The 'Self-Applauding Sincerity' of Overarching Theory, Biography as Ethical Practice, and the Case of Mary van Kleeck," in Helen Silverberg, ed., *Engendering Social Science: The Formative Years* (Princeton: Princeton University Press, 1998), 293–325; Alice O'Connor, *Social Science For What?: Philanthropy and the Social Question in a World Turned Rightside Up* (Russell Sage Foundation: 2007), 41–4; Mary van Kleeck, "Women in the Munitions Industries," *Life and Labor* (June 1918): 113; "Biography of Mary Van Kleeck" Box 3, File "Van Kleeck, Mary (Biographical Data)," USDOL The Woman in Industry Service, Record Group (hereafter RG) 86, National Archives (hereafter NA).

A New Capitalism?

of these new strategies for labor relations to promote a new version of capitalism and greater democratization of industry, this chapter examines the findings of the era's most important site for evaluating the success, failure, and prospects of these programs. Over the course of the New Era, the RSF conducted four in-depth studies that illustrate larger trends in labor experts' examination of labor relations in the 1920s, but with a level of rigor unmatched in other efforts. These investigations took place at the Filene Department Store and the Dutchess Bleachery and included two separate investigations of the Rockefeller plan in the coal and steel industry. Under the leadership of Mary van Kleeck, the RSF published these critical but hopeful studies that informed industrialists and workers' understandings of the benefits and limitations of shop committee and employee representation systems. In general, RSF investigators noted improvements in the living and working conditions of workers employed in firms that adopted new labor relations plans, but they looked skeptically at dramatic claims that such arrangements brought meaningful employee representation to the workplace.

These Van Kleeck-led studies constitute one of the decade's most searching examinations of the dramatic changes under way in the relationship between labor, capital, stockholders, and management. In a substantive way, RSF investigators wrestled with the core of the labor question. They sought to assess the potential of new management strategies to square the democratic promise of the nation with the present structure of industry. Van Kleeck outlined the central problem of the RSF studies and hinted at a broader evolution in social thought wherein intellectuals searched for a means of accommodating capitalism to evolving conceptualizations of the individual or the self:

How can the complex and impersonal character of large-scale modern industry be reconciled with the need of human beings not only to earn a livelihood but to have the satisfaction of self-direction and self-expression in work? In those industries which have sought to find a solution by giving wage-earners as a group some share in management, what have been the actual results in day-to-day practice?[5]

Van Kleeck's questions, investigations, and thoughtful deliberation were part of a larger effort, reaching back to the nineteenth century, to cull meaning from the emergence of capitalism in the United States. As artisans and farmers lost autonomy and independence to markets and bosses, intellectuals moved toward replacing earlier conceptions of the

---

[5] Quoted in Mary La Dame, *The Filene Store* (New York: Russell Sage Foundation, 1930), 35.

virtuous individual as an independent man who was not beholden to a master or market with a new vision of society that emphasized the interdependency of individuals of all classes. According to historian Jeffrey Sklansky, despite growing inequality and greater concentration of the means of production, "liberty as well as equality appeared to depend less on the distribution of property than on popular participation in spiritual and material rewards of industrial progress." In this context, according to Sklansky, both employers and employees were understood to have "shared in the rising prosperity ... while the means of production remained under corporate control." Sklansky sees great danger in this shift, which he associates with the marginalization of political economy and class as categories for understanding economic, social, and political institutions and relations.[6] The RSF studies were not an effort to recover the "republican man" in the modern workplace, but they do, as the Van Kleeck quote reflects, represent part of this larger effort among labor experts, intellectuals, and investigators to find some means of recognizing the individual's worth and role in a modern industrial economy.

Van Kleeck and the RSF were hardly alone in their efforts to interrogate efforts to mediate the growing chasm between citizenship and labor by way of diffusion in the management of industries. Labor and industrial relations experts during and immediately after the war looked widely for practices and policies that might bring about a new, more democratic, organization of industry. Between 1915 and 1922, the *Monthly Labor Review*, a publication of the Department of Labor that reprinted articles from a wide variety of sources, published more than 100 studies describing various attempts to increase worker representation in the management of industry. John L. Lewis confidant and advisor W. Jett Lauck, University of Wisconsin economist John R. Commons, and journalist Ray Stannard Baker all produced lengthy surveys of industrial democratic and employee representation schemes.[7] Many of these observers agreed

---

[6] Jeffrey Sklansky, *The Soul's Economy: Market Society and Selfhood in American Thought, 1820–1920* (Chapel Hill: University of North Carolina Press, 2002), 3. See also Robert H. Wiebe, *Self-Rule: A Cultural History of American Democracy* (Chicago: University of Chicago Press, 1995) and James Livingston, *Pragmatism and the Political Economy of Cultural Revolution, 1850–1994* (Chapel Hill: University of North Carolina Press, 1994).

[7] W. Jett Lauck, *Political and Industrial Democracy, 1776–1926* (New York: Funk and Wagnalls Company, 1926); John R. Commons et al., *Industrial Government* (New York: The Macmillan Company, 1921); Ray Stannard Baker, *The New Industrial Unrest: Reasons and Remedies* (Garden City, NY: Doubleday, Page and Company, 1920). On industrial democracy, see Joseph A. McCartin, *Labor's Great War: The Struggle*

with Lauck, who contrasted earlier conceptions of industrial democracy that stressed the conflicting interests of workers and employers with a "new regime" that substituted "cooperation for conflict, confidence for distrust, and helpfulness for competition and restriction."[8]

As Van Kleeck more than others knew well, New Era efforts to cultivate new variations on capitalism that enhanced a feeling of partnership in industry took place against a backdrop of continued change in the organization of American industry, whereby managers and corporate leaders became increasingly accountable to faceless shareholders rather than propriety capitalists. Management's relative anonymity and the more disparate power structure in the ownership and finance of modern industry complicated even well-meaning efforts to expand the scope of workers' influence in industry. Diffusion – to use a tem employed by Van Kleeck and many others in the New Era – was not just an aspiration for new management schemes on the shop room floor; it was also reality for disparate individuals and institutions to whom those who administered, managed, and worked capital were responsible. To state this in more concrete terms, in an earlier era, if you had an issue with a proprietary capitalist's enterprise – say Carnegie Steel – you knew who to take it up with. In a modern corporation, shareholding spread ownership among a multitude of largely passive individual stockholders with next to no control over the actual running of the firm.

Van Kleeck gave voice to the dilemmas that grew out of this change in the structure of capitalism. For instance, in a confidential memo to John Glenn lamenting the repudiation of cooperative plans by company stockholders and investors in two companies examined by the Russell Sage Foundation, Van Kleeck asked, "What, after all, should be the relation of stockholders to the directing of policy of a company?"[9] Van Kleeck

---

for *Industrial Democracy and the Origins of Modern Labor Relations, 1912–1921* (Chapel Hill: University of North Carolina Press, 1997); Gary Gerstle, *Working-Class Americanism: The Politics of Labor in a Textile City, 1914–1960* (New York, 1989); Milton Derber, *The American Idea of Industrial Democracy, 1865–1965* (Urbana: University of Illinois Press, 1970); Steven Fraser, "Dress Rehearsal for the New Deal: Shop-Floor Insurgents, Political Elites, and Industrial Democracy in the Amalgamated Clothing Workers Union," in Michael Frisch and Daniel Walkowitz, eds., *Working Class America* (Champaign: University of Illinois Press, 1983), pp. 212–255; and many useful chapters in Nelson Lichtenstein and Howell John Harris, eds., *Industrial Democracy in America: The Ambiguous Promise* (Cambridge: Cambridge University Press, 1993).

[8] Lauck, *Political and Industrial Democracy*, 115.
[9] Mary van Kleeck to Glenn, January 1, 1929, Box 103, Folder 1591, Filene Study Correspondence, MVK Papers.

did not struggle with these issues alone. In his consideration of "new capitalism," Harry W. Laidler, the executive director for the League for Industrial Democracy, identified the "separation between ownership and control" as the most "striking development of the new capitalism." General Electric's Owen D. Young observed that the "modern business organization of large size" has "completely divorced ownership from responsibility. Now ownership has little or no relation to the conduct of the business."[10]

Here, we can see Young, Laidler, and Van Kleeck wrestling with a set of questions similar to that of Gardiner Means and Adolf Berle. In their 1932 book, *The Modern Corporation and Private Property*, Berle and Means observed the emergence and consequences of the rise of the modern corporation, where ownership and control had been separated. Berle and Means warned against the powerlessness of largely passive stockholders who had little control over the corporate managers who ran the firm on a day-to-day basis. Van Kleeck and the RSF investigators she led observed similar changes in capitalism, but they shifted the emphasis to a different set of questions. Rather than emphasize aspects of the fiduciary responsibility of corporate managers to shareholders, Van Kleeck and her fellow investigators worried, instead, that managers were too beholden to shareholders and fixated on short-term profits. In this context, they feared stockholders would force the abandonment of any effort by management to improve working conditions and worker compensation if they came at the expense of profit. What they found in their investigations confirmed many of these same concerns.[11]

INTERROGATING NEW CAPITALISM: THE RSF STUDIES

Spurred by postwar managerial innovations, the RSF conducted four investigations of employer-initiated programs to transform labor-capital relations in manufacturing and service industries. Established in 1907 by Margaret Olivia Sage, the widow of a wealthy speculator and financier, the RSF had a long-standing interest in the labor question reaching back to its early years when it financed a path-breaking investigation of life in industrial Pittsburgh, which was published as a six-volume report, the

---

[10] Harry W. Laidler, "The New Capitalism and the Socialist," *Annals of the American Academy of Political and Social Science* 149 (May 1930): 12–13.
[11] Adolf Berle and Gardiner Means, *The Modern Corporation and Private Property* (New York: Columbia University Press, 1931).

Pittsburgh Survey. The four investigations conducted in the 1920s by the RSF did not attempt to provide a representative sample of early 1920s labor relations practices; rather, RSF investigators used these studies as vehicles to examine critically some of the most highly touted experiments in progressive labor relations.

The RSF allocated unmatched resources of money, time, and labor to develop a body of expertise on labor relations in the 1920s. In their investigations, RSF representatives spent months interviewing managers and workers, attending meetings, and examining company records. Although fine studies of industrial democracy, welfare capitalism, and cooperation in industry were completed by Commons, Lauck, and many others, no other investigation in the 1920s approached the RSF's in its commitment to the topic or access to the inner workings of the plans. Despite some employer objections to the analysis produced, the studies were used by a wide variety of periodicals, academics, policy makers, business, and worker groups as definitive assessments of what could be accomplished through negotiation and cooperation at the level of the firm. According to Van Kleeck, the studies aimed to "present the facts for the benefit of others who may be thinking of adopting or developing similar plans, believing that to be the best method to find ways for improving industrial relations."[12]

Three of the studies were published in 1924, including examinations of shared management plans in the steel, coal, and textile industries. The final RSF industrial investigation, published in 1930, shifted the analysis from the manufacturing industry to the rapidly expanding service and distribution sector, which employed an increasing number of women workers in pink- and white-collar occupations. Experiences with labor unrest and unionization varied. Though some unions did exist in the bleachery investigation, the employers viewed them as contributors to the democratizing process. As a group, service employees in the Filene Department Store did not develop a tradition of unionization, and, as Van Kleeck noted, the employee organizations that did exist were "developed on the initiative of the employers not of the employes."[13]

---

[12] Mary van Kleeck to W. L. Mackenzie King, January 7, 1921, Box 15, MVK Papers. Van Kleeck made similar statements in a number of correspondences, articles, and speeches, including Van Kleeck to A. Lincoln Filene, June 9, 1921, Box 103, Folder Filene Study Correspondence, MVK Papers.

[13] La Dame, *The Filene Store*, 40. On the effort to organize department store employees, see Susan Porter Benson, *Counter Cultures: Saleswomen, Managers, and Customers in American Department Stores, 1890–1940* (Urbana: University of Illinois Press, 1986),

The context for the steel and coal industry investigations was very different. Workers before and after World War I engaged in an unsuccessful struggle to establish a union in the Rockefeller-owned Colorado Fuel and Iron Company. In response to violent and well-publicized confrontations, John D. Rockefeller, Jr. worked clumsily at first with industrial relations expert Mackenzie King in an attempt to build a system of employee representation that would provide labor peace without collective bargaining. Taken together, the investigations of these experiments pointed to the difficulties in implementing democratic plans in large, modern corporations, but they also conveyed employer recognition of the increasing obsolescence of older managerial philosophies associated with the drive system and small-scale proprietary capitalism. This was particularly true in the department store, where, as historian Susan Porter Benson has described, counter workers derived power from their near autonomous relationship with customers, forcing managers to rely on "persuasion not command" in their supervision of workers.[14]

THE FILENE DEPARTMENT STORE AND DUTCHESS BLEACHERY INVESTIGATIONS

The Filene Department Store and the Dutchess Bleachery each had interesting attributes that recommended them to the RSF for investigation. Its visibility and durability, as well as the Filene brothers' familiarity with the mission of philanthropic inquiry, made the department store an ideal candidate for RSF investigation. Since the store's founding in 1898, the Filene family publicized the progressive plan in an effort to promote industrial cooperation and extend the rights of citizenship into the workplace. Newspapers, magazines, academic publications, and labor relations texts all gave considerable attention to the Filenes' handiwork. The Filene family also encouraged nonprofit investigation of private interests.[15] Edward A. Filene was a leader in the movement to use philanthropy and nonprofits as a means of investigating and proposing solutions to public, and in particular industrial, problems. In 1910, he established the

---

269; William R. Leach, "Transformations in a Culture of Consumption: Women and Department Stores, 1890–1925," *JAH* 71 (September 1984): 319–42.

[14] Benson, *Counter Cultures*, 288. On the role of these studies in light of changes at RSF, see O'Connor, *Social Science For What?*, 4 and 13–70.

[15] Van Kleeck and Miss Bernice M. Canon, a leader at Filene's, exchanged a number of letters in 1921 discussing whether the family would be willing to allow the RSF to examine its cooperative plan. Mary van Kleeck to Cannon, May 27, 1921 and Cannon to Mary van Kleeck, June 13, 1921, Box 103, Folder 1591, Filene Study Correspondence, MVK Papers.

Cooperative League – renamed the Twentieth Century Fund in 1922 – as a progressive philanthropic organization to promote "the investigation and study of any and all matters relating to civic democracy and industrial democracy."[16] Finally, though there had been many efforts to establish cooperative systems in manufacturing industries, the institution of a program for industrial democracy in a nonmanufacturing industry heightened Van Kleeck and the RSF's interest in the program.[17]

Whereas the Filene experiment was deeply rooted in the company's culture, the Dutchess Bleachery provided investigators with an opportunity to examine the implementation of a program that attempted to pivot labor-capital relations almost on a dime. More so than the Filene investigation, such an experiment would have been highly relevant to observers considering such plans for already existing firms. Additionally, the Dutchess Bleachery provided RSF investigators with an opportunity to examine an ambitious plan providing employees with wide powers to participate in determining their working and living conditions. Garner Print Works and Bleachery (GPWB), a holding company in New York City, owned the Wappinger Falls mill. After purchasing the mill in 1909, GPWB quickly discovered that neglect and "discipline with a vengeance" by the previous owners, as RSF investigator Ben Selekman described it, had alienated workers and the community. GPWB made an effort to work with employees in the plant, but failed to invest in the already dilapidated company-owned housing. Continued poor labor relations and the need to increase production during World War I forced company leaders to again consider their relationship with employees. After a survey of conditions by the treasurer, company leaders developed a plan to improve management's understanding of workers, educate workers on the entire production process, and increase the stability of employment. Van Kleeck

---

[16] Edward C. Elliot and M. M. Chambers, *Charters of Philanthropies: A Study of the Charters of Twenty-Nine American Philanthropic Foundations* (New York: The Carnegie Foundation for the Advancement of Teaching, 1939), 671; Adolf Berle, *Leaning Against the Dawn: An Appreciation of the Twentieth Century Fund and its Fifty Years of Adventure in Seeking to Influence American Development toward a more Effective Just Civilization* (United States of America: The Twentieth Century Fund, Inc., 1969); Gerald W. Johnson, *Liberal's Progress: Edward A. Filene, Shopkeeper to Social Statesman* (New York: Coward McCann, 1948); Meg Jacobs, "Constructing a New Political Economy: Philanthropy, Institution-Building, and Consumer Capitalism in the Early Twentieth Century" in Ellen Condliffe Lagemann, ed., *Philanthropic Foundations: New Scholarship, New Possibilities* (Bloomington: Indiana University Press, 1999), 101–18; James Gilbert, *Designing the Industrial State: The Intellectual Pursuit of Collectivism in America, 1880–1940* (Chicago: Quadrangle Books, 1972).

[17] La Dame, *The Filene Store*, 48.

described the firm's owners as sincere in their efforts to provide a "more democratic as well as a more personal basis for human relations in industry." Van Kleeck hoped that the RSF study would "lead to equally far-seeing experiments in other industrial establishments."[18]

The character of the department store and bleachery work forces provided an opportunity for understanding the expectations of women and immigrant workers. Whereas the steel and coal industries were dominated by men, 70 percent of department store employees were women. The presence of a number of women in management positions further separated Filene's from many industrial experiments in the United States. The report noted women in many "better paid" positions, including division and outside shop managers as well as heads of the Training Department, Expense Control Department, Personal Service Bureau, Clothing Information Bureau, Comparison Department, and Bureau of Standards.[19] The bleachery employed a smaller number of women, only 30 percent of the operatives, but it had a large number of Italian workers, many of whom, according to company leaders, did not speak English.[20]

Three experienced RSF investigators conducted the Filene and Dutchess investigations. Edwin E. Smith and Mary La Dame conducted the Filene study, with La Dame writing the final draft. La Dame had worked in department stores, including the Filene Department Store, for six years prior to her involvement with the Bureau of Salesmanship Research of the Carnegie Institute of Technology, where she developed and implemented psychological tests for sales personnel. La Dame joined the RSF Department of Industrial Studies two years before the beginning of the Filene study in August 1921.[21] Van Kleeck served as a mentor to Edwin Smith, who would later play an important role in the implementation of New Deal labor policy. Smith had contributed to a number of earlier RSF investigations, including examinations of the Dennison Manufacturing Company and the Works Council of the Rock Island Arsenal. Smith left the RSF after the completion of the investigation to become an employment manager for the Filene Company, a position he occupied for a short time before becoming a special assistant to A. Lincoln Filene. Smith would later

---

[18] Ben M. Selekman, *Sharing Management With Workers* (New York: Russell Sage Foundation, 1925), xiv.
[19] La Dame, *The Filene Store*, 93.
[20] Selekman, *Sharing Management With Workers*, 32–3.
[21] La Dame, *The Filene Store*, 41–2. See also John M. Glenn, Lilian Brandt, and F. Emerson Andrews, *Russell Sage Foundation, 1907–1946* (New York: Russell Sage Foundation, 1947), 358–9, 383, 387, 392, 395, 650, and 680.

join the Division of Economic Research of the National Labor Relations Board (NLRB) and, along with David Saposs, play a shaping role in the NLRB's controversial decisions between 1936 and 1940.[22] Ben Selekman conducted the bleachery study. Selekman joined the RSF Department of Industrial Studies in 1916 and conducted a number of important investigations, including a study of industrial disputes in Canada, published in pamphlet form in the teens. Ten years later, Selekman used a revised and expanded form of that investigation to fulfill the requirement for his doctorate at Columbia University.[23] Sylvia Kopald Selekman, Ben Selekman's spouse, published articles in a number of trade union journals, worked for the Labor Bureau Inc. (LBI), and completed her dissertation at Columbia, published as *Rebellion in the Labor Unions*.[24]

The cooperation of company officials was critical for RSF investigators, who needed access not only to workers and managers but to company records that revealed the development of and changes in representation plans. For the Filene investigations, investigators attended meetings and interviewed some of the nearly three thousand employees. To verify findings and provide an opportunity for criticism of the reports, RSF investigators submitted initial drafts of the investigations to employees, employers, and managers.[25] To conduct the bleachery investigation, Selekman spent several weeks in 1921 in Wappingers Falls, where he interviewed workers, managers, and members of the community. Although it was one of the largest mills of its kind in the country, the mill employed only 600 workers (450 men and 150 women).[26] Selekman also had access to past meeting minutes and was able to attend the meetings of the various boards that made up the shared management system.[27] To supplement Selekman's work, the RSF's Sadie Engel used company records to

---

[22] La Dame, *The Filene Store*, 41–2 and Glenn, Brandt, and Andrews, *Russell Sage Foundation, 1907–1946*, 379, 383; United States House of Representatives, *Intermediate Report of the Special Committee of the House of Representatives*, 76th Cong., 1st sess., 1940; Christopher Tomlins, *The State and the Unions: Labor Relations, Law, and the Organized Labor Movement in America, 1880–1960* (Cambridge: Cambridge University Press, 1986).

[23] Ben Selekman, *Postponing Strikes: A Study of The Industrial Disputes Investigation Act of Canada* (New York: Russell Sage Foundation, 1927).

[24] Van Kleeck wrote a number of laudatory letters of introduction for the Selekman family after Ben Selekman resigned from the RSF to travel through Europe. Mary van Kleeck to To Whom It May Concern, March 8, 1927 and Mary van Kleeck to Rene Sand, March 9, 1927, Box 19, Folder 376, MVK Papers.

[25] La Dame, *The Filene Store*, 20 and 22.

[26] Selekman, *Sharing Management With Workers*, 1.

[27] Glenn, Brandt, and Andrews, *Russell Sage Foundation, 1907–1946*, 382.

conduct a statistical study of output before and after the introduction of the shared management plan.[28] The statistical study was unable to definitively determine what weight to give various variables in increasing production, but managers and investigators agreed that there had been a definite increase in production since the introduction of the plan.

Of all the plans investigated by the RSF, the Dutchess Bleachery provided the most comprehensive program for employee representation. In 1918, the bleachery adopted a plan for labor relations featuring three boards established by employers with representatives chosen by workers empowered to reshape the relationship between managers, firm owners, and workers. The Board of Operatives was made up of nine annually elected employees from each of the mill's departments and an executive secretary nominated by the Board of Management. The partnership plan empowered the Board of Operatives to administer welfare and community programs – including the management of the village clubhouse, playground, educational programs, athletic field, and publication of *Bleachery Life*, a company-funded newspaper – and carry grievances to management on behalf of workers. The Board of Management, which determined wages, hours, and budgets, included the six employees chosen by the Board of Operatives as well as six representatives chosen by management from a pool of stockholders and managers. This Board of Management made its decisions within the parameters established by firm owners and the textile industry. For instance, in 1919, the manager of the bleachery informed the board of a nine-thousand-dollar-per-week payroll budget and then allowed the board to determine the rate of pay and the length of the workweek per employee. The board decided on a reduction in hours from fifty-four to forty-eight per week and a 15 percent increase in wages.[29]

According to investigators, the cooperative effort in the bleachery yielded a number of tangible results for mill workers and the company. The Board of Management legislated a one-week paid vacation, improved working conditions, housing repairs, sanitary water at home, and a "sinking fund" that provided unemployment compensation to workers during slack times or injury. When demand for textiles decreased during the postwar downturn, the Board of Management cut wage rates by 12 percent, but, perhaps in a nod to the lessons learned at Pullman, only after the company agreed to decrease rent on company housing by

---

[28] Selekman, *Sharing Management With Workers*, xiv, 101.
[29] Ibid., 54–5.

an equal amount. During flush times, a profit-sharing system provided workers with dramatic benefits. In 1919, workers received a bonus of $150 to $400. According to Selekman, future bonuses did not return to 1919 levels, but years later the employees still "speak wistfully and gratefully about the large amounts they received as bonus in 1919."[30] The plan also allowed for wage adjustments for individual occupations. For instance, box shop workers complained that their wages fell well below the industry standard. After an investigation of other employers, the Board of Management adjusted box workers' wages so that they made slightly more than the industry average. Investigators and the company contended that the success of the plan was reflected in a more flexible and agreeable work force and a dramatic decrease in the labor turnover, which tumbled from 56.5 percent in 1919 to 19.9 percent in 1921.[31]

Van Kleeck and Selekman were effusive in their praise of the bleachery's shared management plan, but they recognized that its small size and recent creation limited the transferability of the plan to other industries and firms. In her introduction to the study, Van Kleeck wrote, "Because of the sincerity of those who devised the plan in seeking a more democratic as well as a more personal basis for human relations in industry than has hitherto prevailed and because of their courage in putting it into operation, the Dutchess Bleachery has achieved a place of leadership."[32] In his conclusion to the study, Selekman gushed that the bleachery was "one of the most advanced, most sincere, and most comprehensive schemes of industrial relations introduced into industry on the initiative of the employers." In marked contrast to what he and Van Kleeck would find in the Filene investigation, Selekman suggested that the plan brought to light "the absentee-landlord in a new role – that of promoting a democratic relationship among the various branches of an enterprise."[33] In a series of articles for the labor press describing various attempts at industrial democracy, Socialist Party leader Norman Thomas hailed the bleachery experiment as an "unusually comprehensive" effort to give workers representation in the management of a traditionally low-wage industry.[34]

The dramatic improvement investigators identified in the bleachery stood in contrast to the mixed results described in the RSF investigation of the long-standing Filene Department Store experiment. The RSF

---

[30] Ibid., 89–90.
[31] Ibid., 101.
[32] Ibid., xiv.
[33] Ibid., 131.
[34] Norman Thomas, "Democracy for Industry," *LEJ* 62 (May 1927): 358.

investigation of the Filene store described a once promising program to increase worker participation that had been compromised by the complications of growth and by a Filene family dispute that occurred after the completion of the investigation. More than any other investigation, the Filene study demonstrated the difficulty of maintaining a democratic system of labor relations in a business where ownership's control was becoming increasingly diffuse and workers had no independent organization to represent their interests. Consistent with firm owner Edward Filene's larger concern with promoting consumption by workers as a salve for business cycle and labor problems, the program aimed to decrease waste in industry so as to increase the value of wages for all workers through lower prices for consumer goods.[35]

Rather than a system of shared control of industry, the Filene plan provided employees a voice in the determination of issues usually assigned to personnel and welfare departments, such as health insurance, savings and loan, education, and social activities. According to investigators, this distribution of responsibilities had the effect of relieving "executives of considerable burden of responsibility" for personnel issues.[36] The Filene Co-operative Association (FCA), established by Edward A. and A. Lincoln Filene in September 1903, had a staff of approximately fifty employees who participated in a number of committees and assisted in determining policy on a range of issues identified by management. The FCA Council governed the association with the assistance of five subordinate boards, including the Arbitration, Credit Union, Benefit Society, Clinic, and Employee Restaurant boards. According to its constitution, the FCA was designed to "give its members a voice in their government, to increase their efficiency and add to their social opportunities, [and] to create and sustain a just and equitable relation between employer and employee."[37]

Although the plan lacked opportunities for employee involvement in the determination of many company policy decisions, RSF investigators found that the cooperative program did demonstrate the effectiveness of intra-firm arbitration boards in remedying employer and employee grievances. La Dame described the FCA's arbitration board as constituting

[35] Lincoln Filene, "How About Retail 'Price Cutting?'" *AF* 35 (September 1928): 1067–72.
[36] La Dame, *The Filene Store*, 227. Also on the Filene experiment see, Meg Jacobs, *Pocketbook Politics: Economic Citizenship in Twentieth Century America* (Princeton: Princeton University Press, 2005), 80; Sanford M. Jacoby, *Modern Manors: Welfare Capitalism Since the New Deal* (Princeton: Princeton University Press, 1997), 15.
[37] Ibid., 47.

"significant participation in the management of the business."[38] The board membership expanded from its creation, but with one exception it was made up entirely of FCA members elected by fellow employees.[39] The board functioned as a jury that would hear and rule on arguments provided by representatives of the company and the worker. The scope of the board's oversight included dismissal, employee bookkeeping mistakes, hours, promotions, and vacation pay. An analysis of 308 rulings between 1901 and 1907 and between 1913 and 1926 suggested that the board exercised a fair amount of autonomy, siding evenly with management and employees and experiencing little in the way of interference from management in the implementation of its decisions.[40] In cases of dismissals, the board ruled in favor of the employee sixty-one times and the company seventy-one times. In cases involving employee bookkeeping mistakes, the board found in favor of the employee on eighty-seven occasions and the company forty-six times.[41]

In addition to reporting these arbitration achievements, RSF investigators drew attention to the success of the FCA in decreasing working hours. Between 1902 and 1913, the FCA voted to cut weekend summer hours and establish new holidays. Though noting the role of management in suggesting certain hours reductions, La Dame indicated that the FCA had "taken some initiative and with definite gains for itself."[42] Workers in general provided "enthusiastic comments" that indicated "they respect the decisions of the Board as fair and just."[43] In an accounting of the advantages and disadvantages of the board for workers, La Dame wrote, "The Board is an institution in which nothing is to be lost and everything to be gained."[44]

Despite these successes, investigators concluded that a poorly explained bonus system, a lack of willingness to discuss wages, and an uninterested if not hostile cadre of new managers compromised the success of the plan. Though the management never engaged the FCA in a serious discussion of wages, it did attempt to use profit-sharing and a bonus system to motivate workers. Although all employees were supposed to be motivated and benefit from the system, the study found that the plan inspired executives

[38] Ibid., 237.
[39] Ibid., 290.
[40] Ibid., 270-8 and 237-58.
[41] Ibid., 274.
[42] Ibid., 143.
[43] Ibid., 279.
[44] Ibid., 285.

but not lower-level employees. According to executives, employee dissatisfaction turned on workers' inability to understand the complexity of bookkeeping strategies of the company (i.e., depreciation) and the impact of tax policies on the company's bottom line.[45] The lack of a transparent and equitable device for determining worker productivity further diminished workers' trust in the system. As a result, workers came to see the "bonus as an expected gift" and "an expression of Management's good will and desire to share its prosperity with those who had helped to create it" rather than as a reflection of worker productivity.[46] In a theme common to both the Filene and Rockefeller plans, investigators found that manager and low-level executive animosity toward the program and its participants further diminished the system's effectiveness. A retiring FCA president indicated that employees asked to participate frequently responded that they "would like to give the time to it," but they had observed "that people who give their time to the F. C. A. get in wrong with their executive, get transferred or are eventually out of a job."[47]

The demise of the Filene experiment demonstrated the difficulty of employing even a modest form of democratization in an economy increasingly moving from proprietary capitalism to corporate capitalism, where companies were owned by stockholders who privileged bottom-line and stock-price issues over the day-to-day functioning of the firm. During the investigation, some workers expressed dismay that cooperative spirit had waned as the company grew and the decision-making center moved further and further away from the manager-worker nexus. A chief executive who had worked for the company for more than twenty years noted that the new managers did not "absorb the ideas of the Filenes," and "as the business and the number of workers increased, the spirit of the old store seemed to disappear." According to the executive, the problems of the company also changed in this period as it became "bigger, more specialized and more technical."[48] This led to a sense among employees that a distant management controlled even those decisions once the domain of the FCA. Previously, the company had avoided this arrangement for fear that "absentee ownership" was "perilous to the achievement of the aims of the business."[49]

---

[45] Ibid., 187.
[46] Ibid., 185.
[47] Ibid., 340.
[48] Ibid., 92.
[49] Ibid., 78.

A New Capitalism?

If growth and technical complexity compromised the Filene plan, tension among firm owners decimated it. A. Lincoln Filene and Edward A. Filene, the sons of store founder William Filene, owned 52 percent of company stock and had agreed to vote together on management issues in order to keep control of the firm in the family and to support the labor relations program. Van Kleeck reported that non-family partners convinced A. Lincoln Filene to vote with them on issues critical to the direction of the company, which gave control of firm decision making to a group much less interested than the founder in democratizing the workplace. By 1929, the experiment was effectively over as new managers made what Van Kleeck described as "very radical and disappointing changes in the store."[50]

THE ROCKEFELLER PLAN IN THE COAL AND STEEL INDUSTRY

The Rockefeller employment plan was widely recognized as the most important and controversial employer-initiated effort to provide workers with a voice in industry. According to the *Machinists' Monthly Journal*, by 1925 the plan had been "adopted in hundreds of other plants."[51] Rockefeller ordered the development and adoption of the plan following open warfare between the company and its employees in 1913 and 1914 and a scathing interrogation by the United States Commission on Industrial Relation's Frank Walsh revealing that Rockefeller had encouraged labor policies leading to the deaths of striking miners and their families. After

---

[50] Mary van Kleeck to Glenn, January 1, 1929. Changes in the cooperative plan included the following: the FCA could not nominate members to the Board of Directors; the Executive Committee was eliminated; the council appointed the executive secretary of the FCA, and the management approved the decision – the opposite had been true in the original plan. Mary van Kleeck to Glenn, August 27, 1929. The result of these changes, according to Van Kleeck, was that "the business as a whole has become like any other retail store and no longer has the forward-looking objective toward which Mr. E. A. Filene was working." Mary van Kleeck to Glenn, January 1, 1929. A. Lincoln Filene made a concerted effort to persuade Van Kleeck and the RSF not to publish the report by insisting that the report was out of date and did not fairly represent the plan as it presently existed. Van Kleeck insisted that the report was up to date and provided a rich source of information on the difficulties in building and maintaining a cooperative plan. A. Lincoln Filene to Mary van Kleeck, April 9, 1929; Mary van Kleeck to Filene, April 15, 1929; A. Lincoln Filene to Mary van Kleeck, April 18, 1929; Mary van Kleeck to A. Lincoln Filene, April 20, 1929. All of these letters can be found in Box 103, Folder 1591 and 1592, Filene Study Correspondence, MVK Papers.

[51] "Sage Foundation Report," *MMJ* 37 (February 1925): 69; Brody, *Workers in Industrial America: Essays on the Twentieth Century Struggle* (New York: Oxford University Press, 1993), 55.

the strike and the ensuing controversy, Rockefeller searched – or at least hired people to search – for a more humane method of governing industry. Former Minister of Labour and later Premier of Canada W. L. Mackenzie King drafted a cooperative plan for Rockefeller's Colorado Fuel and Iron Company (CFIC) and Minnequa Steel Works, which employed some five thousand mine and seven thousand steel workers. Mackenzie King joined Rockefeller in asserting that "a lack of personal relationships between directing management and employes ... was the true point of origin of the bitter conflict of the coal strike in Colorado."[52] To remedy this problem, the RSF described the plan as an attempt to "apply in industry the mechanism of republican government in political life."[53]

As part of an effort to hold off the United Mine Workers (UMW) and sanitize his family's image before an increasingly skeptical public, Rockefeller adopted a plan he promoted as a "comprehensive 'Industrial Constitution'" for Colorado Fuel and Iron employees. The Rockefeller plan, which refused to recognize unions, governed the workplace for workers in twenty-five coal mines, two iron mines, two lime quarries, and one steel mill. With the exception of the iron mines in Platte, Wyoming, all of the mills and mines were located in Colorado. Rockefeller submitted the employee representation system for the mines to employees of the CFIC in 1915. The plan divided the mines into four districts with each district electing its own representatives. Employees elected one representative for every 150 workers to represent them at quarterly and annual meetings, with a minimum of two representatives per mine. Every four months, the company president would call a district conference to discuss issues identified in the plan. The plan established four joint committees

---

[52] Ben Selekman and Mary van Kleeck, *Employes' Representation in the Coal Mines* (New York: Russell Sage Foundation, 1924), xxvii; J. A. P. Haydon, "A 'Close-Up' of Canada's Prime Minister – Mackenzie King," *MMJ* 38 (December 1926): 550–1, 607; For King's understanding of industrial relations, see W. L. Mackenzie King, *Industry and Humanity* (Boston: Houghton Mifflin Company, 1918). In studies and in the title, the RSF spells *employees*' as *employes.*'

[53] Selekman and Van Kleeck, *Employes' Representation in Coal Mines*, xxviii. For more on the strike and its consequence, see Graham Adams, Jr., *Age of Industrial Violence 1910–1915: The Activities and Findings of the United States Commission on Industrial Relations* (New York: Columbia University Press, 1966), 146–75; George Suggs, Jr., *Colorado's War on Militant Unionism: James H. Peabody and the Western Federation of Miners* (Detroit: Wayne State University Press, 1972); James Weinstein, *The Corporate Ideal and the Liberal State* (Boston: Beacon Press, 1968), 191–9; Howard M. Gitelman, *Legacy of the Ludlow Massacre: A Chapter in American Industrial Relations* (Philadelphia: Temple University Press, 1988); and Thomas G. Andrews, *Killing for Coal: America's Deadliest Labor War* (Cambridge: Harvard University Press, 2010).

in each district, including Safety and Accidents; Sanitation, Health, and Housing; Recreation and Education; and Industrial Cooperation and Conciliation.[54] Each committee included three miners' representatives and three representatives chosen by the company president.

Arriving just weeks after the end of a failed coal and steel workers' strike for union recognition, Selekman found that the cooperative effort and employer good will yielded improvements in workers' living conditions and health care. RSF investigators noted that the employees' representation plan "vitalized the interest of the managers and the stockholders in all ... practical aspects of an employe's [sic] life in a mining camp."[55] The Sanitation, Health and Safety Committee and the Recreation and Education Committee helped introduce some of the more immediate improvements in workers' lives. Workers "unanimously" identified "better houses, better sanitary care of the camps, better schools, and the building of clubs and bath houses as improvements since the introduction of the plan in 1915."[56] Health and medical services also improved. The Sanitation, Health and Safety Committee succeeded in removing an "unsatisfactory physician" and in raising funds from workers' monthly wages to fund hospital improvements. Even among workers unhappy with many aspects of the cooperative plan, RSF investigators found employees "well satisfied with the medical service." One worker noted that the hospital was "a good place" that "I don't mind giving my money to."[57]

Improvements in health care, safety, and living conditions provided some evidence that management was willing to work with employees to improve aspects of conditions in the mines and mining communities. Even so, the representation plan's method of wage determination provided a clear example of the limitations of the plan and further evidence that unions affected labor relations in nonunion firms. The CFIC plan did not allow for the negotiation of wages; in fact, the company left wage determination to competitors outside of Colorado. In practice, "competitors' wages" were defined as those wages that the United Mine Workers had agreed to with the Midwestern mine owners that made up the Central Competitive Field.[58] The result of this policy was, according to the RSF,

---

[54] Selekman and Van Kleeck, *Employes' Representation in Coal Mines*, 61–4; Mary van Kleeck, "Procedure Followed in Studying the Industrial Representation Plan of the Colorado Fuel and Iron Company," *JPR* 4 (August–September): 133–54; and "Employees' Representation in Industry," *MLR* 20 (April 1925): 21–6.
[55] Selekman and Van Kleeck, *Employes' Representation in Coal Mines*, 144.
[56] Ibid., 99.
[57] Ibid., 133.
[58] Ibid., 387.

a divided loyalty of mine workers who were "not ungrateful for the new policy of the CFIC and its tangible manifestations in good housing," but who recognized that "they need the protection of representatives outside the company, because they have discovered that men employed in the company are impotent to protect themselves." As investigators noted, the company's willingness to depend on standards set by the UMW not only curtailed the power of CFIC employees to modify working conditions, but it also dramatically limited the ability of the cooperative plan to shape the formulation of "standards for industry as a whole," which on many of the most important labor relations issues continued to be set by workers and employers in union fields.[59]

In developing the plan, King and Rockefeller conceptually reached back to an earlier period of more modest distance between firm owner and worker, both physically and socially. But in modern industry the actual practice of managing workers' daily lives took place far beyond the gaze of executives and stockholders, who used profit – not communication or worker contentment – as the final barometer of success. As in the Filene investigation, RSF investigators found that middle management and foremen's unwillingness to embrace dramatic changes in their working conditions and scope of authority compromised the effectiveness of the plan. A prominent executive conceded that managers did not always adhere to the spirit of the plan and attributed this failure to a generational split among local officials, many of whom were products of "old school" managerial strategies.[60] Leading CFIC advocates of the representation plan attempted to increase the transparency of managers' decisions and reduce the autocratic practices of previous mine managers, but the wide geographic distribution of the mines meant that local administrators maintained much control over daily personnel decisions.

Though it would have been cold comfort to the company given the overall skeptical tone in the report, investigators did find some evidence that the plan had at least tempered superintendents and foremen's autonomy and authority. Superintendents complained, "Management is protecting the miners better than it protects its superintendents and foremen."[61] Many workers asserted, "The superintendent used to say to a man, 'You can take your tools and go.' He wouldn't have to tell him why. A man had no redress. Now they can't discharge us that way."[62] Additionally,

[59] Ibid., 389.
[60] Ibid., 108.
[61] Ibid., 109.
[62] Ibid., 99.

investigators concluded that the plan had succeeded in eliminating the practice of foremen "selling" good jobs to compliant workers.[63]

In its damning assessment of the effectiveness of the plan, however, RSF investigators concluded unambiguously that new managerial strategies and practices did not lead to the promise of greater industrial democracy or shared management. RSF investigators readily agreed that conditions in the mines and surrounding communities improved, particularly in company towns; even so, investigators questioned the degree to which this symbolized democratization of decision making. In areas of education, housing, safety, and camp life, investigators concluded that "the work of the joint committees has revealed the fact that these changes are due primarily to the initiative of management. Neither in the written plan nor in practice do the employes' representatives have responsibility for decisions."[64] Even on paper, RSF investigators concluded, the plan introduced "no radical change in the status of employes by extending to them a share in any phase of the management or by defining terms of partnership."[65] In a 1924 memo to the RSF's John Glenn, Van Kleeck noted that the Colorado plan provided workers with "merely opportunity for conference and for the airing of grievances." "It is upon managerial officials, directed by the stockholders, that decisions rest," Van Kleeck concluded.[66]

In addition to undermining supporters of the plan's more dramatic claims, the study is useful for other reasons as well. Not only does it provide important insights into cooperative labor relations plans, the process by which the report was vetted and published suggests a notable degree of autonomy by philanthropically funded labor investigators. Even more so than in the Filene case, Rockefeller and CFIC officials challenged RSF investigators findings, but Van Kleeck held firm on the report's methodology and damning conclusions. In the introduction to the two CFIC reports, Van Kleeck and Selekman noted that John L. Lewis and the United Mine Workers approved of the report, but Rockefeller and company officials did not. Company officials wanted the names of employees interviewed by RSF investigators in order to verify the employee dissatisfaction described in the report, but RSF investigators had assured workers that their names "would be held in strict confidence." Instead, to

---

[63] Ibid., 104.
[64] Ibid., 147.
[65] Ibid., 80.
[66] Mary van Kleeck to Glenn, July 24, 1924, Box 23, File 461 Mem. 1924, MVK Papers.

verify Selekman's findings, Van Kleeck personally re-examined contested cases, and her findings "confirmed the essential facts upon which Mr. Selekman's report was based."[67] Mackenzie King took aim at Selekman personally and on his focus on company leaders' unwillingness to negotiate with the United Mine Workers. King complained to Van Kleeck that Selekman's "prejudice against the Plan because of the failure" of the CFIC to make an agreement with the UMW "is so self-evident throughout the whole study" that "its usefulness is vitiated pretty much from beginning to close."[68] Later correspondence suggests that Van Kleeck assuaged some of King's concerns, but not to the point where Rockefeller and company officials felt comfortable endorsing the report.[69]

The labor press hailed the RSF study as an authoritative rebuke of the fraudulent democracy propagated by the Rockefeller plan. Since its introduction, unions and their supporters had heaped derision on the Rockefeller plan for its failure to engage in collective bargaining with the UMW. In 1919, William Z. Foster, writing in the *Journal of Electrical Workers and Operators*, condemned the plan as an effort "to befuddle the workers and defeat the Miner's Union."[70] With the publication of the RSF report, unions had fresh data that allowed them to question the effectiveness of the plan. In describing the report, the *Machinists' Monthly Journal* credited the plan with improving "working and living conditions," which "are more wholesome and happy for the miners," yet the journal drew attention to the report's conclusion that "the miners are not satisfied that their representatives have the power to protect them in decisions regarding wages and other conditions at work."[71] The strongest criticism came from the UMW, which referred to the plan as a "farce" and insisted that "the only protection they [CFIC employees] can depend

---

[67] Selekman and Van Kleeck, *Employes' Representation in Coal Mines*, xxxiii.

[68] King also took exception with Selekman's earlier study of the Canadian Industrial Disputes Investigation Act, which King described as "so prejudiced that it destroyed the value of much painstaking and useful investigation." King to Mary van Kleeck, January 17, 1921, Box 15, MVK Papers.

[69] King to Mary van Kleeck, January 17, 1921; Mary van Kleeck to King, January 22, 1921; Mary van Kleeck to King, January 24, 1921; King to Mary van Kleeck, February 2, 1921; King to Mary van Kleeck, March 9, 1921; Mary van Kleeck to King, March 16, 1921; King to Mary van Kleeck, March 18, 1921; King to Mary van Kleeck, April 2, 1921; and Mary van Kleeck to King, July 8, 1921, all in Box 15, MVK Papers.

[70] William Z. Foster, "Suicide of a Company Union," *JEWO* 19 (September 1919): 59. For similar early assessments of the plan in the trade union press, see Samuel Gompers, "The Company Union Fraud," *IMJ* 59 (January 1923): 15; Robert W. Dunn, "A Company Union in Oil," *LA* 10 (April 1926): 15–16.

[71] "Sage Foundation Report," *MMJ* XXXVII (February 1925): 69–70.

ILLUSTRATION 4.1. Russell Sage Foundation Cartoon from March 1, 1925 cover of the *United Mine Workers Journal* portraying the RSF as attacking the Rockefeller plan. The cartoon was republished in a number of different trade union periodicals, including the March 20, 1925 issue of *Justice*. The image appears courtesy of the United Mine Workers of America Archive.

upon is the United Mine Workers of America."[72] The UMW celebrated the published report for delivering "the wallop which leaves the celebrated plan badly twisted and disfigured".[73]

CONCLUSION: A NEW CAPITALISM?

Consideration of the models described in this chapter alongside the Hooverites' vision of the American workplace suggests a gradual rethinking under way in the New Era, as long-standing assumptions about the conflicting interests of labor and capital were giving way, or at least facing challenge. For the Hooverites, the idea of a new capitalism embodied a belief that workplace cooperation between employees and employers could and did benefit all, in the form of increased economic growth, stability, profits, wages, and consumption. How this translated to the actual work process on the shop room or department store floor remained unclear. Hoover and his allies simply presumed that efficiency-minded managers and employers would maintain control over the production process; they were the experts, after all. Having agreed that the goal was to increase productivity in the interests of all, they took for granted that workers could be relied on to work in tandem with managers and employers toward that goal. The successful effort to cut waste on the B&O Railroad described in the previous chapter suggested that this shared goal could come to pass even in union shops where conflict among employees and with management had very recently been the rule.

The vision for a new capitalism that King, Filene, and Van Kleeck brought to the construction and evaluation of the programs described in this chapter was more characteristic of traditional models that stressed industrial democracy and shared governance of the workplace. Such efforts were based less on the assumption of a common set of interests between employers and employees in increasing efficiency and more on a conflict model that had long dominated the industrial relations discourse. When Van Kleeck set out the terms for evaluating new capitalist labor relations, she used a particular language and set of concepts to measure their success, namely power, control, and wealth. And on the first two of these, architects of conservative labor relations plans like the Rockefeller

---

[72] Felix Pogliano, "Miners Reject Reduction," *UMWJ* 32 (July 15, 1921): 11.
[73] "Investigation of Rockefeller Industrial Plan by Sage Foundation Reveals It to be a Real Failure," *UMWJ* 36 (February 15, 1925): 1–2; AFL, "Rockefeller's Company 'Union' Discredited By Impartial Probe," *AFL:WNS* 14 (February 28, 1925): 1.

plan would have agreed that their plans were designed to facilitate the "diffusion of control" – to use Van Kleeck's phrasing from her letter to Haristoy – in industry. Rockefeller, the Filenes, and the bleachery may have been more or less genuine in their commitment to this goal, but all would have agreed that their plans were meant to empower workers to shape important aspects of their work life experience.

Van Kleeck maintained that any meaningful change in capitalism required that workers have a strong, independent, and collective voice in determining under what conditions and for what terms they labored. King and Van Kleeck both seemed to share a hope that such a voice could be fostered by effective communication between employers and employees complemented by a meaningful plan to give workers control in the "direction and management of industry." All four of these experiments revealed, however, that such efforts were rooted in an individual employer's willingness to give up control. The future did not look promising for such efforts. The rise of corporate capitalism, where more disparate ownership again diffused power, this time as stockholders replaced the proprietary capitalists as the evaluators of the bottom line, made this model less workable. Despite their best efforts, Van Kleeck and the industry leaders who built these experimental plans were never able to satisfactorily answer Van Kleeck's increasingly relevant query: "What, after all, should be the relation of stockholders to the directing of policy of a company?"[74]

Such a grim assessment of new capitalism made Van Kleeck a dissenting voice in an era when so many industrial relations experts, in describing the relationship between labor and capital, emphasized the success of shared goals and cooperation. This should not suggest, however, that Van Kleeck was somehow a marginal player in New Era economic and public policy circles, far from it, in fact. Between her terms at the RSF, she served within the Department of Labor as the first director of what would become the Women' Bureau, where she brought this same emphasis on examining the changing structure of capitalism to her examination of women's developing roles in the nation and the economy.

---

[74] Mary van Kleeck to Glenn, January 1, 1929, Box 103, Folder 1591, Filene Study Correspondence, MVK Papers.

5

Gender Research as Labor Activism

The Women's Bureau in the New Era

> It is not, after all, because they are women, but because they are the low wage group that we must study their problems and discover the basis for determining their wages.
>
> – Mary van Kleeck[1]

> The women of today, as well as their employers ... want facts, and if the facts are presented strongly and clearly they will get action. But the facts must be collected first, and the field is open and crying for attention from scientists and health experts as well as from industrial engineers.
>
> – 1921 Women's Bureau Bulletin[2]

On June 5, 1920, Congress established the Women's Bureau (WB), charging it to "formulate standards and policies which shall promote the welfare of wage-earning women, improve their working conditions, increase their efficiency, and advance their opportunities for profitable employment."[3] Support for the WB was such that the House passed the bill by a vote of 255 to 10, and the Senate passed it without a recorded vote, though the *Monthly Labor Review* noted that "there was some opposition."[4] During a decade when policy makers celebrated the fruits

---

[1] WB, "What Industry Means to Women Workers," *Bulletin* 31 (Washington, DC: GPO, 1923): 5.
[2] WB, "Health Problems of Women in Industry," *Bulletin* 18 (Washington, DC: GPO, 1921): 9.
[3] 66th Cong., H. R. 13229, "An Act to Establish in the Department of Labor a Bureau to be Known as the WB," republished in all WB bulletins during the 1920s.
[4] "WB in the United States Department of Labor," *MLR* 11 (July 1920): 174–5; Congress, House Committee on Appropriation, *Sundry Civil Bill, 1920, Part 2,* 65th Cong., 3rd sess., February 10, 1919, 1556–71; "Woman Now Directs Nation's Women Workers,"

of economic abundance garnered with only the lightest touch from the state, WB leaders and investigators saw gender research as a form of labor activism that would advance the cause of all workers. No other organization in the federal government thought harder about how policies could be constructed to protect workers, irrespective of gender, from the continued harsh reality of employment in American industry. Along the way, advocates of protective legislation for women sought not only to protect the particular interests of women workers, but also to drive a wedge through a post-*Adkins* understanding of the "right to contract" and to expand the number of issues that should be seen as affected with a public interest.[5] As the WB made clear, the "woman worker" included a diverse body of citizens with varied workplace experiences and racial and ethnic backgrounds who could not be parsed out of or differentiated from the larger labor question. While recognizing that women encountered "certain peculiar difficulties" in industry, Mary van Kleeck argued, "We must of course agree that women workers are not to be considered a group apart, for they are part of the labor problem as workers and not as women."[6]

Such an approach put the WB in a unique position during the New Era. In addition to Hooverites and neoclassical economists' rejection of labor standards, organized labor dismissed statist policies as an attempt to supplant the role of unions in protecting male workers. On the issue of women workers, the American Federation of Labor (AFL) welcomed

---

NYT, February 3, 1918, 56; and Alice Kessler Harris, *In Pursuit of Equity: Women, Men, and the Quest for Economic Citizenship in Twentieth Century America* (New York: Oxford University Press, 2001), 35–42. The WB was originally named the Woman in Industry Service (WIS) and designed as a emergency war program that would develop public policies concerning women and connect women workers with wartime employment. In hearings and the press, the WIS was referred to as the WIS, the WB, and the Women's Committee. I refer to the organization before it achieved formal bureau status in 1920 as the WIS. After 1920, I refer to it as the WB.

[5] For an analysis of the National Consumer League's efforts to use female protective legislation as an opening wedge, see Kathryn Kish Sklar, "Two Political Cultures in the Progressive Era: The National Consumers' League and the American Association for Labor Legislation" in Linda K. Kerber, Alice Kessler Harris, and Kathryn Kish Sklar, eds., *U.S. History as Women's History: New Feminist Essays* (Chapel Hill: University of North Carolina Press, 1995), 51. On the political mobilization of women more generally, see Elisabeth S. Clemens, *The People's Lobby: Organizational Innovation and the Rise of Interest Group Politics in the United States, 1890–1925* (Chicago: University of Chicago Press, 1997), 184–234.

[6] Mary van Kleeck, "Women's Invasion of Industry and Change in Protective Standard," *Proceedings of the Academy of Political Science in City of New York* 8 (February 1919): 11.

protective legislation seeing women as temporary entrants into the labor market who were unable to organize in self-defense. Meanwhile even in progressive circles, leaders such as Paul Douglas, who, as we have seen, championed the need for labor standards, continued well into the New Deal to cling to a masculine understanding of economic citizenship and argue that women were not part of the "real labor supply."[7] None of these groups viewed the problems women workers faced as symptomatic of the difficulties faced by all workers, nor did many of them see labor standards as a useful means of addressing the larger labor problem. The WB dissented from the conventional wisdom on both of these points, arguing instead for the centrality of wage-earning women's experiences to any understanding of the larger and evolving labor question.

As this and the next two chapters will make clear, the WB and its supporters were not alone in this ambitious and extraordinarily consequential effort to diversify the "labor question." The WB was joined in this struggle by an emerging group of social scientists, government, and nonprofit investigators who used dramatic demographic change brought on by wartime and postwar demands for labor in industry to challenge the public's understanding of not just women, but also African American, Mexican immigrant, and Mexican American workers. This emerging body of experts came to their many and diverse investigations with a shared understanding that the experiences, goals, and expectations of many groups of workers in the United States had been ignored, marginalized, or – by intent or ignorance – distorted. Further, they believed that the public and policy makers' ignorance of these groups had consequences that were indeed extraordinary. If wide swathes of the public and policy makers formulated the "labor question" so that it pertained only to white, male, largely native-born workers, then any attempt to "answer" that question would ignore the experiences of women and workers of color. Given what we know about the uneven implementation of New Deal and postwar economic and labor policies, the WB and others' concerns over an undiversified labor question were no doubt well founded.

In addition to advancing the cause of what Alice Kessler Harris and others have described as social justice feminism, the WB's work should also be understood as part of the dramatic expansion in the institutional capacity of research organizations in government, business, labor, and nonprofit sectors that sought to remake labor relations and shift

---

[7] Kessler Harris, *In Pursuit of Equity*, 97.

the boundary between public and private issues.[8] These organizations devoted increasing energies and resources to making sense of the labor question and to considering and debating whether statist or voluntary measures would be the most effective means of promoting a fair distribution of the nation's economic abundance. Among many of these groups a general understanding emerged, recognizing the potential of workers as employees and consumers to contribute to a more rational, fair, and stable form of capitalism. By the mid-1920s, when court decisions and modest enforcement mechanisms inhibited statist solutions to workers' problems, the WB supplemented its advocacy of labor standards by joining other labor experts in promoting and experimenting with voluntary measures to encourage employers to improve working conditions as a method for increasing worker efficiency, promoting a more just workplace, and decreasing labor turnover.

From the Gilded Age through the 1920s, the federal government's role in addressing the labor problem expanded, but it did so rather unevenly and episodically, in response to various pressures and to the general ambiguity regarding what government should do in the field of industrial relations. As a result, there was ample room for the WB's labor activism to include more than advocating statist solutions to the problems faced by women workers. Though the WB continued throughout the decade to encourage and provide justification for labor standards, its leaders also sought to remake the public's understanding of the female labor question. The frequency with which the WB's investigations appeared in major publications suggests that many Americans were eager for new ways of thinking about wage-earning women who were entering the work force in greater numbers, staying in the work force longer, and working in new fields. Reports of WB investigations appeared frequently and prominently in many publications, including the *Atlantic Monthly, Good Housekeeping, The Annals, Survey, General Federation Magazine, Life and Labor, The Independent, Business Personnel, Ladies Home Journal, Women's Press, Americana Annual, Washington Post, Journal of Industrial Hygiene, Congressional Digest,*

---

[8] On social justice feminism, see Kathryn Kish Sklar, Anja Schüler, and Susan Strasser, *Social Justice Feminists in the United States and Germany* (Ithaca: Cornell University Press, 1998), 5–11. Important variations on this theme can be found in other scholars' work, including Dorothy Sue Cobble, *The Other Women's Movement* (Princeton: Princeton University Press, 2004) and Anelise Orleck, *Common Sense and a Little Fire: Women and Working Class Politics in the United States, 1900–1965* (Chapel Hill: University of North Carolina Press, 1995).

New Republic, Nation, New York Times, and numerous trade union and academic journals.

Historians, particularly social historians attempting to reconstruct the lives of working women, have drawn on the WB's investigations. Much less has been written about the institution itself, the issues it confronted, the practices it did and did not imagine, or its importance in shaping public conceptions of women workers. Historian Judith Sealander produced the only historical institutional analysis of the WB that takes into account its early years. Sealander largely dismissed the WB's efforts as "small, poorly funded, or temporary – losers in a broker state best attuned to the needs of powerful constituencies."[9] Sonya Michel conflates the goals of the Children's Bureau with the Women's Bureau, writing that it "served to reinforce" the Children's Bureau's "conceptual as well as bureaucratic division of labor," which Michel characterizes as a "kind of tunnel vision when it came to women: they were important only in their role as mothers."[10] Historian Alice Kessler Harris, in a recent work considering the twentieth-century struggle for economic citizenship, writes that the effort to establish the WB and gain passage for the Sheppard-Towner Act might look "like a two-pronged commitment to women's mothering and wage earning lives," yet it "appears upon closer examination to be part of the same effort to sustain women's domesticity."[11] In her analysis of the WB as an institution, Kessler Harris describes an "ambiguity" in the Women's Bureau's position on women in the work force that is not borne out by a careful analysis of WB reports and bulletins.[12]

In fact, there was little ambiguity among WB leaders and investigators, whose own experiences and investigations cast considerable doubt on the notion that a man's wage – to the extent there was a working man in the household at all – would support a family. As the *New York Times* reported in its analysis of WB and National Industrial Conference Board (NICB) studies, the WB "has shown often that there are thousands of women in manufacturing, as in other industrial divisions, permanently employed and highly skilled, and who are supporting dependents quite

---

[9] Judith Sealander, *As Minority Becomes Majority: Federal Reaction to the Phenomenon of Women in the Work Force, 1920–1963* (Westport, CT: Greenwood Press, 1983), 9. On the WB after World War II, see Kathleen Laughlin, *Women's Work and Public Policy: A History of the Women's Bureau, U.S. Department of Labor, 1945–1970* (Boston: Northeastern University Press, 2000).

[10] Sonya Michel, *Children's Interests/Mothers' Rights: The Shaping of America's Child Care Policy* (New Haven: Yale University Press, 1999), 93.

[11] Kessler Harris, *In Pursuit of Equity*, 35.

[12] Ibid., 42.

as much as their male fellow workers."[13] Nor did the leaders of the WB believe it was possible or desirable that all working women should leave the workplace and return to unpaid household labor. Rather, the WB worked to replace hoary conceptions of the woman worker that emphasized women as exclusively temporary entrants into the labor market with an understanding that stressed the permanence and indispensability of women workers and of their wages to a modern industrial and increasingly consumer-oriented economy. Particularly in the early years, as WB leaders fought for institutional survival, they occasionally used motherhood and the protection of the home as justification for investigations, but a closer look at WB studies indicates that these seasoned investigators had no illusions about women workers' imminent return to the home. Although the expertise the WB created was gendered, in that it focused on women, the WB understood the problems of women workers to be the problems of all poor workers employed in difficult and often dangerous occupations. In time, the WB came to see itself as a vehicle for promoting labor standards that could protect all workers, irrespective of gender.[14]

Since the late 1980s, historians considering the impact of gender on public policy and women's rights have moved beyond the "false dichotomy of equality vs. difference" for understanding the ideologies, strategies, and aims of advocates of women as mothers, homemakers, and workers.[15] By turning attention to an analysis of the layered nature of

---

[13] "Finds Women's Pay far less than Men's," *NYT*, October 2, 1927, W21. See also Lorine Pruette, "Women in American Industry Reach 8,500,000," *NYT*, November 6, 1927, XX4; "Married Women Workers Doubled in 30-Year Period," *NYT*, December 14, 1928, 46; "The Ratio of Married Women in Industry is Increasing," *NYT*, February 26, 1928, 129; "Finds Woman's Lot is Growing Harder," *NYT*, January 6, 1929, 29; "Women Wage Earners," *AF* 33 (March 1926): 273–4; Cara Cook, "Women Workers," *AF* 33 (April 1926): 454; Mary Anderson, "Mary Anderson on Women's Work," *AF* 33 (May 1925): 333; Mary Anderson, "The Women Workers," *AF* 32 (November 1925): 1073; S. P. Breckinridge, "The Home Responsibility of Women Workers and the Equal Wage," *JPE* 31 (August 1923): 536; Mary Anderson, "Importance of Women in Industry," *The Personnel Journal* 6 (February 1928): 329–30; Mary Anderson, "Recent Investigations by Government Bureaus," *NCSW* (April 1920): 140–2; and "Demands Working Housewives be Included in Coming Federal Census on Employment," *NYT*, July 18, 1929, 3; "The Two-Job Woman," *NYT*, July 19, 1929, 13.

[14] For a similar assessment of the struggle for protective legislation, but with a focus on the National Consumer's League, see Kish Sklar, "Two Political Cultures in the Progressive Era," 51.

[15] Eileen Boris and S. J. Kleinberg, "Mothers and Other Workers: (Re)Conceiving Labor, Maternalism, and the State," *Journal of Women's History* 15 (Autumn 2003): 91; Joan W. Scott, "Deconstructing Equality-versus-Difference: Or, the Uses of Poststructuralist

citizenship in the United States that more adroitly considers gender and race and recognizes the broad and diverse effort of reformers to push for social justice, this shift helped scholars transcend the earlier literature that tried to put advocates and opponents of protective legislation into either maternalist or equal rights amendment camps.[16] While this earlier model worked for understanding the Children's Bureau and the National Women's Party, it did not help historians to make sense of organizations, like the Women's Bureau, that campaigned for labor standards and economic justice for women workers, but with an eye on more ambitious economic and social reforms. Further, this analysis of the work of the WB in the 1920s should be understood as part of a larger effort by Dorothy Sue Cobble and others to build a bridge between the first wave of feminism that focused on achieving suffrage and the second wave that emerged in the 1960s.[17]

Theory for Feminism," *Feminist Studies* 14 (Spring 1988): 32–50. The earlier conception of protective legislation viewed labor standards for women as the product of a long-standing separate spheres discourse – a "domestication" of a sphere of policy making, to use Paula Baker's terminology. See Paula Baker, "The Domestication of Politics: Women and American Political Society, 1780-1920," *AHR* 89 (June 1984): 620–47. During the 1990s, a number of historians and political scientists explored policy making through the lens of separate spheres and maternalism. See Theda Skocpol, *Protecting Soldiers and Mothers: The Political Origins of Social Policy in the United States* (Cambridge: Cambridge University Press, 1992); Seth Koven and Sonya Michel, "Womanly Duties: Maternalist Politics and the Origins of Welfare States in France, Germany, Great Britain, and the United States, 1880-1920," *AHR* 95 (October 1990): 1067–1108; Linda Gordon, *Pitied But Not Entitled: Single Mothers and the History of Welfare* (Cambridge: Harvard University Press, 1995; reprint New York: Free Press, 1994); Robyn Muncy, *Creating a Female Dominion in American Reform, 1890-1935* (New York: Oxford University Press, 1991).

[16] For a review of the move from maternalism to citizenship in work on gender/race and public policy, see Eileen Boris, "On the Importance of Naming: Gender, Race, and the Writing of Policy History," *Journal of Policy History* 17 (2005): 75–92. See also Boris and Kleinberg, "Mothers and Other Workers: (Re)Conceiving Labor, Maternalism, and the State"; Kish Sklar, Schüler, and Strasser, *Social Justice Feminists in the United States and Germany*; Kessler Harris, *In Pursuit of Equity*; and Joanne L. Goodwin, *Gender and the Politics of Welfare Reform: Mothers' Pensions in Chicago, 1911-1929* (Chicago: University of Chicago Press, 1997), 8–11. Many of these works draw explicitly on T. H. Marshall's analysis of ideas of citizenship from the eighteenth to the twentieth century. T. H. Marshall, *Class, Citizenship, and Social Development*, with an introduction by Seymour Martin Lipset (New York: Doubleday & Company, Inc., 1964), 65–122. For an analysis that takes into account the influence of race, class, gender, and nation of origin on the changing nature of "a braided citizenship" in the United States, see Linda Kerber, "The Meaning of Citizenship," *JAH* 84 (December 1997): 833–54.

[17] Cobble, *The Other Women's Movement*, 7. See also Wendy Sarvasy, Beyond the Difference Versus Equality Debate: Post-Suffrage Feminism, Citizenship and the Quest

The WB's opposition to the Equal Rights Amendment and support for protective legislation was not rooted in a maternalist project, such as that of the Children's Bureau, which had a "principled opposition to maternal employment."[18] From the start, WB directors Mary van Kleeck and Mary Anderson emphasized the need to place women workers in the context of broader trends in economic development and opportunity. As mentioned in the previous chapter, before Van Kleeck was called into the service of the state during the war, she had transformed the Russell Sage Foundation's Department of Industrial Studies from an investigatory body focused exclusively on women to one that examined all workers. When future director Mary Anderson organized the first government-sponsored meeting of trade union women in October 1918, the participants did not call for maternal protection; they called for equal pay for equal work, a minimum wage that provided for women and their dependents, and equal opportunity for training in the skilled trades.[19]

Despite a budget that largely stagnated between 1923 and 1929, the WB combined an analysis of government data with onsite investigations and assistance from nonprofit organizations such as the National Consumers League (NCL) and Women's Trade Union League (WTUL) to construct a body of public labor knowledge that integrated black and white industrial wage-earning women into the larger labor question and provided insight into the conditions of all poor workers who struggled to escape difficult, dangerous, and low-paying occupations. Between 1918 and 1929, the WB published seventy-two bulletins ranging in length

---

for a Feminist Welfare State," *Signs* 17 (Winter 1992): 329–62; Sybil Lipschultz, "Hours and Wages: The Gendering of Labor Standards in America," *Journal of Women's History* 8 (Spring 1996): 114–36; and J. Stanley Lemons, *The Woman Citizen: Social Feminism in the 1920s* (Urbana: University of Illinois Press, 1973).

[18] Michel, *Children's Interests/Mothers' Rights*, 91.

[19] "Conference of Trade-Union Women Under Auspices of U.S. Department of Labor," *MLR* 8 (November 1918): 190–1. See also Mary Anderson, "Will Women Retire from Industry with Return of Peace," *Proceedings of the Academy of Political Science in the City of New York* 8 (February 1919): 13–16; Mary Anderson, "Wages for Women Workers," *Annals of the American Academy of Political and Social Science* 81 (January 1919): 123–9; Mary van Kleeck, "Federal Policies for women in Industry," *Annals of the American Academy of Political and Social Science* 81 (January 1919): 87–94. The WTUL, which maintained a very close connection to the WB through Anderson, echoed these demands in its publications and annual meetings. "Seventh Biennial Convention of the National Women's Trade Union League," *MLR* 9 (July 1919): 267–72. For a similar assessment of the WB's advocacy of women's workplace rights, not only in the 1920s but after World War II, see Julia Blackwater, *Now Hiring: the Feminization of Work in the United States, 1900–1995* (College Station: Texas A&M University Press, 1997), 78–9, 135–7.

from an 8-page summary of standards for the employment of women to a 498-page detailed analysis of the impact of labor legislation on the employment of women. These studies combined a close analysis of data generated by government, firms, and nonprofits with onsite investigations, including personal interviews of workers and employers. During World War I, the Woman-in-Industry Service (WIS), the wartime predecessor agency led by Van Kleeck, answered specific, often urgent policy questions concerning women in industry. After the war, among other things, the WB responded to requests by state governments and nonprofit organizations that desired to use knowledge to construct and to promote public policies to protect women workers, but did not have the resources or skills to conduct detailed investigations.

EMPOWERING EXPERTISE: THE CREATION OF THE WOMEN'S BUREAU

Prior to the establishment of the Women's Bureau, the federal government made numerous efforts to institute an organized inquiry into the condition of women workers at home and in industry. In 1907, the Bureau of Labor Statistics (BLS) under Charles Neill launched a massive investigation of women and children workers that culminated in the publication of the nineteen-volume *Report on the Condition of Woman and Child Wage-Earners*. Testifying before a joint hearing of Congress, Mary van Kleeck noted that the BLS report "showed very clearly conditions throughout the Nation which required not simply an investigation but continuous attention on the part of the Federal Government." Partially as a result of the report, Congress in 1912 created, within the Department of Commerce and Labor, the Children's Bureau as well as a more informal Women's Division within the BLS.[20] The Children's Bureau had the strong backing of what historian Robin Muncy called the "female dominion" led by settlement house workers, and it flourished within the Department of Labor (DOL).[21] The Women's Division, on the other hand, faced a lack of funding and the neglect of BLS leaders. The division had its supporters, including the *New Republic*, which strongly sanctioned the work of the

---

[20] Congress, House and Senate, Joint Meeting of House Committee on Labor and Senate Committee on Education and Labor, WB, 66th Cong., 2nd sess., 4 and 5, March 1920, 62; and Mary Anderson, "Recent Investigations by Government Bureaus," NCSW (Chicago: University of Chicago Press, 1920): 140–1.

[21] In March of 1913, President Taft signed a bill that established the Department of Labor as a cabinet-level department.

underfunded but extremely productive Women's Division for its "practical, sound, and readily utilizable" investigations.[22] Even so, according to WB historian Judith Sealander, Neill "frequently diverted money from the division's meager budget to other bureau investigations." Lack of support – not just in financial terms, but in political terms as well – reached a crisis level when female agents working on a report on unemployment in Boston "charged that their statistics had been tampered with by the time the study reached print and so refused to sign the completed copy." The agents resigned and no replacements were hired.[23] When the division disappeared in 1916, the *New Republic* condemned the BLS that concluding that "The gist of the whole matter is that the powers that be" in the Bureau "are not interested in women."[24]

Despite the failure of the Women's Division, advocates of women workers such as the Women's Trade Union League and the National Consumers' League continued to lobby for a permanent government body devoted to the discovery and improvement of the condition of women workers. The entrance of large numbers of women into the work force during World War I combined with the suffrage movement to provide an opening that allowed these groups to break through a wall of congressional apathy. As part of the effort to mobilize workers for the war effort, the War Labor Administration established the Woman in Industry Service (WIS). Originally designed as an emergency war program that would develop public policies concerning women and connect women workers with wartime employment, the WIS received funding in 1919 for an additional year as part of an effort to ease the transition to a peacetime economy.[25]

From its inception, WIS supporters advocated that the service be transformed into a permanent bureau within the DOL. When testifying before the House Appropriations Committee in February 1919, WIS director Mary Van Kleeck described the need for a special bureau specifically designed to address the "special problems" of women workers:

---

[22] "What Uncle Sam Does not Do for Women in Industry," *NR*, July 29, 1916, 325.
[23] Sealander, *As Minority Becomes Majority*, 16. In her testimony before Congress, Van Kleeck did not mention Neill's interference with the Boston study, but she did describe budget and status problems within the BLS's Women's Division. Congress, House and Senate, Joint Meeting of House Committee on Labor and Senate Committee on Education and Labor, WB, 62.
[24] "What Uncle Sam Does not Do for Women in Industry," *NR*, 325.
[25] House, Committee on Appropriation, *Sundry Civil Bill*, 1920, 1556–71. "Woman Now Directs Nation's Women Workers," 56.

If women were earning as high a wages as men; if they were working as short hours as men; if they were working under proper conditions and with entire equality in their bargaining power we would not need a women's bureau, because then it would be natural that every single thing done in the Department of Labor would direct itself to women as well as to men.[26]

In 1920, Senator William Kenyon (R-Iowa) of the Committee on Education of Labor and Congressman Philip Campbell (R-Kansas) introduced a bill to establish the WB as a permanent bureau within the DOL. Although no groups or individuals testified against the establishment of the WB, some congressmen were reported to have had reservations about the need for a separate bureau.

In the context of the recently achieved suffrage, advocates for the establishment of a permanent Women's Bureau did not suffer from the lack of political support that plagued other wartime agencies, such as the Division of Negro Economics (DNE). The chair of the Woman's Executive Committee of the National Republican Committee, Rosalie Loew Whitney, described a party survey of Republican women across the country that found "in every place ... women believed it was necessary to have such a women's bureau in the Department of Labor."[27] When asked about the number of women she represented, Whitney bluntly replied, "I hope it will be very large next November."[28] Also testifying on behalf of the WB, Mrs. George Bass of the Women's National Committee of the National Democratic Party estimated that she represented "about 25,000,000" and that she did not know how "many that left for the other side."[29] Bass sought to place the WB in a larger context of government allocations to other issues. According to Bass, "The appropriation for the prevention of hog cholera was $600,000, while $40,000 has been given for women. The Texas cattle tick received $700,000 ... and to study the animal husbandry and improving the breeds of domestic animals, $300,000." Bass concluded, "I think that the Women's Bureau in the Department of Labor, which asks for the modest appropriation of $150,000 to undertake a work of the most absolutely vital importance – I think they are rather modest in their request. I believe that you should grant it."[30] In June 1920, Congress agreed and established

---

[26] House, Committee on Appropriations, *Sundry Civil Bill*, 1564–5.
[27] Congress, Joint Meeting of House Committee on Labor and Senate Committee on Education and Labor, *WB*, 41.
[28] Ibid., 42.
[29] Ibid., 44.
[30] Ibid., 46.

the Women's Bureau as a permanent arm of the Department of Labor, charging it to formulate standards, improve working conditions, increase the efficiency of, and advance the opportunities for the nation's women industrial workers.

Although most of the women who peopled the WB were longtime government investigators, their efforts can and should be considered part of the creation of the modern social and policy sciences. Indeed, observing their effort to create a body of social knowledge provides yet another opportunity for historians to broaden our conception of the social sciences and to observe how skilled and professional specialists expanded the institutions of social inquiry well beyond the modern, male-dominated university. In her work on the history of the social sciences, Helen Silverberg successfully challenges the distinction between academic social scientists and shapers of other forms of social knowledge, thus widening social science history to include institutions created and led by academically trained women locked out of male-dominated universities. Silverberg accurately describes the "rich network of social research settings outside the university built by female social scientists "to serve their own sense of the social science."

Indeed, the success of the WB raises important questions about laments by Silverberg and Sealander alleging that women's labor investigators were hampered by a narrow experience, limited by class as well as gender. Silverberg argued that "the range and scope of their participation ... had been reduced and narrowed to such female-dominated fields as home economics, social work, and school-based guidance counseling."[31] Regarding the WB's staff and leadership, Sealander claimed that they were "more likely to have seen the drawing room of the Henry Street Settlement House in New York City than to have seen a corporate boardroom or union executive's office." Without powerful ties to business and labor groups, Sealander concluded, these labor experts "had no chance to effect improvements in the working conditions of the woman worker."[32]

Such characterizations slight the skills and experience of WB staffers and minimize the importance of the WB in the development of labor policy discourses in the 1920s. The WB staff was indeed commissioned initially to examine the condition of women workers in particular. Yet

---

[31] Helen Silverberg, "Introduction: Toward a Gendered Social Science," *Gender and American Social Sciences: The Formative Years* (Princeton: Princeton University Press, 1998), 3.
[32] Sealander, *As Minority Becomes Majority*, 28.

the staff transformed that institution into an important vehicle for deliberation on the larger labor question and on the place of statist and voluntary measures reflecting social and political values in determining the conditions under which American workers labored. It is more accurate to characterize these women as experienced government statisticians, investigators, and administrators who created an innovative policy-making role for themselves within state bureaus and, as of World War I, in the federal government.

In fact, much like early leaders of the Bureau of Labor Statistics, who gained experience in various state labor bureaus before playing a shaping role in the construction of federal government labor statistics, Women's Bureau leaders arrived with high levels of education and important experience in state government and the nonprofit sector.[33] Assistant Director Agnes L. Peterson had previously supervised the Minnesota Department of Labor's law enforcement division, the "first [U.S.] special agency to function as a division or bureau to have administrative and law enforcement responsibilities pertaining to the employment of women and children."[34] Statistician and editor of the Editorial Division Elizabeth A. Hyde had held statistical and research positions with the Census Office, Carnegie Institution, U.S. Immigration Commission, U.S. Commission on Industrial Relations, National War Labor Board, and *Monthly Labor Review*. Ethel Best and Caroline Manning planned and carried out WB field studies. Best came to the WB after serving as president and director of the Neighborhood House in Westchester County and working as a special investigator in the New York Women in Industry Service. Manning earned an M.A. in English at Radcliffe in 1906 and held a fellowship at the Women's Educational and Industrial Union in Boston, where she worked undercover as an "unskilled woman" in order to investigate the condition of women workers. She left Boston in 1913 to "make a tenement house inspection in Philadelphia for the city board of health." Later

---

[33] For an analysis of similar staffing patters in the Bureau of Labor Statistics and its predecessors in the federal government, see Alexander Keyssar, *Out of Work: The First Century of Unemployment in Massachusetts* (Cambridge: Cambridge University Press, 1986); Mary O. Furner, "Knowing Capitalism: Public Investigation and the Labor Question in the Long Progressive Era," in Mary O. Furner and Barry Supple, eds., *The State and Economic Knowledge: The American and British Experiences* (Cambridge: Cambridge University Press, 1991), 246–68; and James Leiby, *Carroll Wright and Labor Reform: The Origin of Labor Statistics* (Cambridge: Harvard University Press, 1960).

[34] All WB staff background from Eleanor Nelson (comp.), Public Information Division Articles 1918–1955, WB, Box 11, File 331, Record Group (hereafter RG) 86, National Archives at College Park, MD (hereafter NA).

in the same year, she took a position as an investigator with the Bureau of Women and Children of the Minnesota Department of Labor. She moved to the Children's Bureau in 1918, but transferred to the Women's Bureau in 1920. Special agent and editor of the Division of Public Information Mary V. Robinson came to the WB with an A.B. from Goucher College, a year of graduate work at Johns Hopkins, training in journalism studies at New York University, two years of teaching at Westhampton College, and Red Cross work in France during the war.

Most, but not all, of the WB's leaders had middle-class backgrounds. Mary Anderson, appointed director of the WB by President Wilson with the endorsement of a wide variety of political and labor groups, was one of the few WB leaders to have risen from the working class.[35] In 1889, at the age of seventeen, the Swedish-born Anderson had emigrated to the United States with her family. She held a number of jobs, among them as a dishwasher in a Michigan lumber camp and a stitcher in an Illinois shoe factory. Her union involvement began in 1894 when she joined the International Boot and Shoe Workers' Union, where she served as a local president and sole female member of the union's executive board. In 1903, she joined the Women's Trade Union League, serving as an investigator, organizer, and representative to the United Garment Workers. In 1916, Anderson embarked upon the government stage of her career when she was appointed assistant secretary of WIS. When Van Kleeck left the service in 1919, Anderson became director.[36]

[35] M. Carey Thomas (president of Bryn Mawr College) to President Wilson, March 28, 1921; Margaret Drier Robins (former president of WTUL) to Secretary James J. Davis, March 21, 1921; Secretary Wilson sent a number of responses to organizations and individuals who endorsed Anderson, but whose original letters were not preserved. Secretary of Labor to Harriet Taylor Upton (vice-chairman National Republican Committee), March 25, 1921; Secretary of Labor to Mary W. Dewson (National Consumers' League), March 23, 1921. All letters General Records of the Department Labor, General Records, 1907–1942 (chief clerk's office), file 156/6 Mary Anderson, 1918–1923, RG 174, NA.

[36] "Mary Anderson" in Gary M. Fink, ed., *Biographical Dictionary of American Labor* (Westport: Greenwood Press, 1974), 88–9; Mary Anderson as told to Mary Winslow, *Woman at Work* (Minneapolis: University of Minnesota Press, 1951; reprint Westport: Greenwood Press, 1973). The voluminous correspondence between Van Kleeck and Anderson and other WB leaders provides evidence of Van Kleeck's continued influence on the WB well beyond the end of her tenure as director in 1920. Officially, Van Kleeck served as chairman of the WB Technical Committee, along with Mrs. Frank B. Gilbrath and Charles P. Neill (former BLS commissioner). On the committee, see letter to Anderson from Technical Committee and signed by Van Kleeck, April 2, 1926, Box 71, Folder WB Correspondence. Letters between Van Kleeck and Anderson convey a warm friendship and wide agreement on labor issues. The tone of the letters suggests Van Kleeck continued to play a mentoring role to Anderson, who frequently sought out Van Kleeck's advice and approval. For correspondence between Anderson and Van Kleeck, see Boxes 64 and

The varied training and demonstrated skill of WB investigators did not translate into generous appropriations. Anderson and supporters of the WB constantly struggled for a larger appropriation and greater pay equity for female government workers. The WB's budget, always a source of complaint in Anderson's annual reports, started at $40,000 in 1920, increasing to $75,000 in 1921 and to $108,000 by 1929. Anderson's annual report only occasionally mentioned the number of staffers employed each year, but a 1926 study of women in government service indicated that the WB employed 45 women, compared to 120 in the Children's Bureau and 33 in the Bureau of Home Economics.[37] Anderson frequently stressed the difficulty of attracting qualified women given congressional limitations placed on wages. As a reclassification of federal employees loomed in 1923, Anderson wrote, "The staff of the bureau has increased from 39 to 47" with "24 new appointments and 16 separations from the service." Anderson attributed this high turnover to an eighteen-hundred-dollar-per-year cap on agent salaries, which she contended made it impossible "to hold agents who have far more advantageous offers for similar employment outside of government service."[38] A large number of WB employees classified as fact collectors and analysts benefited from the 1923 reclassification, which resulted in a dramatic increase in the number of WB employees making more than eighteen hundred dollars, from five in 1921 to twenty-two in 1925, or nearly 50 percent of those employed by the WB.[39]

REDEFINING WOMEN WORKERS AS BREADWINNERS

Despite its limited budget, the WB's investigations demonstrated the progress of women workers in industry, the vast diversity of working women's experiences in industry, and the fact that wage work was nothing new to women workers. The WB took aim at conceptualizations of women

---

71, all in Mary Van Kleeck Papers, Sophia Smith Collection, Smith College (hereafter MVK Papers).

[37] The report listed one male employee in the WB. His salary was less than $1,860 per year. WB, "The Status of Women in the Government Service," *Bulletin* 53 (Washington DC: GPO, 1926), 5–6, 45.

[38] WB, *Fifth Annual Report of the Director of the WB* (Washington, DC: GPO, 1923), 20. See also, WB, *Third Annual Report of the Director of the WB* (Washington, DC: GPO, 1921), 22 and "The WB," *Survey Graphic* (April 16, 1921): 74.

[39] WB, "The Status of Women in the Government Service," 39–41, 44–5.

workers as temporary entrants into the labor market, referring in a 1920 report, for example, to the contributions of a "seasoned, hard-drilled army of women workers" to the war effort. Rejecting the view that these workers were new to industry, the WB stressed, "Necessity had long before dragged these women into the ranks of labor in factory, mill, office, and store, and had subjected them to the stern discipline of daily tasks performed under the lock-step system of modern industrial organization."[40] While attacking the idea that women were employed in large numbers only in times of national emergency, the WB succeeded in demonstrating the diversity of experiences of women workers and in scrutinizing the failure of employers to reward women workers equally for their experience and indispensable contribution to the war effort.

To advertise women workers' success in expanding the scope of employment opportunities into professional and manufacturing occupations, the WB described dramatic shifts in women workers' employment away from domestic and personal service occupations and toward clerical and manufacturing work.[41] The percentage of women over the age of ten employed in domestic and personal service occupations fell from 7.3 percent in 1910 to 5.4 percent in 1920. The WB noted that this trend was particularly prominent for black women, who "entered factory employment in large numbers during the war."[42] The most dramatic changes in women's employment occurred in manufacturing industries. Between 1910 and 1920, the number of women workers employed as semiskilled operatives in the iron and steel industries and automobile factories increased by 145 and 1,408 percent respectively. This broadening of the occupational fields employing women was reflected in comparisons between 1900 and 1920 census data, which indicated that the number of occupations employing fifty thousand women or more increased from nineteen to thirty.[43] In some of these industries, such as clerical work, cigar and tobacco factories, and the lumber and furniture industries, the

---

[40] WB, "The New Position of Women in American Industry," *Bulletin* 12 (Washington, DC: GPO, 1920), 16.
[41] WB, "The Occupational Progress of Women," *Bulletin* 27 (Washington, DC: GPO, 1922), 3.
[42] Ibid., 8–9.
[43] Industries with fifty thousand women workers in 1910 included servants, dressmakers, milliners, schoolteachers, boarding house keepers, stenographers and typists, musicians, nurses, laundresses, clothing factory operatives, and textile mill operatives. "New" industries that in 1920 employed fifty thousand women workers included saleswoman, bookkeepers and cashiers, retail dealers, cigar factory operatives, shoe factory operatives, clerks in stores, and clerks in offices. WB, "The Occupational Progress of Women," 19–20.

WB's analysis revealed that women, between 1900 and 1920, were supplanting male workers.[44]

By pointing to progress made by women workers and their longstanding participation in wage labor, the WB took aim at the "Pin-Money Fallacy," also challenged by more recent scholarship, which dismissed the centrality of female wage labor by suggesting that young women worked "to make a little extra money and will soon get married and be on 'easy street' for the rest of her life." WB editor Mary N. Winslow concluded, "Every investigation which touches wage-earning women piles up the evidence that women are working more often than not to eke out some husband's or father's insufficient wage and make it adequate for the family needs."[45] Examining women workers in Kansas, WB investigators found that nearly half the women in industry were over the age of twenty-five, and an equal number were over the age of thirty and under the age of twenty.[46] In a study of the Household Census Schedules for Passaic, New Jersey, WB investigators found that nearly half the women residents worked for wages, and one-half of these working women "were or had been married."[47] In 1925, the WB produced a four-city study that found little evidence to support the idea that women were only temporary participants in the labor force; in fact, of the nearly forty thousand women workers examined, over three-fifths were at least twenty-five years old and more than one-half were or had been married.[48] Examining the presence of children in homes with breadwinning women, the WB found that more than 50 percent of working women had children.[49]

---

[44] WB, "The Occupational Progress of Women," 26–30; WB, "Facts about Working Women," *Bulletin* 46 (Washington, DC: GPO, 1925), 6–7.

[45] WB, "Health Problems of Women in Industry," 3; Mary Anderson, "Recent Investigations by Government Bureaus," NCSW (Chicago: University of Chicago Press, 1920), 141; Mary Anderson, "Women in Industry," *AF* 32 (May 1925): 333–5; WB, "Women in Kentucky Industries," *Bulletin* 29 (Washington, DC: GPO, 1923), 80–5; WB, "The Share of Wage-Earning Women in Family Support," *Bulletin* 30 (Washington, DC: GPO, 1923); WB, "Family Status of Breadwinning Women In Four Selected Cities," *Bulletin* 41 (Washington, DC: GPO, 1925); WB, "Women in Ohio Industries," *Bulletin* 44 (Washington, DC: GPO, 1925), 8; WB, "Women Workers and Family Support," *Bulletin* 49 (Washington, DC: GPO, 1925).

[46] WB, "Women's Wages in Kansas," *Bulletin* 17 (Washington, DC: GPO, 1921), 21, 53–82.

[47] WB, "The Family Status of Breadwinning Women: A Study of Material in the Census Schedules of a Selected Locality," *Bulletin* 23 (Washington, DC: GPO, 1922), 4.

[48] WB, "Family Status of Breadwinning Women in Four Selected Cities," 8–9.

[49] Ibid., 17.

LABOR INQUIRY AS ACTIVISM THROUGH GENDERED AND RACE KNOWLEDGE

The WB was a far more aggressive advocate for wage justice and against job discrimination than has been recognized. The agency prominently reported not only that experience in a trade or job did not automatically lead to an increase in wages, but also that wage gains appeared to depend on the race, age, occupation, and location of women workers. Rhode Island employers did reward experienced women in industries such as rubber manufacturing, where women with more than twenty years of experience earned 80 percent more than their fellow workers with less than six months of experience.[50] White women workers in Kentucky with five years on the job received credit for experience, earning on average $14.10 per week, a significant increase compared to $10.75 for new workers. Yet there was hardly any experience premium for black women with five or more years of experience, whose weekly earnings of $10.40 differed negligibly from the average of $9.80 black women with no experience earned for similar work.[51] This lack of remuneration for experience received by black women in Kentucky industries was consistent with the Women's Bureau's findings in Alabama and Tennessee.[52]

Age discrimination was also documented. An analysis of New Jersey wages and experience found "a steady increase in earnings with each year of additional experience, except for the women who had worked 15 years and over, whose median earnings were slightly less than those of the women who had worked ten and under fifteen years."[53] In Delaware, women with one to five years of experience could expect to see rising incomes through their fifth year in the trade, after which wages leveled off before climbing again for women with more than fifteen years of experience.[54] An analysis of wages in Kansas found little fluctuation in wages, concluding that women between thirty and fifty years old "cannot hope for such rapid increases in her wage as she experienced in earlier years."[55] The WB conducted one study that directly compared the wages

---

[50] WB, "Women in Rhode Island Industries," *Bulletin* 21 (Washington, DC: GPO, 1922).
[51] WB, "Women in Kentucky Industries," 55–7.
[52] WB, "Women in Alabama Industries," *Bulletin* 34 (Washington, DC: GPO, 1924), 54; WB, "Women in Tennessee Industries," *Bulletin* 56 (Washington, DC: GPO, 1927), 44.
[53] WB, "Women in New Jersey Industries," *Bulletin* 37 (Washington, DC: GPO, 1924), 33.
[54] WB, "Women in Delaware Industries," *Bulletin* 58 (Washington, DC: GPO, 1927), 35–6.
[55] WB, "Women's Wages in Kansas," 31.

of women workers with those of men workers. In 1920, the WB issued a study of women workers in government service that revealed that women working in government received significantly lower wages than their male counterparts.[56]

Regarding racial discrimination, WB studies provided important comparative data that conveyed a deep inequality between black and white women workers. Both labored under difficult conditions for little pay, but WB research described black women workers as a separate class of laborers, with a high labor force participation rate, who worked in the most difficult and dirty occupations for a fraction of the wages of working-class white women. A study of Georgia workers in 1922 revealed median weekly earnings for white women of $12.20, but of only $6.20 for black women. This incongruity held true for annual earning as well, with white women's median earnings at $748 and black women's at $413.[57] Differences in occupations accounted for some of this wage inequality, but it persisted in knit goods and manufacturing where black and white women worked in the same occupations and firms. These differences were most pronounced in garment industries, where white workers' median weekly earnings were $12.20 and black women's only $3.90, indicating to WB investigators a "considerable discrimination against Negro women."[58] In many plants across several states, the WB found when employers used a piece-rate system "the rates were lower for Negro than for white women workers."[59]

Given these disparities, it is not surprising that economic instability hit black women workers disproportionately hard. In one of the few WB surveys with more than one data point for wages, an investigation of wages in Missouri revealed that between January 1921 and April 1922, when the economy began slowly to climb out of the postwar depression, white women's median wages fell from $12.90 to $12.65 per week, whereas black women's fell dramatically more, from $9.35 to $6.00.[60]

[56] WB, "Women in Government Service," *Survey Graphic*, June 12, 1920, 378.
[57] WB, "Women in Georgia Industries," *Bulletin* 22 (Washington, DC: GPO, 1922), 7.
[58] Ibid., 31.
[59] Ibid., 32. For other studies that included similar data on wage discrepancies between black and white women, see WB, "Women in Arkansas Industries," *Bulletin* 26 (Washington, DC: GPO, 1923), 6, 27–47; WB, "Women in Kentucky Industries," 29–57; WB, "Women in South Carolina Industries," *Bulletin* 32 (Washington, DC: GPO, 1923), 12–14; WB, "Women in Alabama Industries," 52–70; WB, "Women in Tennessee Industries," 5, 39–44; WB, "Women in Delaware Industries," 68; and WB, "Women in Mississippi Industries," *Bulletin* 55 (Washington, DC: GPO, 1926), 5, 18.
[60] WB, "Women in Missouri Industries," *Bulletin* 35 (Washington, DC: GPO, 1924), 8.

An analysis of the relationship between the WB and black women workers provides another opportunity to reassess the importance and the radicalism of the WB by contemporary standards. Historians of the WB have overstated the degree to which it ignored black women workers. In fact, the WB was one of the few institutions consistently publicizing the tremendous hardships and injustices experienced by black women workers struggling to gain a foothold in industrial occupations. During World War I, Van Kleeck worked actively with Director of the Division of Negro Economics (DNE) George E. Haynes and Secretary of Labor Wilson to appoint a black woman to the staff of the WIS. Van Kleeck's efforts led to the appointment of Helen Irvin to the WIS staff as a special assistant, though Haynes and the DNE directed much of her work.[61] Irvin came to the WIS with considerable experience, having graduated from Howard University and completed graduate work in "economics, vocational guidance, and psychology" at both Chicago and Pennsylvania. Her work with the Food Administration and Red Cross provided her with experience in both nonprofit and government sectors.[62]

Historians have portrayed Anderson's leadership of the WB as significantly less attentive to black women workers' issues than Van Kleeck's.[63] This perception is true to a point. Anderson worked in a tradition of labor inquiry that tended to diminish the importance of household labor and ignore the work of predominantly African American agricultural workers in the South.[64] Architects of the WB wrote these prejudices and blindspots into the act creating the WB. The act establishing the WB charged that it "shall have authority to investigate and report to the

---

[61] For more on Van Kleeck's advocacy of Irvin and the need for labor expertise concerning black women, see Mary van Kleeck, "New Standards for Negro Women in Industry," *Life and Labor* (June 1919): 134–5; Van Kleeck to Secretary Wilson, September 3, 1918, Van Kleeck to Secretary Wilson, April 18, 1919, WB, File Correspondence of the Director, 1918–1920, Van Kleeck, A-M, RG 86, NA. On Van Kleeck's continued interest in issues concerning black workers and her relationship to the National Urban League, see Guichard Parris and Lester Brooks, *Blacks in the City: A History of the National Urban League* (Boston: Little, Brown and Company, 1971), 200–3. In 1932, Emma Penn Shields completed her M.A. at New York University with a thesis entitled "Vocational Adjustment Problems of Negro Women in New York City." Doxey A. Wilkerson, "Section D: The Vocational Education and Guidance of Negroes," *Journal of Negro Education* 9 (April 1940): 265.

[62] "To Represent Negro Women Wage Earners," *Broad Axe*, December 28, 1918, 5. Also see Francille Rusan Wilson, *The Segregated Scholars: Black Social Scientists and the Creation of Black Labor Studies, 1890–1950* (Charlottesville: University of Virginia Press, 2006), 192–6.

[63] Fink, *Biographical Dictionary of American Labor*, 88–9.

[64] Boris and Kleinberg, "Mothers and Other Workers," 92–3.

said department [Department of Labor] upon all matters pertaining to the welfare of women in industry." As a result, the WB did not examine domestic and agricultural occupations, where, particularly in the South, the majority of black women were employed.[65] Historical anecdotes have not done the WB any favors, either. In their examinations of the WB, Judith Sealander and Phillip Foner recount an episode when civil rights activist Mary Church Terrell approached Anderson hoping to establish a Colored Women's Division in the WB. Anderson dismissed the suggestion, remarking "colored women in industry are not a very large factor."[66]

All this notwithstanding, such references obscure the WB's important work describing the condition of black women workers. From her earliest involvement with the WB, Anderson recognized the difficulties black women faced, particularly in the South. While presiding over the October 4, 1918 meeting of trade union women, Anderson asked that the conference participants consider the issues of "colored women in general but particularly the colored women of the South." Anderson noted the pernicious use of wartime "Work or Fight" laws that compelled men, and in some cases women, to work or be charged with vagrancy. She specifically mentioned the situation in New Orleans, as described to her by Haynes, where "they had picked [black] women up on the street and thrown them in jail and kept them there for any amount of time; and often the next morning they bring them forward before the judge, and they pick them out and they say 'You go to work there; you go to work there; you go to work there, or you go to jail, for thirty or forty or fifty days.'" Anderson indignantly described instances when white women had used such laws to force black women back into domestic occupations.[67]

[65] For the nation, 35.7 percent of black women employed outside the home worked in agricultural occupations and 53 percent worked in domestic occupations. As of the 1920 census, only 7 percent of black women found employment in manufacturing occupations. By the time of the WB's investigations, this number had likely grown as a result of wartime employment and the migration. For more on the long-standing opposition to inquiry into the condition of black workers, see David Levering Lewis, *W. E. B. Du Bois: Biography of a Race* (New York: Henry Holt and Company, 1993); John H. Stanfield, *Philanthropy and Jim Crow in American Social Science* (Westport, CT: Greenwood Press, 1985); Leiby, *Carroll Wright and Labor Reform*; and William T. Moye and Joseph P. Goldberg, *The First Hundred Years of the Bureau of Labor Statistics* (Washington, DC: GPO, 1985).

[66] Quoted in Judith Anne Sealander, "The WB, 1920–1950: Federal Reaction to Female Wage Earning" (PhD dissertation, Duke University, 1977), 39–40; Philip S. Foner, *Women and the American Labor Movement: From World War I to the Present* (New York: The Free Press, 1980), 125–6. For a more recent assessment of the WB's consideration of African American women, see Rusan Wilson, *The Segregated Scholars*, 173–214.

[67] "Trade Union Conference of the Woman in Industry Service of the United States, Department of Labor, 4 October 1918" Reel 4 of Records of the WB of the U.S. DOL, 1918–1965: Part I, frame 1040–2. For a further description of widespread abuse of these

Looking at discrimination as an aspect of labor market mobility and segmentation, WB investigators Helen B. Irvin and Emma Shields produced two pithy studies of black women in industry describing rampant discrimination and shocking wage differentials. Shields, a former student of George E. Haynes, followed the path Pidgeon and Manning took from the Children's Bureau to the Women's Bureau.[68] Irvin and Shield's studies' found that whenever possible black women used a tight labor market as a vehicle to move to jobs with greater autonomy and flexibility than domestic labor. In clerical work, according to Irvin, African American women used the war labor shortage to gain a tentative foothold in positions previously dominated by white women. Though many workers were told after the war that their services were no longer required or that the position was "intended for white workers," others "acquitted themselves in so satisfactory a manner that they were retained" permanently or even promoted.[69]

Despite a contraction in nondomestic occupational opportunities after the war, Irvin found evidence of a "widespread shortage of workers in all branches of domestic service," which led to "great discontent among housewives," some of whom "appear to have gone to the extent of organizing for the purpose of forcing the emancipated Negro housemaid and laundress out of her new industrial position and back to the dissatisfaction of the other woman's kitchen."[70] The results of the 1920 census revealed that the number of black women employed in domestic work fell 11.6 percent between 1910 and 1920.[71] Investigations for the United States Employment Service (USES) and the Woman-in-Industry Service by Elizabeth Ross Haynes confirmed growing unrest and mobility among those black women who continued to work in domestic occupations in the North. "Some very evident changes have come about in personal and

---

laws in the South, see Walter F. White, "'Work or Fight' in the South," *NR*, 1 March 1919, 144–6. On the effort to mobilize black women for the war effort, see William Breen, "Black Women and the Great War: Mobilization and Reform in the South," *Journal of Southern History* 44 (August 1979): 421–40.

[68] Rusan Wilson, *The Segregated Scholars*, 196–200.

[69] DNE, *The Negro at Work During the World War and Reconstruction: Statistics, Problems, and Policies Relating to the Greater Inclusion of Negro Wage Earners in American Industry and Agriculture* (Washington, DC: GPO, 1921; reprint, New York: Negro Universities Press, 1969), 133.

[70] Helen Brooks Irvin, "Conditions in Industry as They Affect Negro Women," in *NCSW* (Chicago: Rogers and Hall Co., 1919), 523; Elizabeth Ross Haynes, "Negroes in Domestic Service in the United States: An Introduction," *Journal of Negro History* 8 (October 1923): 385.

[71] "Occupations for Negroes," *Southern Workman* LII (May 1923): 11.

domestic service during the past twelve months," Haynes reported. "There is much the same restlessness and change from one employer to another; much the same wear and tear on households and housewives."[72]

Building on this body of work, in 1922 Shields produced a study detailing reductions in the black female industrial work force following the war. Shields determined that black women maintained positions in industrial employment, but that, in 40 of the 150 establishments surveyed, employers reassigned black women to lower-skilled positions, and in two plants "management frankly acknowledged that the Negro women were gradually being weeded out."[73] Black women who continued to work in manufacturing occupations often faced more difficult working conditions than their white counterparts. Shields described workplace segregation, longer hours for black employees, unequal pay, employment instability, poor ventilation, and inadequate access to toilets, drinking, and washing facilities. Shields accounted for some of the disparities between white and black workers by pointing to the age of facilities where black women worked. "The dirty factory surroundings of Negro women were partly due, it seemed, to the fact that these women were left in the old factory buildings, which managers considered beyond the hope of cleaning, when new factory buildings were constructed for the white women workers," Shields explained.[74] Of the 150 plants Shields surveyed, 101 employed "white and Negro workers under different conditions."[75] The inequality

---

[72] Haynes was the wife of DNE head George E. Haynes, and she was a graduate student in political science at Columbia University. She served as a dollar-a-year worker for the Woman-in-Industry Service under Van Kleeck and a domestic service employment secretary for USES from January 1920 to May 1922. Elizabeth Ross Haynes grew up in Lowndes County, Alabama, graduated from Fisk with an A.B. in 1903, and attended summer school classes at the University of Chicago in 1905 and 1907. In 1924 she was the first African American elected to the YWCA National Board, and in 1935 was elected co-leader of Harlem's 21st Assembly District. She also served as an executive member of Tammany Hall. John A. Garraty and Mark C. Carnes, eds., *American National Biography*, 1999, s.v. "Elizabeth Ross Haynes"; Elizabeth Ross Haynes, "Two Million Negro Women at Work," *Southern Workman* (February 1922): 66; also Elizabeth Ross Haynes, "Negroes in Domestic Service in the United States: An Introduction," 384–442. The latter publication is Haynes's M.A. thesis in political science at Columbia University. For more on Haynes and the importance of her work, see Rusan Wilson, *The Segregated Scholars*, 200–8.

[73] WB, "Negro Women in Industry," *Bulletin* 20 (Washington, DC: GPO, 1922), 11.

[74] Ibid., 28. Of the firms surveyed, Shields noted fifteen firms employing three thousand black women "in quarters which had been vacated by white women." Shields makes a similar point in Emma L. Shields, "Negro Women and the Tobacco Industry," *Life and Labor* 6 (May 1921): 143.

[75] WB, "Negro Women in Industry," 29.

did not escape black women, who in interviews, according to Shields, "revealed the fact that they had fully observed the differences and felt humiliated and discouraged as a result."[76]

Between 1923 and 1929, the WB did not produce any studies devoted exclusively to black women workers; instead, the WB attempted to integrate black women into its overall examination of women workers. To its credit, the WB recognized that its analysis of black women after 1922 had been scattered. In its 1927–8 annual report, the WB noted:

> Notwithstanding the importance of the subject and the interest it evokes, the bureau, in the 10 years of its existence, had been able to make but one study of the employment of Negro women.... With this great deficiency in mind, all the data concerning Negro women in the reports of State surveys made by the Women's Bureau are being assembled and correlated.[77]

The result in 1929 was a seventy-two-page Women's Bureau study of black women workers in fifteen states that attempted to synthesize published and unpublished WB studies with 1920 Bureau of Census occupational statistics in order to paint a broad picture of black women workers. Unfortunately, due to the scattered chronological and geographical quality of the data, the 1929 study did not provide a particularly clear picture of black women workers in 1929, or in any other year for that matter. Women's Bureau investigator and report author Mary Elizabeth Pidgeon conceded in the conclusion of her discussion of wages, "Differences in time of survey, in type of industry, and in locality narrow the scope of the accurate comparisons that are possible from the data secured."[78]

Though integrating black women into the state studies was an imperfect method, an analysis of WB studies suggests that the WB did an adequate job of including a fairly representative sample of black women employed in *industry* in its studies – that is, in nonagricultural and nondomestic occupations. Table 5.1 compares the percentage of black women in industry according to the 1920 census with the percentage of black women recorded in various WB state surveys. WB surveys were onsite

---

[76] Ibid., 30. See also "American Girl's Travels," *NYT*, April 9, 1922, 90.
[77] "Summary of the Tenth Annual Report of the Director of the WB: Part II, Comments and Recommendations," 1923, Reel 4 of Records of the WB of the U.S. Department of Labor, 1918–1965: Part I, frame 877.
[78] WB, "Negro Women in Industry in 15 States," *Bulletin* 70 (Washington, DC: GPO, 1929), 47. Like other WB investigators, Pidgeon came to the WB with a wealth of experience. She had previously worked with the Children's Bureau as well as the University of Virginia and the University of Chicago. Mary Anderson to Mary van Kleeck, February 10, 1928, Box 71, Folder 1107, "WB-Correspondence," MVK Papers.

TABLE 5.1. *Were African American Women Underrepresented in WB Reports Relative to their Presence in Industry?*

State (Bureau Bulletin #)	Percentage of the female work force over the age of ten that is African American according to Census Bureau – 1920	Percentage of the female workforce over the age of ten that is African American and employed in industries other than domestic or agricultural occupations according to Census Bureau – 1920	Percentage of black women in industry as described in Women's Bureau state and local surveys
Georgia (22)	65	18.9	17.5
Maryland (24)	30.3	7.0	5.6
Kentucky (29)	20.1	10.9	12.6
South Carolina (32)	70.7	17.4	7
Alabama (34)	64.6	17.5	13
Missouri (35)	12.1	2.7	8.6
Illinois (51)	5.4	2.2	4.6
Tennessee (56)	44.8	10.9	8.6
Mississippi (55)	77.2	22.3	18.9
Delaware (58)	25.3	5.0	13.2

investigations conducted by WB investigators who interviewed employers, managers, and foremen; inspected the plants; and personally gathered payroll statistics. The WB's studies underrepresented the percentage of black women industrial workers in Alabama, Georgia, Maryland, South Carolina, Mississippi, and Tennessee and overrepresented the number in Delaware, Illinois, Missouri, and Kentucky.

ADVOCATING LABOR STANDARDS BEFORE AND AFTER *ADKINS*

Armed with data representing the experiences of black and white women workers, the WB worked to persuade policy makers and the public to reconsider prevailing understandings of the labor market and the policies affecting workers. In an era when policy makers celebrated capital's ability to provide for American consumers and experts' skill in managing the business cycle with only the lightest touch from the federal government, WB investigators built up a body of expertise that revealed the uneven nature of this prosperity. Just as significant, however, the WB provided a site where labor reformers and policy makers could explore the potential of statist and voluntary policies to improve the working and living conditions of all American workers, irrespective of gender. From its earliest studies, the WB made clear that its work was about something more than the protection of motherhood. In its review of a 1920 WB study, the *New Republic* observed, "The report reaches the modest conclusion that perhaps the remedy is not to exclude the women from the occupation but to 'exclude' the conditions."[79]

Like many national agencies, the WB struggled with the problem of federalism. A lack of development in federal regulatory powers and a tradition of public regulation of health and safety concerns by state governments forced the WB to work closely with governors and state legislative bodies. The WB found willing and eager cooperation from the states, which looked to the WB to fortify state investigatory efforts and propose legislative means of ameliorating inadequate wages and poor working conditions. Historian William Brock's work on nineteenth-century public policy demonstrates that state governments developed institutions for the regulation and investigation of public health and labor that were eventually adopted by the federal government.[80] In the case of women workers, the situation was in part reversed. Although some states – such as Minnesota and New York, where many WB investigators earned critical training and experience – created institutions or hired investigators to examine the condition of women workers, generally state-level inquiry was not as well developed as the work of the WB.

Upon the WB's establishment, state governments immediately called on the expertise and skill of its investigators to examine the condition of women workers and propose legislation to ameliorate poor working conditions. In doing this work, the WB took on an awesome responsibility. It not only had to "discover" working women and invent a method for dealing with gender and labor; it also had to develop labor standards to protect these workers and monitor the enforcement of laws already enacted, a task further complicated by the fact that the WB did not have the lever of federal legislation at its disposal and had to rely entirely on individual state governments for assistance.

In the late teens and early 1920s, the WB was optimistic about the willingness and effectiveness of states to mandate and enforce wage and hour legislation improving the working conditions of women workers.[81]

---

[79] "Women in Industry," *NR* XXVN (January 26, 1921): 321.
[80] William R. Brock, *Investigation and Responsibility: Public Responsibility in the United States, 1865–1900* (Cambridge: Cambridge University Press, 1984); and William J. Novak, *The People's Welfare: Law and Regulation in Nineteenth Century America* (Chapel Hill: University of North Carolina Press, 1996).
[81] WB, "State Laws Affecting Working Women," *Bulletin* 40 (Washington, DC: GPO, 1924), 1. Also see Mary Anderson, "Women's Work and Wages: The WB and Standards

Even business research organizations such as the NICB that had opposed minimum wage legislation conceded that such laws had pushed up wages for many workers, particularly the lowest paid. In its investigation of minimum wage legislation in Massachusetts, the NICB admitted that wages had increased as a result of legislation, but it insisted that outside of Massachusetts, minimum wage laws had been established at levels about equal to what women were already receiving. Of course, even if this were true, such laws would have had the added benefit of maintaining these wage levels in economic downturns. Anderson and the WB publicly and privately defended the utility of wage legislation. In a letter to Maud Younger of the National Woman's Party, Anderson wrote, "Our minimum wage conferences all tell of these facts. Even with the very poor wage that the wage board sets ... we find that in 95 percent of the cases the minimum wage raises the women's wages."[82] By 1923, thirteen states and the District of Columbia had passed some type of minimum wage legislation. Significant though uneven progress had been made regarding hours regulation as well, and by 1924 only four states had no laws regulating some aspect of the number of hours worked by women.[83]

With a Supreme Court stacked with Taft appointees and hostile to national labor standards save those workers directly involved in commerce and covered by the Adamson Act and the Lafollette Seamen's Act, the WB aided and encouraged state-based efforts to protect workers and publicized evidence of successful attempts to improve working conditions and terms of employment. In doing so, the WB adopted a time-tested method previously utilized by the Bureau of Labor Statistics that aimed

---

of Women's Work," *NCSW* (Chicago: University of Chicago Press, 1921), 285; Mary N. Winslow, "The Effect of Labor Laws on Women Workers," *NCSW* (Chicago: University of Chicago Press, 1927), 312–13.

[82] Mary Anderson to Maud Younger, October 20, 1921, National Woman's Party Papers, Reel 19; Vivien Hart, *Bound by Our Constitution: Women Workers and the Minimum Wage* (Princeton: Princeton University Press, 1994), 113; NICB, *Minimum-Wage Legislation in Massachusetts* (New York: NICB, 1927).

[83] WB, "State Laws Affecting Working Women," 1 and 6. Also see Anderson, "Women's Work and Wages: The WB and Standards of Women's Work," 285; Winslow, "The Effect of Labor Laws on Women Workers," 312–13. WB, "Iowa Women in Industry," *Bulletin* 19 (Washington, DC: GPO, 1922), 19; and WB, "Standard and Scheduled Hours of Work for Women in Industry," *Bulletin* 43 (Washington, DC: GPO, 1925), 11–13. The WB also examined other areas where legislation regulated the employment of women workers, WB, "The Employment of Women at Night," *Bulletin* 64 (Washington, DC: GPO, 1928).

to encourage emulation by laggard states and to offer model legislation that progressive statists in the states could easily adopt.

Frequently, state leaders supporting labor standards called on the WB (and its predecessor, the WIS) to conduct investigations in order to build a body of expertise that would support efforts to establish labor legislation opposed by business interests. In one such instance, Indiana Governor James P. Goodrich, the state's industrial board, and the state wartime council of defense requested that the WB conduct a survey of the state's labor laws and their effects on women workers. An examination of 112 plants employing twelve thousand women workers in November and December 1918 revealed long hours by women workers and a failure of the state to enforce laws regulating the employment of workers under the age of eighteen.[84] The WIS pointed to a number of industries with extraordinarily long workdays, including a sixty-five-hour workweek in a clothing factory, eighty-four hours in a cannery, and eighty-eight hours and forty minutes in an automobile manufacturing plant. After the completion of the report, the Indiana State committee requested that the Women's Bureau and the Children's Bureau organize a conference in Indianapolis to present the study's findings to a larger audience.[85] Governor Goodrich also adopted the investigation's recommendation that the state establish a permanent women's division to regulate hours and working conditions of women in industry.[86] Throughout the 1920s, the WB used state-level investigations similar to the one in Indiana to publicize the best practices of states with established labor standards and to shame states that left women workers unprotected. In its investigation of Indiana, investigators noted that the state was "one of the six states having no law limiting the hours of women over 18 years of age," which

---

[84] WIS, "Labor Law for Women in Industry in Indiana," *Bulletin* 2 (Washington, DC: GPO, 1919), 10, 13–19.
[85] House, Committee on Appropriations, *Sundry Civil Bill, 1920*, 1561.
[86] WIS, "Labor Law for Women in Industry in Indiana," 3. For a similar situation, but in New York, see House, Committee on Appropriations, *Sundry Civil Bill, 1920*, 1561. "Women Work Risk of Women," *NYT*, July 23, 1918, 11. WIS, "Proposed Employment of Women During the War in the Industries of Niagara Falls, N.Y.," *Bulletin* 1 (Washington, DC: GPO, 1918); "Industrial Problems of Women at Niagara Falls: Woman in Industry Service makes Recommendations for Their Solutions," *Life and Labor* (January 1919): 21–2; "Proposed Employment of Women During the War in the Industries of Niagara Falls, N.Y.," *MLR* 8 (January 1919): 231–46. For other wartime studies, see WB, "Standards for the Employment of Women in Industry," *Bulletin* 3 (Washington, DC: GPO, 1919); WB, "Wages of Candy Makers in Philadelphia in 1919," *Bulletin* 4 (Washington, DC: GPO, 1919).

"makes possible abnormally long hours of employment for women."[87] By 1921, Indiana enacted a law restricting hours worked by women in manufacturing.[88]

Prior to *Adkins*, it looked like the WB might make a cottage industry of investigating conditions in states at the invitation of government and nonprofit groups and then proposing state legislation modeled on the Indiana example. For instance, after a number of failures to enact an eight-hour law in Iowa, supporters of the legislation, including the League of Women Voters and the Federation of Women's Clubs along with the state commissioner of labor, requested that the WB conduct an investigation in order to "present arguments" for the legislation "based on the actual conditions" of women workers. The WB identified Iowa as "extreme, though not alone, in its ignoring of the advance in labor legislation as it affects women." "Iowa is one of the six States which do not limit the number of hours, by day or week, that a woman may work; it is one of the 35 states permitting night work without restriction; it is one of the 34 States having no minimum wage legislation," the WB reported.[89] In Virginia, the WB conducted a survey of hours and working conditions at the request of Governor Westmoreland Davis, who, in a letter to Secretary of Labor Davis, suggested that an investigation "would supply valuable information concerning the industrial activities of this State, and would be of especial value as a basis for any legislation that might be enacted in the interest of women engaged in industry."[90]

In other cases, proponents of labor legislation on the state level used WB investigations to attack antilabor standards arguments. For instance, WB research played an important role in the Consumers' League of Ohio and the Ohio Council of Women in Industry effort to undermine

---

[87] WIS, "Labor Law for Women in Industry in Indiana," 4, 11, 26–9.
[88] WB, "Some Effects of Legislation Limiting Hours of Work for Women," *Bulletin* 15 (Washington DC: GPO, 1921), 7. For further evidence of the WB's advisory role to states, see, WB, "Iowa Women In Industry"; WB, "Hours and Conditions of Work For Women in Industry in Virginia," *Bulletin* 10 (Washington, DC: GPO, 1920); WB, "Labor Laws for Women in Industry in Indiana"; WB, "Women in Missouri Industries"; WB, "Women in Rhode Island Industries"; WB, "Women in Alabama Industries"; and WB, "Women in Maryland Industries."
[89] WB, "Iowa Women In Industry," 7–8.
[90] WB, "Hours and Conditions of Work For Women in Industry in Virginia," 6. During and shortly after World War I, writers of WB bulletins often made very specific policy recommendations to state governments based on their investigation. WB, "Labor Laws for Women in Industry in Indiana," 27–9; WB, "Women in Missouri Industries"; WB, "Women in Rhode Island Industries," 13; and WB, "Women in Maryland Industries," 14.

a study by a minimum wage commission established by Ohio state government leaders to investigate the costs and benefits of popular minimum wage legislation. After a short and thin investigation, the commission announced its opposition to a minimum wage law. Drawing in part on WB data, Ellery F. Reed, working with the Consumers' League of Ohio and the Ohio Council of Women in Industry, demonstrated the deficiencies in the original study.[91]

In addition to investigating conditions and proposing labor standards, the WB inspected the enforcement and effectiveness of state labor standards legislation and found mixed results. On one hand, some states provided few tools to enforce legislation, or they utilized labor boards that allowed for the virtual renegotiation of labor standards legislation when violations were discovered. Though the WB insisted that state laws always improved working conditions for some working women, investigators discovered a number of vexing instances when states did not effectively enforce protective legislation or when they excluded occupational groups, such as domestic and agricultural, that employed large numbers of women. The latter situation proved an unfortunate precedent for New Deal policies that excluded these same groups of workers. In 1928, at the end of a decade in which voluntarism was promoted at the highest levels of government, the WB conducted its largest New Era study, a 635-page analysis of minimum wage laws in the United States between 1912 and 1927.[92] A lack of institutional capacity to enforce minimum wage laws led the WB to conclude, "There has been a tendency to subordinate minimum-wage administration and enforcement to other State activities by placing it as a subdivision of a department with multitudinous other duties."[93] Additional enforcement problems occurred in states that used

---

[91] Ellery F. Reed, *An Analysis of the Report of the Ohio Minimum Wage Commission* (Cleveland: Consumers' League of Ohio and the Ohio Council of Women in Industry, 1925); H. B. Hammond, "Review," *AER* (September 1926): 495–7.

[92] In the study, the WB examined thirteen states with minimum wage legislation covering 1,080,257 women workers. WB, "The Development of Minimum-Wage Laws in the United States, 1912–1927," (Washington, DC: GPO, 1928), 14. Some states continued to enforce minimum wage laws after 1923. Of the thirteen states with wage legislation on the books prior to 1923, at least two states (Massachusetts and Washington) continued to enforce wage laws, and New York passed a new piece of minimum wage legislation. The study proved useful to New Dealers who attacked "liberty of contract" rulings, and it was republished by the WB in 1934.

[93] In Colorado, Kansas, Massachusetts, Minnesota, and Washington, the state had abolished independent commissions enforcing and administering labor laws. WB, "The Development of Minimum-Wage Laws in the United States, 1912–1927," 26.

wage boards and commissions to study the cost of living for workers and determine a proper wage level. When these commissions and boards met with employer opposition, they often negotiated wage compromises that did not equal increases in workers' expenses.[94] Clearly, in that policy climate, governments lacked the muscle to stand against recalcitrant employers, even when legislation had been established.

As the most important government body deliberating on labor standards, the WB helped shape the public's understanding of the impact of wage and hour laws in other ways, such as addressing the controversy between advocates of legislated labor standards for women and equal rights activists who claimed such gendered legislation hampered women at work. Though WB leaders' sympathies lay with the usefulness of labor standards, the WB sought a mandate that would allow bringing together an ideologically diverse body of leaders in January 1926 to assess the impact of labor standards. Controversy surrounded the conference, but a compromise resolution was finally adopted requesting that the WB enlist the help of an advisory committee made up of representatives of the National Women's Party (NWP), American Federation of Labor, WTUL, and the League of Women Voters to "make a comprehensive investigation of all the special laws regulating the employment of women, to determine their effects."[95] This particular attempt at cooperation failed, in part as a result of disagreements over whether the testimony should be closed or open to the public, but the WB continued with its investigation. After an extensive study, the WB concluded, "In almost every kind of employment the real forces that influence women's opportunity are far removed from legislative restriction of their hours or conditions of work." Though recognizing that legislation could restrict female workers' opportunities in specific situations (i.e., legislation prohibiting night work), the WB optimistically suggested that confidence in the ability of women to do the work, social mores, and technological change were among the "real forces" determining the future of women in the workplace.[96] Such conclusions flatly contradicted the claims of 1920s equal rights advocates, such as Alice Paul and the NWP, who contended that labor standards

---

[94] Ibid., 370–1. For further evidence of inadequate enforcement, see WB, "Iowa Women in Industry," 36, 50. WB, "Industrial Accidents to Women in New Jersey, Ohio, and Wisconsin," *Bulletin* 60 (Washington, DC: GPO, 1927); WB, "Women in Mississippi Industries," 5; WB, "Women in Delaware Industries," 7–8.

[95] Quoted in "Labor Women Carry Battle to Coolidge," *NYT*, January 22, 1926, 2.

[96] WB, "The Effects of Labor Legislation on the Employment Opportunities of Women," *Bulletin* 65 (Washington, DC: GPO, 1928), xv, 54.

legislation automatically hurt women workers' earnings and opportunities in industry.

Not only did the WB find little evidence that protective legislation hurt women workers; conversely, the WB noted instances when labor standards designed to protect female workers also improved conditions for male workers. In fact, the WB's understanding of the effect of labor standards on all workers raises questions about historians' conception of laws supposedly designed to protect women. Kathryn Kish Sklar has effectively described a strategy employed by the National Consumers League of using legislation concerning women workers as an "entering wedge for the protection of all workers," a situation in which women workers served as surrogate for men.[97] During the 1920s, WB leaders discovered that laws designed to protect women workers benefited male workers who experienced a "corresponding shortening" of their hours when hours were cut for women. In describing this phenomenon, the WB noted that "far from bringing women to work as the unsuccessful competitors of men who could work longer hours, the reduction of hours for women has in many cases given men a 'free ride' to shorter working hours for themselves."[98] Van Kleeck added in a letter to Ethel Smith, "Laws passed to limit the working day for women have resulted in the recovery of leisure for both men and women in the same industry."[99] This may be one of the few instances in which "difference theory" paid off by increasing the actual practice of gender equality.

During its first decade, the WB's effectiveness in advancing the cause of workers turned in part on its ability to adjust to dramatic shifts in the political and legal terrain. Overturning generations of work by labor reformers, the Supreme Court's rejection of federal minimum wage laws in *Adkins v. Children's Hospital* (1923) reopened the debate over the

---

[97] Kish Sklar, "Two Political Cultures in the Progressive Era," 51.
[98] This occurred in forty of forty-nine factories surveyed. WB, "Some Effects of Legislation Limiting Hours of Work for Women," 15–16. See also Winslow, "The Effect of Labor Laws on Women Workers," 315. Many labor experts noted that men and women in industry benefited from labor standards that explicitly protected women. Mary van Kleeck to Lillian Randall, February 1, 1927, Box 18, MVK Papers.
[99] Mary van Kleeck to Ethel M. Smith, January 8, 1923, Box 71, Throughout the New Era, Van Kleeck continued to make the case that men and women benefited from legislation aimed at women. In doing so, Van Kleeck often cited WB data. See Mary van Kleeck to Lilian Randall, February 1, 1927, Box 18, "Working Women in International Fellowship, 1919," Address at First International Congress of Working Women, Washington, DC, October 28, 1919, (particularly page 6) Box 24, File 487, all of the above in MVK Papers.

proper role of the national state in regulating wages. As they had done in previous cases defending protective legislation, the National Consumers League (NCL) and its allies had produced a large brief for this case (two volumes, 453 pages) providing facts defending minimum wage laws.[100] By mid-decade, however, Supreme Court decisions, employers' recognition of the economic benefits of improved working conditions, and the associational ideological bent of Hooverite policy makers impelled the WB to experiment with voluntaristic means of improving working conditions. To accommodate this change in the political terrain while continuing to advocate for workers, the WB increasingly used its research capacity to produce expertise that contributed to a growing body of literature suggesting that higher wages, shorter hours, and better working conditions could promote the interests of the investor and managerial classes by alleviating the problem of labor turnover and increasing worker efficiency for all workers.

Increasingly, the WB stressed that its goal was to enlist "public support for raising standards" and that this could be achieved through any of three methods, including "voluntary action by employers ... trade unions ... and labor legislation."[101] To improve the standards of working women, the WB contributed to a body of expertise generated by business, government, nonprofit, labor, and industry groups that promoted voluntary employer action to decrease hours as a remedy for the growing and expensive problems of labor turnover, worker fatigue, unrest, waste, and absenteeism. As early as 1919, the WB noted an increasing body of evidence suggesting "in the long run output is increased by the shortening of hours" as a result of "better health and hence greater efficiency, less absenteeism, and less 'labor turnover.'"[102] A 1921 study of women workers in states with hours regulations found employers who

---

[100] The use of an extensive brief based on data and research that conveyed the conditions of labor to justices had been part of the strategy in *Muller v. Oregon* 208 U.S. 412 (1908), which included voluminous research on the debilitating effects of long hours, low wages, and poor working conditions on workers. Through briefs focused on women workers, Felix Frankfurter, who as much as anyone used the language of maternalism to defend protective legislation, noted in 1916 that in terms of the evidence in the briefs, "there is no sharp difference in kind as to the effect of labor on men and women." Felix Frankfurter, "Hours of Labor and Realism in Constitutional Law," *Harvard Law Review* (February 1916): 367; Hart, *Bound by Our Constitution*, 103.

[101] WB, "Summary: The Effects of Labor Legislation on the Employment Opportunities of Women," vii.

[102] WIS, "Labor Laws for Women in Industry in Indiana," B 11; Alice Kessler Harris, *Out to Work: A History of Wage-Earning Women in the United States* (New York: Oxford University Press, 1982), 200.

Gender Research as Labor Activism 213

discovered "that by working fewer hours and paying higher wages" they "got better and more efficient girls" and "negligible" labor turnover. The WB described one employer as follows: "Although it probably cost him 5 cents an hour more for each girl he made this up easily in increased production because of greater efficiency, fewer mistakes, a better class of more highly skilled girls, and a lower labor cost because of the small turnover."[103] In 1923, the WB sent a questionnaire to firms that had been surveyed in a 1922 study to gauge progress made in decreasing the number of hours worked by women either through voluntary means or state laws limiting the number of hours for women employees. The WB found that where hours had been reduced and "comparable records have been kept of the output of the plant, before and after the change, it has been shown that ordinarily the business was able to stand the reduction in hours."[104]

A 1926 Women's Bureau 203-page study of lost time and labor turnover in cotton mills provided further evidence supporting the assertion that cutting hours could increase efficiency in the factory and benefit both employers and employees. The WB conducted a substantial investigation, visiting eighteen cotton mills (nine in the North and nine in the South), examining the records of 10,541 workers and interviewing 2,214 women workers. In mills with a ten-hour day or less, men and women lost 13.2 percent of their time; in mills with a work day longer than ten hours, workers' lost time rose to 21.7 percent. Investigators found rates of labor turnover twice as high for women workers in industries with the fifty-five-hour week compared to the forty-eight-hour week; almost this entire turnover (91 percent) was the result of women quitting their jobs.[105]

CONCLUSION

During the latter years of the New Era, the WB made valuable contributions to a discourse on labor relations that emphasized the need to

---

[103] WB, "Some Effects of Legislation Limiting Hours of Work for Women," 10. For additional discussion of progressive employers' support of reduced hours and labor legislation, see WB, "History of Labor Legislation for Women in Three States," (Washington, DC: GPO, 1929), 8–9.

[104] WB, "Standard and Scheduled Hours of Work for Women in Industry," 43; WIS, "Labor Law for Women in Industry in Indiana," 11, 18–20.

[105] WB, "Lost Time and Labor Turnover in Cotton Mills," *Bulletin* 52 (Washington, DC: GPO, 1926), 14–18; and Mary Anderson, "Hours of Work," *AF* 32 (September 1925): 769–72.

use voluntary measures to better working conditions and improve industrial efficiency while protecting individual liberties. But in 1937, the legal and political tide turned again, this time in favor of advocates of protective legislation. Historians and other legal scholars have long debated whether the Supreme Court's decision in *West Coast Hotel Co. v. Parrish* (1937) resulted from Justice Owen Roberts succumbing to "externalist" pressure brought on by FDR's landslide victory in 1936 or instead culminated in a gradual rethinking of the public's right to regulate aspects of the employee-employer relationship, or some more intertwined explanation.[106] The WB's investigations' direct impact on the case history is difficult to discern, but its constant efforts in the New Era to publicize the hardships faced by American workers and to demonstrate the ability of both statist and voluntary means to mediate the more ferocious aspects of the evolving U.S. version of capitalism surely helped to transform Americans' understanding of the constantly shifting "labor problem."

The core question the WB struggled with in the New Era was the same one reformers, legislators, and the courts have wrestled with throughout American history: What issues are considered private and which are legitimate grounds for public action? The imprecise and contested boundary between public and private has shifted often since the New Era. While labor militancy has played a crucial role in pushing previously private concerns into the public domain, the WB's work suggests the need to consider how knowledge, inquiry, and bureaucratic expertise can help shape and reshape the public and policy makers' understanding of issues in flux. The next two chapters demonstrate how other groups of investigators worked alongside the WB to further diversify the labor question so that it more accurately represented the experiences of Mexican immigrant, Mexican American, and African American workers. During its first decade, as it pushed Americans to rethink the role of women workers in the economy and society, the WB provided the most important site in the federal government for discussions of legislated labor standards as a means of improving the quality of life for industrial workers. At a time when many policy makers believed that the labor problem was

---

[106] For an excellent overview of this scholarship and a strong case for a more intertwined explanation, see Laura Kalman, "The Constitution, the Supreme Court, and the New Deal," *AHR* 110 (October 2005): 1052–79. On the WB's role in interpreting the effect of the decision on the labor market and women workers, see Kathleen McLaughlin, "Inquiries on the Minimum Wage Law Flood the WB," *NYT*, April 25, 1937, 6.

being solved by economic prosperity, the WB provided vivid evidence of the uneven nature of this economic ascent and demonstrated how a three-pronged attack – including expanded government regulation, efficiency studies focused on the relationship between improved labor standards and increased productivity, and a consistent argument for recognizing the importance of women's labors to the New Era economy – could improve the quality of life for American workers and promote greater equality amongst all workers.

As the WB's attention to African American women attests, the enormous demographic changes of the era – the Great Migration, the increasing presence of women in industry, the growing importance of Mexican workers in industry after 1910 – were often linked. The continuation of WB funding after the war meant that women workers had an important voice in the federal government, but other groups were not so fortunate.

6

The New "Negro Problem"

> What has been done was done in the search for the truth, that the enthusiasm of reform may be linked with the reliability of knowledge in the efforts to better the future conditions of the city and the Negro.
> – George Edmund Haynes

Short of advancements in the lives of individuals, the nationalization of the "Negro problem" was among the most important changes compelled by the World War I migration of black Americans. In a 1919 report for the Department of Labor (DOL), University of Pittsburgh professor Francis D. Tyson concluded, "The race question is no longer confined to the States below the Mason Dixon line, but is the concern of the whole Nation."[1] The Great Migration and the investigations and inquiries made into its causes and consequences belied the myth that black Americans were satisfied with conditions in the South and, as such, could be addressed as a regional concern. As important, these same forces helped to create a space where a contingent of largely African American government officials, scholars, and nonprofit investigators seized the opportunity to construct a new representation of black Americans on the national stage. In doing so, they supplanted earlier notions of black workers as largely content Southern domestic and agricultural employees with a new vision of an ambitious and mobile work force challenging racism in the workplace and striving for new opportunities in industry.

---

[1] Francis D. Tyson, "The Negro Migrant in the North," in *Negro Migration in 1916–1917* (Washington, DC: GPO, 1919), 155. See also Monroe N. Work, "Taking Stock of the Race Problem," *Opportunity* 2 (February 1924): 45.

As war slashed European immigration, industrial employers became increasingly reliant on labor streams flowing out of the South. Between 1915 and 1921, as many as one million African Americans, mostly between the ages of twenty-one and forty-five, fled oppressive conditions in the South in search of wartime employment and greater freedom in the Northern cities. Continued demand for black workers in industry, originally due to a dramatic decrease of wartime immigration and later to restrictive immigration policies, encouraged another seven hundred thousand to move over the remainder of the decade. The speed of this migration caused public confusion and concern among policy makers and labor experts, who struggled to make sense of an enormous demographic shift taking shape – some feared taking over – before their eyes. Amidst the unprecedented movement of black Americans from the South to the urban North and following violent urban race riots in 1918 and 1919, the *New York Times* reported that the "Negro problem" had "entered upon a new and dangerous phase" that is "in some respects the most grave now facing the country."[2]

During World War I and the New Era, a new class of labor and race experts thrust itself into the public debate over the meaning of monumental changes under way in the African American work force. In doing so, these experts challenged long-standing and deeply racist conceptions of these workers and, like the Women's Bureau (WB), labored steadily to integrate the Negro problem into the public and policy makers' understanding of the broader and shifting labor question. Unlike the state-sanctioned and permanent Women's Bureau, where policy makers served as a client group of sorts, these labor experts fought from positions in government, academia, and new nonprofit agencies to make the case for the relevance of issues related to race in America – issues wide swathes of the American public would have just as soon ignored or treated as marginal or regional concerns. Though they had significant success in using the migration to compel a public rethinking of important aspects of race and race relations, they shared with the Women's Bureau a common frustration in their inability to convince a significant portion of the American public and policy makers that the problems faced by black and – as we will see in the following chapter – Mexican immigrant and Mexican American workers were part of structural problems within the economy. When it came to accounting for the difficulties faced by various groups of workers, too often policy makers and economic leaders

[2] "For Action on Race Riot Peril," *NYT*, October 5, 1919, section 10, page 1.

failed to recognize or simply ignored overwhelming evidence indicating that race and gender inequalities had been woven into the social and economic fabric of American capitalism.

This chapter and the next describe an expanding body of expertise that begins with federal and state governments' World War I-era investigations of migration and racial violence and then shifts to a period of inquiry underwritten by an array of nonprofit institutions. As knowledge of black workers accumulated and the site of investigations shifted, the focus broadened from examining the causes of the Great Migration to a more analytical inquiry into the state of race relations, particularly within the working class. During World War I, the federal government showed a keen if ephemeral interest in black workers. The Division of Negro Economics (DNE) was created within the Department of Labor to answer pressing public questions regarding dramatic changes in the black working class and to coordinate the placement of black workers in war industries. In this period, a cross-racial group of investigators came to mixed conclusions about the causes of the migration. The thrust of their conclusions emphasized the economic causes of the migration and gave less attention to the dire conditions faced by black Southerners that would have provided a vivid context explaining why hundreds of thousands of citizens were so eager to abandon the South when demand for labor in the North increased.

As the site of these investigations moved to the nonprofit sphere and they came to be led by African American social scientists, investigators shifted their attention to conditions in the North, the state of race relations, and the modest but important gains black workers made in industry. For the purposes of this chapter, this shift will be considered by way of the Chicago Commission's inquiry into the causes of the 1919 Chicago Race Riot. In addition to the content of the report, the Chicago investigation is useful in two respects: first, it introduces Charles S. Johnson, who became a leading expert on New Era race relations and a strong proponent of racial justice; and second, it demonstrates a shift in the site of investigations into race relations from the state to the nonprofit sphere. While the governor of Illinois ordered the investigation, the state failed to provide any funding for its work; instead, a group of nonprofit organizations raised the necessary funds to allow the investigation to move forward.[3] As Chapter 7 demonstrates, when the federal and state

---

[3] Martin Bulmer, "Charles S. Johnson, Robert E. Park, and the Research Methods of the Chicago Commission on Race Relations, 1919–1922: An Early Experiment in Applied Social Research, *Ethnic and Racial Studies* 4 (1981): 292.

governments abandoned inquiry into race relations after the war, philanthropic and nonprofit organizations stepped forward in an attempt to fill the void, and in the process helped investigators like Johnson to build up new institutions of inquiry devoted to advancing racial justice.

Throughout the New Era, Johnson and others wrestled with the relationship between previous ethnic groups' assimilation into American society and the African American experience. By the late teens, Johnson's interest in these matters took him to the University of Chicago, where he worked with sociologist Robert E. Park. Park and other Chicago sociologists explained social change as a product of disequilibrium brought on by an "invasion" "such as large-scale migration or technological advances."[4] This model proved particularly useful in explaining ethnic groups' assimilation into U.S. society, which Park argued occurred only after a period of competition, conflict, and accommodation. For Johnson and others concerned with the impact of the Great Migration, the central question that came out of this analysis turned on whether, after a period of competition, conflict, and accommodation, black Americans would ultimately assimilate into broader American society, or alternatively, if the racial barriers constructed by white Americans (among other factors) would block the traditional path to assimilation. As we will see, particularly in the next chapter, Johnson worked relentlessly to shed light on the constructed nature of racism in America and the persistent efforts of white Americans to maintain the racial divide. Joining him in this effort were not just other scholars of the African American experience, but also a cadre of emerging social scientists concerned with the Mexican immigrant and Mexican American experience in the United States. More attention will be devoted to this issue in the following chapter, but it is important to note that this diverse group of scholars was, like Johnson, both working in and drastically revising the Chicago school paradigm of the ethnic cycle.

AN INTRACTABLE CONDITION

Advocates and experts examining black workers faced a daunting set of prejudices and dilemmas. From its start, the World War I migration

[4] Alice O'Connor, *Poverty Knowledge: Social Science, Social Policy and the Poor in Twentieth-Century U.S. History* (Princeton: Princeton University Press, 2001), 49. See also Hans Joas, *Pragmatism and Social Theory* (Chicago: University of Chicago Press, 1993); Fred H. Matthews, *Quest for an American Sociology: Robert E. Park and the Chicago School* (Montreal: McGill-Queen's University Press, 1977); and Stow Parsons, *Ethnic Studies at Chicago, 1905–1945* (Urbana: University of Illinois Press, 1987).

of black workers to Northern cities threatened to undermine an "ideology of black inferiority" that for generations had provided a serviceable understanding of the intractable nature of the Negro condition. The ideology of black inferiority was hardly static, unitary, or free of tension; yet it contained an underlying assumption of racial difference suggesting that African Americans' innate biological or deeply ingrained social characteristics adequately explained their inferior station in American society. In reviewing these beliefs, sociologist and civil rights activist Charles S. Johnson drew a parallel between worn-out ideas concerning women and African Americans. According to Johnson, "Anatomically, mentally, and by an alleged special act of God both [African Americans and women] have been arranged in the scheme of creation a little lower than supreme man of the particular race making the comparison."[5] According to this belief system, racial differences were indelible or "subject to change only by a very slow process of development or evolution."[6]

Prior to the World War I migration, assumptions of racial inferiority led scholars and observers to a variety of conclusions regarding the future of the black race. In a widely heralded American Economic Association publication, Frederick L. Hoffman concluded that a "combination" of Negro "traits and tendencies must in the end cause the extinction of the race."[7] Such conclusions emerged, too, in federal government inquiries. During the Civil War era, Joseph Kennedy, director of the census, boldly argued that the census, "with unerring certainty," pointed to the "gradual extinction" of "the colored race."[8] Other scholars, such as University of Pennsylvania ethnology and linguistics professor Daniel G. Brinton, divided the world's peoples into higher and lower races. Brinton suggested that whites were more inclined to thrive in northern climates, but "the black race finds it hopeless to struggle with the climate above the fortieth Parallel of latitude."[9]

[5] Charles S. Johnson, "Public Opinion and the Negro," *NCSW* (1923): 498.
[6] George M. Fredrickson, *The Black Image in the White Mind: The Debate on Afro-American Character and Destiny, 1817–1914* (Hanover: Wesleyan University Press, 1971), 321, see also 228–55; Persons, *Ethnic Studies at Chicago, 1905–1945*; Daniel Brinton, *Races and Peoples: Lectures on the Science of Ethnography* (Philadelphia: McKay, 1890); Frederick L. Hoffman, "Vital Statistics of the Negro," *Arena* 5 (April 1892); Frederick L. Hoffman, "Race Traits and Tendencies of the American Negro," *Publications of the American Economic Association*, XI (August 1896); John H. Stanfield, *Philanthropy and Jim Crow in American Social Science* (Westport: Greenwood Press, 1985), 16–37.
[7] Fredrickson, *The Black Image in the White Mind*, 251.
[8] Margo J. Anderson, *The American Census: A Social History* (New Haven: Yale University Press, 1988), 69.
[9] Brinton, *Races and Peoples*, 280; Persons, *Ethnic Studies at Chicago, 1905–1945*, 15.

Lack of interest in the Negro problem further reified racist stereotypes among social scientists. In his analysis of race and the social sciences, sociologist John Stanfield suggests that during the early twentieth century the "prevailing opinion among sociologists was that the innate inferiority of blacks made them irrelevant as subjects of inquiry."[10] This was particularly true among Northern social scientists who, prior to World War I, thought of the Negro problem as a Southern, rural, and agricultural problem – not a region or topic that excited great interest in a time when the ramifications of industrialization and immigration set much of the agenda for the emerging discipline of sociology.[11]

Government investigations, even those conducted by sympathetic African American investigators prior to the U.S. entry into the war, did little to suggest that the Negro problem was soon to be a dynamic national issue. In 1916, the Census Bureau's Charles E. Hall, William Jennifer, and Robert A. Pelham had just finished directing a "corp of Negro clerks" in tabulating a nearly 850-page study – based on Bureau of Census (BOC) publications, schedules, and manuscript tables – detailing the economic and social development of the Negro population in the United States between 1790 and 1915.[12] Director of the census Sam L. Rogers described the report as the "most comprehensive statistical report ever published on the subject."[13] The *Journal of Negro History* judged it "a cause of much satisfaction" that "these facts are available so that many questions which have hitherto been puzzling because of the lack of such statistics may now be easily cleared up."[14]

A review of BOC findings provides vivid evidence of the degree to which black Americans had been geographically and occupationally

---

[10] Stanfield, *Philanthropy and Jim Crow in American Social Science*, 23.
[11] Ibid., 16–37.
[12] Department of Commerce, *Negro Population: 1790–1915* (Washington, DC: GPO, 1918); W. B. Hartgove, "The Story of Marian Louise More and Fannie M. Richards," *The Journal of Negro History* 1 (January 1916): 29–30. Pelham was the son of a prominent African American Detroit family.
[13] Department of Commerce, *Negro Population*, 13. Joseph A. Hill, "Recent Northward Migration of the Negro," *MLR* 18 (March 1924): 1–14. To supplement the 1918 report, Hall prepared a second 845-page report covering the years between 1920 and 1932. See Department of Commerce, *Negroes in the United States, 1920–1932* (Washington, DC: GPO, 1935).
[14] "Review," *Journal of Negro History* 4 (April 1919): 235; see also E. A. Goldenweiser, "Review," *AER* 9 (March 1919): 136. In addition to Anderson, *The American Census*, see Carroll Wright and William C. Hunt, *History and Growth of the United States Census* (Washington, DC: GPO, 1900) and A. Ross Eckler, *The Bureau of the Census* (New York: Prager, 1972).

segregated prior to World War I and establishes a baseline for making sense of the revolutionary change that took place during the migration. Geographically, the proportion of African Americans living in the North and South stayed amazingly stable throughout the period considered by the BOC. In 1790, approximately 91.1 percent of African Americans lived in the South; in 1910, that percentage had fallen a mere two percentage points to 89.0.[15] In compiling the most extensive body of census statistics ever gathered concerning black Americans, BOC investigators described increased landownership and improvements in general economic condition, but consistent isolation in agricultural occupations in the South and extremely high relative female labor participation rates among black women.[16] In 1910, 54.7 percent of black women over the age of ten worked for wages, compared to only 19.6 percent of their white counterparts. The percentage of black male agricultural workers remained remarkably steady between 1890 and 1910, with 49.2 and 50.3 percent of black men employed in agricultural pursuits respectively.[17] In professional occupations, the census report found dramatic racial disparities in representation, leading the investigators to conclude that each of the professions, "with the single exception noted [clergy], is undermanned among Negroes."[18]

CELEBRATION AND CONCERN: FIRST STEPS AT MAKING SENSE OF THE MIGRATION

Heightened federal government interest in the "Negro problem" was in part prompted by a mix of confusion, hope, and fear emanating from various sectors of American society affected by the migration. Once under way, speculation concerning the causes and consequences of the migration ran the gamut from laments that such a vast demographic shift would devastate Northern unionized white workers and the Southern economy to celebration of the migration as a strike for elusive economic and social rights. T. J. Woofter, Jr., future research professor at the University of

---

[15] Department of Commerce, *Negro Population, 1790–1915*, 33.
[16] John Cummings, "Negro Population: 1790–1915," in *Negroes in the United States*, 18.
[17] Department of Commerce, *Negro Population, 1790–1915*, 504.
[18] Ibid., 511. There was one black physician for every 3,194 African Americans but one white physician for every 553 whites. In dentistry, there was one black dentist for every 20,560 African Americans, and one white dentist for every 2,070 whites. In law, there were 12,315 African Americans per black lawyer, judge, or justice and one white law professional for every 718 whites.

North Carolina's Institute for Research in Social Science and son of the dean of the School of Education at the University of Georgia, described the migration as a "strike against the plantation regime" in the Southern black belt.[19] Georgia governor Hugh Manson Dorsey lamented, "The economic value of the Negroes has not been fully appreciated, but it will be better understood when plows are idle and farms run to wood."[20] Robert Bagnall, president of the Detroit branch of the NAACP, introduced the issue of civil rights into the discourse in a way white politicians and experts like Dorsey and Woofter avoided. According to Bagnall, "The Negroes who remain in the South will be accorded the rights of men, or else the wealth of the South will perish from the face of the earth."[21] Northern white unions insisted employers had used black workers to break a 1916 packing plant strike in East St. Louis. Early in the migration, the Central Trades Labor Union, facing black replacements for striking aluminum ore workers, demanded employers "retard ... the growing menace" of black labor and, even more sinisterly, "devise a way to get rid of a certain portion of those who are already here."[22]

Union, political, and business leaders may have had a handle on some of the causes and implications of the migration on their local jurisdictions, but responsibility for separating fact from fiction and creating a national explanation of the movement fell principally to the federal government, which was largely ill prepared for such a task. In 1916, the DOL turned to the Census Bureau's Charles Hall and William Jennifer, the two most knowledgeable investigators in the federal government on the emerging Negro problem, "to make a quick inquiry into the causes, extent, and general character of the migration."[23] After a tour of the South for the Department of Labor during the summer of 1916, Hall and Jennifer concluded that the migration had not had yet a significant impact on the labor supply of the North or South. They did suggest that "the situation warranted a more detailed study because the migration's character and

---

[19] T. J. Woofter, Jr., "The Negroe on a Strike," *Journal of Social Forces* 2 (November 1923): 84; Guy Benton Johnson and Guion Griffs Johnson, *Research in Service to Society: The First Fifty Years of the Institute for Research in Social Science at the University of North Carolina* (Chapel Hill: University of North Carolina Press, 1980), 44, 50–1, 53, 104.

[20] Quoted in Robert W. Bagnall, "The Labor Problem and Negro Migration," *Southern Workman* XLIX (November 1920): 518.

[21] Ibid., 523.

[22] Thomas L. Dabney, "Organized Labor's Attitude Toward Negro Workers," *The Southern Workmen* LVII (August 1928): 326.

[23] W. B. Wilson, "Letter of Authorization by the Secretary of Labor," in DNE, *Negro Migration in 1916–17* (Washington, DC: GPO, 1919), 7.

magnitude appeared to be changing rapidly."[24] The continued demand for labor in wartime industries "excited widespread concern for its possible effect upon the prosecution of the war," according to Secretary Wilson, and prompted a "wider and more intensive investigation" of the developing migration.[25]

Willful ignorance of race issues justified by the persistent belief that the Negro problem was a decidedly Southern concern, combined with a long tradition of involvement in these same issues within the nonprofit and philanthropic spheres, compelled Wilson to look beyond the federal government for leadership and expertise. More than in other areas of labor investigation, inquiry into the condition of black and, as we shall see later, Mexican workers depended on the support of philanthropists. In terms of African Americans, this link reached back to the nineteenth century. As a result of the federal government's post-Reconstruction neglect, philanthropic leaders almost autonomously conceived of and constructed education and labor policies to improve race relations and the condition of African Americans. Historian Ellen Condliffe Lagemann chronicles the convening of educational, religious, and philanthropic leaders at Capron Springs, Virginia in 1898 to coordinate their projects. Lagemann outlines three assumptions on which this group built programs:

First, that the education of blacks was a Southern problem; second that it could be handled most effectively if the cooperation of white Southerners were actively solicited; and third, that it would be advisable to view education in relation to regional economic development and within established patterns of relationship between black and white Americans.[26]

---

[24] Henry P. Guzda, "Social Experiment of the Labor Department: The Division of Negro Economics," *Public Historian* 4 (Fall 1982): 13.

[25] Wilson, "Letter of Authorization by the Secretary of Labor," 7.

[26] Ellen Condliffe Lagemann, *The Politics of Knowledge: The Carnegie Corporation, Philanthropy, and Public Policy* (Middletown, CT: Wesleyan University Press, 1989), 124–5. For more on the relationship among philanthropists, social sciences, African American education, and public policy, see O'Connor, *Poverty Knowledge*; Magat, *Unlikely Partners: Philanthropic Foundations and the Labor Movement* Ithaca: Cornell University Press, 1999); Gloria Samson, *The American Fund for Public Service: Charles Garland and Radical Philanthropy, 1922–1941* (Westport, CT: Greenwood Press, 1996); Benjamin G. Brawley, *Doctor Dillard of the Jeanes Fund* (Freeport, NY: Books for Libraries Press, 1971); Joe Martin Richardson, *A History of Fisk University, 1865–1946* (Tuscaloosa: University of Alabama Press, 1980); Stanfield, *Philanthropy and Jim Crow in American Social Science*; Martin Bulmer, "Support for Sociology in the 1920s: The Laura Spelman Rockefeller Memorial and the Beginnings of Modern, Large-Scale Sociological Research in the University," *American Sociologist* 17 (November 1982): 185–92.

As part of this effort, philanthropists developed institutions to promote black leaders who might serve as mediators between white and black society and helped establish research bodies to examine the South as a unique region. For instance, the Rockefeller Foundation's General Education Board and the Jeanes and Slater Funds awarded university scholarships to prospective leaders of the black community. To better understand the unique character of the South, a number of philanthropic organizations funded research institutions, most notably the University of North Carolina's Institute for Social Science.[27]

Secretary Wilson's choice of Dr. James H. Dillard to lead an investigation into the causes and effects of the migration illustrates the long-standing link between nonprofits, philanthropists, and issues related to race, uplift, reform, and labor.[28] Dillard, who served as the president of the Jeanes and Slater Funds and was a member of the Rockefeller Foundation's General Education Board (GEB), was described by Dr. James E. Gregg, principal of the Hampton Institute, as a "trusted friend and untiring helper of the twelve million Negroes in this country."[29] Named after Anna T. Jeanes, a Quaker who donated more than a million dollars to assist in the education of African Americans in the rural South, the fund was established by the Jeanes family after Booker T. Washington (Tuskegee) and Hollis Burke Frissell (Hampton Institute) solicited a donation from Jeanes. John F. Slater established the Slater Fund, similar in mission to the Jeanes fund, with a donation of one million dollars in 1882. The Rockefeller Foundation's General Education Board worked closely with these two foundations and contributed money to their efforts.[30] Dillard's ties to philanthropic foundations and nonprofits ran deep. When he retired in 1929, the John F. Slater Board, after much discussion concerning his well-being among nonprofit and philanthropic leaders, generously provided him with a retirement allowance.[31]

In April 1917, Dillard began his DOL investigation by organizing a group of researchers, four white and one African American, who

---

[27] O'Connor, *Poverty Knowledge*, 67–73; Johnson and Johnson, *Research in Service to Society*.
[28] W. W. Brierley to Dillard, June 16, 1930, General Education Board (hereafter GEB) Collection, Box 268, Folder 2765 James H. Dillard, Rockefeller Archive Center (hereafter RAC). The president of the Slater Fund automatically had a seat on the GEB. Brawley, *Doctor Dillard of the Jeanes Fund*, 57, 68.
[29] James H. Dillard, "The Humanity of Armstrong," *Southern Workman* L (March 1921): 99.
[30] Brawley, *Doctor Dillard of the Jeanes Fund*, 57, 68.
[31] Folders 2764–5 James H. Dillard, Box 268, LSRM Collection, RAC.

conducted short investigations to determine why black workers were leaving the South in such great numbers. The published 157-page DOL study included individual reports on conditions in the South by R. H. Leavell, T. J. Woofter, T. H. Snavely, and W. T. B. Williams, as well as a report of African American conditions in the North by Francis Tyson, with an introduction by Dillard that summarized the report's findings. All the researchers were university trained and had some connection to philanthropic, state, and academic institutions devoted to understanding and assisting black Southerners.[32]

In explaining the migration, all agreed that black Americans experienced dire living conditions in the South. R. H. Leavell, a former professor in Mississippi, used data gathered by the Mississippi State Board of Health for its campaign against malnutrition to show a 23 percent increase, in 1917 alone, in the number of African Americans suffering from pellagra. According to Leavell, "unless intelligently supplemented by supervised production of foodstuffs by the worker for his own use," the wage of an agricultural worker "is not enough to maintain the Negro in a high state of physical efficiency."[33] W. T. B. Williams, the only African American investigator involved in the study, graduated from Harvard and served as field director for the Jeanes and Slater Funds and the Hampton Institute.[34] Williams reported particularly difficult conditions in Alabama and Mississippi, where a 1916 flood had destroyed what remained of a cotton crop already devastated by several years of boll weevil infestation. According to Williams, "the banks, merchants, and planters were unable or unwilling to make further advances to the Negro laborers. Many of the employers turned the Negroes out with nothing to live on."[35]

The burden of educating policy makers and the public on the role racism and violence played in pushing black workers north fell primarily on Williams, who cast the migration as a long-awaited opportunity to achieve a fuller measure of economic opportunity and dignity. According to Williams, "For years no group of thoughtful, intelligent class of Negroes ... have met for any purpose without finally drifting into some discussion of their treatment at the hands of white people." Williams rejected explanations for the migration, embraced by many white Southerners

---

[32] "Note" in DNE, *Negro Migration*, 5. Abraham Epstein, *The Negro Migrant in Pittsburgh* (Pittsburgh: School of Economics, University of Pittsburgh, 1918; reprint New York: Arno Press and the *NYT*, 1969), 5.
[33] R. H. Leavell, "The Negro Migration from Mississippi," in DNE, *Negro Migration*, 25.
[34] "Note," *Negro Migration*, 5; Brawley, *Doctor Dillard of the Jeanes Fund*, 73.
[35] T. J. Woofter, "Migration of Negroes from Georgia," in *Negro Migration*, 93.

and evident in some of the reports by his fellow DOL investigators, that blamed labor agents or a breakdown in communication between white and black Southern leaders for the movement out of the South. According to Williams:

> The average white man, however, seems to have little knowledge or appreciation of this feeling among Negroes.... Indeed, it was rare to find a southern white man who felt, or would at least admit to me, that the South's treatment of the Negro had anything to do with the exodus.[36]

In an attempt to answer claims that the migration could only be explained economically, since social and racial injustices were constant in the South, Williams countered: "There is a vast amount of dissatisfaction among them [black southerners] over their lot. There seemed to be no escape and little remedy for it, so there was no point in stirring up trouble for themselves by publicly railing about their plight." The migration north, according to Williams, provided the "chance long looked for to move out and to better their condition."[37]

Throughout the decade, investigators looking into race relations struggled with how best to describe sources of racial animosity between white and black skilled and unskilled workers, and the prospects for peaceful relations in the future. The Dillard-led report, finished in the early spring of 1918 – after the East St. Louis riots but well before the summer of 1919 – made some modest efforts in this direction. Tyson's contribution to the Dillard report detailed incidences of racial violence, but concluded that, given the size of the migration, "the amount of race friction is remarkably small." When Tyson did find racial conflict in the workplace, he blamed unskilled workers. In fact, he went so far as to reframe the East St. Louis riots as the result of competition among unskilled workers, whereas previous accounts had laid much of the blame on white unions, particularly the American Federation of Labor (AFL) St. Louis Central Trades and Labor Union. In words that would echo in investigations later in the decade, Tyson concluded, "East St. Louis was not a struggle between organized and unorganized labor, but between the white and black unorganized workers crowding for a place on the lowest rung of the industrial ladder."[38]

---

[36] W. T. B. Williams, "The Negro Exodus from the South," 101–2.
[37] Ibid., 102–3.
[38] Francis D. Tyson, "The Negro Migrant in the North," in *Negro Migration in 1916–1917*, 134–5.

The Dillard report received a positive reception tempered by recognition of the vast number of questions regarding the migration that it did not answer. The Department of Labor published five thousand copies and it became, according to George E. Haynes, "practically a textbook – a guide for dealing with problems where the question of Negro migration is involved" for employers and welfare workers in the North and South.[39] This initial study combined with continued migration and race violence stimulated an interest in a more thorough examination of the other half of the migration question, the status of African Americans in the North. In reviewing the Dillard-led study for the *Southern Workman*, a monthly journal published by the Hampton Normal and Agricultural Institute, Monroe Work of the Tuskegee Institute commented that the parts of the study concerned with the impact of migration in the North were "not as comprehensive or conclusive a study as could have been made."[40] The *Journal of Negro History* concurred, writing that the report's analysis of Negroes in the North "is too brief to cover the field adequately."[41] No doubt Work and others had hoped that the report might provide a counterpoint to Southern whites' depiction of conditions in the North. The Southern white press reported high prices, overcrowding, unemployment, cold weather, and broken families in describing conditions in the North, whereas the *Chicago Defender* (or *Pretender*, as it was parodied in Southern white newspapers) described the North as a place where jobs were plentiful and racial violence nominal.[42] According to Work, however, the real value of the study rested in the Department of Labor's recognition of the need to give "special attention to problems connected with Negro Labor." To that end, Work and other black leaders noted approvingly the establishment of the Division of Negro Economics "with a well-equipped Negro at the head of it." This, according to Work, "was the most important result of the investigation."[43]

---

[39] U.S. Congress, Senate Committee on Appropriations, *Legislative, Executive, and Judicial Appropriation Bill*, 1922, 65th Cong., 2nd sess., January 28–February 2, 1921, 98.

[40] Monroe Work, "Negro Migration in 1916–1917," *Southern Workman* XLVIII (November 1919): 614–15.

[41] *Journal of Negro History* 4 (July 1919): 344.

[42] Monroe Work, "The Negro Migration," *Southern Workman* L (May 1924): 204.

[43] Work, "Negro Migration in 1916–1917," 614–15. For further discussion of efforts to curb the migration of black workers to the North, see Bagnall, "The Labor Problem and Negro Migration," 520–1. Bagnall was the rector of St. Matthew's P. E. Church and the president of the Detroit branch of the NAACP. A number of organizations requested that the DOL form a separate division to examine issues affecting black workers. On February 26, 1918, John Shillday (NAACP), Eugene Kinckle Jones (NUL), and James Dillard met with the DOL to discuss the formation of the DNE. See Guzda, "Social

THE RISE AND FALL OF THE DIVISION OF NEGRO ECONOMICS

Indeed, the formation of a division within the DOL dedicated to the rapidly changing "Negro problem" made clear that race issues were once again a national concern. Following the Dillard report, "and partly in consequence of the investigation upon which it rests," Secretary Wilson and the Department of Labor recognized the "advisability of its having continuous expert advice upon economic problems involving wage-earning labor in its relation to the Negroes of the country and their employers, and especially with reference to an effective prosecution of the war."[44] Between 1918 and 1922, the DNE provided migrant and settled African Americans a unique voice in policy circles and helped to fill the void of "knowledge and appreciation," to draw from Williams, of African American conditions and expectations. The *Washington Bee* noted approvingly that the DNE's work shows the "the United Sates Government through the Department of Labor is really solving some of the great problems seriously affecting the economic condition of the Negro Wage earner."[45] Although it was vital to the war and immediate postwar effort to make sense of racial violence and demographic change, the DNE faced constant pressure from members of Congress who did not see the need for an institution of labor inquiry devoted to investigating the conditions of black workers. Despite opposition to its establishment, according to Haynes, Secretary Wilson recognized, "Since Negro wage-earners constitute about one-seventh of the working population it is reasonable and right that they should have representation in council when their interests are being decided."[46]

Experiment of the Labor Department," 15; G. H. Edmunds to Secretary Wilson, March 6, 1918, General Records of the Department of Labor, Box 2, Folder Race Riot E. St. Louis, Ill. 1917, Record Group (hereafter RG) 174, National Archives at College Park, MD (hereafter NA). Edmunds was a black organizer for the United Mine Workers who urged the DOL to investigate black workers, partially to prevent them from being used as strike breakers.

[44] Wilson, "Letter of Authorization by the Secretary of Labor," 8.

[45] "Work of the Division of Negro Economics Commended to Congress," *Washington Bee*, January 28, 1918, 6.

[46] George E. Haynes, "To Avert Friction with Negro Labor," *NYT*, June 15, 1919, section 3, page 9. On the DNE, see also Guzda, "Social Experiment of the Labor Department; James Stewart, "The Rise and Fall of Negro Economics: The Economic Thought of George Edmund Haynes," *AER* 81 (May 1991): 311–14; James Stewart, "George Edmund Haynes and the Office of Negro Economics," in Thomas D. Boston, ed., *A Different Vision: African American Economic Thought, Volume I* (New York: Routledge, 1997), 213–29; Eileen Boris and Michael Honey, "Gender, Race, and the Policies of the Labor Department," *MLR* 111 (February 1988): 26–35; Jane and Henry Scheiber, "The Wilson

Though prompted by war needs, race violence, and migration, the creation of the DNE culminated years of work by civil rights leaders to force the federal government to recognize the distinct economic concerns of African Americans. At the turn of the century, DOL commissioner Carroll Wright, a veteran of the Civil War imbued with New England's commitment to black freedom, had ordered a series of studies concerning black workers that stressed the complexity of post-Civil War African American political-economic development and attempted to ascertain, "with as near an approach to scientific accuracy as possible, the real condition of the Negro."[47] On their own, these Wright-directed studies could hardly have been expected to jettison traditional beliefs in black inferiority; yet they did legitimize federal government inquiry into changes in black communities at a time when most federal government policy makers ignored the issue. They also provided evidence that challenged the "retrogression hypothesis" by demonstrating that despite racism, black Americans were fully capable of assimilating into American industrial society.[48] Unfortunately, the work of W. E. B. Du Bois, who conducted three of the seven studies, and the other turn-of-the-century DOL investigators of black America did not receive the attention it deserved. In fact, correspondence between Du Bois and government officials suggest that some congressmen so feared the impact of government-sanctioned and

---

Administration and the Wartime Mobilization of Black Americans," *Labor History* 10 (Summer 1969): 448–52; William J. Breen, *Labor Market Politics and the Great War*, 126–30; and Judson MacLaury, "The Federal Government and Negro Workers Under President Woodrow Wilson," Paper delivered at Annual Meeting for History in the Federal Government, Washington, DC, March 16, 2000. Also available online at http://www.dol.gove/dol/asp/public/programs/history/shfgproo.html.

[47] W. E. B. Du Bois, "The Negroes of Farmville, Virginia: A Social Study," *Bulletin* 14 (Washington, DC: GPO, 1898), 1. Also see the following DOL publications: W. E. B. Du Bois, "The Negro in the Black Belt: Some Social Sketches," *Bulletin* 15 (Washington, DC: GPO, 1899); W. E. B. Du Bois, "The Negro Landholder of Georgia," *Bulletin* 17 (Washington, DC: GPO, 1901); William Taylor Thom, "The Negroes of Sandy Spring Maryland: A Social Study," *Bulletin* 32 (Washington, DC: GPO, 1931); William Taylor Thom, "The Negroes of Litwalton, Virginia: A Social Study of the 'Oyster Negro,'" *Bulletin* 37 (Washington, DC: GPO, 1901); J. Bradford Laws, "The Negroes of Cinclaire Central Factory and Calumet Plantation, Louisiana," *Bulletin* 38 (Washington, DC: GPO, 1902); and Richard R. Wright, Jr., "The Negroes of Xenia, Ohio: A Social Study," *Bulletin* 48 (Washington, DC: GPO, 1903). See also Francille Rusan Wilson, *The Segregated Scholars: Black Social Scientists and the Creation of Black Labor Studies, 1890–1950* (Charlottesville: University of Virginia Press, 2006).

[48] Maria Farland, "W. E. B. Dubois, Anthropometric Science, and the Limits of Racial Uplift," *The American Studies Association* 58 (2006): 1017–44.

government-legitimized expertise on black workers that Du Bois's report on Lowndes County, Alabama, according to Commissioner of Labor Statistics Ethelbert Stewart, "was destroyed by authorization of Congress in 1921."[49]

As an institution, the DNE had a national presence and brought together some of the most experienced experts on the "Negro problem" from the government and nonprofit spheres. At its height, the DNE employed 134 examiners, 7 secretaries, and 15 state representatives. It had state branches in North Carolina, Virginia, Alabama, Kentucky, Mississippi, Florida, Georgia, California, Ohio, Illinois, Pennsylvania, Michigan, New Jersey, and New York, as well as the District of Columbia. The DNE staffed its offices exclusively with African American employees, some of whom had experience in other federal offices, including Charles Hall and William Jennifer, who moved from the Bureau of the Census and the United States Employment Service (USES) to prominent positions in DNE offices in Ohio and Michigan. The DNE also drew leaders from the nonprofit sector, such as Forrest B. Washington of the Detroit National Urban League (NUL), who served as the supervisor of negro economics in Illinois.[50] To further integrate the efforts of the DOL, DNE, and nonprofit organizations, the department called an informal conference on "Negro Labor Problems" in February 1919 that included representatives of the YMCA, YWCA, NAACP, Phelp-Stokes Fund, Tuskegee Institute, NUL, American Missionary Association, Jeanes-Slater Fund, and Women's Home Mission Council.[51] As with the Women's Bureau, resourceful DNE investigators attempted to overcome a chronic lack of resources by fortifying their own investigations with research by a variety of government and nongovernment institutions of inquiry. The DNE used data and observations from religious

---

[49] See exchange of letters between Du Bois and Stewart, including Du Bois to Stewart, September 18, 1924 and Stewart to Du Bois, September 23, 1924, Correspondence of Mr. Stewart as Commissioner, 1923–1926, Records of the Bureau of Labor Statistics, Box 6, File 79–82, RG 257, NA. For more on Wright's efforts to support research on Negro labor, see James Leiby, *Carroll Wright and Labor Reform: The Origins of Labor Statistics* (Cambridge: Harvard University Press, 1960), 106–7. For more on Du Bois's relationship with the Department of Labor, see David Levering Lewis, *W. E. B. Du Bois: Biography of a Race, 1868–1919* (New York: Henry Holt and Company, 1993), 354–7.

[50] DNE, *The Negro at Work During the World War and During Reconstruction: Statistics, Problems, and Policies Relating to the Greater Inclusion of Negro Wage Earners in American Industry and Agriculture* (Washington, DC: GPO, 1921; reprint, New York: Negro Universities Press, 1969), 68. For more on DNE organization and activities, see "Roosevelt Lauds Our Negro Troops," *NYT*, November 3, 1918, 12.

[51] DNE, *The Negro at Work During the World War and During Reconstruction*, 15–17.

organizations, state advisory boards, local branches of the NUL, USES, Inspection and Investigation Service (a service within the BLS), Census Bureau, YMCA, Red Cross, and state and local governments.[52] Among its supporters, the exclusive employment of African Americans caused some to wonder if the DNE was just another Jim Crow institution, but most black leaders framed its establishment as a victory for black workers and their advocates.[53]

The timing of the DNE's establishment resulted in a situation where the division in effect "pirated" the role of employment coordinator from USES, thus establishing an important position for itself as a clearinghouse for expertise on the swiftly changing "Negro labor question." On August 1, 1918, the secretary, through the War Labor Administration, fortified the mission of USES by giving it the "responsibility of recruiting and placing the common labor in war industries employing 100 or more workers."[54] By August, however, the DNE had already established a domain for itself as an agency of black employee recruitment, investigation, and coordination. USES, the Women's Bureau, and many other government and private organizations looked almost exclusively to the DNE for leadership and expertise on issues concerning black workers, and employers and employees looked to it as a source for coordinating employment for black workers, particularly in war industries.

To lead the DNE, Secretary Wilson appointed George E. Haynes to the director's position. Haynes came to the DNE with a strong academic record and close ties to philanthropic and nonprofit organizations that had and would remain key to every phase of the inquiry into the New Era Negro question. Haynes was born in 1880 in Pine Bluff, Arkansas and educated at Fisk (B.A. in 1903), University of Chicago (summer, graduate-level course work), and Yale, where he studied under sociologist William Graham Sumner and completed his M.A. in sociology in 1904. After four years of work with the Colored Department of the International Committee of the YMCA, Haynes returned to graduate school at the New York University School of Philanthropy (later renamed the Columbia School of Social Work) and later Columbia, where in 1912 he completed his doctorate in sociology under German-trained economist Samuel

---

[52] Ibid., 41.
[53] Guzda, "Social Experiment of the Labor Department," 17–18.
[54] DNE, *The Negro at Work During the World War and During Reconstruction*, 22. William Breen, *Labor Market Politics and the Great War: The Department of Labor, the States, and the First U.S. Employment Service, 1907–1933* (Kent, OH: Kent State University Press, 1997), 127–8.

McCune Lindsay.[55] Prior to leading the DNE, Haynes helped found the National Urban League and served as its executive secretary, a post later held by Eugene Kinckle Jones. NUL executive secretary L. Hollingsworth Wood – a Quaker who often worked as the intermediary between the NUL and philanthropic organizations such as the LSRM – reported to the Memorial that he, along with a group of white and African American leaders, met with and "induced the Secretary [Wilson] ... to appoint" Haynes to head the DNE.[56]

Haynes's early work suggests a recognition of the dreadful conditions faced by black workers in the North, but also a belief in eventual assimilation. Published in 1912 as *The Negro at Work in New York City*, Haynes's dissertation helped him secure a position at Fisk University, where he organized and served as chair of the Department of Social Sciences until 1918.[57] Though black workers continued to be segregated in domestic and personal services, Haynes's early work revealed that by 1900 an increasing number found employment in more skilled occupations such as tailors, masons, engineers, and firemen. Haynes wrote that these promising changes "must be accounted for on the ground that slowly the walls of inefficiency" and prejudice "which have confined Negroes to the more menial and lower-paid employments are being broken down."[58] In analyzing the conditions of black workers in the North, Haynes conducted some of the earliest work on the conditions and difficulties facing black families in Northern cities. According to Haynes, the problems facing

---

[55] Dissertation published as George Edmund Haynes, *The Negro at Work in New York City: A Study in Economic Progress* (New York: Columbia University, Longman's, Green and Co., 1912; reprint, New York: Arno Press and the NYT, 1968). On Haynes's education and leadership of the DNE, see Wilson, *The Segregated Scholars*, 61–5, 83–9, and 120–35.

[56] L. Hollingsworth Wood to LSRM, December 17, 1918, Folders 1002–1010, Series 3, Box 99, Folder 1005, LSRM Collection, RAC. For more on the debate over who should lead the DNE, see Guzda, "Social Experiment of the Labor Department," 16–18. On Haynes's contentious and decisive separation from the NUL, see Nancy J. Weiss, *The National Urban League, 1910–1940* (New York: Oxford University Press, 1974), 134.

[57] For more on George Haynes, see also Wilson, *The Segregated Scholars*; Jesse Thomas Moore, Jr., *A Search for Equality: The National Urban League, 1910–1961* (University Park: Pennsylvania State University Press, 1981), 42–59; Guichard Parris and Lester Brooks, *Blacks in the City: A History of the National Urban League* (Boston: Little Brown, 1971); Jessie Carney Smith, ed., *Notable Black American Men* (Detroit: Gale Research Inc., 1999), 528–32; Weiss, *The National Urban League, 1910–1940*; "In the Service of His People," *Journal of Negro History* 6 (April 1921): 107–8; and John A. Garraty and Mark C. Carnes, eds., *American National Bibliography* s.v. "George E. Haynes."

[58] Edmund Haynes, *The Negro at Work in New York City*, 70.

black families grew out of larger social and economic problems, particularly low wages, high rents, racism, segregation, and much higher rates of female labor force participation, which combined to create conditions where "the family [is] unable to protect itself from both physical and moral disease."[59]

As director of the DNE, Haynes struggled to accomplish two seemingly contradictory tasks, attention to which help frame the work of investigators and advocates of African American and Mexican workers described in this chapter and the next. First, he needed to provide a representation of black workers that made clear that they could work competently in industry, labor alongside white workers, and demonstrate the potential for upward mobility. Second, he needed to give voice, and indeed to redefine as a national concern, the plight of black Americans who confronted not only workplace discrimination but savage and often deadly violence. Nowhere was the difficulty of this task more apparent than in the DNE's efforts to explain the 1919 riots in the days after the riot ended. As in Tyson's earlier examination of the relationship between white and black workers in Northern industry, the DNE chose to characterize the relationship as, by and large, one of cooperation rather than conflict. Haynes suggested that variables such as the "acute housing situation" in Chicago and politicians' willingness to use race to inflame white voters were the immediate causes of the riots. Haynes's report described workplace tension, particularly in the stockyards, as a secondary cause of the riots, suggesting that there were "many evidences of good feeling and cooperation between white and colored workers."[60] Simultaneously, the DNE condemned the violence perpetrated by white mobs and called on the federal government to act. DNE investigators noted a widespread feeling among all classes of African Americans that "the Federal Government should do something to remedy their condition."[61] Reconciling the need to publicize racial injustice while presenting a representation of black – and, as we will see in the next chapter, Mexican and Mexican American – workers as efficient contributors to the modern industrial workplace would continue to strain advocates for black and Mexican workers throughout the decade and beyond.

Despite racial violence, DNE investigators made clear that given time, opportunity, and training, black workers would rise into semiskilled and

[59] Ibid., 89.
[60] DNE, *The Negro at Work During the World War and During Reconstruction*, 28.
[61] Ibid., 29 and George E. Haynes, "The Negro Laborer and the Immigrant," *Survey Graphic* (May 14, 1921): 209–10.

skilled occupations. During the war, DNE investigators provided ample evidence that black workers gained a toehold in many unskilled and semi-skilled industrial occupations across a range of industries. To make clear that with necessary training black workers could rise out of the ranks of unskilled labor, investigators pointed to black workers' experience in foundries, for example, noting that Southern foundries had for "more than a generation" employed black men in skilled occupations such as molders. As a result, in some cases black skilled workers in Northern works logged more hours and had a higher hourly pay than their white counterparts.[62]

Employer acceptance of black workers in industry was implicit in all of this data, but during its short life the DNE began to experiment with another line of attack that the NUL would sharpen after the war, specifically, using employer satisfaction as an important measuring stick of black workers' success in industry. In fact, Haynes highlighted the general "satisfaction with Negro Labor" among employers surveyed. In a letter to the NAACP's Walter White listing black workers' accomplishments in industry, Haynes described a Detroit automobile firm, where fifty black workers replaced seventy white workers of mixed ethnicity and surpassed the white workers' productivity by 300 percent while slashing the number of overtime hours worked. Similarly, an Illinois casting company employing some 174 black employees reported that they constituted "some of our best workers. Our experience with colored help has been quite satisfactory and we expect to continue to employ it."[63]

Choosing to appeal to employers was significant. Facing often violent resistance from white workers, black workers and their advocates were dealt a weak hand, to be sure, and appealing to solidarity with white workers must have appeared futile if not delusional, but Haynes's strategy of comparing black workers with white workers came with consequences that were not immediately evident. First and foremost, advocating for black workers in this fashion alienated exclusionary craft unions; this indeed was the point in some cases. After all, if craft unions worked actively to exclude black workers from certain trades, then appealing

---

[62] DNE, *The Negro at Work During the World War and During Reconstruction*, 42.
[63] George E. Haynes to Walter F. White, Assistant Secretary, NAACP, November 12, 1919, Papers of the NAACP: Part 10, Peonage, Labor, and the New Deal, 1913–1939. Reel 9 Group 1 Series C, Administrative File Cont. Group 1 Box 319. File: General Labor, September 1919–December 1919, Library of Congress (hereafter LOC). See also, "Roosevelt Lauds Our Negro Troops," *NYT*, November 3, 1918, 12; and "Tells of Negroes' Role in War Work," *NYT*, May 8, 1921, 131.

directly to employers might open up opportunities in industry or in the unions themselves, if only craft unions could be compelled to recognize that racist practices created a reservoir of workers eager to supplant union members. But appealing directly to employers and stressing employability left black workers and their advocates vulnerable in other areas. At its core, this argument suggested that black workers were somehow different, though in a good way, from their white counterparts; they were, for instance, more productive and less likely to unionize. As shown in the next chapter, when Mexican workers gained a foothold in Northern and Eastern industry, they too faced stiff resistance, and some of their advocates experimented with emphasizing difference as well. This time, however, the difference would be reconfigured as between black and Mexican workers and the ease with which Mexican workers could be integrated into the labor force relative to the more "disruptive" presence of their black counterparts.

Despite important work by the DNE, the division faced increasing scrutiny by members of congressional appropriations committees, who questioned the necessity of a government body focused on investigating a single group of workers. When the department appealed to the Appropriations Committee for DNE funding in 1919, an unnamed conferee made the bogus claim that Secretary Wilson, in creating the DNE, had "usurped powers mandated to Congress in creating a public agency," thus making the DNE unconstitutional.[64] It quickly became apparent that Secretary Wilson did not have the political support to defend the DNE. As a result, "the committee upheld the point of order" and the DNE moved closer toward extinction.[65]

The fight to establish a permanent DNE continued into the early 1920s. The African American press campaigned for the continuation of the DNE's work in some permanent institutional form similar to the Women's Bureau. The *Southern Workman* editorialized that African Americans "should have able representatives who may sit at the council tables and know what is going on and be in position to give some sane and timely advice."[66] By the time President Warren Harding took office in 1921, however, Haynes and his assistant, Karl Phillips, the only remaining DNE employees, were working part time with the BLS's Investigation and Inspection Service. Haynes continued to testify before the congressional

---

[64] Guzda, "Social Experiment of the Labor Department," 33.
[65] Ibid., 34.
[66] "Wise Federal Action," *Southern Workman* XLVIII (February 1919): 51–2. See also "Negro Workers during the World War," *Savannah Tribune*, March 12, 1921, 4.

appropriations committees through 1922 in hopes of reinstating funding for the DNE, but without success. In a 1921 appropriations hearing, Representative Walter W. Magee (D-NY) challenged Haynes on the need for the DNE, asking if there should be a "division of Italian economics, a division of Jewish economics, a division of Polish economics, a division of Indian economics, and so on down through all the races that make up this cosmopolitan people?" Haynes responded that the black population in the United States was "segregated from the white population ... as no other group is." Magee's rejoinder was indicative of policy makers' willingness to close their eyes to the problems that only two years earlier had erupted in some of the worst urban violence in American history: "There is no segregation up there so far as I can see."[67]

This, of course, was nonsense, and civil rights activists worked steadily and at times with success to integrate black workers' concerns and experiences into larger policy debates. For instance, when E. E. Hunt and Herbert Hoover parceled out invitations to the President's Conference on Unemployment (PCU) in 1921, they did not include an African American among the invitees. This omission was noticed. In August and early September, Hoover, Harding, and Davis all received letters from individuals and organizations – including the *Chicago Defender*, Ida M. Tarbell, the American Baptist Home Mission Society, members of Congress, and various branches of the NUL – asking that an African American representative be included on the committee. E. E. Hunt initially rebuffed these requests, writing that Hoover did not intend that the conference "will be made up of groups." But by September 29, Hoover relented and asked Haynes to join the PCU's Committee on Community, Civic, and Emergency Measures chaired by Colonel Arthur Woods, and he asked Phillip Brown of the Department of Labor to give expert testimony at the public hearings of the conference.[68]

Such efforts suggest the importance activists attached to African American representation in all aspects of government. Haynes and others

[67] Congress, House Committee on Appropriations, *Sundry Civil Appropriation Bill, 1921. Part 2: Statement of Mr. George E. Haynes and Mr. Karl F. Phillips*, 66th Cong., 2nd sess., March 20, 1920, 2164. Phillips does not appear to have made any statements during the hearing.
[68] These letters can be found in Box 642, Folders: "Unemployment Conferences: Members Suggested Colored 1921" and "Unemployment Conference Members, R-T," Commerce Papers, Herbert Hoover Presidential Library, West Branch, IA (hereafter HHPL); "RR Church to Secretary James J. Davis," Box 651, Folder Unemployment, Labor Department, 1921, April–September, Commerce Papers, HHPL. See also "Unemployment Conference: Negro Representation," *Southern Workman* L (November 1921): 488–9.

would argue repeatedly before Congress and the nation for the importance of the DNE. The strategic institutional tasks adopted by the DNE undoubtedly made its eventual disappearance all the more troubling to those interested in, first, creating a state-legitimized body of labor knowledge concerning African American workers and, second, guaranteeing that black workers' concerns would remain a national concern. Testifying in 1920 before the House Committee on Appropriations, Haynes suggested that the DNE's examinations of African American participation in industry were "the only bases of information on this subject available on which employers and others can build programs and plans of action."[69] Haynes argued for the importance of the DNE's work to the larger government and testified that "the Woman-In-Industry Service, the Investigation and Inspection Service, the Children's Bureau, the Conciliation Service, the bureau of Industrial Housing and Transportation, and other branches of the department were served in a cooperative way in their dealing with Negro wage earners."[70] Ultimately, these arguments did not persuade congressmen who consistently argued that black labor issues were addressed by other institutions within the federal government.

And to a degree this was true, but policy makers failed to recognize that, as Haynes suggested, this was in no small measure *because* of the work of the DNE and the links its leaders had established in other departments. As described in the preceding chapter, during and immediately after World War I, the DNE and the Women's Bureau worked hand in hand to conduct path-breaking investigations by Helen B. Irvin and Emma Shields that publicized the struggles and progress of black wage-earning women. Cooperation between the WB and the DNE provided an institutional space where the work of a group of trained labor experts concerned with black women workers could momentarily flourish, and demonstrated the DNE's ability to make public the conditions of workers often ignored by government investigators. With the disappearance of the DNE, the Department of Labor lost Haynes, Irvin, Shields, and other important voices. Nonetheless, at least in the case of the WB, DNE studies came at a formative moment. Indeed, they helped to place black women's issues within the purview of the WB and partially account for the WB's somewhat successful effort to include these industrial workers' experiences

---

[69] Congress, House Committee on Appropriations, *Legislative, Executive, and Judicial Appropriation Bill, 1922*, 66th Cong., 3rd sess., December 21, 1920, 1304. Haynes would restate this claim before Congress on a number of occasions, often with evidence from employers who wrote to him commending the DNE's work.
[70] Ibid., 1305.

into an analysis of the labor question in the 1920s. Observers recognized immediately the significance of the loss of the DNE. In examining the postwar unrest, T. J. Woofter described the need for a "more careful study of the situation," which could "be done best by some neutral organization such as the United States Department of Labor possessed during the war in its Division of Negro Economics."[71] Hopes for the reemergence of a DNE-like organization persisted. In September 1930, NUL Director T. Arnold Hill wrote to Secretary of Commerce Robert T. Lamont requesting that federal agencies pay particular attention to the unique position of African American labor in industry. According to Hill, "It is recognized that the problems of Negro workers, like those of women and children, show peculiar difficulties: and for this reason I take it we have a Women's Bureau and a Children's Bureau in the Department of Labor."[72] Woofter, Hill, and others lamented the loss of the DNE, but it was not immediately clear who could take up the task. In fact, the loss of the DNE meant nonprofit organizations would, in large part, bear the responsibility for explaining the ongoing migration and its consequences.

THE RED SUMMER AND THE EMERGENCE OF CHARLES S. JOHNSON

As the nation struggled to make sense of the wave of postwar race riots, prevailing ideas about black workers and the nature of the color line in America received greater attention, not just from the federal government, but on a state and local basis as well. In Chicago, the presence of strong African American-led institutions like the NUL, *Chicago Defender*, and parts of the Democratic Party, combined with a long-standing inquiry by University of Chicago sociologists like Robert Park into assimilation, helped create a space for a new sort of inquiry examining the intersection of race, class, and ethnicity. The lack of state funds for the Chicago Commission on Race Relations's investigation and its reliance on nongovernment funding make it a symbol of the rather sudden shift in inquiry

---

[71] T. J. Woofter, "The Negro and Industrial Peace," *Survey Graphic* (December 18, 1920): 421. Civil rights organizations campaigned for the continuation of the DNE's work as well: see NAACP to Hon. James W. Good (IA-Rep), March 30, 1920, Papers of the NAACP, Part 10: Peonage, Labor and New Deal, 1913–1939; Reel 10 Group 1 Series C, Administrative File, Group 1 Box 319, File: General Labor, January 1920–July 1920, LOC.

[72] T. Arnold Hill to Robert P. Lamont, September 3, 1930, General Records of the Department of Commerce, Office of the Secretary, Subject Files of the Assistant Secretary of Commerce, E. E. Hunt, 1921–1931, Box 20, File: Economic Status of the Negro, RG 40, NA.

from the government to the nonprofit sphere. In the final report, the commission noted that when Governor Frank O. Lowden appointed the commission, the Illinois legislative session had already ended and would not convene again until January 1921. To meet the financial needs of the committee, the commission noted, "a group of citizens offered to serve as a co-operating committee to finance the Commission's inquiry and the preparation and publication of its report."[73]

A true statement as far as it goes, but the lack of state funding was more than just an issue of timing. From the beginning, Governor Lowden made it clear that no state funding, even from the governor's emergency fund, would be forthcoming; instead, the governor planned to rely on the generosity of wealthy Chicagoans. Lowden went so far as to agree that "if all else failed," he would find nonstate funding to "see that the commission had money for its work."[74] Initial attempts to raise money were somewhat successful. In mid-September 1920, the *Chicago Defender* asked black Chicagoans to "regard it their duty to help support the project." The *Defender* reported that already some twenty-two thousand dollars had been raised and spent, but that an additional eight thousand dollars was still needed.[75] The commission and its allies did eventually cobble together the necessary funding to complete the investigation, relying in particular on a series of loans and a two-thousand-dollar donation from Julies Rosenwald. Settling the final costs of the report, however, required that Lowden follow through on his offer. At a luncheon he organized in April 1921 after he had left office, Lowden gave one thousand dollars to help the commission pay its final bills.[76] With the demise of the DNE, this would be the new model for funding inquiry into the "Negro problem."

As a lead investigator and an author of the Chicago Commission report on the 1919 Chicago race riot, Charles S. Johnson emerged in the postwar era as one of the leading experts on African Americans and race relations. Johnson was born in 1893 in Bristol, Virginia, where his father served as a Baptist minister for forty-two years. After completing his degree at Virginia Union University in 1916, he entered graduate school at the University of Chicago, where he worked with sociologist

---

[73] This group included James B. Forgan (chairman), Abel Davis (treasurer), Arthur Meeks, John J. Mitchell, and John G. Shedd. They were assisted by R. B. Beach and John F. Bowman, both of the Chicago Association of Commerce. Chicago Commission on Race Relations, *The Negro in Chicago* (Chicago: University of Chicago Press, 1922), xvii.

[74] For an excellent history of the effort to fund the commission, see Arthur I. Waskow, *From Race Riot to Sit-In, 1919 and the 1960s* (Gloucester, MA: Peter Smith, 1975), 67–70.

[75] "Race Commission Asks the Public to Help," *Chicago Defender*, September 18, 1920, 12.

[76] Waskow, *From Race Riot to Sit-In, 1919 and the 1960s*, 70.

Robert Ezra Park, who also served as the president of the Chicago Urban League. Johnson's Chicago education was interrupted by his service in France during World War I, but he returned to Chicago in 1919 in time to observe the early stages of the Great Migration and the 1919 race riot.[77]

During the summer of 1919, Governor Lowden appointed a twelve-member committee, with six white and six black members, to investigate "Chicago during the period of the riot."[78] The idea of bringing together white and black leaders was not new, but the Chicago Commission on Race Relations brought these leaders together on a more equal footing than had been the case in Southern interracial commissions, where whites dominated the discourse and agenda. Howard University sociologist Kelly Miller contrasted the National Inter-racial Commission's work with the report of the Chicago Commission, which he characterized as "the only document of its kind based upon the joint study and reflection of the two races co-equal in numbers, competency, and authority."[79] Released in 1922, the Chicago report was produced too early to utilize the 1920 census occupational data, but it made full use of the Census Bureau's *Negro Population: 1790–1915* report, the Thirteenth Decennial Census (1910), DNE reports, Chicago Urban League workplace investigations, U.S. Census of Manufacturers (1914), and Emmett J. Scott's *Negro Migration During the War*.[80] To gain more specific information on black workers, the report effectively utilized a survey method similar to the one Du Bois had employed earlier in his own DOL investigations,

---

[77] On Johnson, see Richard Robins, "Charles Johnson," in James E. Blackwell and Morris Janowitz, eds., *Black Sociologists: Historical and Contemporary Perspectives* (Chicago: University of Chicago Press, 1974), 56–84; Wilson, *The Segregated Scholars*, 145–58; Weiss, *The National Urban League, 1910–1940*, 216–17; David Levering Lewis, *When Harlem Was in Vogue* (New York: Knopf, 1981), 46; Richard Robbins, *Sidelines Activist: Charles S. Johnson and the Struggle for Civil Rights* (Tuscaloosa: University of Mississippi Press, 1996); William Banks, *Black Intellectuals: Race and Responsibility in American Life* (New York: W. W. Norton & Company, 1996), 73–82; Patrick J. Gilpin and Marybeth Gasman, *Charles S. Johnson: Leadership Beyond the Veil in the Age of Jim Crow* (Albany: State University of New York Press, 2003); Matthew William Dunne, "Charles Johnson and Southern Liberalism," *The Journal of Negro History* 83 (Winter 1998), 1–34. For an analysis of the University of Chicago and its importance, see Alice O'Connor, *Poverty Knowledge*, 74–98; Joas, *Pragmatism and Social Theory*; Matthews, *Quest for an American Sociology*; and Parsons, *Ethnic Studies at Chicago, 1905–1945*.

[78] Chicago Commission on Race Relations, *The Negro in Chicago*, xvi.

[79] Kelly Miller, "The Negro in Chicago," *American Journal of Sociology* 29 (January 1924): 499.

[80] Emmett J. Scott, *Negro Migration During the War* (New York: Arno Press and the *NYT*, 1969; first published in 1920), vii.

including the use of questionnaires to identify firms with black workers and follow-up visits to examine their conditions of employment.[81]

The report provided evidence of black workers' successful integration into industrial occupations and identified white workers and middle managers as the chief obstacles to black workers' upward mobility. As we will see in the next chapter, later in the decade and as the head of the National Urban League's Department of Industrial Studies, Johnson conducted empirical studies of workplace race relations throughout the country in which he sharpened his critique of white workers as the source of racial intolerance while continuing to draw attention to the malleability of race relations and the potential for improvements. These investigations increasingly differentiated workplace interracial relations, which varied from friendly to antagonistic, from labor market interracial relations, which appeared to grow more and more antagonistic in the Northeast and Midwest as the labor market tightened after the war and employers increasingly recognized the ability of black workers to accomplish the same tasks as whites, often at a lower wage.

Despite racial violence and intolerance in the North, the report's emphasis on opportunities available and taken up by African Americans served as an implicit critique of the ideology of black inferiority. The report unambiguously demonstrated the opportunities created by work in Northern industry and variability in relations between white and black Chicagoans. Chicago commission investigators stressed employer satisfaction with black labor, the presence of amiable race relations in some firms, and expanded occupational opportunities in Northern industries. Even after the riot, black migrants in Chicago described "greater freedom and independence in Chicago," particularly in living, working, political, legal, and leisure spheres.[82] As in the DNE reports, investigators stressed the employability of black workers. The commission found a "remarkable increase" between 1915 and 1919 in the number of black workers employed in manufacturing, clerical occupation, and laundries.[83] Black women in particular benefited from the tight wartime labor market. According to the commission, prior to the war "Negro women were popularly thought of as a class of servants unfitted by nature for work calling for higher qualifications," but employers confronted with a labor shortage found that black women "were as

---

[81] Chicago Commission on Race Relations, *The Negro in Chicago*, 361.
[82] Ibid., 98–9.
[83] Ibid., 362.

teachable as white women and became as efficient workers after receiving the necessary training."[84]

The report also worked to contradict the idea that black workers were incapable of working in industrial occupations and that black and white workers could not work together. Employers surveyed by the commission described black migrants as efficient, reliable, and trainable and relations between white and black workers as amiable. The commission concluded, "The volume of evidence before the Commission shows that Negroes are satisfactory employees and compare favorably with other racial groups."[85] When asked, "Has your Negro labor proved satisfactory?" 118 of the 137 firms questioned "reported that Negro labor had proved satisfactory."[86] In biracial workplaces, employers and black workers alike indicated favorable relations between white and black workers on the job. Although white workers were not surveyed and therefore not treated as subjects of inquiry, of the 865 black workers studied less than one percent "complained of disagreeable treatment by white workers."[87] When the commission surveyed employers in 137 firms employing 22,337 black workers, only two reported that "race friction was a disturbing factor in their plants."[88]

Further undermining the ideology of black inferiority, the report pointed to the ambition of black workers in the face of persistent discrimination. While the earlier DOL reports worked mostly to explain the forces driving migration, Johnson's inquiry provided the first opportunity to hear from these workers themselves. As the report made clear, black workers in Chicago wanted, and felt they deserved, to be treated as equals. The long-term satisfaction of migrants with work in Chicago turned on what one worker referred to as "hope on the job," or the possibility that black workers might have the opportunity to gain better positions and higher wages over time. The report found satisfaction with hours, wages, and treatment among recent migrants, but black Chicago workers employed in the city longer than two years complained of a "lack of opportunity for advancement or promotion."[89] These workers leveled the vast majority of

---

[84] Ibid., 385.
[85] Ibid., 378.
[86] The industries satisfied with black workers employed a total of 21,640 black workers, while those that expressed dissatisfaction employed only 697 black workers. Ibid., 373–8.
[87] Ibid., 385.
[88] Ibid., 394.
[89] Ibid., 387.

their workplace complaints at the foremen, particularly in the foundries and iron and steel mills. Most of these complaints described the foremen's contribution to lower piece rates, greater employment instability, lack of upward mobility, and general mistreatment. To illustrate the point, investigators pointed to a foundry where an abusive foreman had made it his mission to "drive all the 'niggers' from the department."[90] In the stockyards, and railroad dining car and Pullman service, black workers described company rules that barred black workers "from positions for which they were better qualified than the white men who held them." The commission concluded that black workers' "complaints were largely variations on the same theme – race discrimination."[91] The commission noted mounting frustration among black workers, particularly those who had been in the North for years, who experienced a racial barrier imposed by unions, fellow workers, foremen, and employers. The commission found that stories reflecting discrimination traveled quickly through the black community, "which is constantly growing more race conscious."[92]

Implicit throughout the report is the notion that the future of race relations rested not on inevitabilities, but on choices. In what amounts to an appeal to what Gunnar Myrdal would later describe as the American Creed, the report made the case that employers, unions, and workers made the choice to discriminate or not to discriminate. Setting the stage for a line of inquiry later taken up by Johnson and the NUL, the commission devoted more than a third of its labor analysis to an examination of relations between black workers and unions. Investigators found some unions that embraced black workers, while others forbad their admittance either through constitutional writ or established practices.[93] Unions' policies concerning black workers varied. The eight AFL affiliates and the four railway brotherhood unions (not affiliated with the AFL) built in constitutional provisions that excluded black workers from union membership. The Machinists' Union and International Brotherhood of Electrical Workers did not include exclusionary clauses in their constitutions, but practiced, according to the commission, "exclusion of an unwritten law." Unions admitting black workers into white locals

---

[90] Ibid., 389.
[91] Ibid., 390–2.
[92] Ibid., 403.
[93] Ibid., 420. Other unions that fell into this category included the Amalgamated Sheet Metal Workers' International Alliance and the United Association of Plumbers and Steam Fitters of the United States and Canada.

experienced generally good relations with black workers, but efforts to bring black workers into unions were frustrated by employers who would pay black workers at a lower wage or actively use racism as a tool to divide workers. On occasions when unions fought for these workers, some employers responded by suggesting that if they were going to have to pay equal wages, they would "get a good white man" to do the job.[94] Regarding women workers, the commission found a degree of ambivalence in union shops where black women were "retained at a beginning wage for an unreasonable time after acquiring satisfactory skill and production." Though the Women's Trade Union League was made aware of the condition, the commission found that "no well-directed effort has ever been made to unionize colored workers in the garments trades, except when they have been called in as strikebreakers to replace white workers."[95]

Although it showed variation in relations between black workers and unions, the report rejected organized labor's claim that black migration hurt unions. When the commission examined labor leaders and white workers' contention that employers imported black workers to replace white workers, it found "no evidence of any value was discovered to support them."[96] When asked to provide evidence of recruitment by companies, AFL president Samuel Gompers pointed to the use of some thirty thousand black workers during the 1919 steel strike. Commission investigators tersely suggested that even if such recruitment had taken place, the riot occurred well before the steel strike and so recruitment "could not have affected the situation out of which the riot came." They concluded, "Labor leaders insist that employers in the Chicago district imported Negroes from the South, notwithstanding their inability to cite facts in support of the belief."[97] The commission's dismissal of organized labor's position had the effect of sharpening an emerging labor market debate between the AFL and advocates of black workers that would intensify through the decade as the NUL increasingly took aim at organized labor's discriminatory efforts to protect white workers from competition with blacks workers.

---

[94] Ibid., 415.
[95] Ibid., 367.
[96] When the commission questioned the general superintendents of Armour, Morris, Swift, and Wilson plants, they all "declared emphatically that their companies had not engaged in any encouragement of migration." Ibid., 363.
[97] Ibid., 364.

Widely heralded by both the white and black press, the public reception of the report suggests how significant inquiry had become, in the minds of many, to addressing the New Negro problem. Pointing specifically to the report on the first page of its inaugural issue, the National Urban League's *Opportunity* underscored, as it would throughout the rest of the decade, the importance of this sort of investigation and publicity to the larger goal of breaking down long-held ideas about race: "Traditions and taboos backed by centuries of unquestioned acceptance have overshadowed the relations of races like ghosts seeking the privilege of a new embodiment."[98] Describing the report as "of national value, and not merely of local application in its findings," the *New York Times* echoed this sentiment. The *Times* quoted approvingly the report's conclusion that racism directed against African Americans is "due to circumstances of position rather than to distinct racial traits." "If the public is brought to share this conviction," the *Times* concluded, "we shall have gone a long way toward doing the right thing by the twelve million negroes in America."[99]

CONCLUSION

Although it proved ultimately unsuccessful, the struggle to establish a state-sanctioned research arm in the civil rights movement demonstrates the importance movement leaders and organizations placed on inquiry and expertise legitimated by the state. In conducting their investigations, the DNE and Chicago Commission constructed an institutional and discursive space for rethinking the "Negro labor problem" in the 1920s and gathering empirical evidence on a group of workers usually ignored by social scientists in academia and government agencies. Here, a new group of experts had an important opportunity, limited in some respects by a reliance on outside organizations for funding, to take the first steps toward reconceptualization of the "Negro problem," develop a language for discussing the problem, identify a mode of analysis, and formulate solutions to the "problem." As a result, these experts took significant steps toward replacing pseudo-scientific notions of biological inferiority with a tentative variation of the Chicago school assimilationist model, emphasizing in this incarnation the malleability of race relations.

[98] "The Chicago Race Commission," *Opportunity* 1 (January 1923): 3. For similar praise from the NAACP, see Augustus Granville Dill, "'The Negro in Chicago': The Report of the Chicago Commission on Race Relations," *Crisis* 25 (January 1923): 113.
[99] "Fair Play for the Negro," *NYT*, September 26, 1922, 16.

These investigations also helped in the vital effort to nationalize the "Negro problem" by rejuvenating a tradition of state-led inquiry into black workers that had its recent roots in the Wright-Du Bois investigations. In the process, the DNE made black labor issues a concern of the federal government. When congressmen dismissed the DNE as redundantly addressing issues the DOL had already considered, they at least implicitly recognized that black labor issues were a concern of the federal government, not a peculiarly Southern condition and exclusively a state and local concern. As Graham Romeyn Taylor, executive secretary of the Chicago Commission concluded, "No longer can the South say that it alone knows the problem and should be left to solve it in its own way; nor can the North longer point the finger of scorn at the states which previously maintained almost a monopoly of violations against the Negro."[100]

Though less explicitly than in the case of Mary van Kleeck and Mary Anderson and the leaders we will encounter in the next chapter, investigators and advocates like Johnson and Haynes worked in this period to make the experiences of black workers integral to any understanding of the larger labor question. Congressmen who refused to support the continuation of the DNE's work and unions that rejected the notion that black workers' concerns were vital to the overall labor movement were among those who frustrated this effort. With little to no support from unions or the state, leaders like Johnson turned increasingly back to the nonprofit and philanthropic sector for the financial resources they needed to continue their work. By the mid-1920s, however, interest in the migration of black Americans from the South would be linked to another migration stream, this one from Mexico and the Southwest and stimulated by many of the same "pull" forces that had made the Great Migration possible.

---

[100] Graham Romeyn Taylor, "Public Opinion in Problems of Race and Nationality," *NCSW* (1923): 493; Graham Romeyn Taylor, "Race Relations and Public Opinion," *Opportunity* 1 (July 1923): 197–200; Work, "Taking Stock of the Race Problem," 45; and Leonard Outwaite, statement at "Social Science Research Council, Hanover Conference, 1928," 210–11, Folder 1894, Box 330, Series 5, Social Science Research Council Collection, RAC.

"It's great to be a problem" by J. W. Work
Crisis, November 1920, Vol. 21 No. 1

It's great to be a problem,
A problem just like me;
To have the world inquiring
And asking what you be.
You must be this,
You can't be that,
Examined through and through;
So different from all other men,
The world is studying you.

My grandfather cursed my father;
For Noah cursed Ham, you know;
Therefore, my father's children,
The rocky road must go.
We can't turn here,
We can't turn there,
Because the world's in doubt,
What we would do,
Where we would go,
What we would be about.

I'm sullen if I speak not,
I'm insolent if I speak;
Must curb my aspirations,
I must be lowly, meek.
I can't eat here,
I can't sleep there,
Must "Jim Crow" on full fare;
The world can't know
What I would do,
If I were treated square.

It's great to be a problem, a problem just like me;
To have the world inquiring
And asking what you be.

7

Promising Problems

Working toward a Reconstructed Understanding of the African American and Mexican Worker

> False notions, if believed, false preconceptions, may control conduct as effectively as true ones.
> – Charles Johnson, NCSW (1923)

> Many of the important features of Negro life and interracial relations have in the past been the subject of imperfect knowledge and acrimonious debate rather than of scientific inquiry.
> – "Race Relations and Negro Work"[1]

> Unless the Mexican immigrant in the United States is made articulate, unless his economic contribution to the development of the western United States is recognized and rewarded, unless his needs and interests are considered from his own point of view, any attempt to solve the problem will lack the most vital of all values, the human value.
> – Ernesto Galarza, NCSW (1929)

Continued interplay among labor, race, ethnic, migration, and immigration concerns during and after World War I created a space where advocates and experts on Mexican and African American workers could press for a new public understanding of each of these groups' place in U.S. society. By the early 1920s for black workers and by mid-decade in the case of Mexican workers, an emerging body of "labor and race scholars" used this moment of uncertainty, characterized by racial violence and dramatic demographic change, to challenge prevailing notions

---

[1] "Race Relations and Negro Work, 1926–27," Series 3, Box 101, Folder 1021 Negro Problems 1927–1929, 1, Laura Spelman Rockefeller Memorial Collection (hereafter LSRM), Rockefeller Archive Center (hereafter RAC).

about race and ethnicity in America. Informed by on-the-ground inquiry into actual conditions, they demonstrated that the "Mexican problem" and the "Negro problem" were national, not regional, concerns. These investigators and advocates strove to diversify the labor question so that it more clearly reflected the growing importance of, and difficulties faced by, black and Mexican workers in industry. Their effort to reveal migrants and immigrants as "real workers" achieved some important success, particularly in promoting the rethinking of ideas about the legitimacy of race and ethnicity as identifying categories, in relations to character and capability, and about the cultural assumptions active in the structuring of race relations. Perhaps most important, these inquirers' efforts persistently demonstrated that the presence and persistence of the color line in America was a *choice*, not an inevitability, much of it consciously made and remade by those with the power and the will to ensure that the nation remained deeply divided.

Remedying these problems required individuals and institutions – particularly organized labor and the federal government – to recognize the concerns of these often new industrial workers and to take concrete steps to ameliorate issues of racial injustice in the workplace and beyond. Like the Women's Bureau (WB), the National Urban League (NUL) demanded action by the federal government. If the federal government had found a legitimate role for itself as an enforcer of the Eighteenth Amendment, they argued again and again, then surely it could find the courage to defend the Fourteenth and Fifteenth Amendments as well. When it came to organized labor, advocates for these workers became increasingly exacerbated by the inability of white workers to recognize that a failure to organize black workers and confront racism in the house of labor eroded union power.

As in the case of earlier work by the WB and the Division of Negro Economics (DNE), a significant amount of this activism focused on examining, disclosing, and – on the basis of fact-based attitudinal analysis – undermining assumptions about black and Mexican workers specifically and about race relations generally. These efforts were based on the belief that better public knowledge of the aspirations, abilities, and accomplishments of minority racial groups would lead to improvements in race relations.[2] Conversely, they argued that the overt racism of the

---

[2] Historian Joe Trotter characterizes the examination of the Great Migration in this period as dominated by a "race relations imperative." See Joe William Trotter, Jr., "Black Migration in Historical Perspective: A Review of the Literature," in Joe William Trotter, Jr., ed., *Great Migration in Historical Perspective: New Dimension of Race, Class, and Gender* (Bloomington: Indiana University Press, 1991), 5.

period was in part the result of distortions disseminated by movements and figures who – either intentionally or unthinkingly – repeated stereotypes containing false assumptions that influenced conduct. As Charles Johnson argued at the 1928 meeting of the National Conference of Social Work (NCSW), "False notions, if believed, false preconceptions, may control conduct as effectively as true ones."[3] Faith in the power of inquiry to inform and correct was shared by philanthropic and nonprofit organizations that helped to facilitate this research, such as the Social Science Research Council (SSRC), which funded important investigations into the movement of Mexican immigrant, Mexican American, and black workers. The chairman of the SSRC, economist Wesley Mitchell, concurred with Johnson's sentiments, writing in support of such efforts, "There seems to be no group of social problems in which men's attitudes have been characterized by a larger measure of emotion and a smaller measure of science."[4]

The efforts of these investigators have not been fully understood. Carey McWilliams, in his survey of the New Era Mexican problem, noted a dramatic increase in attention to the issue during the decade, but he described the research in this period as a "depressing mass of social data ... consistently interpreted in terms of what it revealed about the inadequacies and the weaknesses of the Mexican character." These alleged weaknesses included a lack of thrift, enterprise, and "leadership, discipline, and organization," as well as voluntary segregation.[5] Yet, although such anti-Mexican sentiment did indeed permeate a significant section of the literature on Mexican workers in this period, McWilliams overlooked an emerging body of expertise on Mexican immigrants and Mexican Americans that worked to undermine these same stereotypes. The work of organizations such as the National Urban League provides evidence of a similar trend under way in research on African Americans.

---

[3] Charles S. Johnson, "Public Opinion and the Negro," *NCSW* (1923): 498.

[4] Mary van Kleeck, foreword to *The Negro in American Civilization: A Study of Negro Life and Race Relations in the Light of Social Research* by Charles S. Johnson (New York: Henry Holt and Company, 1930), vii. Both Van Kleeck and Johnson were involved in an advisory committee of the SSRC. At the 1928 SSRC Hanover Conference, Johnson and Van Kleeck presented material outlining the type of work completed on the Negro problem as part of a larger effort to consolidate and better organize this line of inquiry. "Social Science Research Council, Hanover Conference, 1928," 199–205, Folder 1894, Box 330, Series 5, SSRC Collection, RAC.

[5] Carey McWilliams, *North from Mexico: The Spanish-Speaking People of the United States*, new edition, updated by Matt S. Meier (New York: Greenwood Press, 1990), 188–9.

McWilliams may have missed much of the decade's interesting work on the Mexican problem, but he was on to something of importance when, in his 1948 *North from Mexico*, he asserted that much of the work was "deeply colored by the 'social work' approach," which he characterized as one with a "morose preoccupation with consequences rather than causes."[6] Yet despite McWilliams's negative attitude, many of the experts and investigators examining the Negro and Mexican problems found an audience before the NCSW. This affinity was in part the result of the difficulty they had in cultivating audiences elsewhere, but their presence also suggests that the NCSW was a fairly intellectually diverse and ambitious body in this period, one willing to take on a variety of issues related to race, ethnicity, and gender that other organizations marginalized or simply ignored. Where McWilliams was mistaken was in his conflation of the views of these experts on race and labor who spoke before the NCSW with the ideas of those social workers who embraced more behavioral – as against social and structural – explanations for poverty. As mentioned in the introduction, during the 1920s (as opposed to the 1930s) the field of social work was sufficiently in play to sustain an analysis of poverty that included social or political economy within its purview, alongside explanations that focused on the behavior of individuals. The work of Johnson on the Negro problem, Paul S. Taylor and Ernesto Galarza on the Mexican problem, and Mary Anderson and Mary van Kleeck on the issue of women in the work force all pointed to problems in American industry and society that were not caused by – and could not be ameliorated by altering – the behavior of the party being discriminated against.

McWilliams's assessment of social work as a tradition of inquiry does help us better understand the importance of institutions and their locations. Whereas the formation of the Women's Bureau provided Van Kleeck, Anderson, and others the institutional space and state-sanctioned legitimacy to speak out on a range of issues affecting women workers, advocates of African American and Mexican workers were left searching for a similar platform. Lacking a bastion within the state, they turned to nonprofit and philanthropic organizations that took up issues the federal government tried to ignore or simply dismissed. Their efforts within these alternative settings served to illuminate the distinctive character – the inclusions and omissions extant – institutionalists have characterized as the building of the American regulatory and administrative state.[7]

[6] Ibid., 188.
[7] See footnote fourteen in the introduction for key works that inform my understanding of the relationship between institutional capacity, inquiry, investigation, and the policymaking process.

This chapter begins by describing how policy makers and investigators came to link the Negro problem and the Mexican problem as migration and immigration from the South, Southwest, and Mexico continued during and after World War I. The destabilizing impact of these demographic changes created an opportunity for investigators and advocates – now working in or with funding from nonprofits and philanthropic organizations such as the NUL, the SSRC, and the Laura Spelman Rockefeller Memorial (LSRM) – to compel a rethinking of long-held and deeply racist assumptions concerning black and Mexican workers in the United States. These investigators, described in the second and fourth sections of the chapter, took full advantage of this opportunity. However, as the third section of the chapter suggests, the relative position of black and Mexican workers complicated matters for these advocates and investigators. Increasingly, they wrestled with how to portray the industrial progress of each group relative to the other. While they found undeniable evidence of hard-earned success experienced by black and Mexican workers in industry, they also exhibited palpable concern that with the closing of immigration from Europe, black and Mexican workers might be left to compete for only the least desirable jobs in industry and agriculture.

Taken together, the work of the experts and advocates described in this chapter can be best understood as an effort to transform what had long been understood as the intractable condition of Mexican and African American agricultural and domestic laborers into a national and increasingly industrial and urban problem. As J. W. Work's poem implies, it is better to be a "problem" – "To have the world inquiring. And asking what you be" – than to be a condition, whose inferior station in American society was taken as given and seen as not meriting inquiry. Drawing on timeless American notions of freedom while calling attention to insurmountable contradictions in American democracy, these inquirers then pointed the way to the most effective and just means of ameliorating these promising problems. Only when the policy makers, organized labor, employers, and the public came to recognize the permanence, ambition, and ability of these workers could the nation have a clear understanding of the larger labor question.

FRAMING THE POSTWAR IMMIGRATION DEBATE

Dramatic demographic changes and racial conflict made possible, indeed compelled, a rethinking of immigration policy and prevailing assumptions about racial groups and race relations. After the war, African American internal migration continued, as did the flow of Mexican workers. During the war, Mexican workers stepped up a migration stream precipitated by political unrest in Mexico traced back to the Mexican Revolution in 1910 and the mounting demand for agricultural and industrial labor in the United States. As head of the wartime Food Service Administration and as part of a successful effort to expand wartime agricultural production, Herbert Hoover strongly and successfully advocated for a loosening of immigration restrictions. The number of Mexicans in the United States skyrocketed from two hundred twenty-two thousand in 1910 to four hundred seventy-eight thousand by 1920 and then approximately six hundred thirty-nine thousand by 1930.[8] The majority of Mexican immigrants and Mexican Americans worked and lived in the Southwest, but between World War I and the onset of the Great Depression more than fifty-eight thousand found work in Midwestern industry and agriculture.[9] Slashed European immigration, rising real wages, and changes in the workday stimulated this demand. For instance, when U.S. Steel shifted to the eight-hour day, the industry turned increasingly to Mexican and African American labor. Eugene G. Grace of Bethlehem Steel indicated to the *New York Times* that the tight labor situation for the company had improved "owing to immigration from Mexico and the migration of the negro from the South to the North." By 1923, the works had hired at least twenty-five hundred Mexican workers.[10] Harvard economist Thomas Nixon Carver warned that immigration from Mexico posed the "greatest menace" to the "present tendencies toward the diffusion of prosperity." "Immigration of cheap labor from any source," according to Carver, "tends to depress wages and to concentrate rather than to diffuse wealth.... Cheap labor means poverty."[11]

A persistent belief among policy makers that Mexican workers returned to Mexico meant that the Mexican problem received somewhat less attention than the Negro problem, but by mid-decade an emerging group of experts began working to reshape the public's understanding of the experiences, aspirations, and abilities of Mexican immigrants and Mexican Americans in the United States. The Mexican and Negro problems were often deeply intertwined by policy makers and by those who

---

[8] David G. Gutiérrez, ed. *Between Two Worlds: Mexican Immigrants in the United States* (Wilmington: Scholarly Resources Inc., 1996), xiii.
[9] Zaragosa Vargas, *Proletarians of the North: A History of Mexican Industrial Workers in Detroit and the Midwest, 1917–1933* (Berkeley: University of California Press, 1993), 1.
[10] "Steel Wage to Rise as Hours Decrease," *NYT*, July 27, 1923, 15.
[11] T. N. Carver, "The Changing Economic Status of Labor," *General Management Series: Numbers 34–53, 1926* (New York: Kraus Reprint Corporation, 1967), 6–7.

worked to challenge prevailing ideas concerning the present and future of race relations. Increasing national concern over this latest incarnation of the Negro problem sensitized some policy makers in the federal government to the troubled history of American black-white race relations and also to the prospect, as they saw it, of heightened racial conflict along a different racial interface if Mexican immigration continued.[12] In the halls of Congress, Representative Albert Johnson (R-WA), chair of the Committee on Immigration and Naturalization, made this linkage clear in 1926 hearings contemplating limits on Mexican immigration. Pointing to the growth of the Mexican population, Johnson worried that the "white people of the lands ... shall be dwarfed ... by a different type of people getting on the lands, producing other citizens who will get into the body politic." Johnson elaborated on the nature of his concerns, along the way alluding cryptically to the gravity of the situation by referencing the demographic outcome for the earlier introduction of black people into the territory that became the United States:

> The committee knows from its studies that the largest number of black people ever brought in any one year to the United States was less than 8,000. Who would have thought at that time that a fearful racial problem would have come, leading to a great war, from the introduction of those blacks? This committee knows that 1 person in every 12 in the United States is black skinned. We can see problems here that we do not discuss, but which are dangerous and troublesome.[13]

For a problem too "dangerous and troublesome" to discuss, the perceived national peril that accompanied a continuation of Mexican immigration to the United States received significant public airing. In hearings

---

[12] The reference to the "latest incarnation" of the Negro problem is meant to acknowledge the rise of a very different Negro problem in the 1890s South that was precipitated by the potential for an interracial alliance of poor white and black sharecroppers by way of the Populist movement. The discrete nature of these two Negro problems was recognized even at the time. Historian Arthur Schlesinger, at the 1928 SSRC Hanover Conference, described how "the Populist movement began to split the ranks of the Democratic Party in the South in the early nineties." By the mid-1890s, Schlesinger noted, white Democrats solved this problem by reuniting, agreeing that a more concerted effort was needed to disenfranchise the African American vote, and clarifying that the Democratic Party was a white man's party. There is no evidence, so far as I can assess, that the investigators and policy makers at the time viewed the rise of the World War I era Negro problem as connected to what occurred in the early 1890s. "Social Science Research Council, Hanover Conference, 1928," 205–6, Folder 1894, Box 330, Series 5, SSRC Collection, RAC.

[13] Statement of Albert Johnson in U.S. Congress, House Committee on Immigration and Naturalization, *Hearings on Seasonal Agricultural Laborers from Mexico*, 69th Cong., 1st sess., 1926, 39. For similar sentiments, see also House Committee on Immigration and Naturalization, *Immigration from Countries of the Western Hemisphere*, report prepared by Albert Johnson, 71st Cong., 2nd sess., 1930.

two years earlier, Congressman John C. Box (D-TX) queried Mr. S. P. Frisselle, a California supporter of continued Mexican immigration in the interest of agriculture, "Have you ever known how the country or read of one in history which filled the body of its citizenship with underling labor that did not have some dire consequences, just such as the South had from bringing black labor from Africa?" Though Frisselle insisted Mexicans were not immigrants, as they were not "coming here for permanent residence," Box answered his own question with a firm, "I have not."[14] Box continued with this line of thinking in 1928, when he argued: "All the strife that we had for 50 years before the Civil War ... we have reaped as the consequences of a great race question." Box then equated the immigration debate with the constitutional convention: "The country has adopted [a] restrictive [immigration] policy. If it had adopted it in the constitutional convention, if it had been possible to do so, the country would have been a hundred percent better off right now."[15]

The tortured search for solutions to the New Era race and labor problems that satisfied employers' need for labor without undermining a racialized understanding of citizenship was laid bare in the decade's frequent congressional hearings and debates concerning the issue. In 1926, 1928, and 1930, Congressman Box led unsuccessful efforts to restrict immigration to the United States from nations in the Western hemisphere that had not been included in the decade's earlier immigration restriction acts. To balance the interests of industry and those who fought to eliminate Mexican immigration, some advocates for continued migration went so far as to suggest clearly unconstitutional solutions to the "problem" of Mexican settlement in the United States. In 1926 hearings, for instance, Congressman Bird Vincent, who represented a downstate Michigan district with a significant number of sugar beet farmers, asked skeptically, "Have we got to adopt a plan of bringing in folks and saying to them 'you are different from everybody else; you have to work at one thing, or you go.' Can we start with that principle?" Despite the growers' demands, many on the committee seemed skeptical regarding the

[14] Ibid., 26.
[15] Quoted in David Gutiérrez, *Walls and Mirrors: Mexican Americans, Mexican Immigrants, and the Politics of Ethnicity* (Berkeley: University of California Press, 1995), 53. For a specific discussion of the Mexican problem in the 1920s, see David Montejano, *Anglos and Mexicans in the Making of Texas, 1836–1986* (Austin: University of Texas Press, 1987), particularly chapter eight. On the link between race and citizenship as it pertained to Mexicans and Mexican Americans, see Natalia Molina, "'In a Race All Their Own:' The Quest to Make Mexicans Ineligible for U.S. Citizenship" *Pacific Historical Studies* 79 (2010): 167–201.

prospects for such a system. Noting that Mexicans were "already developing citizenship," Chairman Johnson pointed out that the children of these workers born in the United States had "rights and cannot be kicked out." Perhaps unaware of the Fourteenth Amendment, I. D. O'Donnell, representing farmers of Wyoming and Montana, cavalierly suggested that Congress was "big enough to create a board or organization, or enact some law to control it." Seizing the opening, Box asked incredulously, "You think when the Constitution of the United States vests him with citizenship because of birth we could deport him?" Undeterred, O'Donnell continued along these lines, suggesting that given the overall population of the nation, the relatively small number of Mexican immigrants would matter little. To this Johnson replied that a similar belief had been held about the early phases of Chinese and Japanese immigration to the West Coast.[16]

Congressional discussions like these underscored the public nature of immigration and migration concerns and suggested an opportunity to provide the public and policy makers with a fuller and more accurate assessment of who ultimately bore responsibility for racial conflict in the United States. With the disappearance of the DNE, inquiry into changes in the African American population increasingly moved outside of the state and into the nonprofit sphere. Various advocates for a new understanding of the cultures and aspirations of Mexican nationals and Mexican Americans adopted a similar approach, looking to burgeoning nonprofits such as the Social Science Research Council for support. This necessary turn to non state institutions was damaging in some degree, in that it left investigators without the legitimacy only the federal government could provide. But it was also liberating, in that investigators in nonprofits could more clearly and directly address controversial issues related to racism, race relations, and the uneven nature of citizenship in New Era America, often with less concern over procuring and sustaining congressional funding.

[16] *Seasonal Agricultural Laborers from Mexico*, Hearing Before the Committee on Immigration and Naturalization, House of Representatives 1926, 68–72, 94–5. To varying degrees, other scholars have framed the rise of various "problems" arising out of the migration and immigration of various groups as, among other things, related to public health concerns. See, for instance, Natalia Molina, *Fit to Be Citizens? Public Health and Race in Los Angeles, 1879–1939* (Berkeley: University of California Press, 2006); Nayan Shah, *Contagious Divides: Epidemics and Race in California's Chinatown* (Berkeley: University of California Press, 2001); William Deverell, *Whitewashed Adobe: The Rise of Los Angeles and the Remaking of Its Mexican Past* (Berkeley: University of California Press, 2005).

Together the two bodies of experts who studied African American and Mexican groups made the case that the problems arising out of these two migration streams were both economic and social. Contemporary scholarly work in sociology and the actual experience of successive generations of Western European immigrant populations suggest that past immigrant groups could hope to assimilate into the larger white population over time, eventually rising to more advantaged positions in the occupational scale. Meanwhile, Mexican and black workers were faced with racial barriers that in some respects actually increased during a decade when policy makers and the public rethought the United States' relationship to the rest of the world. As these investigators and advocates made clear, black and Mexican workers made great economic strides in the New Era and in many situations found employers and white fellow employees who tolerated an integrated workplace. Nonetheless, persistent racism and discrimination challenged the notion that, with time, new groups would have the opportunity, if they so chose, to assimilate fully into the broader society. For integration to occur, these experts increasingly argued, white Americans would have to be much more forthright in addressing racial barriers to integration that were actively constructed and maintained by those with the power and will to ensure that the nation remained divided on racial and ethnic lines.

The nature of expert inquiry concerning African Americans changed significantly over the decade. Violent racial conflict during and following the war pushed labor experts to go beyond largely descriptive studies and delve into race relations in a more substantive way. As observed in the previous chapter, state governments took the lead in this area and established commissions to investigate the wartime and postwar surge in racial violence in cities such as East St. Louis and Chicago.[17] The growing importance of the nonprofit sector to black labor inquiry was evident in these federal and state investigations, which drew heavily from nonprofit

---

[17] For examples and analysis of World War I-era race riot investigations, see Chicago Commission on Race Relations, *The Negro in Chicago* (Chicago: University of Chicago Press, 1922); State of Illinois, Council of Defense, Committee on Labor, *The Race Riots at East St. Louis* (Washington, DC: GPO, 1918); and U.S. House of Representatives, 65th Cong., 2nd sess., *Report of the Special Committee Authorized by Congress to Investigate the East St. Louis Riots at East St. Louis* (Washington, DC: GPO, 1918). For analysis of these studies, see Elliot M. Rudwick, *Race Riot at East St. Louis, July 2, 1917* (Carbondale: Southern Illinois University Press, 1964); James R. Grossman, *Land of Hope: Chicago, Black Southerners, and the Great Migration* (Chicago: University of Chicago Press, 1989); and William M. Tuttle, Jr., *Race Riot: Chicago in the Red Summer of 1919* (New York: Atheneum, 1979).

organizations such as the National Urban League in filling their ranks of investigators. Local NUL branches provided expertise to state and federal agencies concerned with black workers. For instance, the Department of Labor paid the salary of an NUL executive to supervise the "industrial details of the United States Employment Service for Negroes with the aid of an assistant furnished by the United States Employment Bureau."[18] Following the war, the termination of the DNE left a gaping hole in policy makers' resources for making sense of issues affecting black workers. This gap forced innovative experts and advocates of black workers to construct non state institutions of labor inquiry with the assistance of nonprofit and philanthropic organizations such as the National Urban League, the Laura Spelman Rockefeller Memorial, and the Carnegie Corporation. They managed to make a virtue out of a necessity, though: in many respects, this amounted to the most ambitious and substantive phase of New Era inquiry into the Negro question.

The work of the newly formed SSRC deserves special mention in this context because it funded the most important inquiries into the Mexican problem during the era, but also because it attempted to link the dramatic demographic changes in the black and Mexican populations. The SSRC's Committee on Scientific Aspects of Human Migration (renamed the Committee on Population in 1927) was chaired by Edith Abbott and grew out of earlier studies by the National Research Council, though the SSRC studies focused much less on race as a biological concept and more on how socioeconomic factors explained the relative position of groups.[19] According to anthropologist Casey Walsh, the SSRC saw the migration of African Americans and Mexicans as related and chose to fund one group of studies on Mexican immigration by Paul S. Taylor, Mario Gamio, and Robert Redfield, and another on African American migration. Indeed, the SSRC clearly saw the issues as ongoing and linked, identifying the "Negro and Mexican migrations of the past decade" as issues of "great importance, which should be studied while the movement is still in progress."[20] Though the SSRC would eventually sponsor

[18] Newsletter from Eugene Kinckle Jones to Mr. John D. Rockefeller, May 28, 1919, Series 3, Box 99, Folder NUL 1918-1922, 2, LSRM Papers, RAC.
[19] For insight into the SSRC's early deliberations on whether to take up these very controversial issues, see "Report of Joint Conference of the Committee on Problems and Policy of the SSRC," 32-41 and 77-100, Folder 569, Box 53, Series 3, Accession 25, LSRM Papers, RAC.
[20] SSRC, "Report of the Committee on Scientific Aspects of Human Migration," December 18, 1926, Folder 1134, Box 191, Subseries xix, Series I, SSRC Papers, RAC. The report was written by committee chair Edith Abbott.

a far-reaching study by Johnson on the Negro problem that culminated in the publication of *The Negro in American Civilization*, this happened only after a multiyear study of the African American migration from the South by Frank Ross was abandoned due to Ross's inability to deliver a publishable report.[21] Given the attention that Taylor, and Gamio to a lesser degree, received upon publication of their respective reports, it is interesting to contemplate how the SSRC's work on these two related "problems" might have been able to shape the public and policy makers' understandings of these issues had Ross's study come to fruition in a timely manner.[22]

Nonetheless, given the importance of Gamio, Taylor, and Redfield's work on issues related to immigration from Mexico, the SSRC's work is significant. Though Gamio described in some detail racism encountered by Mexicans in the United States and explained how such experiences made assimilation unlikely, his 1926–7 study suffered from his constant effort to straddle "the line between racial and socioeconomic approaches."[23] Gamio had studied at Columbia with Franz Boas, a fierce critic of scientific racism, but his analysis of Mexicans in the United States too often suffered from preoccupation with the Indian and *mestizo* culture

---

[21] Mary van Kleeck chaired the National Interracial Conference committee in charge of the Johnson study. The NIC, NUL, and the SSRC's Advisory Committee on the American Negro (renamed the Advisory Committee on Inter-Racial Relations) cooperated in efforts to investigate and improve race relations and the condition of African Americans. See Will W. Alexander to Dr. Arnold Bennett Hall c/o Dr. Charles E. Merriam, March 26, 1927; George E. Haynes, "Memorandum on Survey of Investigations of Problems of the Colored Race in the United States to be carried on under the auspices of the NIC Prepared for the Advisory Committee on Interracial Relations of the SSRC. March 23, 1927"; and Charles S. Johnson, "Memorandum on Proposed Field Activity of the Research Committee of the NIC," all to be found in pages 20–30, Folder 1765, Box 307, Subseries 1, Series 2, Accession 1, SSRC Papers, RAC.

[22] I am most grateful to Casey Walsh for providing me with a copy of his unpublished study of the SSRC's migration studies. Casey Walsh, "The Social Science Research Council and Migration Studies (1922–1933)." See also Casey Walsh, "Ethnic Acculturation: Manuel Gamio, Migration Studies, and the Anthropology of Development in Mexico, 1910–1940," *Latin American Perspectives* 31 (September 2004): 118–45. On the NRC's Committee on Scientific Problems of Human Migration, see Clark Wissler, *Final Report of the Committee on Scientific Problems of Human Migration*, Folder 633, Box 59, Series 3, Accession 25, LSRM Collection, RAC; and Charles Yerkes, "The Work of Committee on Scientific Problems of Human Migration, National Research Council," *JPR* 3 (October 1924), 189–96. Wissler observes in his report, "It may be remarked that the newly organized Social Science Research Council set up a committee of its own, under the same title, and took over the projects and recommendations of our Committee relating to the social sciences." Wissler, *Final Report of the Committee on Scientific Problems of Human Migration*, 14.

[23] Walsh, "Ethnic Acculturation," 125.

of immigrants, which he deemed determinative of Mexican immigrants' inferior status in American and Mexican society. Gamio implied that it was not that all Mexicans were culturally inferior, but rather mainly those from whom the immigrant stock was derived.[24] In part due to the selective reading it likely received, Gamio's work would have largely confirmed many policy makers' and much of the white public's assumptions about Mexican inferiority, and in a perverse way helped to justify it.

The second of the three outstanding scholars of Mexican immigration funded by the SSRC was Robert Redfield. Redfield did not complete his PhD until the summer of 1928, and his work, by that point, had moved on to examining postrevolutionary Mexico; nonetheless, his understanding of the significance of inquiry in shaping the public's understanding of race and connections to the larger network of investigators concerned with Mexican immigration merit mention. Following his service in World War I as an ambulance driver in France and a short postwar stint at Harvard, Redfield returned to Chicago in 1919, completing his J.D. at the University of Chicago in December 1921. A short and unfulfilling career in municipal law ended when his father-in-law, Robert E. Park, offered to finance a trip in the fall of 1923 for Redfield and his wife, Greta, to Mexico. Here, Redfield witnessed village life in postrevolutionary Mexico and came into contact with a number of influential Mexican intellectuals, most importantly Gamio. By early 1924, Redfield, with Park's enthusiastic support, had decided to leave the law and pursue a PhD in anthropology at the University of Chicago. Redfield biographer Clifford Wilcox reports that Redfield's early graduate work – funded by the LSRM by way of a Local Community Research Committee grant – focused on the Mexican population in Chicago with the aim of providing "basic information about the social and cultural backgrounds of immigrants that would assist social workers in their efforts to help immigrants assimilate."[25] These early investigations did not result in a published report or paper, and Redfield soon turned his attention to Mexico. His late-twenties Tepoztlán study – financed by the SSRC – and later work examined the three districts Gamio had identified as "now furnishing the most immigrants to the United States."[26] Though there is less on

---

[24] On Gamio, see also George Sanchez, *Becoming Mexican American: Ethnicity, Culture, and Identity in Chino Los Angeles, 1900–1945* (New York: Oxford University Press, 1993), 120–2 and David A. Brading, "Manuel Gamio and Official Indigenismo in Mexico," *Bulletin of Latin American Research* (1998): 75–89.
[25] Clifford Wilcox, *Robert Redfield and the Development of American Anthropology* (Lanham: Lexington Books, 2004), 30.
[26] Walsh, "The Social Science Research Council and Migration Studies," 25.

Redfield's ideas about civil rights in the 1920s, his work on Mexicans in Chicago and involvement in the post–World War II struggle for African American civil rights suggests that he would have been in agreement with New Era investigators, such as Johnson and Taylor, on the importance of inquiry in addressing racial conflict. For instance, in addressing Redfield's understanding of race in the context of his testimony in *Sweatt v. Painter* (1950), historian Kathryn Jane Kadel argues that Redfield "thought of race in socially constructed rather than as biological terms," and that he "left no possibility for applying his expertise as a social scientist in the quest for" civil rights "untapped."[27]

Of the three investigators, Paul S. Taylor produced the work that was and remains the most important. A 1922 University of California, Berkeley PhD who joined the economics faculty upon graduation, Taylor produced a more detailed, nuanced, and ultimately useful study of Mexican workers in the United States between 1927 and 1929 that helped to undermine many of the prevailing assumptions concerning Mexican Americans and Mexican immigration to the United States. In doing so, Taylor added his voice to that of an emerging group of labor and immigration experts who, like those who reexamined the Negro problem, sought to take advantage of a period of dramatic change to reshape Americans' understanding of the labor question. Through his research and publications, Taylor fought to undermine several damaging assumptions about people of Mexican descent in the United States. The SSRC worked with Taylor in these efforts, charging him not only to investigate the character of the Mexican population in the Southwest, but also to follow Mexicans into Colorado and the Great Lakes region. Rather than portraying these immigrants and migrants as temporary laborers sequestered in low-skill and low-pay occupations, the SSRC directed Taylor to describe "the ladder upon the rungs of which Mexicans are commencing to climb to higher levels in our economic life."[28] When Taylor went beyond the monograph with his

---

[27] Kathryn Jane Kadel, "Little Community to the World: The Social Vision of Robert Redfield, 1897–1958" (PhD dissertation, Northern Illinois University, 2000), 142.

[28] Edith Abbott, "Report to the Chairman of the Social Science Research Council from the Committee on Scientific Aspects of Human Migration, March 31, 1927," 3, Folder 1765, Box 307, Subseries 1, Series 2, Accession 1, SSRC Papers, RAC. Abbott served as chair of the Committee on Scientific Aspects of Human Migration (renamed the Advisory Committee on Population in 1927). The Abbott-chaired committee was itself a "special committee" of the larger Committee on Problems and Policy, which even in its name provides a sense of how the SSRC viewed this work. By 1927, there were ten special committees, including the Advisory Committee on Interracial Relations and the Advisory Committee on Industrial Relations. The committee structure and organization shifted frequently. Helen Richardson wrote the original proposal that led to Taylor's investiga-

findings in order to reach a wider audience through publications such as *Survey Graphic*, the SSRC's Robert Lynd congratulated him, writing, "You are doing a genuine service in making the material you have gathered available to this wider group ... dollar for dollar the Council has reason to be extraordinarily satisfied with its investment in the study of Mexican Immigrants under you."[29]

As in the case of African Americans, stereotypes of Mexican and Mexican Americans had fierce public advocates, this time from two separate camps: immigration restrictionists who opposed, and agricultural and other interests who advocated, continued migration from Mexico. Together, these partisans developed a three-part understanding of the Mexican problem that proved relatively serviceable for their varied purposes through the mid-1920s. First, hoping to undermine policy makers' concerns over the potential of continued migration to further complicate race problems in the United States, the agricultural interests that advocated continued migration argued that Mexican workers were not immigrants at all; instead, this group contended, Mexicans in the United States were a discrete group of temporary workers who had a "homing instinct" that made their return to Mexico inevitable. Testifying on behalf of agricultural interests in California, S. F. Frisselle described "the Mexican" as a "homer." "Like the pigeon he goes back to roost."[30] Return to Mexico was, of course, not a total myth. Given discrimination in the United States and the relatively open border, unsurprisingly, many Mexicans who came to the United States in search of work did return, but the intent of propagating the "homing" idea was to ease anti immigrant concerns, not to provide an empirically accurate characterization of the situation. For Mexican Americans and their advocates, such depictions undermined efforts to achieve the full rights of citizenship in the United States. Moreover, restrictive immigration polices such as the 1917 Immigration Act had unintended consequences. By regulating the

---

tion. See Helen Richardson, "Investigation of Mexican Immigration and Casual Labor in the United States," Folder 563, Box 52, Series 3, Accession No. 25, LSRM Papers, RAC.

[29] Lynd served as assistant to SSRC chairman Wesley Mitchell. Robert S. Lynd to Taylor, May 5, 1931, Carton 10, Folder 1 Correspondence, Paul S. Taylor Papers, UC Berkeley Bancroft Library, Manuscripts Collection. For an overview of Taylor's work, see Abraham Hoffman, "An Unusual Monument: Paul S. Taylor's Mexican Labor in the United States Monograph Series," *Pacific Historical Review* 45 (May 1976): 255–70; and Linda Gordon, *Dorothea Lange: A Life Beyond Limits* (New York: W. W. Norton and Company, 2009), particularly 140–54.

[30] U.S. Congress, House Committee on Immigration and Naturalization, *Hearings on Seasonal Agricultural Laborers from Mexico*, 6.

movement of Mexicans in and out of the United States through policies such as literacy tests and fees, these policies actually increased the number of Mexican immigrants in the United States. According to George Sanchez, "The unintended consequences of policies designed to make immigration more difficult were to encourage those already in the country to stay, thus transforming what had been a two-way process into a one-way migration."[31]

Second, those both in favor of and opposed to this migration viewed Mexican workers in general, as historian Mark Reisler has argued, as docile, indolent, and backward. Whereas restrictionists found these characteristics un-American and threatening, anti restrictionists identified these characteristics as "splendid prerequisites for the type of labor they required."[32] Farmers in the Southwest cast Mexican workers as docile and well suited to the difficult work in the fields, tied to one employer by way of "cheap" wages that made quitting economically infeasible. Writing in the *Saturday Evening Post*, Charles Teague, himself a California farm owner, described Mexican workers as uniquely suited to hot, heavy, and seasonal work that "white labor refuses to do and is constitutionally unsuited to perform." For those who might consider bringing in "Puerto Rican [sic] Negroes or Filipinos" to do the work, Teague noted the added advantage that a significant portion of Mexican workers returned home and did not need "to be supported through the periods when there was no work to do."[33]

[31] Sanchez, *Becoming Mexican American*, 68.
[32] Mark Reisler, "Always the Laborer, Never the Citizen: Anglo Perceptions of the Mexican Immigrant during the 1920s," in David Gutiérrez, ed., *Between Two Worlds: Mexican Immigrants in the United States* (Wilmington: Scholarly Resources Inc., 1996), 25. See also Kathleen Mapes, "'A Special Class of Labor': Mexican Im(Migrants), Immigration Debate, and Industrial Agriculture in the Rural Midwest," *Labor: Studies in Working-Class History of the Americas* 1 (Summer 2004): 65–88; Gutiérrez, *Wall and Mirrors*, 47–68; Sanchez, *Becoming Mexican American*; Neil Foley, *The White Scourge: Mexicans, Blacks, and Poor Whites in Texas Cotton Culture* (Berkeley: University of California Press, 1997), 40–63; Camille Guerin-Gonzales, *American Workers and American Dreams: Immigration, Repatriation, and California Farm Labor* (New Brunswick: Rutgers University Press, 1994), particularly 25–47; and Mae Ngai, *Impossible Subjects: Illegal Aliens and the Making of Modern America* (Princeton: Princeton University Press, 2003), 56–90.
[33] Charles Teague, "A Statement on Mexican Immigration," *Saturday Evening Post* 107 (March 10, 1928), 169–70. The *Saturday Evening Post* frequently addressed this issue in the 1920s; see Raymond A. Mohl, "The *Saturday Evening Post* and the 'Mexican Invasion,'" *Journal of Mexican History*, III (1973), 131–8. Regarding longtime *Post* columnist Kenneth Roberts, one of the most persistent critics of immigration from Mexico and Mexican Americans, see Sylvia Whitman, "The West of a Down Easterner: Kenneth Roberts and the Saturday Evening Post, 1924–1928," *Journal of the West* (January 1992): 94–5.

Third, the Mexican worker was reported to lack ambition, thus posing no threat to enterprising American workers. Rather than hoping to move from low-paying and arduous work in agricultural labor to better-paying manufacturing work, Mexican workers preferred agricultural labor and would not – in fact, could not – compete with white and white-ethnic industrial workers. As Louisiana congressman Riley J. Wilson put it, "The Mexican does not save money and has no ambition to own any land. He is a gambler and he is always broke and always looking for more wages, and therefore you have a constant population that does not develop good citizenship or become landowners."[34]

The depictions of Mexican workers varied between those of outright restrictionists who wanted to end immigration from Mexico and those of employers in agriculture and industry who required workers who would labor for low wages. Whereas agricultural interests saw something redeeming in continuing immigration from Mexico and the Southwest, advocates of a dramatic reduction in this stream saw danger. As historian Mae Ngai characterized this tension, "Anti-Mexican rhetoric invariably focused on allegations of ignorance, filth, indolence, and criminality."[35] Both groups, however, decidedly agreed that Mexican workers should not be eligible for citizenship. While encouraging Congress to rethink U.S. immigration policy as it concerned Mexico, the *New York Times* concluded that it was "folly to pretend that the more recently arrived Mexicans, who are largely of Indian blood, can be absorbed by and incorporated into the American race."[36]

The quality of the migrant population was not the only issue under discussion among experts and policy makers. In examining the immigration policy in the 1920s, historian Daniel J. Tichenor has argued that "neither legal nor illegal Mexican inflows prompted great concern among national policymakers."[37] In fact, considerable attention was given to the issue of Mexican labor among national policy makers in the New Era, but there was also a discernable shift in the nature of this discussion, nurtured by emerging bodies of evidence that challenged widely held behavioral, racial, and cultural assumptions about the nature of immigration from Mexico.

---

[34] U.S. Congress, House Committee on Immigration and Naturalization, *Hearings on Seasonal Agricultural Laborers from Mexico*, 25.
[35] Ngai, *Impossible Subjects*, 53.
[36] "Singling Out Mexico," *NYT*, May 16, 1930, 19.
[37] Daniel J. Tichenor, *Dividing Lines: The Politics of Immigration Control in America* (Princeton: Princeton University Press, 2002), 172.

What changed in this debate was not the presence of concern with the issue, which was debated frequently and heatedly throughout the 1920s, but rather the assumptions about the relationship of Mexican workers to issues central to the larger labor question continually under discussion during the New Era, including citizenship, permanence, upward mobility, skill, and aspirations. Recognition that prevailing beliefs about the nature of Mexican immigration were inaccurate began very slowly to percolate in the postwar era as opponents of this immigration stream warned that Mexican workers had moved well beyond their presumptive place as temporary laborers in agricultural, domestic service, and railroad occupations in the Southwest. Early in the 1920s, former Texas congressman James L. Slayden noted with concern that three-quarters of immigrants from Mexico came in illegally and found work as far north and east as Minneapolis and Chicago. Slayden, like others in Congress and beyond, equated Mexican workers with African Americans, noting that both groups were "gregarious" and had "developed a taste for the movies and the white lights."[38]

By the late 1920s, experts such as Ernesto Galarza, Emory Bogardus, Manuel Gamio, and Paul Taylor worked to supplant earlier behavioral assumptions, replacing them with a more nuanced representation of the Mexican and Mexican American experience that undermined many of the beliefs held by both restrictionists and non restrictionists. While the contention that a wide swath of the work force arriving from Mexico planned to and did return to Mexico proved accurate, new data challenged representations of the Mexican worker as an individual who worked short bouts of exclusively unskilled labor, only invariably to return to Mexico. For those who planned permanent residence, as David Gutiérrez, Gabriela Arredondo, and others have clearly demonstrated, the path to citizenship for Mexican and Mexican Americans – to the extent that one was sought – was "fundamentally different" from that of European immigrants.[39] By mid-decade, the arguments of restrictionists and anti restrictionists alike crumbled in the face of continued immigration from Mexico, interregional migration, and permanent settlement within the United States. The combination of threatened presumptions about the nature of this immigration stream and increases in the overall Mexican and Mexican American population residing in the United States

[38] James L. Slayden, "Some Observations on Mexican Immigration," *Annals of the American Academy of Political and Social Science* 93 (January 1921): 122–3.
[39] Gabriela F. Arredondo, *Mexican Chicago: Race, Identity, and Nation, 1916–39* (Chicago: University of Illinois Press, 2008), 106.

led to increased calls for restrictions on immigration from Mexico. Those who believed that "playing the race card" would promote restriction also turned to making a more concerted effort to identify people of Mexican descent as nonwhite.

RECONSTRUCTING THE PUBLIC PERCEPTION OF THE NEGRO PROBLEM

The effort to maintain a national focus on the Negro problem did not die with the conclusion of the Chicago investigation or the demise of the DNE. In place of state-sponsored investigations, the NUL led a contingent of organizations, scholars, and researchers funded by philanthropic foundations such as the Laura Spelman Rockefeller Memorial, SSRC, and, Carnegie Foundation that constructed a body of labor knowledge comparable to that created by the DNE and the Women's Bureau. An eight-thousand-dollar grant by the Carnegie Foundation in 1921 provided initial funding for the NUL's Department of Research and Investigation. In response to a 1924 plea from L. Hollingsworth Wood, the LSRM appropriated five thousand dollars as a "special contribution" in addition to its annual NUL appropriation for "research and investigations conducted by the League."[40] By 1926, the NUL budgeted more than twenty-three thousand five hundred dollars toward research and investigation, making it by far the largest department in the NUL.[41] The establishment of the NUL department and Charles Johnson's appointment as director of research was well received.[42] The *Southern Workman* asserted that Johnson's research and investigations "should receive the active support of every open-minded man and woman, because it aims to assemble and interpret the facts of American life as they have a bearing

---

[40] L. Hollingsworth Wood to Beardsley Ruml, Series 3, Box 99, Folder 1006 NUL, 1923–1924, LSRM Collection, RAC. In 1921, the Carnegie Corporation provided a special three-year grant of eight thousand dollars per year to the NUL in order to form the Department of Research and Investigations. John D. Rockefeller, Jr. gave the Department of Industrial Relations forty-five hundred dollars between 1925 and 1931.

[41] Leonard Outhwaite to Hollingsworth Wood, June 4, 1926, Series 3, Box 99, Folder 1007 NUL 1925–6, LSRM Collection, RAC. For more on funding of the NUL in general, see Nancy Weiss, *The National Urban League, 1910–1940* (New York: Oxford University Press, 1974), 156–8.

[42] Implicit recognition of the value of NUL work came from a number of interesting unpublicized donations, including an "anonymous" 1931 donation of $500 by President Hoover to the NUL, which made Hoover one of the more generous individual contributors to the NUL at a time of declining donations from other quarters. "National Urban League," December 16, 1931, Series 3, Box 100, Folder 1014 NUL Reports, LSRM Collection, RAC.

on the welfare of Negroes." The Tuskegee Institute's Monroe Work pointed to "the tremendous educational value to the Nation" evident in Johnson's work.[43] When they needed information on the migration and African American workers, NAACP leaders such as Walter White turned to the NUL. NAACP leaders did not find this arrangement entirely satisfactory. Historian David Levering Lewis describes an internal evaluation that led Mary Ovington to complain that the *Crisis* had never produced a "good piece of research" and that *Opportunity* "was now the magazine in ascendant."[44] Even readers of the *Crisis* recognized it was deficient in this area. William N. Jones, a reader from Baltimore, wrote, "I believe an industrial department with an aggressive program would greatly augment the work of the organization."[45]

The NUL was not new, of course, to its role as an authority on black workers. During and immediately after World War I, employers and government officials often turned to the NUL for assistance. Historian James R. Grossman's analysis of the Chicago branch of the NUL describes the difficulties the NUL faced in the North, where it was expected to serve "three masters": "It advised industrialists and helped them to increase productivity; it improved conditions for migrants"; and it encouraged migrants to be openly ambitious – a trait white Southerners had suppressed and "labeled arrogance."[46] Other philanthropic organizations also contributed to this effort and drew on the body of experts gathered

[43] "The Urban League," *The Southern Workman* LI (January 1922): 4–5.
[44] David Levering Lewis, *W. E. B. Du Bois: The Fight for Equality and the American Century, 1919–1963* (New York: Henry Holt and Company, 2000), 155. See also T. Arnold Hill, executive secretary of the Chicago Urban League to Walter F. White, assistant secretary NAACP, November 14, 1919, Reel 9, Group 1, Series C, Administrative File Cont. Group 1 Box 319, File: General Labor, September 1919–December 1919, Papers of the NAACP: Part 10, Peonage, Labor, and the New Deal, 1913–1939, Library of Congress (hereafter LOC); L. Hollingsworth Wood to LSRM, December 17, 1918, Series 3, Box 99, Folder 1005, LSRM Collection, RAC.
[45] William N. Jones, "NAACP and Labor," *Crisis* 34 (April 1927): 59. A number of NUL employees assumed supervisory positions within the DNE; see "Appeal of the NATIONAL LEAGUE ON URBAN CONDITIONS AMONG NEGROES to the Laura Spelman Rockefeller Memorial," December 1918, Series 3, Box 99, Folder: NUL 1005, 1918–1922, LSRM Collection, RAC.
[46] Grossman, *Land of Hope*, 204. On the NUL, see also Touré F. Reed, *Not Alms But Opportunity: The Urban League and the Politics of Racial Uplift, 1910–1950* (Chapel Hill: University of North Carolina Press, 2008); Jesse T. Moore, *A Search for Equality: The National Urban League, 1910–1961* (University Park: Pennsylvania State University Press, 1981); Weiss, *The National Urban League, 1910–1940*; and Francille Rusan Wilson, *The Segregated Scholars: Black Social Scientists and the Creation of Black Labor Studies, 1890–1950* (Charlottesville: University of Virginia Press, 2006), particularly chapter four.

around the NUL and the now defunct DNE. For instance, as Johnson transitioned from the NUL to Fisk University, the SSRC helped fund a study by the National Interracial Conference eventually published as Johnson's *The Negro in American Civilization*. Notably, George E. Haynes, former DNE director, served as the executive secretary of the committee with Van Kleeck as chair and Johnson as the research secretary.[47]

The NUL's reliance on philanthropists for much of its funding left the organization open to the criticism that its officers were mere "Negro administrators of white philanthropy," as Sterling Spero and Abram Harris suggested in their 1930 study, *The Black Worker*.[48] Indeed, foundation leaders did more than simply fund investigations. Through their funding choices and reviewing of proposals, they played a key role in shaping the development of knowledge concerning black workers and communities. A 1926 LSRM report conceded, "It should be borne in mind that the amount of work undertaken [by the NUL] has to a certain extent been determined by a deliberate Memorial policy."[49] But Harris and Spero went much too far in their dismissal of the NUL's work

---

[47] Van Kleeck, "Foreword," v–xi; and Rusan Wilson, *The Segregated Scholars*, 160.

[48] Spero and Harris included interracial committees in this category as well. Sterling Spero and Abram Harris, *The Black Worker: The Negro and the Labor Movement* (New York: Columbia University Press, 1931), 464–5. Of some interest, Spero, who received a fellowship from the SSRC in 1925 and renewed in 1926, appealed to an advisory committee of the SSRC for funding in the late 1920s and none other than Charles Johnson presented the project to the committee. His request was denied based on a "lack of definitive information concerning the results of his previous work [presumably his two-year research fellowship] on this subject, and his methods and plans for the future." "Minutes of the Advisory Committee on Interracial Relations of the Committee on Problems and Policies of the SSRC held in Washington, January 22, 1927," Folder 684, Box 64, Series 3, LSRM Papers, RAC. He was apparently quite persistent in this unsuccessful effort; see Leonard Outhwaite to Wesley Mitchell, February 28, 1928, Folder 685 Box 64 Series 3, LSRM Papers, RAC. Though focusing more on the leadership of the LSRM and other philanthropic organizations, John H. Stanfield takes a similarly critical view; see John H. Stanfield, *Philanthropy and Jim Crow in American Social Science* (Westport: Greenwood Press, 1985).

[49] "Race Relations and Negro Work, 1926–7," Series 3, Box 101, Folder 1021: Negro Problems 1927–1929, LSRM Collection, RAC. On funding sources for the NUL in this period, see Weiss, *The National Urban League, 1910–1940*, 155–62. On the LSRM, see Martin Bulmer and Joan Bulmer, "Philanthropy and Social Science in the 1920s: Beardsley Ruml and the Laura Spelman Rockefeller Memorial, 1922–1929," *Minerva* 19:3 (Autumn 1981): 347–407; Martin Bulmer, "Support for Sociology in the 1920s: The Laura Spelman Rockefeller Memorial and the Beginnings of Modern, Large-Scale, Sociological Research in the University," *The American Sociologist* 17 (November 1982): 51–4; Marc C. Smith, *Social Science in the Crucible: The American Debate over Objectivity and Purpose, 1918–1941* (Durham: Duke University Press, 1994); and Stanfield, *Philanthropy and Jim Crow in American Social Science*, 61–96.

and in their willingness to lump all recipients of philanthropic aid into one category. Whereas previous foundation-funded research and labor policy development had accommodated Southern racist traditions, the work of the NUL in the 1920s candidly analyzed impediments to black workers' upward mobility and assigned blame to a number of white-led organizations.[50] In fact, Johnson's analysis of the causes of black worker problems in industry resembled W. E. B. Du Bois's controversial labor analysis more than it did that of Booker T. Washington, another important recipient of foundation aid often charged with public appeasement of white racism. Part of the explanation for this had to do with timing. The confusion surrounding the impact of the Great Migration on American society and the absence of other institutions to make sense of what was going on provided a window for Johnson and others to engage in a broader inquiry into race and labor relations than had been possible in the pre–World War I South.

As director of research and investigation, Johnson functioned as editor of the NUL monthly *Opportunity*. Scholars have often characterized *Opportunity* as a vehicle to publicize the achievements of Harlem Renaissance artists and, in Johnson's words, "to inculcate a disposition to see enough of interest and beauty in their own lives to rid themselves of the inferior feeling of being Negro." But the journal also served as an outlet for publicizing the work of the research department.[51] In the

[50] For examinations of the relationship between philanthropists and the groups and organizations they funded, see Barry D. Karl and Stanley N. Katz, "Foundations and Ruling Class Elites," *Daedalus* 116 (March 1987): 1–40; Barry D. Karl and Stanley N. Katz, "The American Private Philanthropic Foundation and the Public Sphere 1890–1930," *Minerva* 19 (Summer 1981): 236–70; Donald T. Critchlow, "Think Tanks, Antistatism, and Democracy: The Nonpartisan Ideal and Policy Research in the United States, 1913–1987," in Mary O. Furner and Michael Lacey, eds., *The State and Social Investigation in Britain and the United States*, 279–322; David Hammack, "Foundations in the American Polity, 1900–1950," in Ellen Condliffe Lagemann, ed., *Philanthropic Foundations: New Scholarship, New Possibilities* (Bloomington: Indiana University Press, 1999), 43–68; David Hammack and M. Stanton Wheeler, *Social Science in the Making: Essays on the Russell Sage Foundation, 1907–1972* (New York: Russell Sage Foundation, 1994); Alice O'Connor, *Poverty Knowledge*; James Smith, *The Idea Brokers: Think Tanks and the Rise of a New Policy Elite* (New York: The Free Press, 1991), and Ellen Condliffe Lagemann, ed., *Philanthropic Foundations: New Scholarship, New Possibilities* (Bloomington: Indiana University Press, 1999).

[51] L. Hollingsworth Wood to Beardsley Ruml, Box 99, Folder 1006 NUL, 1923–1924, LSRM Collection, RAC; Charles S. Johnson, "The Rise of the Negro Magazine," *Journal of Negro History* 13 (January 1928): 18. For more on the journal and Johnson's role as a chronicler and advocate of the Harlem Renaissance, see Lewis, *When Harlem Was in Vogue*, particularly 113–18, 179, 198–9. In the second volume of his biography of Du Bois, Lewis describes a sudden change in *Opportunity* as it "switched within a couple

first edition of *Opportunity*, Eugene Kinckle Jones wrote that the journal would "try to set down interestingly but without sugar coating or generalizations the findings of careful scientific surveys and the facts gathered from research."[52] Reflecting on the mission of the monthly in 1928, Johnson wrote:

> The policy of the magazine as it has developed has emphasized the objectives of making available for students, writers and speakers dependable data concerning the Negro and race relations for their discussions, with the thought that truth carries its own light, that accurate and demonstratable facts can correct inaccurate and slanderous assertions that have gone unchallenged.[53]

After two years of publication, *Opportunity* had a monthly circulation of six thousand, which included more than 100 public and university libraries. As a testament to the usefulness of the journal to social scientists, Jones reported "over forty classes in sociology use it for reference."[54] From the LSRM's perspective, *Opportunity* furnished "the medium through which synopses" of NUL studies "are published and distributed."[55]

NUL investigators and contributors, often from NUL branch offices, examined wages and hours, but they also worked to reveal the nature of the color line and the decisive role white workers played in maintaining it. By surveying the state of race relations across industries and regions, they demonstrated that a color line did exist, but that the line varied significantly. Johnson, in particular, never fully rejected the Chicago school model, which suggested that interracial tension would diminish as white-ethnic and black workers assimilated to the common mores of

---

of issues from being a forum for the cutting-edge articles of distinguished social scientists and educators to become the premier review for literary and artistic effusion of the so-called New Negro." Lewis is correct to point to a shift in the periodical, particularly after 1926 when the research department struggled for funding, but I find that in the biography – and in *When Harlem Was in Vogue* – Lewis overemphasizes the shift, not only in *Opportunity* but in Johnson's thinking as well. Though Johnson was one of the key players in the Harlem Renaissance, he developed an equally important role as the leading expert on the "Negro labor problem" in the 1920s. For Lewis's characterization of *Opportunity*, see Lewis, *W. E. B. Du Bois*, 156.

[52] Eugene Kinckle Jones, "Cooperation and '*Opportunity*,'" *Opportunity* 1 (January 1923): 5. Also quoted in Lewis, *When Harlem Was in Vogue*, 95.

[53] Johnson, "The Rise of the Negro Magazine," 19.

[54] Kenneth Chorley to Beardsley Ruml, February 5, and Eugene Kinckle Jones to Laura Spelman Rockefeller Memorial, January 15, 1925, both in Series 3, Box 99, Folder 1007 NUL 1925–1926, LSRM Collection, RAC.

[55] "Race Relations and Negro Work, 1926–27," Series 3, Box 101, Folder 1021 Negro Problems 1927–1929, 4, LSRM Collection, RAC. For an overview of the NUL's investigations, see Weiss, *The National Urban League, 1910–1940*, 216–33.

modern industrial society; even so, he insisted that white workers' willingness to work side by side with black workers and accept them as a legitimate part of the labor market was the decisive factor in the future of the color line.

The NUL's commitment to evaluating the condition of black America and race relations through the lens of African American workers increased during the decade. By mid-decade, T. Arnold Hill, formerly of the Chicago NUL, joined the national office as head of the Department of Industrial Relations, while Johnson's Department of Research and Investigation expanded its scope to include greater attention to the relationship between organized labor and black workers. In explaining the increased attention to these issues, the NUL cited an "embarrassing poverty of information of any sort" and the potential for this vacuum in the public's understanding of black workers specifically, and of race relations more generally, to be filled by "careless generalizations which contribute nothing but confusion and more trouble to this issue."[56]

To fill this void, the NUL conducted a series of studies describing how understanding that racism was socially constructed helped to explain the relative lack of occupational mobility among black workers. In Johnson's studies of workplace race relations in the Midwest, Northeast, and South, he found greater emphasis on de jure segregation in border states such as Missouri, Kentucky, and Maryland, where "the necessity has been felt for being explicit on absolute segregation in residential areas, enforcing the issue with an ordinance."[57] Johnson cited Allison Muir, personnel executive of the General Electric Company, who confirmed a hardening of racial divisions "the nearer you get to the Mason Dixon Line." According to Muir, in Birmingham you would find white workers who preferred to work with skilled black workers rather than "poor white trash," but in "Baltimore the white workers demand separation in everything."[58] Johnson found that white workers maintained degrees of segregation

[56] "The New Industrial Outlook," *Opportunity* 3 (May 1925): 133. For a somewhat similar take on Johnson and the research work of the NUL in the 1920s, see Richard Robbins, *Side Lines Activist: Charles Johnson and the Struggle for Civil Rights* (Jackson: University Press of Mississippi, 1996), 46–8. Johnson would remain in this position until 1928, when he divided his time between the NUL and the Interracial Conference Committee. In the fall of 1928, he moved to Fisk University, where he became the head of the department of social science, though he remained a contributing editor to *Opportunity*. Elmer Anderson Carter replaced Johnson as editor in October 1928 and Ira De Reid assumed the position of director of research and investigations.

[57] Charles S. Johnson, "Negroes at Work in Baltimore, MD: A Summary of the Report on the Industrial Survey of the Negro Population," *Opportunity* 1 (June 1923): 12–19.

[58] Ibid., 12.

through grassroots activism and through institutional means that limited black workers' access to particular occupations. Among barbers, motion picture operators, horse-shoers, public accountants, and portable engineers, state examining boards exercised "a very rigid selection and by this means have been known to hold down the number of Negroes' licenses."[59] In other cases, white workers' militant refusal to work alongside black workers proved an adequate deterrent to the employment of black labor. In its work with employers, the NUL's Department of Industrial Relations found that the "almost invariable answer given by an employment manager to one seeking jobs for Negroes is 'Our white employees will not work with them.'"[60]

In these urban studies, the NUL did the most sophisticated work of the decade in analyzing the costs of industrial segregation. Johnson and the NUL utilized the method Du Bois had used in *The Philadelphia Negro* of comparing the occupational distribution for white and black workers to demonstrate the degree to which discrimination isolated black workers in low-skilled and low-paying occupations.[61] In his study of Baltimore, Johnson found that despite being only 14.8 percent of the total population, black workers made up 65.6 percent of domestic and personal service workers and 47 percent of unskilled workers.[62] In a survey of black workers in St. Louis for the NUL, William V. Kelly found that although black male workers found employment in most industries, they were "generally doing porter's work and are so underpaid that the woman in the family must find a job to supplement the income of the man." As Kelly observed regarding St. Louis, "It is far easier for a [black] woman to find employment than it is for a man." In an observation that foreshadowed controversial work that focused more on the black family and less on structural deficiencies in the economy by scholars including E. Franklin Frazier and later Daniel Patrick Moynihan, Kelly suggested that this arrangement "gives rise to serious social problems within the family."[63]

[59] Ibid., 18.
[60] "Outline of Work and Activities of the Industrial Relations Department of the National Urban League, March 15th, 1925–May 31st, 1926," Series 3, Box 99, Folders NUL 1007, 1025–1926, LSRM Collection, RAC; T. Arnold Hill, "Labor," *Opportunity* 7 (January 1929): 23.
[61] For an analysis of Du Bois's *Philadelphia Negro*, see O'Connor, *Poverty Knowledge*, 33–9. The NUL studies might provide us with a link between Du Bois's turn-of-the-century work and St. Clair Drake and Horace R. Cayton's work in *Black Metropolis: A Study of Negro Life in a Northern City* (Chicago: University of Chicago Press, 1945).
[62] Johnson, "Negroes at Work in Baltimore, MD," 14.
[63] William V. Kelly, "Where St. Louis Negroes Work," *Opportunity* 5 (April 1927): 116. For similar sentiments in the period, see E. Franklin Frazier, "The Scourges of the Negro

To remedy these problems, advocates for a new understanding of the situation of black workers cultivated a more narrowly focused, three-pronged message – one to the federal government, one to employers, and another to organized labor – meant to underscore the central point that a clear understanding of the "labor question" required that black workers' concerns and experiences be recognized and their rights defended.

If Hoover and his allies felt confident that major public problems could be addressed through investigation and voluntary action, activists and experts concerned with the Negro problem concurred that any effort to address racial injustice required a clear understanding of the problem, but they, like the Women's Bureau, were less reticent when it came to the need for statist intervention. In fact, throughout the decade and on many fronts, they argued that such an intervention was imperative. In the weeks after the 1919 Chicago race riot, Chicago poet and journalist Carl Sandburg published a series of articles for the *Chicago Daily News* examining the riot. Later in the year, when Sandburg published these articles as a book, he closed the text with a call for federal action from NAACP chairman Joel E. Spingarn. In language that echoed throughout the decade, Spingarn argued, "The fact must now be emphasized that the race problem is not local, but is a national question. It should have federal attention, and there should be federal aid."[64] Over the course of the decade, activist and experts made the case for direct action to defend the constitutional rights of black Americans. On housing, they praised Supreme Court decisions that made unconstitutional efforts by cities to use planning and zoning to codify segregated neighborhoods. They demanded protection from lynching by way of a constitutional amendment that would force the federal government to protect the lives of African Americans. And they demanded that the federal government enforce the Fifteenth Amendment, protecting the right of African Americans to vote. Tactically, the adoption and enforcement of the Eighteenth Amendment provided civil rights activists with a new tool. If federal and state governments in the North

---

Family," *Opportunity* 4 (July 1926): 210–13, 234; Forrester B. Washington, "The Effect of Changed Economic Conditions Upon the Living Standards of Negroes," *NCSW* (1928): 471–3. For more on the relationship between research on the black family and policy makers' understanding of poverty, see O'Connor, *Poverty Knowledge* and Andrew J. F. Morris, *Limits of Voluntarism: Charity and Welfare from the New Deal through the Great Society* (Cambridge: Cambridge University Press, 2009).

[64] Carl Sandburg, *The Chicago Race Riots July 1919* (New York: Harcourt, Brace, and Howe, 1919), 79.

and South could arrive at a rough consensus on the constitutionality of the government's right to reach into the lives of American citizens in order to deny them a drink, then surely this provided ample justification to protect the most basic right of all: the right to vote. *Opportunity* asked, "If the 18th [Amendment] is enforced as a moral issue and at great expense, what is to become of morality if the 14th and 15th Amendments are ignored?" The answer to this question boiled down to little less than the rule of law: "The Negro problem in politics can be simplified by stating it as the problem of whether or not it is safe to teach disrespect for our government laws."[65]

The message to employers and unions was similar, but the tone was not. Like the DNE, the NUL reached out to employers, often with testimonials from other employers challenging older notions of black workers as inferior and substituting a description of the successful efforts of black migrants to learn new trades, work efficiently, and remain loyal to employers, particularly during periods of labor unrest when white workers walked off the job. While these NUL reports outlined progress, they recognized that the effort to bring black workers into industry would take work and that there was evidence of places where – for lack of training and discipline or as a result of hostility from employers, unions, or white employees – black workers had struggled. The overriding message to employers, however, focused on the progress and ability black workers had shown when given the opportunity and training necessary to succeed on the job.[66]

---

[65] "Moral Issues of the Campaign," *Opportunity* 6 (September 1928): 259. See also "Nullification," *Opportunity* 5 (April 1927): 97–8; "The 14th, 15th, and 18th Amendments," *Opportunity* 6 (March 1928): 67–8; and "Rum and Race," *Opportunity* 6 (May 1928): 32.

[66] For a sampling of employers' assessment of black workers' performance, see "A Summary of 1920 Accomplishments of the National Urban League," Series 3, Box 99, Folder 1005 NUL, 1918–1922, LSRM Collection, RAC; Edgar E. Adams, "Assimilation into Industry," *Opportunity* 4 (February 1926): 56–7; Charles S. Johnson, "The Negro Population of Waterbury, Connecticut: A Survey by the Department of Research and Investigations of the National Urban League," *Opportunity* 1 (November 1923): 302; "The South Studies the Migrant in the North," *Opportunity* 2 (June 1924): 2; Eugene Kinckle Jones, "Negro Migration in New York State," *Opportunity* 4 (January 1926): 10; "Industrial Employment of the Negro in Pennsylvania," *MLR* 22 (June 1926): 1225; T. Arnold Hill, "Labor," *Opportunity* 7 (January 1929): 23; John T. Clark, "Negro in Steel," 4 (March 1926): 87–8; and "Negroes as Workers," *Opportunity* 4 (March 1926): 90. For an analysis of the relationship between immigrant and black workers, see Charles S. Johnson, "Substitution of Negro for European Immigrant Labor," *NCSW* (Chicago: University of Chicago Press, 1926): 317–27.

More interesting, however, is the case the NUL made to organized labor. If the NUL offered employers the carrot, they unapologetically threatened organized labor with the stick. Though they occasionally referenced places where black workers made good union members, the thrust of the NUL's investigations into organized labor focused on identifying discriminatory practices of unions and drawing attention to places where black workers eroded organized labor's power.[67] Although "economic necessity" had "overcome in large measure the prejudices of employers," the NUL argued, organized labor remained an impediment to racial integration.[68] In many respects, the AFL's unwillingness to organize black workers served as a useful foil for experts and advocates who used it to demonstrate clearly the absurdity of ignoring the centrality of black labor to a realistic understanding of modern industrial American society. While AFL leaders argued that few of their member unions actually denied black workers membership, the NUL mocked a craft union model that increasingly in practice, if not policy, resulted in exclusively white, skilled unions. Such a misunderstanding of the labor market persisted in unions, black workers' advocates argued, despite clear evidence that organized labor needed to expand its understanding of the labor market to include workers of color and unskilled workers.

If the AFL hoped that the problems for organized labor brought on by the Great Migration would pass, the NUL argued that this was a turning point for unions, not an ephemeral problem. In a 1928 *American Federationist* article, Hill described the movement of black Americans north while noting that they were settling in urban industrial cities and now made up one-eighth of industrial workers. Hill described these workers as being at a crossroads – if they joined unions they became less valuable to employers: if they chose not to join, they jeopardized the position of all workers.[69] The choice of overriding importance, however, once

---

[67] For evidence that the NUL wanted better relations, see "Labor and Race Relations," *Opportunity* 4 (January 1926): 4–5. On the relationship between the NUL and AFL, see also Weiss, *The National Urban League, 1910–1940*, 203–15.

[68] "The New Industrial Outlook," *Opportunity* 4 (February 1926): 37.

[69] T. Arnold Hill, "Negro Labor," *AF* 35 (December 1928): 1452–6; T. Arnold Hill, "The Negro in Industry," *AF* 32 (October 1925): 915; T. Arnold Hill, "The Dilemma of Negro Workers," *Opportunity* 4 (February 1926): 39. For more on the NUL as an advocate for unionization of black workers and critic of organized labor's policies toward black workers, see the following articles: "A Successful Negro Labor Union," *Opportunity* 1 (May 1923): 21; "Negro Miners in the Coal Strike," *Opportunity* 2 (July 1924): 195; Abram L. Harris, "The Plight of the Negro Miners," *Opportunity* 3 (October 1925): 303, 312; T. Arnold Hill, "The Negro in Industry, 1926," *Opportunity* 5 (February 1927):

again, was the one facing white workers and unions, who discriminated against black fellow workers at their own peril. Howard University sociologist Kelly Miller nicely described the dilemma black workers faced: "Logic aligns the Negro with Labor, but good sense arrays him with capital."[70]

Along these same lines, Johnson and others noted frequently that organized labor's fear of black workers undermining union strength was well founded and that black workers had materially benefited from crossing picket lines. White workers' "fear is warranted," Johnson argued in an article for *Survey Graphic*, "for not only is there a menace to union objectives in the availability of Negro workers, but it has so happened that many of the greatest advances which Negroes have made in industry ... are due to strikes and their part in breaking them."[71] The problem, as Thomas L. Dabney phrased it, turned on white workers' efforts "to acquire class consciousness while remaining race conscious."[72] Implicitly arguing that the problems of white workers were largely the same as those faced by black workers, the NUL directly criticized the AFL's craft union structure, which failed to serve white and black workers alike. Noting the paltry results of the AFL's Southern campaign and the unions' inability to organize even 10 percent of the nation's workers, *Opportunity* editorialized that the AFL "then not only has failed to unionize the black worker; it has failed to unionize the white worker."[73] Privately, NUL leaders questioned the quality of AFL leadership. T. Arnold Hill wrote to Chicago settlement leader Mary McDowell, "I confess I question the courage of some of the leaders – in fact I believe that some of them would like to

---

51–2; Helen G. Norton, "The Brookwood Conference on Negro Labor," *Opportunity* 5 (August 1927): 244–5; Claude A. Barnett, "We Win a Place in Industry," *Opportunity* 7 (March 1929): 82–6; "The AFL and the Negro," *Opportunity* 7 (November 1929): 335–6; "A Cause for Apprehension," *Opportunity* 7 (October 1929): 304.

[70] "Labor and Race Relations," 4–5; Hill, "The Dilemma of Negro Workers," 39. While hardly apologizing for racism in the ranks of and leadership of organized labor, A. Phillip Randolph argued that the path to progress for black workers lay in organizing and unionization. See A. Phillip Randolph, "The Negro and Economic Radicalism," *Opportunity* 4 (February 1926): 62–4.

[71] Cited in Jesse O. Thomas, "The Negro Industrialist," *NCSW* (1928): 459 and William L. Evans, "The Negro in Chicago Industries," *Opportunity* 1 (February 1923): 15.

[72] Thomas L. Dabney, "Southern Labor and the Negro," *Opportunity* 7 (November 1929): 345.

[73] "The AF of L and the Negro," *Opportunity* 7 (November 1929): 335; "President of the A. F. of L. Replies," *Opportunity* 9 (December 1929): 367. Green's reply is published in the same edition on pages 381–2.

see a change in organized labor but as usual they are afraid to proceed in this direction."[74]

In the longer term, the NUL's appeal to unions can be cast as a success. After all, when John L. Lewis organized the CIO, he explicitly reached out to the NUL and other civil rights organizations in order to assure them that labor's cause was the cause of black and unskilled industrial workers throughout the nation. The near term, however, was a different story. As the NUL noted, the number of African American local unions plummeted from 169 in 1919 to 21 in 1929, representing an overall decline in the percentage of black locals among the total union movement from 18.7 percent to 5.4 percent.[75] Meanwhile, the AFL remained indifferent to rethinking the union's goals and membership, even to the point of rejecting the NUL's offer in both 1925 and 1926 to pay for half the salary for a "competent Negro who would work under [AFL president William Green's] direction" to smooth the relations between black workers and the union.[76] In a 1926 article for *Opportunity* entitled "Why Belong to the Union," Green gave a generic sales pitch for unionization that could have been written of any group of workers, demonstrating a lack of interest in the unique issues facing black workers.[77] Other union leaders, such as one of the intellectual forces in the AFL, John P. Frey, were outright hostile to the needs of black workers. In a 1929 speech before the National Interracial Conference and published in *American Federationist*, Frey, adopting the same rationale Congress had used in rejecting calls to make the DNE a permanent department, argued that black workers suffered no injustices that had not been experienced by Polish, Italian, Jewish, or Russian workers, and added that black leaders impeded attempts by organized labor to organize black workers.[78]

---

[74] T. Arnold Hill to Mary McDowell, July 21, 1926, Series IV Industrial Relations Department, Box 4, File "J-P" 1926–1934, NUL Papers, LOC.

[75] Further evidence that the AFL abandoned black workers in this era can be found in the number of black paid organizers on staff, which fell from three in 1911 to zero in 1929. Ira De A. Reid, "Lily-White Labor," *Opportunity* 8 (June 1930): 172.

[76] T. Arnold Hill, "Open Letter to Mr. William Green, President, American Federation of Labor," *Opportunity* 8 (January 1930): 57 and T. Arnold Hill to Mary McDowell, July 21, 1926, Series IV Industrial Relations Department, Box 4 File "J-P" 1926–1934, NUL Papers, LOC.

[77] William Green, "Why Belong to the Union?" *Opportunity* 4 (February 1926): 61–2.

[78] John P. Frey, "Attempts to Organize Negro Workers," *AF*, 36 (March 1929): 296–305; "The American Federation of Labor and the Negro," *AF* 36 (July 1929): 241. For similar suggestions of a lack of progress by decade's end, see T. Arnold Hill, "The Present Status of Negro Labor," *Opportunity* 7 (May 1929): 144–5.

CONSIDERING THE RELATIVE POSITION OF THE NEGRO AND MEXICAN WORKER

Not surprising, given Johnson's training with Robert Park as well as the changing demographics of the work force, the NUL was not satisfied with looking solely at black-white relations. When Johnson turned his attention to workplace race relations in Los Angeles, he found further evidence of the malleability of interracial labor relations. In part to debunk myths concerning black workers' suitability for particular occupations, Johnson drew attention to the diversity of occupations where black workers found work, including railway, management, and manufacturing occupations.[79] Better relations between white and black employees partially accounted for greater opportunities. According to Johnson, despite "understandable" and "well founded" employer fears of friction between black and white laborers, little disorder occurred in firms with a mixed work force. Johnson noted with some surprise, "No outstanding instance of racial disorder resulting from the use of Negro and white labor in the same plants came to the attention of this study."[80] In plants with an interracial work force, Johnson found evidence that the objection to black workers "is not a permanent or deeply serious contingency" and "further evidence that the objection has faded after a short period of contact."[81]

For advocates of racial justice for African Americans such as Johnson, constructing an argument that confronted white worker and union racism was relatively straightforward, but the analysis became considerably more complicated when a third or forth racial group was introduced into the mix. Looking comparatively at the experiences of a diverse working class, Johnson identified similarities in the experiences of black and Mexican workers who struggled to break into skilled occupations. In addition to obstacles posed by racism, Johnson attributed the difficulty these two groups of workers faced in gaining employment in skilled occupations in part to a lack of "industrial background." "Like the Southern Negroes," Mexican workers in California "have been agricultural," he explained.[82]

But lack of industrial experience told only part of the story. Johnson took great interest in examining how the addition of large numbers of

---

[79] Charles S. Johnson, *Industrial Survey of the Negro Population of Los Angeles* (no publisher, 1926), 41; Charles S. Johnson, "Negro Workers in Los Angeles Industries," *Opportunity* 6 (August 1928): 235; and "Instincts in Industry," *Opportunity* 5 (June 1927): 158.
[80] Johnson, "Negro Workers in Los Angeles Industries," 238.
[81] Johnson, *Industrial Survey of the Negro Population of Los Angeles*, 36.
[82] Ibid., 29.

Asian, Mexican immigrant, and Mexican American workers led to further variability in the drawing of the color line. It appeared to Johnson, for instance, that in iron, steel, brick, clay, and gas manufacturing, Mexicans greatly outnumbered African Americans, while in railroad work and public service, blacks outnumbered Mexicans.[83] Johnson found that the relationships among white, Mexican, and black workers varied radically across plants and firms. He reported, "White workers in one plant have demanded Mexicans and in another refused to work with them; insisted on separate lavatories in plants and accepted unsegregated ones in others; objected to Mexicans in one place and accepted Negroes in another."[84]

Johnson did not work alone in wrestling with these issues. At this critical juncture, as both populations were in flux, there was an active process of evaluating the position of each group relative to the other. While there was certainly evidence of white workers' resistance in the West to working alongside Mexican workers, the widespread and virulent grassroots resistance that had become so obvious in white attacks on black workers and residents in East St. Louis, Chicago, and in other locations of race riots was not present. In fact, some investigators suggested, sometimes very subtly but at times not, the Mexican and Mexican American experience of workplace discrimination in the United States was quite distinct from that of black Americans. For instance, in observing increased confusion over race issues in Texas as the population of Mexicans increased dramatically, sociologist and economist Max Sylvannus Handman – another PhD from the University of Chicago – succinctly observed, "The theory that the Mexican is a white man is receiving its acid test." Although Handman noted that the United States had no experience in handling nonwhite peoples as "anything but a subordinated or isolated group," he also recognized that Mexicans, in the treatment they received and demanded, were distinct from African Americans and becoming more so as they increasingly put down roots.[85]

Taylor and Gamio, too, wrestled with the comparability of the Mexican experience with that of earlier European immigrants and black Americans. When it came to finding a comparative immigrant experience in residential

[83] Ibid. and Johnson, "Negro Workers in Los Angeles Industries," 234–40.
[84] Ibid., 238. For further examples, see Johnson, *Industrial Survey of the Negro Population of Los Angeles*, 45–6. Charles S. Johnson, *The Negro in American Civilization: A Study of Negro Life and Race Relations in the Light of Social Research* (New York: Henry Holt and Company, 1930): 78–9.
[85] Max Sylvannus Handman, "The Mexican Immigrant in Texas," *NCSW* (1926): 336; Max Sylvannus Handman, "The Mexican Immigrant in Texas," *Southwestern Political and Social Science Quarterly* 8 (1926): 334.

patterns, Taylor concluded that while Mexicans and Americans occupied the same "natural geographic area," the "race-class-culture line of separation" for Mexicans made the African American experience, rather than the Northern European, a more apt comparison.[86] For Gamio, however, skin color, low pay, and a tradition of subservience among the class of Mexicans who came to the United States assured that they would remain in the "lowest American social strata," with the exception of African Americans. Gamio noted, "It should be recognized ... that the race prejudice which exists toward the Mexican has never been so pronounced or exaggerated as that felt toward the Negro."[87]

Experts on both the Mexican and Negro problem, then, had to decide to what degree they wanted to emphasize commonalities and differences between these two groups of workers who were just then entering industry in significant numbers. This, to put it mildly, was a tricky business. Both groups made the case for assimilation and all recognized major changes in the demographics of the labor force, but they struggled with how to depict the progress of one group relative to the other. To be sure, the evidence on this question was mixed and there was no consensus even within studies. For instance, Taylor's painstaking multivolume study, *Mexican Labor in the United States*, contained a close analysis of relations among black, white, white-ethnic, and Mexican workers that stressed variability in these relationships depending on region, workplace, management, and makeup of the work force, among other factors. Such variability left the general characterization of these relationships open to interpretation.

Whereas Johnson emphasized malleability and variation in race relations over time and space, some experts on Mexican immigrant and Mexican American workers suggested that while these workers felt the brunt of white worker racism, they had experienced considerably less resistance than black Americans in integrating white workplaces and neighborhoods, and in many cases themselves felt racial antipathy toward black workers. Describing a divergence from the African

---

[86] Paul S. Taylor, *Mexican Labor in the United States: Imperial Valley* (Berkeley: University of California Press, 1928), 83.

[87] Manuel Gamio, *Mexican Immigration to the United States: A Study of Human Immigration and Adjustment* (Chicago: University of Chicago Press, 1931; reprint New York: Dover Publications, Inc., 1971), 156. Taylor, too, found evidence to suggest that there was less racial prejudice directed at Mexican relative to black workers. Paul S. Taylor, *Mexican Labor in the United States: Chicago and the Calumet Region*, University of California Publications in Economics, vol. 7, no. 2 (Berkeley: University of California Press, 1932), 109.

American experience in Northern housing, Taylor – writing now for a broader audience in *Survey Graphic* – found less segregation in Northern cities than in the Southwest. Taylor noted that Mexicans in the Midwest and East lived in neighborhoods either abandoned or currently occupied by European immigrants. Contrasting what he had encountered in the Southwest, Taylor concluded that Mexican workers' housing "reflects the position Mexicans themselves hold among the other immigrants in northern industry; it is less distinctive and less isolated than that which, as members of *la raza*, they occupy in the Southwest."[88] J. Blaine Gwin of the Associated Charities in El Paso and the American Red Cross noted that while Mexicans "tend to congregate in sections by themselves," these "sections are not so closely defined as the sections where the colored race is found."[89]

The effort to distinguish between the reception of Mexicans/Mexican Americans and African Americans extended to the workplace. Gwin described less racial antipathy toward Mexican workers, suggesting, "Nowhere has the race question been raised where Mexicans work side by side with other peoples."[90] In his examination of the Imperial Valley, Taylor further noted "a dislike which Mexicans profess to living among colored people."[91] Though he had no sympathy for either African Americans or Mexican Americans, Congressman Slayden too described a "jealousy and dislike" between these groups brought on in part due to classification of Mexicans as white in Southern states.[92]

On the issue of Mexican workers replacing or succeeding black workers in industry, uncertainty reigned, but the stakes and investigators' interest were unquestionably high. If black workers could be shown moving into more skilled positions as Mexican workers entered the workplace, then Johnson and others could point to industrial progress for black Americans, who were taking the next step toward assimilation. But if Mexican workers were supplanting black workers in industry, that case

---

[88] Paul S. Taylor, "Mexicans North of the Rio Grande," *Survey Graphic* LXVI (May 1, 1931): 197, 200.
[89] J. B. Gwin, "Social Problems of Our Mexican Population," *NCSW* (1926): 331.
[90] Ibid., 330.
[91] Taylor, *Mexican Labor in the United States Imperial Valley*, 23. Taylor would find corroborating evidence to support this point. See Paul S. Taylor, *Mexican Labor in the United States: Bethlehem, Pennsylvania*, University of California Publications in Economics, vol. 7 no. 6 (Berkeley: University of California Press, 1931), 17; Paul S. Taylor, *An American Mexican Frontier* (Chapel Hill: University of North Carolina Press, 1934).
[92] Slayden, "Some Observations on Mexican Immigration," 124.

would be more difficult to make. Indeed, Johnson pointed to the former phenomenon, noting that Mexican workers were taking jobs in regions abandoned by white and black farmers or industrial jobs first taken up by black migrants during the war. According to Johnson, "As yet there is but little actual competition, the Mexicans taking the least desirable jobs, pushing up Negroes one grade as the Negroes in turn pushed up the foreign born, who in turn pushed up the native whites."[93] Taylor concurred in general but with some significant qualifications. He found that between World War I and 1928, the situation varied among industries and as a result of company recruitment strategies, but that there was evidence of Mexicans replacing black workers. The more significant and larger trend, however, was in the dramatic increase in the proportion of black and Mexican workers in industries like steel and meatpacking. The overall trend, Taylor concluded, suggested that it was "clearly the 'whites' who have been replaced during this longer period."[94]

A closer look at the work of Johnson, Taylor, and others reveals an even more complicated and significant story concerning interracial and ethnic relations in industry. Advocates for black and Mexican workers could take comfort in evidence suggesting that traditional patterns of immigration and assimilation had trumped racism in industry. But there was evidence of a more troubling scenario that suggested competition for entry-level positions between Mexican and black workers. Roden Fuller, for instance, found a "gradual displacement of Negro labor by Mexican labor in the main occupations open to both throughout" Texas, New Mexico, and Arizona.[95] Handman added that the "displacement of the Negro by the Mexican on railroad construction is proceeding at a rapid pace."[96] The *Kansas City Advocate*, an African American newspaper, was more blunt, warning that the increasing presence of Mexican cotton pickers constituted a "permanent menace to Negro cotton hands, who are used to American standards of living."[97] After years of hearings assessing

---

[93] Johnson, *The Negro in American Civilization*, 37; Charles S. Johnson, "Some Economic Aspects of Negro Migration," *Opportunity* 5 (October 1927): 297–9.

[94] Paul S. Taylor, "Some Aspects of Mexican Immigration," *JPE* 38 (October 1930): 615; Paul S. Taylor, *Mexican Labor in the United States* (Berkeley: University of California Press, 1931), 48.

[95] Roden Fuller, "Occupations of the Mexican-Born Population of Texas, New Mexico, and Arizona, 1900–1920," *JASA* 23 (March 1928): 66. For similar – though often inconclusive – sentiments, see Handman, "The Mexican Immigrant in Texas," 335–6; Hill, "The Negro in Industry," 52.

[96] Handman, "The Mexican Immigrant in Texas," 336.

[97] "Mexican Labor Menaces Negro Cotton Pickers," *Kansas City Advocate*, January 1, 1926, 7; [untitled editorial], *Western Outlook*, February 25, 1928, 4.

the impact of Mexican immigration to the United States, Congressman Albert Johnson concurred: "Evidence showed that where the Mexican competes with the American negro, the latter is invariably the loser."[98] In a chilling finding that must have alarmed Johnson, he too described employers in cities with a large Mexican population who believed that black workers could perform satisfactorily if given a chance, but who also, since white workers refused to work with African Americans, found it more convenient to hire Mexicans instead.[99] As the doors to immigrants closed during the 1920s, the possibility that black and Mexican workers could be sequestered at the bottom of American industry competing for the most meager of wages and opportunities surely troubled advocates for racial justice.

REMAKING THE PUBLIC IMAGE OF THE MEXICAN PROBLEM

If the relative progress of black and Mexican workers posed a dilemma for experts and advocates of each of these groups, there was unquestioned agreement on the efficacy of using new expertise and knowledge as a means of attacking long-held and racist stereotypes. As in the case of black workers, many of whom also came from rural and farming backgrounds, one of the first tasks was to debunk the idea that Mexicans lacked the ability and aspiration to move out of unskilled manual labor. Taylor and others drew on employers' testimonials and aggregate occupational data to make this point. For instance, at Bethlehem Steel, President Eugene Grace described recently arrived Mexican workers as "doing better than expected"; while most were working as unskilled laborers, "some have done so well that they have been advanced."[100] Grace reported to the *New York Times* that the company had found the twenty-five hundred Mexican workers it employed in the wake of the shift to the eight-hour day to be "desirable workers."[101] Others joined Taylor in emphasizing the upward mobility of Mexican workers. Robert McLean of the Board of National Missions in Los Angeles boldly proclaimed that the "Mexican

---

[98] House Committee on Immigration and Naturalization, *Immigration from Countries of the Western Hemisphere*, 4.
[99] Johnson, "Negro Workers in Los Angeles Industries," 239. See also Ira De A. Reid, "Negro Life on the Western Front," *Opportunity* 7 (September 1929): 275. See also David R. Roediger and Elizabeth D. Esch, *The Production of Difference: Race and the Management of Labor in U.S. History* (Oxford: Oxford University Press, 2012), particularly 170–204.
[100] Taylor, *Mexican Labor in the United States, Volume II*, 13.
[101] "Steel Wage to Rise as Hours Decrease," *NYT*, July 27, 1923, 15.

is the Atlas who holds upon his broad shoulders the industrial world in the Southwest."[102] Gwin further undermined the stereotypes of Mexican workers, adding that they had "shown ability to develop as skilled workmen if given time and patient instruction."[103]

Few stereotypes of the Mexican worker came under more consistent skepticism than the hard-to-kill "homing" thesis. Agricultural interests were deeply invested in the myth that Mexican workers automatically and reliably returned to Mexico, which justified the openness of the border. But they were not alone in this concern. As the congressional discussion referenced in this chapter's introduction suggests, many white Americans were vexed by the implications for American racial identity if still another dark-skinned group were allowed to settle in the United States and eventually claim full rights of citizenship. Undeterred, Taylor and others developed a two-pronged attack that aimed, first, to describe the Mexican problem as a national concern, and, second, to demonstrate the folly of voluntary or coercive efforts to eradicate an ethnic Mexican population from the United States in light of the powerful internal and external factors inviting them into the country.

Like the DNE and Johnson, Taylor and others demonstrated repeatedly that the Mexican problem was a national rather than merely a regional concern. Echoing the case made by the DNE concerning the nationalization of race issues, Taylor detailed the tremendous increase in the number of Mexican workers in Northern industry and compared the migration of Mexican workers to the Great Migration. "In the long run," he concluded, "there is probably about as much, but no more, reason to regard the Mexican population as confined to a region than the Negro population."[104] In reporting his investigation of the Imperial Valley during the spring and summer of 1927, Taylor described a settled and permanent Mexican population that was "vastly more important numerically than the group which crosses the line for seasonal work ... and of infinitely greater social significance to the Unites States, for these are becoming a permanent part of the culture of the valley."[105] Along these same lines and earlier than most, Ernestine M. Alvarado of the New York YWCA argued strongly as early as 1920 for greater integration of Mexican immigrants into the social, economic, and educational fabric of the nation. According

---

[102] Robert McLean, "Mexican Workers in the United States," *NCSW* (1929): 536.
[103] Gwin, "Social Problems of Our Mexican Population," 329, 330.
[104] Taylor, "Some Aspects of Mexican Immigration," 612.
[105] Taylor, *Mexican Labor in the United States*, 19.

to Alvarado, Mexicans workers would be a "very useful element" in the "social life and prosperity of the nation," if only unions, workers, schools, and employers would treat them and their children fairly.[106]

Similar to the NUL's strategy of using organized labor to undermine any understanding of the labor question that did not include African Americans, advocates for Mexican workers worked to diversify the labor question by attacking the homing myth. As early as 1921, Gwin argued that coercive mechanisms to force Mexican immigrants to return had almost entirely failed and that "no one knows where" more than 20 percent of the workers admitted to the United States under wartime measures were. Preliminary estimates by the American Consul at Chihuahua suggested that only 50 percent of those who migrated ever returned and, more broadly, that more peaceful conditions in Mexico had "no effect" on immigration to the United States.[107] Addressing the NCSW in 1929, McLean spoke about the "pious hope" that, left alone, the Mexican problem would take care of itself as Mexicans returned to Mexico. Specifically addressing the congressional hearings concerning the Box and Harris bills, McLean described interviews with Mexican workers who not only planned to stay in the United States as a result of their children's preference and the higher wages available, but who overwhelmingly supported immigration restrictions to prevent further competition from new Mexican immigrants. McLean concluded, "The roots of our Mexican population are down too deep in our social and economic soil to permit of the possibility of a return."[108] California Department of Industrial Relations investigator Louis Bloch's analysis of actual and reported immigration of Mexicans added that "only a very small number of Mexicans return to their native land."[109]

---

[106] Ernestine M. Alvarado, "Mexican Immigration to the United States," *NCSW* (1920): 479–80.

[107] J. B. Gwin, "Immigration along Our Southwest Border," *Annals of the American Academy of Political and Social Science* 93 (January 1921): 128, 129.

[108] McLean, "Mexican Workers in the United States," 534–5.

[109] Louis Bloch, "Facts about Mexican Immigration before and since the Quota Restriction Laws," *JASA* 24 (March 1929): 60. For a sampling of similar analyses, see Emory S. Bogardus, "The Mexican Immigrant and Segregation," *The American Journal of Sociology* 36 (July 1930): 77; Charles A. Thompson, "Mexicans – An Interpretation," *NCSW* (1928): 502; Ernest Galarza, "Life in the United States for Mexican People: The Experience of a Mexican," *NCSW* (1929), 399–404; Glenn E. Hoover, "Our Mexican Immigrants," *Foreign Affairs* (October 1929): 3–4; Secretary of Labor James J. Davis to Senator William J. Harris, December 28, 1928, File 23 Migration Study Box 13, Paul S. Taylor Papers, Bancroft Library Manuscripts Division; and Taylor, *Mexican Labor in the United States: Bethlehem, Pennsylvania*, 23–4.

Challenges to the homing thesis had an effect, even in Congress. When S. M. Nixon, a representative of southeastern Texas farmers, argued before the House Committee on Immigration and Naturalization in 1926 that "Mexicans go south when the cold weather sets in," the chair of the committee was skeptical. Drawing on recently concluded investigations by the Department of Labor, Chairman Albert Johnson challenged Nixon's assertion, noting that "of those who came in legally for the fiscal year ending last July, only a small proportion went back."[110] Testimony before the Committee on Immigration and Naturalization in 1929 led Johnson to conclude on behalf of the committee that the assertion that "most of the Mexicans coming to the United States returned to Mexico after temporary, seasonal employment" could not be "sustained" given recent evidence of these workers' consistent employment in Chicago, Indiana, Pennsylvania, "and elsewhere far removed from the southern border."[111]

Investigators' increased attention to the expectations and aspirations of the children of Mexican immigrants also helped to undermine traditional understandings of Mexicans and Mexican Americans while pointing to injustices against them that made citizenship in the United States impossible and, in some respects, undesirable from the point of view of the migrant. The work of sociologist Emory Bogardus provides an excellent example of this shift in thinking. Like Johnson, Bogardus earned his PhD in sociology under Park at Chicago. He moved to the University of Southern California in 1911 and in 1915 established a sociology department, and five years later, a school of social work. Bogardus's work pointed to the occurrence under way of a generational shift within the Mexican American community. Earlier generations of immigrants had maintained a cultural if not a physical tie to their homeland based on frequent return to Mexico in some cases and on a cultural nationalism born of ethnic pride and obstacles to gaining the full rights of American citizenship. In the 1920s, however, a second generation of American-born Mexican Americans wrestled with a more braided identity. Echoing to a degree the Chicago "ethnic cycle" model of assimilation, Bogardus argued that this generation "is no longer satisfied with his parental culture; he feels himself a part of the United States and would like to be accepted as such."

[110] House Committee on Immigration and Naturalization, *Seasonal Agricultural Laborers from Mexico*, 45.
[111] House Committee on Immigration and Naturalization, *Immigration from Countries of the Western Hemisphere*, 3–4.

Rejecting antiquated and pedestrian conceptions of the Mexican problem and, like Johnson, pointing to the constructed nature of the color line, Bogardus argued against faith in the ephemeral nature of a Mexican presence in the United States and for an understanding of the Mexican American experience that paralleled Du Bois's description of dual identity. According to Bogardus, "To be American-born of intelligent Mexican parents and to be versed in American culture, but at the same time to be viewed as Mexican, a 'foreigner.' And sometimes unjustly to be called a 'dirty greaser' causes the second generation Mexican to lose faith in us and in our country, even in humanity."[112] Bogardus used American racism itself to explain why some Mexican migrants had less interest in citizenship. Comparing the experience of U.S. citizens in Mexico with that of Mexicans in the United States, Bogardus reasoned that rejecting citizenship in one's native land would lead to one less layer of protection: "By remaining a citizen of Mexico and by calling on the Mexican consul for assistance the Mexican immigrant often can secure justice, whereas if he becomes an American citizen, he feels helpless."[113]

Some reviewers of Taylor's SSRC studies expressed frustration with his failure to develop a clear hypothesis to go along with the voluminous data he had collected, but by the end of the decade Taylor, joined by a cadre of new voices on Mexican workers, published a number of articles that undermined the foundation of 1920s assumptions about Mexican immigration.[114] The May 1931 edition of *Survey Graphic*, titled "Mexicans in Our Midst: Newest and Oldest Settlers of the Southwest," featured a mix of social science and cultural celebration that – though certainly not as consistently laudatory of Mexican culture and its contribution to American life – echoed the magazine's celebration of the Harlem Renaissance in its March 1925 edition edited by Alain Locke and Johnson. The 1931 edition brought together the leading experts, including

---

[112] Emory S. Bogardus, "Second Generation Mexicans," *Sociology and Social Research* 13 (January 1929): 276–83. Emory S. Bogardus, "The Mexican Immigrant and Segregation," 74–80. For a more skeptical view of Bogardus than I have presented, see Sanchez, *Becoming Mexican American*, 97, 101.

[113] Bogardus, "The Mexican Immigrant and Segregation," 78. For more on the relationship between conditions in the United States and the desire for citizenship, see the investigation conducted for the Interchurch World Movement by G. Bromley Oxnam and summarized in G. Bromley Oxnam, "The Mexican in Los Angeles from the Standpoint of the Religious Forces of the City," *Annals of the American Academy of Political and Social Science* 93 (January 1921): 130–3.

[114] For one such review, see Walther T. Watson, "Mexican Labor in the United States: Dimmit County, Winter Garden District, South Texas," *The American Journal of Sociology* 37 (September 1931): 312–13.

McLean, Taylor, and Gamio as well as an extraordinarily talented group of artists, including Diego Rivera, Jose Clemente Orozco, Ansel E. Adams, and Georgia O'Keeffe. The volume had a reflective quality to it. This mood, Taylor suggested, was a result of the economic downturn, increased nativist sentiment, and stepped-up effort to maintain control of the border, which indicated that "the epoch of Mexican mass migration is now closed."[115] Once again rejecting the notion that the Mexican presence was, or ever had been, an ephemeral phenomenon, contributors to the volume described the many contributions ethnic Mexicans had made and were making to American economic and cultural life.

Far from lacking a clear outlook on the Mexican problem, Taylor's anchoring article systematically decimated nearly all of the restrictionist and anti restrictionist arguments concerning the status, aspirations, and abilities of Mexican workers in the United States, while at the same time underscoring the alienating impact of discrimination. Taylor drew, with hearty approval from the SSRC, on his extensive investigation to provide a broad overview of the importance of Mexican labor to American agriculture, but he also described the foothold these workers had achieved in Northern industries, including steel, packing, and automobiles. Taylor explicitly rejected the anti restrictionist case that Mexican workers were somehow only capable of agricultural labor, arguing that they "show capacities seldom attributed to them by their agricultural employers." Rather than viewing Mexican workers as somehow outside traditional immigration patterns, Taylor placed this migration stream and employment trajectory in the context of European immigrants and black migrants who entered industry first as unskilled and low-paid workers before moving into better-paying semiskilled positions. Taylor noted that most of these workers were "still on the lowest rung of the ladder, but appreciable numbers are rising to the ranks of the semi-skilled" and earning higher wages.[116]

In the field of education, Taylor explicitly argued against notions of Mexican intellectual inferiority resulting from Indian or *mestizo* lineage. Here, too, Taylor's research is suggestive of larger shifts in the analysis that clearly broke with older ideas concerning the determinative nature of race in explaining the aspirations and abilities of different racial and ethnic groups. Where other observers had attributed the slow educational

---

[115] Taylor, "Mexicans North of the Rio Grande," 205.
[116] Ibid., 140. See also Max Sylvannus Handman, "San Antonio: The Old Capital City of Mexican Life and Influence," *Survey Graphic* 19 (May 1931): 166.

progress by Mexican youth to racial inferiority, Taylor argued that "social and economic grounds," including poor schools and the need for child contributors to family wages, provided a sufficient explanation. Again and as in the NUL's analysis, this was not a story of racial inevitabilities, but of choices: in this case, the choice the larger American public had made to subsidize the price of food by paying immigrant farm workers low wages and to discriminate against Mexican youth in education. While acknowledging that the vast majority of immigrants were some combination of Indian and *mestizo*, Taylor argued that the children of these working-class immigrants had "made brilliant records in high schools and even colleges, at times ranking as valedictorians."[117] In an effort to subvert the collection of useful fictions expounded by employers who defended Mexican immigration as a way of recruiting cheap and docile laborers who had few aspirations aside from agricultural labor, Taylor quoted one landowner who lamented, "If the Mexicans learn English, they don't work so well; if they get educated a little they don't make such good farm hands."[118] As for the idea that Mexicans were inherently docile, Taylor offered up several instances of worker resistance to low wages and concluded, "The 'docility' of Mexican laborers, so frequently extolled by employers who seem to have believed them racially strike-proof, is not to be taken too literally."[119]

In many respects, Ernesto Galarza embodied themes reflected in Bogardus and Taylor's analysis of generational change. By decade's end, Galarza began to emerge as one of the most forceful and durable advocates for an understanding of the Mexican problem rooted in the experiences of Mexican immigrants. In spearheading this effort to re-represent Mexicans and Mexican Americans and to challenge received conceptions of the race, Galarza drew attention to Mexican immigrants who had already settled in the United States, their problems, and their vital economic contributions. Born in Mexico in 1905, Galarza came to California with a wave of immigrants who left Mexico during the rise of the Mexican Revolution. After graduating from Occidental College, he was awarded a scholarship to Stanford, where he earned a master's degree in political science and history. Before the National Conference of Social Work in 1929 and in the 1931 Taylor-edited *Survey*, Galarza explicitly took up the cause of articulating the Mexican problem from

---

[117] Taylor, "Mexicans North of the Rio Grande," 200–1.
[118] Ibid., 136.
[119] Ibid., 202.

the point of view of the Mexican immigrant who had already settled in the United States. Galarza argued, "Unless the Mexican immigrant in the United States is made articulate, unless his economic contribution to the development of the western United States is recognized and rewarded, unless his needs and interests are considered from his own point of view, any attempt to solve the problem will lack the most vital of all values, the human value."[120]

Galarza reasoned that the absence of an accurate understanding of Mexican workers resulted from three factors, namely disorganization, disillusionment, and consistent effort to discredit all peoples of Mexican descent. Galarza described a level of disorganization rooted in the persistent poverty that compelled Mexican workers to move frequently, inhibiting community formation. Identifying Mexicans as a disillusioned people resigned to disappointment and "without benefit of lobby," Galarza nicely evoked philosopher John Dewey in his *Survey* article, suggesting that the person of Mexican origin in the United States "is what John Dewey might call a pathetic public with its tragic problem."[121] Signaling a still more dramatic break with Gamio's racial determinism, Galarza took aim at efforts to diminish the contributions of Mexican immigrants based on their background. Frustrating assimilationist efforts, according to Galarza, was a consistent effort to paint Mexican contributions to American culture and society as "representative of a degenerate Indian stock" and somehow outside "the 'practical' spirit of the times."[122] By focusing on white Americans' efforts to resist Mexican integration, Galarza worked to repudiate and rewrite the Chicago school "ethnic cycle" model outlined by Park and Thomas. In Galarza's description, disorganization remained and persisted, but disillusionment replaced acculturation, which discrimination against Mexicans precluded.

As a young immigrant in his late twenties and early thirties, Galarza, more effectively than anyone else in the period, made conspicuous the many problems associated with the one-dimensional portrayal of the Mexican as singularly a low-skilled worker. Such an understanding was particularly problematic for the children of immigrants who occupied, according to Galarza, a "difficult borderland through which it seems that all second generation immigrants must pass." Those who had the opportunity to attend public schools rejected the hard labor taken up by their

---

[120] Galarza, "Life in the United States for Mexican People," 404.
[121] Ibid.; Ernest Galarza, "Without Benefit of Lobby," *Survey Graphic* LXVI (May 1, 1931): 181.
[122] Galarza, "Without Benefit of Lobby," 181.

parents and experienced a cooling of affinity for Mexico. Instead, and in words that echoed Alvarado's call before the NCSW in 1920 and those of experts on African Americans who made a similar effort, they embraced much that was American, but as a result of prejudice they were unable to secure a "place in the social scheme of their adopted country."[123]

CONCLUSION

Johnson's reflections on the relationship between conceptions and conduct in the chapter's epigraph suggest the importance that all of these investigators placed on the need for a body of knowledge that relied upon empirical investigation to challenge the basic ideas about race groups that helped to prop up and justify the so-called scientific racism woven into the fabric of New Era American society. Johnson summed up the significance of these efforts and the stakes if they were unsuccessful: "The riots in Washington, Atlanta, Chicago, East St. Louis, and Omaha, are striking examples of accumulated resentments, unchallenged mutual beliefs, the one race [has] about the other. If these beliefs can be made accessible for examination, there is hope that many of them may be corrected."[124]

By drawing attention to variations across industries, workplaces, and regions, these experts demonstrated that segregation, racism, and discrimination supported by bogus science were choices, not inevitabilities or conditions. The color line they described came about due to specific and alterable choices made by groups of Americans with the power to construct, and the time and will to maintain, a deeply divided nation. The nationalization of the Negro and Mexican problems aided their efforts to use knowledge and expertise as a tool for justice. Their methods were objective, but their motives were hardly scientific. If the Mexican and Negro problems could be described as regional concerns, they could easily be ignored, but when they became an American problem, the stakes were much higher for policy makers, who were beginning to ratchet up the rhetoric against the emerging Soviet threat. By drawing attention to the national injustices visited upon Mexican immigrants, Mexican Americans, and African Americans, this group of social scientists and their supporters worked in a tradition of publicizing the insupportable contradictions in American democracy and race relations that would culminate in works such as Gunnar Myrdal's 1944 epic study of American race

---

[123] Galarza, "Life in the United States for Mexican People," 402.
[124] Johnson, "Public Opinion and the Negro," 498.

relations, *American Dilemma*, which drew heavily upon such studies.[125] Indeed, the issues identified by the experts and advocates in this and the preceding two chapters informed the work of future generations of scholars and activists, who continued to draw attention to the persistence of color and gender lines, the recalcitrance of unions, and the links between labor rights and civil rights.[126]

Investigators and advocates of women, Mexicans Americans, and African Americans experienced less success in their effort to diversify the labor question so that it more accurately reflected the experience of these quite "real workers." This failure was clear to the experts and advocates. For instance, before the SSRC's annual Hanover Conference in August 1928, Will Alexander argued that given African Americans' place in industry, "any study of the American labor problems must take this element into consideration." Unfortunately, he lamented, "Up to the present time, this has not been done to a large extent."[127] As described in the introduction to this volume, this failure came with dire and enduring consequences well into the twentieth century, ranging from the discrimination embedded in the Fair Labor Standards Act and the Wagner Act to the uneven implementation of the Social Security Act that tilted hard in the favor of white men.

In the end, however, these efforts were also meant to pose a challenge to all Americans, and in doing so they fit nicely into the long history of the civil rights movement. In an address before the New York State Conference of Charities and Corrections in 1925, Eugene Kinckle Jones summed it up nicely: "We are engaged in America in an experiment of national life which at present is an example to the rest of the world. We have made great strides forward in handling most all of the social problems we face. Probably we have made less progress in solving the problem of race contacts than in any other direction." Then, in language that linked Abraham Lincoln and Frederick Douglass's challenge to America

---

[125] For a recent analysis of Myrdal's approach and significance, see Alice O'Connor, *Social Science For What?: Philanthropy and the Social Question in a World Turned Rightside Up* (New York: Russell Sage Foundation, 2007), 66–70.

[126] On the long civil rights movement, see, among the many recent examples, Zaragosa Vargas, *Labor Rights Are Civil Rights: Mexican American Workers in Twentieth-Century America* (Princeton: Princeton University Press, 2005) and Dorothy Sue Cobble, *The Other Women's Movement* (Princeton: Princeton University Press, 2004).

[127] "Social Science Research Council, Hanover Conference," page 196, Folder 1894, Box 330, Series 5, SSRC Collection, RAC. For a similar, more recent observation concerning agricultural proletariat who in New Deal legislation were excluded "from the legal definition of 'worker,'" see Ngai, *Impossible Subjects*, 136.

in the nineteenth century to the modern civil rights movement, Jones tied the civil rights struggle to the survival of American democracy in a way that would have resonated with Anderson, Van Kleeck, Galarza, and others in this period: "The opportunity for statesmanship service to humanity is ours. The obligation is ours. We cannot pass on to posterity the responsibility for work which we should assume. The challenge of democracy is before us. The Negro is probably the real test of democracy in America. Shall this democracy endure?"[128]

[128] Jones, "Negro Migration in New York State," 11.

Conclusion

Production has eliminated the more acute tensions associated with inequality. And it has become evident to conservatives and liberals alike that increasing aggregate output is an alternative to redistribution.
– John Kenneth Galbraith, *The Affluent Society* (1958)[1]

If the greatest free nation in the history of mankind has to get down on its knees in fear of something as abstract and as arbitrary as these so-called free-market forces, well then, we're through. We might just as well haul down the flag, lock up the Capitol, go home, and admit that we don't have the courage or the imagination to govern ourselves.
– Hubert Humphrey (1976)[2]

On December 3, 1929, E. E. Hunt addressed the American Society of Mechanical Engineers concerning *Recent Economic Changes*. Hunt adopted a more tempered tone than he had in June of that year when he contemplated the opening of the cornerstone of the soon to be constructed Commerce Building. In this December speech, Hunt embraced the past decade's "higher standard of living," increases in "productivity and buying power," and "balance of production and consumption." But with an eye on the speculative bubble that had burst on Wall Street less than two months prior, Hunt tempered claims that a "new era" had been achieved and clearly saw the emerging crisis as a testing ground for Herbert Hoover's philosophy and policies. He returned again and again

---

[1] John Kenneth Galbraith, *The Affluent Society: 40th Anniversary Edition* (New York: Houghton Mifflin Company, 1998), 80.

[2] Cited in Jefferson Cowie, "The Ghost of Full Employment," *American Prospect*, September 29, 2010. http://www.prospect.org/cs/articles?article=the_ghost_of_full_employment.

in the address to the question of "economic balance," even suggesting that the national economy could be pictured as "one of the common playthings of childhood – a seesaw."

The seesaw is never still. Forces on both sides of the balance are always changing, so that one end of the beam is tipping a little bit up and the other a little bit down at any given moment. Yet there may be a rough equilibrium if the forces acting on the two ends of the beam are so directed as to neutralize each other. The delicate balance may be preserved if we know what the forces are and how they may be controlled.

Hunt did not specify the parties at either end of the seesaw, if he had any in mind at all, but his list of threats to this economic balance were long and timeless – speculation, waste, price manipulation, ignorance of economic principles, selfish greed, inadequate leadership, and "the perils of a disregard of the common interest by either labor or management." Hunt's tone suggested both a quiet confidence and a sense of unease. He noted a marked moderation in the business cycle since the post–World War I recession and attributed this stability to "certain countervailing tendencies" developed in the 1920s, including a new emphasis on conservation, waste elimination, and economic stabilization. Concerning the unfolding crisis, Hunt praised President Hoover's "prompt" and "revolutionary" efforts in 1929 to intervene in the economy in order to "counteract the effects of a dip in the business cycle by the stimulation of private and public construction, by the maintenance of general buying power, and by the preservation of industrial peace."[3]

An examination of this speech and the New Era more generally invites many comparisons to what came before and after. Recently, many observers have noted similarities between the twenties and events and choices that led up to the current Great Recession. Indeed, there are some important parallels, particularly when we consider issues such as increasing income inequality, crisis in the banking and financial sectors, stock speculation, the housing market, and a general overriding sense that – as Carmen M. Reinhardt and Kenneth S. Rogoff have described the periods preceding both crises – "this time is different."[4] While recognizing the importance of these observations and comparisons, *American Labor and*

---

[3] E. E. Hunt, "Economic Changes in 1929," *Mechanical Engineering* 52 (February 1931): 105–6.
[4] Carmen M. Reinhart and Kenneth S. Rogoff, *This Time is Different: Eight Centuries of Financial Folly* (Princeton: Princeton University Press, 2009).

Economic Citizenship argues that an understanding of the New Era is important for other reasons as well.

In the New Era, we can see a powerful new vision of capitalism taking hold, one quite different from the capitalism of the late nineteenth and early twentieth century. This transformation was not primarily the product of some form of unintended or less-than-conscious evolution. The tumultuous period surrounding World War I both coincided with and helped precipitate the convening of an intellectually and institutionally diverse group of highly trained experts, investigators, and reformers who moved confidently forward against the most vexing of public problems. They worked sometimes together, occasionally at cross purposes, and at times in ways that seemed disconnected entirely from each other. They took up an ambitious range of issues and problems woven deeply into the fabric of U.S. history and the nation's most enduring political-economic discourse. They queried how best to order the economy, what constitutes a fair society, who is entitled to the full rights of American economic citizenship, and what expectations Americans of varied backgrounds can, should, and do have of the U.S. version of capitalism.

These long-debated issues took on new relevance in light of the violent labor and race conflict, demographic change, and economic instability surrounding World War I. But as the decade unfolded, deliberation on these questions increasingly took place on a terrain quite different from that of the war era, one characterized by rising real wages, relative labor peace, and unevenly shared but still quite significant prosperity. Under these circumstances, New Era strategies for managing the economy had, many believed, ushered in a new form of capitalism that answered the labor question by replacing long-standing concerns centered on the problematic relationship between economic concentration and democracy with a new vision of a highly productive and expanding consumer-driven economy. Simultaneously, advocates for an expansion of rights to long marginalized groups exploited demographic change brought on by the war to compel a rethinking of long held, and usually deeply racist and sexist assumptions concerning African American, Mexican immigrant, Mexican American, and women workers. This convergence stimulated new thinking about the economy, informed by concerns rooted in the recent instability but hopeful that a combination of inquiry and thoughtful deliberation could bring about a more fair society.

Their efforts yielded significant and durable results. The New Era was clearly a pivotal period for the movement of consumption and growth to the center of reflection upon American culture, economic thought, and policy. During the New Era, the Hooverites worked to supplant a conflict model of labor-capital relations with one that described workers as partners in industry and, more importantly and durably, consumers eager to share in the fruits of increased productivity. The American Federation of Labor and Hoover's recognition that consumer spending was the key to stabilizing the economy became an important part of the framework for American economic policy in the New Deal and through the growth decades after. Though aspects of current economic development might vex them, Hunt, Hoover, John P. Frey, Florence Thorne, Jürgen Kuczynski, Marguerite Steinfeld, and others no doubt would have nodded in agreement at current concerns over the impact of consumer confidence and consumer spending on economic stability and national welfare. Just as significantly, they would have looked skeptically at corporate liberal claims made in the period prior to World War I that maintenance of the price system required a degree of scarcity.

Hunt, Hoover, and others worked in the New Era to replace concerns about the distribution of wealth and income with a new emphasis on the power of economic growth and consumption to address, as they might have phrased it, the "more acute tensions associated with inequality." As the Galbraith quote in the epigraph at the opening of this chapter suggests, this emphasis on expansion rather than redistribution may have gone underground in the 1930s, but it reemerged in the 1940s in ways that would have sounded quite familiar to New Era policy makers. The significance of the New Era in this process has not been fully appreciated. Historian Kathleen Donohue suggests, and Alan Brinkley seems to concur, that not until the 1940s did experts square the interests of consuming citizens with those of business. According to Donohue, "By the end of the war [World War II] most liberals had become convinced that a disciplined capitalism would provide consumers with an abundance of high-quality goods while simultaneously providing capitalists with ample profits."[5] I place this transition a generation earlier, in the New Era. Though they differed on other issues – specifically on how best to "discipline" or "balance" capitalism, as Donohue and Hunt respectively refer to it – Hoover and union advocates embraced similar visions of capitalism that emphasized the desirability of a stable but constantly growing economic system

---

[5] Kathleen G. Donohue, *Freedom from Want: American Liberalism and the Idea of the Consumer* (Baltimore: Johns Hopkins University Press, 2003), 6. Also see Alan Brinkley, *The End of Reform: New Deal Liberalism in Recession and War* (New York: Vintage Press, 1995).

where capital and labor worked in tandem to increase efficiency, profits, wages, and consumption. In failing to adequately interrogate the question of income inequality, Hoover and his followers were able to perpetuate their belief that the fruits of economic abundance were being evenly shared. Appropriately skeptical that organizations such as the Bureau of Labor Statistics and the National Bureau of Economic Research (NBER) could be trusted to produce and interpret expertise that represented the interests of American workers, the American Federation of Labor (AFL) Research Bureau and the Labor Bureau Inc. (LBI) made a concerted effort to significantly revise policymakers' knowledge in this critical area.

More than just better statistics would be needed to correct the income inequality that we now know plagued the New Era. Hunt's mention of "countervailing tendencies" tempts one to see in Hooverite thought a sort of antecedent to what John Kenneth Galbraith described in his 1952 *American Capitalism* as "countervailing powers." Galbraith's "countervailing powers" assumed the presence of competing groups – buyers and sellers broadly conceived so as to include, for example, unions, retailers, cooperatives, and producers – who had sufficient power to prevent the domination of one group over the others.[6] For Galbraith, the state, particularly in the New Deal, assisted in "the development of countervailing power," but, for Hoover, the state was a facilitator among groups of shared and common – not competing – interests.[7] Hoover assumed that, given recent economic changes, modest interventions could stabilize the "seesaw." The closest followers of Hoover held an almost unshakable belief that labor and capital shared a common interest in increasing production and consumption and that these goals could be achieved through thoughtful deliberation and investigation. If individuals or groups of workers or capitalists embraced policies in conflict with this "common interest," a public and thorough investigation would reveal the recalcitrant party and ensure an efficient and equitable resolution of the conflict. Consciously or not, the Hooverites constructed investigations and then legitimized bodies of knowledge that confirmed this understanding of the New Era economy. Particularly in the early part of the decade, the Hooverites focused most of their rhetorical and analytical attention on the production half of the "production-consumption" model. Decreasing

---

[6] John Kenneth Galbraith, *American Capitalism: The Concept of Countervailing Power* (Boston: Houghton Mifflin Company, 1956), 108–34, particularly 114–17.
[7] Ibid., 128. Galbraith described this assistance as "perhaps *the* major domestic function of government." Emphasis in original. See also ibid., 135–53.

waste in industry, advocating standardization, and promoting inter- and intra-firm and industry-wide coordination monopolized the attention of early 1920s Hooverites. This left the coordination of production with consumption up to employers, who determined what goods to produce and what wages to pay.

The Hooverites' focus for much of the New Era on the production side of things, it turned out, was a mistake. Faith that the economy had been transformed into a vehicle for producing a cornucopia of consumer goods blinded powerful Hooverites to the too-slow development of consumer goods industries and the disproportionate rewards for increased production that went to capital, rather than to the workers who were supposed to provide an "insatiable" market for goods. In his recent examination of wages and productivity, economic historian Alexander Field finds that although New Era wage earners benefited from low unemployment and access to consumer credit, "labor shared hardly at all in the very large productivity gains in manufacturing during the 1920s." It is "fair to say," Field concludes, "that capital reaped almost all of the gains from productivity growth in the 1920s."[8] If employers had increased wages in proportion to increased productivity, as the AFL urged, workers might plausibly have been able to absorb the increasing number of goods through consumption; but this would have required, first, that wages be increased accordingly and, second, as Alvin Hansen pointed out, that increased production come ever more intensely in the form of goods consumable by workers. Neither turned out to be the case, and, as Hansen warned, this spelled disaster by the end of the decade. The NBER, the most influential economic policy institution of the decade, largely ignored the issue of income inequality, and when it did consider it, as in Morris A. Copeland's work in *Recent Economic Changes*, the NBER largely got it wrong. Hooverites' important observations regarding organized labor's contribution to waste in industry blinded them to the important role unions played in forcing employers to maintain or to raise wages. Here, the leading economists and engineers that populated federal agencies and the NBER and FAES could have learned much from a careful reading of RSF, LBI, and AFL studies that demonstrated both that many workers benefited from unions' ability to push up nonunion workers' wages and that workers' earnings were not keeping up with the

---

[8] Alexander J. Fields, "Economic Growth and Recovery in the United States: 1919–1941," forthcoming in Nicholas Crafts and Peter Fearon, eds., *The Great Depression of the 1930s: Lessons for Today* (Oxford: Oxford University Press, 2013).

ability of industry to produce. Further, the Mary van Kleeck-led studies by the RSF suggested a change in the organization of firms that left less discretion to the very managers and owners who were supposed to render to labor the high wages necessary to maintain demand.

The Great Depression made clear the inadequacies of a system that relied so heavily on the discretion of employers for "balance" and "discipline." In the New Deal era, policy makers recognized that high wages were not woven into the fabric of the U.S. economy and that some statist social and economic policies and union coercion were required to ensure some approximation of a "fair" society that achieved a consumption level commensurate with the nation's rapidly expanding ability to produce goods. This critique of New Era ideas about capitalism had a long lineage reaching back most recently to Progressive Era reformers and through New Era statist liberals. In the New Era, individuals such as Van Kleeck, Mary Anderson, and Paul Douglas and organizations like the Women's Bureau and the National Urban League (NUL) hammered home the need for statist policy solutions to raise wages, improve working conditions, and break down deeply entrenched racist and sexist practices. They rejected neoclassical economists' faith that the market, absent frictions, would fairly distribute the fruits of increased productivity and efficiency. And they found the philosophical underpinnings of *Adkins* hopelessly out of date. These labor experts used their positions in academia, government, and nonprofits to call attention to the consequences of fundamental changes in the organization of industry, and to inequalities in wealth and power exacerbated by recent economic changes.

Taking advantage of dramatic demographic changes in the work force that heightened public concern, advocates and experts studying women, African American, and Mexican workers attempted to diversify the labor question in the New Era so that it more accurately captured the experiences of these groups of workers. The NUL in particular presented organized labor and the public with a clear choice: either work with us to dismantle a color line that divides Americans on the basis of race, or live with the consequences of a racially divided labor force. Aiming to correct misrepresentations, the Women's Bureau challenged outmoded and inaccurate depictions of the woman worker as an exclusively temporary entrant into the labor force and made clear that women were indeed "real workers." Taken together, these many and diverse efforts made the case that any comprehensive set of polices for reforming, as well as stabilizing, capitalism had to take into account the continued and growing importance of women and racial minorities to the American economy.

Economic growth and curbs on immigration no doubt provided opportunities for these workers. But growth alone, it was clear to this diverse group of investigators and experts, could not address the injustices faced by African American, Mexican American, and women workers. They argued instead for a more diversified understanding of economic issues that more accurately reflected the broad range of experiences and problems faced by an increasingly diverse work force. The obstacles these workers faced, they made clear, were the product of choices made by Americans with the will and the power to ensure that the nation remained divided. Racism and sexism were choices made in the present and could not be excused or papered over with worn-out ideas about the "condition" of a race or the proper place of women. Only forthright action by the larger public along with labor organizations, business, and the state could ameliorate these public, national, and increasingly international concerns. By drawing attention to the national injustices visited upon African American, Mexican American, and women workers, these experts helped establish a tradition of publicizing the insupportable contradictions in American democracy and race relations that would continue in the postwar era in the work of social scientists such as Gunnar Myrdal who, along with others, drew heavily on this New Era work. This effort to expose racist and discriminatory practices, as Mary Dudziak has demonstrated, took on new relevance from the Truman to Johnson administrations when the Negro problem, in particular, became an international as well as domestic concern.[9] Advocates such as Ernesto Galarza, who first gained standing in the New Era, would continue to mix inquiry and activism to make the case for Mexican immigrant and Mexican American rights well into the 1960s.[10]

Though these efforts would undeniably prove useful in forcing Americans to address racial and gender inequality in later decades, the failure to diversify the labor question in the New Era had devastating consequences in the form of New Deal policies that, as Ira Katznelson and others have demonstrated, provided far more robust benefits for white, male workers than they did for women and racial minorities.[11] The

---

[9] Mary Dudziak, *Cold War Civil Rights: Race and the Image of American Democracy* (Princeton: Princeton University Press, 2002).

[10] Galarza's works are many, but see in particular Ernesto Galarza, *Merchants of Labor: The Mexican Bracero Story* (San Jose: Rosicrucian Press, 1964) and *Barrio Boy* (Notre Dame: University of Notre Dame Press, 1971).

[11] Ira Katznelson, *When Affirmative Action Was White: An Untold History of Racial Inequality in Twentieth Century America* (New York: W. W. Norton and Company, 2005).

state largely turned a deaf ear to the plight of these more marginalized workers, but the story is quite different when it came to organized labor, particularly as it concerns African American workers. The increasing presence and activism of black workers in industry combined with persistent attacks on unions by organizations like the NUL did bear fruit in the 1930s. Though the color line persisted, as did violent tension between black and white workers, the CIO and other unions did explicitly recognize the necessity of making a concerted effort to reach out to minority workers and the organizations, like the NUL and NAACP, that purported to represent them. Similarly, the campaign for labor standards yielded tangible results in part because organized labor came to support intervention in the labor market in unprecedented ways through the Social Security Act, Fair Labor Standards Act, and Wagner Act.

A slightly different story emerges concerning the legacy of New Era expertise on the conditions of Mexican immigrant and Mexican American workers. The successful effort by Taylor and others to undermine the stereotype of the Mexican worker as a temporary entrant into the labor force, and indeed the nation, had mixed consequences. A growing recognition of the increasing numbers and permanent residence of Mexican and Mexican American workers in the United States created opportunities to make claims on the rights of American citizenship, but it also led to increasing calls for greater vigilance in securing the U.S. border with Mexico. When the "Mexicans in our midst," to use *The Survey*'s description, had been understood as only temporary sojourners taking on the most difficult and dangerous work in the Southwest, Congress took relatively modest steps, despite the cries of Congressman Box and others that it do more. The combination of the hard times brought on by the Great Depression and the erosion of this earlier depiction of the Mexican worker, however, led to increasing calls for some method of controlling, if not eliminating through deportation, this segment of the labor force. In the early 1930s, the Mexican problem did indeed become a national and public concern, but the results were pernicious, including the often indiscriminate and at times violent repatriation of more than four hundred thousand Mexicans and Mexican Americans.

Finally, an examination of the New Era helps us to better understand both continuities in the period from the New Era through the post–World War II period and the significance of dramatic changes in the political economy of the United States rooted in economic policy and thought since the 1970s. The recognition of a need to align growing productivity with consumption provides the continuity. What W. W. Rostow termed the "age of high mass consumption" and others called the "golden era of capitalism," between roughly 1948 and 1973, witnessed productivity and wage gains moving largely in tandem – an impressive achievement that served consumers and producers well.[12] In the 1920s, productivity, particularly in manufacturing, increased dramatically. Cars rolled off the assembly lines from single-storied factories in unprecedented numbers, factory floors were reorganized to take advantage of increasing access to electricity, and various appliances increasingly made their way into American homes.[13] As Field has demonstrated, these productivity improvements in the manufacturing sector in the twenties anticipated more across-the-board improvements in the thirties. According to Field, the "golden age of U.S. productivity growth" between 1948 and 1973 "can be seen as a period reflecting the extension and persistence of trends and technological foundations established during the interwar period."[14] Given what we now know about these dramatic productivity gains in manufacturing, it is less surprising that in the New Era a near consensus emerged that the continuation of the decade's prosperity rested on the "balance between production and consumption." The effort to balance productivity gains with wage increases was a significant innovation in economic thought and policy and one that – along with relatively high rates of unionization, continued improvements in productivity, U.S. manufacturing dominance, increasing international financial stability, Cold War era government spending, and the unleashing of consumer demand pent up by World War II, among other factors – contributed to the nearly three decades of economic growth and rising household income that followed World War II. The problem, as the Great Depression in part demonstrated, and New Deal and Keynesian economic policy worked to correct, turned on finding the most effective and fair mechanism for maintaining demand.

The New Era and New Deal periods share a common belief that something needed to be done to align consumption with production. Advocates for policies that squared production and consumption came, eventually, to embrace a more central role for the state in these efforts. For instance, by 1945, AFL president William Green – who in the New

---

[12] W. W. Rostow, *The Stages of Economic Growth: A Non-Communist Manifesto* (Cambridge: Cambridge University Press, 1960) and Robert L Heilbroner and Wilberg, *The Making of Economic Society, Thirteenth Edition* (Boston: Pearson, 2012), 122–37.
[13] Alexander J. Field, *A Great Leap Forward: 1930s Depression and U.S. Economic Growth* (New Haven: Yale University Press, 2011), 44–8.
[14] Ibid., 106.

Era had argued against government involvement in the determination of wages – embraced federal government policies for guaranteeing "the maintenance of a high national income ... [and] equilibrium between producing and consuming power."[15] For Green and the AFL in particular, this was a significant departure from organized labor's rejection of statist labor policies proposed in the New Era by the Women's Bureau and Paul Douglas. But when situated in the context of organized labor's relatively sophisticated efforts to square production and consumption in the New Era, this shift might be better characterized as an adjustment in method in order to achieve a shared goal identified in the twenties by politicians, policy makers, and union and business leaders.

Such philosophical continuity between the New Era and New Deal should give pause to anyone who might want to draw clear parallels between the New Era and the period since the 1970s. Central to New Era economic thinking was this idea that a balance should be achieved between "production and consumption." Hoover and his allies' methodology for achieving this result now appears wildly naïve, but the idea that not only should production and consumption be squared but that policy makers should do something – though they could and did disagree about the means – to ensure that it did, seems quite distant today. Beginning in the 1970s, as Daniel Rodgers has recently observed, policy makers increasingly came to embrace the idea of "the market" as the most appropriate method of allocating resources and distributing production. "The term 'market'" in the last quarter of the twentieth century, Rodgers persuasively argues, came to stand for "a way of thinking about society with a myriad of self-generated actions for its engine and optimization as its natural and spontaneous outcome."[16] The New Era was a time of prosperity and increased opportunity on many fronts for Americans of varied backgrounds, but as the nation stumbled out of World War I, few would have cast their lot with something as abstract and chaotic as "the market." As Hunt said in December 1930, evoking a child's seesaw, "[T]here may be a rough equilibrium if the forces acting on the two ends of the beam are so directed as to neutralize each other. The delicate balance may be preserved if we know what the forces are and how they may

---

[15] Brinkley, *End of Reform*, 224; Fink, *Progressive Intellectuals and the Dilemmas of Democratic Commitment*, 102. Original William Green, "Protecting Our American System of Freedom: If I Were an Industrial Manager," *Vital Speeches of the Day*, January 15, 1945.

[16] Daniel Rodgers, *Age of Fracture* (Cambridge: Belknap Press of Harvard University, 2011), 41.

be controlled."[17] Since the 1970s, concern for sustaining a middle class and its consumption function in the United States has been exchanged for the argument that U.S. wages have to be competitive with those of workers offshore, and that unions and work rules were the causes of U.S. job loss. The divergence since the 1970s in productivity and wages, along with the rapid increase in income and wealth inequality, would seem to argue against ceding so much power in maintaining a balanced economy to the idea of the market.

---

[17] Hunt, "Economic Changes in 1929," 105.

Archival Sources and Abbreviations

Bancroft Library, University of California at Berkeley
    Paul S. Taylor Papers
    Ernesto Gamio Papers
Catholic University
Department of Labor Library
Department of Commerce Library
George Meany Memorial Archives (GMMA)
Herbert Hoover Presidential Library, West Branch, Iowa (HHPL)
    Pre-Commerce Period, 1895–1921
    Commerce Period, 1921–1928
    Campaign and Transition Period, 1928–1929
    Presidential Period, 1929–1933
    Special Collections, 1750–Present
    Durand, Edward Dana, 1906–1959
    Gompers, Samuel: Collection, 1917–1924
    Hinsdale, Lester J.: Collection, 1895–1934
    Hunt, Edward Eyre: Collection, 1904–1959
Manuscript Division, Library of Congress, Washington, DC (LOC)
    American Federation of Labor Records
    Brotherhood of Sleeping Car Porters Papers
    Otto S. Beyer Papers
    Stuart Chase Papers
    James J. Davis Papers
    Felix Frankfurter Papers
    John P. Frey Papers
    Arthur H. Gleason Papers
    National Association for the Advancement of Colored Peoples Papers
    National Consumers League Papers
    National Urban League Papers

National Trade Union League of America Papers
A. Phillip Randolph Papers
Rockefeller Archive Center, Sleepy Hollow, New York (RAC)
    General Education Board Archives (1901–1964)
    Laura Spelman Rockefeller Memorial Archives (1918–1930)
    Rockefeller Foundation Archives, 1910 (1912–2000)
    Russell Sage Foundation Records, 1885 (1907–1982)
    Social Science Research Council Archives (1924–1990)
    Leonard Outwaite Papers (1929–1977)
    Raymond B. Fosdick Papers, (1919–1934) –1951
Sophia Smith Collection, Smith College, Northampton, Massachusetts
    Mary van Kleeck Papers, 1883–1972 (MKV Papers)
Howard University
    E. Franklin Frazier Papers
    Mary Church Terrell Papers
National Archives at College Park College Park, MD (NA)
    Record Group 29. Bureau of the Census (RG 29)
    Record Group 40. General Records of the Department of Commerce (RG 40)
    Record Group 73. Records of the President's Organization on Unemployment Relief, 1928–1933 (RG 73)
    Record Group 86. Women's Bureau (RG 86)
    Record Group 174. General Records of the Department of Labor (RG 174)
    Record Group 257. Bureau of Labor Statistics (RG 257)
State Historical Society of Wisconsin, Madison, Wisconsin (WSHS)
    American Federation of Labor Papers
    David Saposs Papers

Index

Page numbers followed by an "f" indicate a figure. Page numbers followed by a "t" indicate a table.

Abbott, Edith, 259, 262n28
Achinstein, Asher, 96
activism, gender and race research as, 32
Adkins v. Children's Hospital, 15, 29, 99, 208, 212, 301
Advisory Committee on Interracial Relations, 260n21, 262n28
Advisory Committee on the American Negro, 260n21
The Affluent Society (Galbraith), 8
AFL. *See* American Federation of Labor (AFL)
agricultural industry, 33, 200, 256, 265, 285
Alchon, Guy, 25, 27, 115
Alexander, Will, 293
Alford, L.P., 70
Alvarado, Ernestine, M,, 285–6
American Association for Labor Legislation (AALL), 47, 51, 54–5, 118
American Clothing Workers, 147
American Dilemma (Myrdal), 292–3
American Economic Association, 98, 104, 106, 132
American Federation of Labor (AFL): black workers and, 276–8; brain drain in, 116; consumer economics in relation to, 9; indexes of, 134–5; relations with intellectuals, 130;
Metal Trades Department, 89; at National Industrial Conference, 39; purpose of, 111; Research Bureaus, 27, 120, 122, 299; relations with research organizations, 118–119; relations with Rockefeller, 67n101; on social wages, 126; wage policy of, 126; wage theory of, 114, 115; on women workers, 181–2
American Federationist, 120, 133, 276
American Statistical Association meeting, 1928, 112–13
Anderson, Elmer, 272n56
Anderson, Mary: background of, 193; on black women, 200; leadership of, 199; legacy of, 294; on wages, 206; at the WD, 187
The Annalist, 55
assimilation, 219, 258
"associational state," 27
Atterbury, W.W, 121f, 148, 149f
automobile industry, 114, 117, 138

Bagnall, Robert, 223
Baker, Paula, 186n15
Baltimore and Ohio Railroad Company (B&O) experiment: benefits of, 146–8, 151; cartoon about, 149f; development of, 145; implementation of, 146; opposition to, 148–50;

origin and purpose of, 141–2; significance of, 154, 178; Willard at, 144–5
Bankers' Trust Co. of New York City, 88
Barnett, George, 100, 103
Bass, George, 190
Benson, Susan Porter, 162
Berle, Adolf, 160
Bernstein, Michael, 65, 106n82
Berridge, William A., 69
Best, Ethel, 192
Bethlehem Steel, 254
Beyer, Otto S., 122, 143–8
BIIS. *See* Bureau of Immigration and Immigration Service (BIIS)
black inferiority, ideology of, 33, 220, 243, 246
black women workers: census data on, 222; efforts to unionize, 245; in industry, 203–4t; Kelly on, 273; in manufacturing, 200, 208; occupations of, 201, 202; unions and, 245; WB's relations with, 198–200
The Black Worker (Harris and Spero), 269
black workers: assimilation of, 219; attitudes toward, 216, 217, 220–1, 242–4; census data on, 221–2; conditions of, 218, 226; demand for, 217; Frey on, 278; industries of, 280; Mexican workers compared to, 236, 279–84; migration of, 216; mobility of, 272; occupations of, 273; organizing of, 250; representation of, 216; as strike breakers, 277; relations with unions, 244–5, 303; white workers compared to, 235–6; women compared to, 220. *See also* black women workers; "Negro problem"
Bleachery Life, 166
Bloch, Louis, 286
Board of Management at Dutchess Bleachery, 166–7
Board of Operatives at Dutchess Bleachery, 166
Bogardus, Emory, 266, 287–8
boot and shoe industry, 61
Box, John C., 256, 257
Brinkley, Alan, 8, 298
Brinton, Daniel G., 220
Brissenden, Paul, 102n71
Brock, William, 205
Brookwood Labor College, 122, 129

building trades, 73–4, 142, 143
Bureau of Census (BOC), 221, 241
Bureau of Immigration and Immigration Service (BIIS): NBER in relation to, 67; on organized labor, 62–4; under Stewart, 58–9; on strikes, 61; on wages and hours, 61–4; on workday issues, 60–1. *See also* immigration and immigrants, Mexican
Bureau of Labor Statistics (BLS): makeover of, 82; *Report on the Condition of Women and Child Wage-Earners*, 188; statistics of, 89–90; wage data of, 58–64, 85–7; on wages, 83
business cycle problem. *See* economic stability and instability
Business Cycles and Unemployment, 68

Cabot Fund, 51
capitalism. *See* New Era economy and economics
Carnegie, Andrew, 37, 267
Carr, Elma B., 90, 95–6
Carter, Elmer Anderson, 272n56
Carver, Thomas Nixon, 155n2, 254
Catchings, Waddill, 130, 131, 132–3
Census Bureau, 221, 241
Central Trades Labor Union, 223
change index for prices, 86
Chase, Stuart, 122
Chicago Commission on Race Relations: on black women, 242–3; funding for, 239–40; members, 241; report of, 242–6; significance of, 218, 246–7
Chicago Daily News, 274
Chicago Defender, 228, 237, 239, 240
Children's Bureau, 187, 188, 194
CIO (Committee of Industrial Organizations), 19, 303
Clark, John Bates, 80–1, 131
Clark, John Maurice, 79, 97–8, 99, 100
Clinton, William J., 36
Cobble, Dorothy Sue, 186
Cohen, Joseph L., 102
Cohen, Lizabeth, 3n6, 20
Collins, Robert, 7
Colorado Fuel and Iron Company plan and study: benefits of, 173; cartoon about, 177 f 4.1; nature of, 172–3; origin of, 171–2; response to, 176–7f; results of, 173–5, 178–9; significance of, 175
Committee on Education and Labor, 40

Index

Committee on Elimination of Waste in Industry, 43
Committee on Immigration and Naturalization, 255, 287
Committee on Industrial Relations, 262n28
Committee on Problems and Policy, 262n28
Committee on Women's Work, 156
Commons, John R., 86, 112, 161
Commonwealth Steel, 50
comparative ethnic studies, 279-284
Conference of Charities and Corrections, 293
conflict model labor relations: nature of, 40; prevalence of, 35-6; shift away from, 114-15, 298; under Wilson, 38
construction industry, 73-4, 142, 143
Consumer Price Index (CPI), 89-90
consumers and consumption: AFL in relation to, 9; attitudes toward, 75; Hunt on, 1; impact on New Era, 297-8; legacy of, 304-5; production and, 8, 30; purchasing power of, 72, 127-9, 135; rise in, 3-4; role of, 9; underconsumption, 116n5; wages in relation to, 10; workers as, 115. *See also* economic growth; production and productivity
Consumers' League of Ohio, 208-9
Cooperative League, 163
cooperative management plan at B&O: benefits of, 146-8, 151; cartoon about, 149f; development of, 145; implementation of, 146; opposition to, 148-50; origin of, 141-4
cooperative management plans: B&O, 141-51; Colorado Fuel and Iron Company's, 171-8; Dutchess Bleachery's, 166-7; Filene's, 168-71
Copeland, Morris A., 72, 300
corporate liberalism, 27-8
corporate vs. proprietary capitalism, 13
corporatism, voluntary. *See* voluntary corporatism
cost of living: calculation of, 84-5; data, 88, 95-6, 118; index, 135; studies on, 95-7; wages linked to, 126-7
cotton mill study of the Women's Bureau, 213

Council of Economic Advisors (CEA), 113, 153
craft unions, 236, 276, 277
Crisis, 4, 248, 268
Cunningham, William J., 70-1
Currarino, Roseanne, 17

Dabney, Thomas L., 277
Daily Worker, 150
Davis, James J., 30, 35, 56-8
Davis, Westmoreland, 208
democracy in relation to industry, 16-17, 162, 297
Democratic Party, 255n12
demographic changes, impact of, 253-4, 255
Dennison, Henry, 74, 112
Department of Labor (DOL): Dillard at, 225-6; Hooverites in relation to, 56-7; *Monthly Labor Review*, 158; relations with NUL, 259; role of, 39; Women's Division, 188. *See also* Division of Negro Economics (DNE); Women's Bureau (WB)
Dewey, John, 1, 2-3, 26, 291
diffusion of management, 159-60
Dillard, James H., 225-8
discrimination. *See* Equal Rights Amendment; labor standards for women; racism and racial discrimination
Distribution of Wealth (Clark), 80-1
diversification of the labor question: alliances for, 214; failure in, 293; legacy of, 302; need for, 16-17, 182; results of, 17
Division of Industrial Studies, 156
Division of Negro Economics (DNE): characteristics of, 231-2; Congress on, 15-16; end of, 34, 239, 240, 259; funding for, 236-7; Haynes studies, 234-6; origin and purpose of, 33, 218, 229-30, 232; relations with other agencies, 232; significance of, 246; staff of, 231; success of, 17-18; support for, 190; relations with WB, 199, 238. *See also* Great Migration; Haynes, George E.; "Negro problem"
DOL. *See* Department of Labor (DOL)
domestic work, 200, 201-2
a domestication of a public policy, 186n15
Donohue, Kathleen, 8-9, 109n92

Dorsey, Hugh Manson, 223
Doten, Carroll Warren, 47
Douglas, Paul: background of, 92; critics of, 93–4, 103; on NICB and BLS, 90; on productivity, 112; on standard of living, 104–5; on unemployment insurance, 19; on unions, 107–8; *Wages and the Family*, 100; on wages and wage policy, 29, 30, 79, 91, 97; on women workers, 20, 182; on workers, 110
Drury, Horace B., 48, 51, 52, 53
Du Bois W.E.B., 4, 230–1, 270, 273
Dubofsky, Melvyn, 40, 57
Dunlop, John, 44
Durand, Dana, 152
Dutchess Bleachery experiment, 163–7

East St. Louis riots, 227
economic growth: consumption in relation to, 75; ideology of, 29–30; immigration and, 302; postwar, 112–13; power of, 298–9; and prosperity, 28. *See also* production and productivity
economic stability and instability: AFL in relation to, 9; black women in relation to, 198; *Business Cycles and Unemployment*, 68–9; characteristics of, 3–4; Hunt on, 296; solutions for, 115–16; threats to, 296; wages linked to, 127–9, 132–3, 134, 135
economic stagnation, 80
Economics of Overhead Costs (Clark), 98–9
Edgeworth, F.Y., 87
Edmunds, G.H., 229n43
education of mexican workers, 289–90
eight hour day. *See* workday issues
Eighteenth Amendment, 16, 250, 274
Electric Alloy Steel Company, 50
Emergency Fleet Corporation, 89
employee representation programs. *See* cooperative management plans
employment stability, 62n88
Engel, Sadie, 165
Equal Rights Amendment, 187
European immigrants, 18, 266
Evans, Clark, 122
Evans, Glendower, 95
expertise and investigation, the use of: Dewey on, 1, 2–3; Haynes on, 216; historical aspects of, 5–6; institutionalization of, 111; legacy of, 302, 303; origin and purpose of, 48–9; role in New Era, 14–15; significance of, 246, 284, 292–3. *See also* research bureaus

Facts for Workers, 123–4, 125, 127
Fair Labor Standards Act, 116, 303
Fairchild, Henry Pratt, 84–5
family allowance system, 101, 102–3
Faulkner, R.P., 112
Federal Public Health Service (FPHS), 49
federalism and the Women's Bureau, 205
Federated American Engineering Societies, 42–6, 51–2
Feis, Herbert, 124
feminism, social justice, 182
Field, Alexander, 11, 300, 304
Fifteenth Amendment, 274–5
Filene department store: characteristics of, 162, 163, 164; FCA of, 168–9, 170, 171n50; Filene, A.L., 171n50; Filene, E.A., 35, 162–3, 168, 171; study of, 165–6, 168–71
Final Report of the Committee on Scientific Problems of Human Migration (Wissler), 260n22
Fischer, Irving, 86, 94
Ford, Henry, 114, 117
Fordism, 114
Foster, William T., 130, 131, 132–4
Fourteenth Amendment, 16, 29, 257
Frazier, E. Franklin, 273
freedom of contract doctrine, 99, 109
Frey, John: alliances of, 131; on black workers, 278; career of, 130; at NBER, 66–7; on wages, 76
Frisselle, S.P., 256, 263
Fuller, Roden, 283
Furner, Mary, 22, 29

Galarza, Ernesto: on immigrants, 23, 249; legacy of, 294, 302; on Mexican problem, 21, 290; significance of, 291
Galbraith, John Kenneth, 8, 295, 299
Gamio, Mario: compared ethnic studies of, 280–1; on "homing myth," 286–7; significance of, 266; at SSRC, 259; SSRC studies of, 260
Garner Print Works and Bleachery (GPWB), 163

Index

Gary, Elbert H., 49, 50–1, 54, 119, 121f
Gay, Edwin E., 64, 73
GEB (General Education Board) of the Rockefeller Foundation, 225
gender and race issues compared, 32, 220, 252
gender and wages, 61–2
gender research as activism. *See* Women's Bureau (WB); Women's Bureau research
General Electric Company, 272
Gilbrath, Mrs. Frank G., 193n36
Glenn, John, 13
Goldmark, Josephine, 48, 49
Gompers, Samuel, 67n101, 120, 129
Goodrich, James P., 207
Grace, Eugene G., 254, 284
Great Merger Movement, 28
Great Migration: causes of, 218, 226, 227; Dillard study of, 225–8; DNE in relation to, 18; impact of, 216–17, 219–20, 276–8; response to, 222–3; role of unions, 245; Ross study of, 260; SSRC study of, 259; statistics on on wages, 4; Trotter on, 250n2. *See also* Chicago Commission on Race Relations
Great Recession, 296
Green, William, 120, 122, 141, 278, 304, 305
Gregg, James E., 225
Gries, John, 73–4
Grossman, James R., 268
Gwin, J. Blaine, 282, 285

Habermas, Jürgen, 5n14
Hall, Charles E., 221, 223–4
Handman, Max Sylvannus, 280, 283
Hanover Conference (1928), 18, 255n12, 293
Hansen, Alvin: on changing workforce, 116; on production, 13; on productivity, 300; on wage increases, 105–6; on wages, 79–80, 93–4, 104; on wages and prices, 92n35
Harding, Warren, and Harding administration, 6, 42, 50, 52, 56
Haristoy, M. Just, 154, 155
Harris, Abram, 269–70
Harris, Alice Kessler, 182, 184
Hart, David, 36
Hawley, Ellis, 9, 26–7, 28

Haynes, Elizabeth Ross, 201, 202n72
Haynes, George E.: on 1919 riots, 234; background of, 232–3; dissertation of, 233–4; on DNE, 229, 236–8; DNE studies of, 234–6; on knowledge, 216; at National Interracial Conference, 269; significance of, 247; van Kleeck in relation to, 199, 269
"high-wage doctrine," 77
Hill, T. Arnold, 272, 276–7
Hoffman, Frederick L., 220
"homing myth," 285–9
Hoover, Herbert: at 2nd Industrial Conference, 40–1; capitalism of, 37–8; DNE and, 237; in FAES, 42; governance of, 36; on immigration, 254; on individualism, 26; labor relations views, 41; NBER in relation to, 65–6; relations with NUL, 267n40; time capsule of, 1; on workday issues, 50. *See also* New Era economy and economics; *Recent Economic Changes (REC)*
Hooverites: characteristics of, 26, 37–8, 75–7; "Hoovering" by, 35n2; relations with NBER, 68; Populists compared to, 7–8; significance of, 299–300; supporters of, 76; use of expertise and investigations, 55–6; vision of, 13–14
Hopkins, Mary D., 49
Horner, R.H., 59
housing discrimination, 274
Humphrey, Hubert, 295
Hunt, E. E.: on African American representation in government, 237; on Davis, 57; on depression, 152; DNE and, 237; on expertise, 23; on "Hoovering," 35n2; on market forces, 305–6; on NBER, 66; on *Recent Economic Changes*, 1–2, 69, 70, 295; on wages, 125
Hyde, Elizabeth A, 192

immigration and immigrants, Mexican: agricultural industry on, 33, 256, 265, 285; attitudes toward, 251, 255; children of, 287, 290, 291–2; citizenship for, 266; European immigrants compared to, 18, 266; Galarza on, 249; "homing myth" re:, 285–9; impact of, 253–4; increase in, 254; *New York Times* on, 254;

public health concern re:, 257n16; restrictionists, 263–4; in RSF studies, 164; SSRC studies of, 259–60, 261. See also Mexican and Mexican American workers; Mexican problem; Taylor, Paul S.
income inequity: adjusting, 72; Hooverites and, 299; Hooverites on, 298; increase in, 306; NBER and, 300; recognition of, 11–12
indexes: AFL's, 134–6; CPI, 89–90; *The Making and Using of Index Numbers*, 87; significance of, 87n21
industrial relations plans, 156–9. See also cooperative management plans
industrial waste, 41–7
inquiry and investigation, use of. See expertise and investigation, the use of
insurance, social, 102
International Association of Machinists, 143–4
International Brotherhood of Electrical Workers, 244–5
International Molders Journal, 130
International Typographical Union (ITU), 125
interracial relations studies, 279–84
Irish Colts, 4
Irvin, Helen, 199, 201, 238
"It's Great to be a Problem" (Work), 248

J. Walter Thompson Company, 135n65
Jacobs, Meg, 8, 13, 116n5, 126, 153n127
Jeanes, Anna T., 225
Jennifer, William, 223–4
Johnson, Albert, 255, 284, 287
Johnson, Charles S.: on assimilation, 219; background of, 240–1; career of, 272n56; compared ethnic studies of, 279, 281, 283; Du Bois compared to, 270, 273; *Negro in American Civilization*, 260; at NUL, 267; on *Opportunity*, 271; on preconceptions, 249, 251; on race and gender, 220; on race relations, 242; significance of, 33, 218, 247; on use of expertise, 292; relations with van Vleeck, 251n4
Johnston, William H., 143–4
Jones, Eugene Kinckle, 271–2, 293–4
Jones, F.W., 84–5

Jones, William N., 268
Jordan, Virgil, 91
Journal of Electrical Workers and Operators (JEWO), 119, 148, 149f, 176
Journal of Negro History, 221
Justice, 177 f 4.1

Kadel, Kathryn Jane, 262
Kansas City Advocate, 283
Katznelson, Ira, 302
Kazin, Michael, 143
Kelly, William V., 273
Kennedy, Joseph, 220
Kenyon, William S., 41, 190
Kessler-Harris, Alice, 20, 110n93, 182, 184
Keynes, John Maynard and Keynesian economic policy, 8, 13, 80, 304
Kimball, Dexter S., 73
King, Mackenzie, 162, 172, 174, 176
King, Wilford, 72, 86
Kuczynski, Jürgen, 122, 127n39, 135, 139, 141–4
Kuhn, Thomas, 5
Kuznets, Simon, 12

La Dame, Mary, 164, 168–9
Labor Age, 111, 121f
Labor Bureau Inc. (LBI): activities of, 105, 123–4; labor's share studies of, 137–8; origin and purpose of, 122; origin of, 115; on profits, 139–41; role of, 120; significance of, 299; on waste in industry, 43
Labor Herald, 150
labor management cooperation. See cooperative management plans
labor shortage, 3
labor standards for women: advocacy for, 183; alliances for, 205–6; analysis of, 186; enforcement of, 209; legislation for, 208–11. See also Women's Bureau (WB)
labor's share index, 134–6
labor's share studies, 137–8
Lagemann, Ellen Condliffee, 224–5
Laidler, Harry W, 154, 160
Lamberson, Francis, 91, 93–4
Lauck, Jett, 20n37, 152, 153, 158–9, 161
Laura Spelman Rockefeller Memorial (LSRM): leadership of, 269n48; on

NBER, 66; relations with NUL, 267; on NUL, 269, 271; Outhwaite at, 18; on race relations, 249
League for Industrial Democracy, 160
Leavell, R.H., 226
legislation, 94–5, 100, 109. *See also* labor standards for women
Lever, E.J., 150
Lewis, David Levering, 268
Lewis, John L., 278
liberalism, corporate, 27–8
liberalism, statist, 29
Linder, Marc, 127n39
Lindsay, Samuel McCune, 50
Livingston, James, 80, 108
Lloyd, Henry Demarest, 58
Locomotive Engineers Journal, 128, 150
Lowden, Frank O., 240, 241
lumber industry, 137
lynchings, 274
Lynd, Robert and Helen, 23, 117, 263

MacGregor, D.H., 102–3
Machinists' Monthly Journal, 128, 171, 176
Machinists' Union, 244–5
Magazine on Wall Street, 76
The Making and Using of Index Numbers, 87
Manning, Carol, 192–3
marginal productivity theory, 113, 131
"market," the term of, 305
Marshall, Alfred, 87
Marx, Karl, 127n39
maternalism, 186n15
McDowell, Mary, 277
McGoun, A.F., 12
McKay, Claude, 4
McLean, Robert, 286
McWilliams, Carey, 251–2
Means, Gardiner, 160
Meeker, Royal, 82, 85, 87, 103
metal trades, 150n120
Metal Trades Employers Association, 101
Mexican and Mexican American workers: advocates for, 19; in agriculture, 33–4; attitudes toward, 264–6; black workers compared to, 279–84; European immigrants compared to, 18, 280–1; industries of, 280. *See also* immigration and immigrants, Mexican; Taylor, Paul S.

Mexican Labor in the United States (Taylor), 281
"Mexican problem": attitudes toward, 284–5; Galarza on, 290–1; legacy of research on, 303; linked to "Negro problem," 18, 253, 254–5, 259–60; McWilliams' research on, 251–2; nationalization of, 249–50, 285, 292; solutions to, 250. *See also* immigration and immigrants, Mexican
Michel, Sonya, 184
Middletown (Lynd), 117
Miller, Kelly, 241, 277
Mills, Frederick, 71–2
Milnes, Nora, 102n71
minimum wage: enforcement of, 209–10; freedom of contract in relation to, 109; legislation, 94–5; support for, 100, 102. *See also* wage determination; wages
Mitchell, Wesley: *Business Cycles and Unemployment*, 68; Hoover in relation to, 65; *The Making and Using of Index Numbers*, 87; on NBER, 67; NBER and, 64, 65, 81–2; opponents of, 88; on REC, 69; on research, 251; role in New Era, 9; Rubinow in relation to, 78; significance of, 30; on statistics, 82, 85
The Modern Corporation and Private Property (Means and Berle), 160
Money, 132
Money Illusion (Fischer), 94
Monthly Labor Review, 87, 158, 180, 192
Morgan, J.P., 121f
Morris, Andrew, 21
Moynihan, Daniel Patrick, 273
Muir, Allison, 272
Muncy, Robin, 188
Muste, A.J., 117, 129
Myrdal, Gunner, 244, 292–3, 302

National Association for the Advancement of Colored People (NAACP), 19, 223, 235, 268, 274, 303
National Association of Manufacturers, 114
National Bureau of Economic Research (NBER): relations with DOL, 27; financing of, 66–7; on income distribution, 72; Mitchell at, 81–2; origin and purpose of, 64–5, 67;

REC, 73–4; reports by, 67–8; significance of, 39; weaknesses of, 300
National Conference on Social Work (NCSW), 21, 252
National Consumers League (NCL), 212
The National Income and its Purchasing Power, 72
National Industrial Conference Board (NICB): BLS compared to, 90–1; in cartoon, 121f; Faulkner at, 112; origin of, 39; statistics of, 88; on wages, 206
National Interracial Conference, 260n21, 269
National Manufacturers Association Committees, 121f
National Urban League (NUL): on 12-hour day, 54–5; budget of, 267; relations with CIO, 278; relations with DOL, 259; Johnson at, 242; legacy of, 302; nature of, 271–2; on "Negro Problem," 250; relations with non-profits, 267–70; research department of, 267, 272; role in "Negro problem," 259; significance of, 301; relations with unions, 18; on white workers, 16. *See also* Johnson, Charles S.; *Opportunity*
National Urban League studies: purpose of, 271; results of, 272–3, 274–6, 279; on unions, 276–8
National War Labor Board (NWLB), 118
National Women's Party (NWP), 186, 206, 210
NBER. *See* National Bureau of Economic Research (NBER)
NCL (National Consumers League), 212
The Negro at Work in New York City (Haynes), 233
Negro in American Civilization (Johnson), 260
Negro Migration During the War (Scott), 241
Negro Population: 1790–1915 (Census Bureau), 241
"Negro problem": experts on, 217; funding for, 246, 247; Johnson, A. on, 255; linked to "Mexican problem," 253, 254–5, 259–60; nationalization of, 18, 216, 247, 249–50, 292; *NYT* on, 4; solutions to, 250, 274–6. *See also* Division of Negro Economics (DNE); Great Migration; Johnson, Charles
Neil, Charles, 188, 193n36
neoclassical economics, 12, 88, 113
new capitalism. *See* New Era economy and economics
New Deal era, 8, 301, 304–5
New Era economy and economics: challenges to, 14–16; characteristics of, 2, 6–7; Great recession compared to, 296; Laidler on, 154; leaders of, 9; legacy of, 29, 298; nature of, 36, 75; New Deal compared to, 304–5; origin of, 6–7; proprietary capitalism in relation to, 12, 13; significance of, 297–306; van Kleeck on, 154–5, 178–9. *See also* consumers and consumption; economic growth; Hooverites
New Republic, 117, 189, 205
New York Times (NYT): on Chicago Commission report, 246; on immigration, 254, 265; on Mexican workers, 284; on "Negro problem," 4; on Women's Bureau, 184
NICB. *See* National Industrial Conference Board (NICB)
Nixon, S.M., 287
non-profit and philanthropic organizations: DNE in relation to, 239, 240; at Filene's, 162; government study in relation to, 24–5; NUL's relations with, 267–70; in race and ethnicity research, 252; in race relations studies, 218–19, 224; role of, 7; role on "Negro problem," 258–9, 267–9; significance of, 269. *See also* Russell Sage Foundation (RSF); Social Science Research Council (SSRC)
North From Mexico (McWilliams), 251n4
NWP (National Women's Party), 210
NYT. *See New York Times* (NYT)

O'Connor, Alice, 21
O'Donnell, I.D., 257
Ogburn, William Fielding, 24
Olney, Martha, 10
Opportunity: on 18th Amendment, 275; on AFL, 277; Ovington on, 268; purpose of, 270–1; on research, 246; on unions, 278; van Kleeck in, 32

organized labor. *See* unions
Outhwaite, Leonard, 18
overhead costs linked to labor, 98
Ovington, Mary, 268

Paper Trade Journal, 35, 74
Park, Robert E., 219, 239, 261–2
Paul, Alice, 210–11
Persons, William M., 92
Peterson, Agnes L., 192
Philadelphia Daily News, 75
philanthropic and non-profit organizations. *See* non-profit and philanthropic organizations
Pidgeon, Mary Elizabeth, 203
"Pin Money Fallacy," 196
Pittsburgh Survey, 47, 161
Poggi, Gianfranco, 5
Pollak Foundation for Economics, 130
Populist movement, 255n12
Populists compared to Hooverites, 7–8
Pound, Ezra, 2
Press Assistants Union, 141
price data, 86
production and productivity: consumption and, 9, 30; Galbraith on, 8; indexes, 134–5; marginal productivity theory, 113, 131; standard of living linked to, 106; TFP, 11; wages linked to, 112, 113, 118, 132, 300, 304
profits: in cartoon, 121f; corporate vs. proprietary, 12; LBI studies on, 139–41; *Profits*, 132, 133; sharing of, 167; wages linked to, 108–9, 152
proprietary to corporate capitalism, shift from, 13
protective legislation for women. *See* labor standards for women
public role/concern in economic and labor issues: Clark on, 97–8, 100; Dewey and, 26; under Hoover, 37, 41, 76–7; on wages, 94–5, 97, 102, 109, 212; on workday issues, 25, 37, 47–8, 55–6
purchasing power linked to wages, 72, 127–9, 135

race and gender issues compared, 32, 220, 252
race relations, study of: compared to gender issues, 252; LSRM on, 249; origin and purpose of, 217–19; Trotter on, 250n2. *See also* Chicago Commission on Race Relations
racial inferiority, ideology of, 220
racism and racial discrimination: against black women, 201–3; of blacks and Mexicans, 280; in Chicago report, 244; in housing, 274; ideologies, 220; against Mexicans, 260; remedying, 249–50; resistance to, 4; role in Great Migration, 226; of social scientists, 221; stereotypes, 221, 251, 263, 284–5; in unions, 250; by unions, 276–8; violence and, 227; WB data on, 197–8
railroad industry, 141–7
Railway Clerk, 147–8
real wages: Douglas on, 104–5; Kuczynski on, 151–2; purpose of, 30; rise in, 10
Rebellion in the Labor Unions (S. Selekman), 165
Recent Economic Changes (REC) (NBER): Copeland in, 300; Hunt on, 1–2, 70, 295–6; production-consumption in, 27; response to, 69, 70; significance of, 67, 71, 73–4
redbaiting, 114, 129, 130
Redfield, Robert, 259, 260, 261–2
Reed, Ellery, 209
Reinhardt, Carmen, 296
Reisler, Mark, 264
Report on the Condition of Women and Child Wage-Earners, 83, 188
research bureaus: AFL's, 115, 120, 122; cartoon about, 121f 3.1; expansion of, 182–3; *Facts for Workers*, 123; ITU's, 125n31; NUL's, 272; origin of, 119–20; role of, 120; studies by, 137
Richardson, Helen, 262n28
riots, 33, 218, 227, 234, 274
Roberts, Kenneth, 264n33
Robinson, Mary V., 193
Rockefeller, John D., 67n101, 162, 225, 267n40
Rockefeller plan. *See* Colorado Fuel and Iron Company plan
Rogers, Daniel, 114, 305
Rogers, Sam L., 221
Rogoff, Kenneth S., 296
Rorty, M.C., 66
Ross, Dorothy, 22, 24
Ross, Frank, 260
Rostow, W.W., 303–4

rubber industry, 137
Rubinow, Isaac, 78, 81, 83, 94–5
Ruml, Beardsley, 69
Russell Sage Foundation (RSF): activities of, 31; cartoon about, 177 f 4.1; John Glenn of the, 13; legacy of, 301; studies by, 160–1; van Kleeck at, 154–6. *See also* Colorado Fuel and Iron Company plan and study; Dutchess Bleachery experiment; Filene department store

Sage, Margaret Olivia, 160
Sanchez, George, 264
Sandburg, Carl, 274
Saposs, David, 122, 129n45
Saturday Evening Post, 264
Scattergood, Margaret, 138
Schlesinger, Arthur, 255n12
Scott, Emmett J., 241
Seager, Henry R., 89n27, 156
Sealander, Judith, 184, 189, 191
Second Industrial Conference, 40
secular stagnation, 80
Selekman, Ben, 163, 165
Selekman, Sylvia Kopald, 165
shareholders, 31, 155, 159–60, 170
Shields, Emma, 201, 202, 238
shift system investigations, 51–2
Shipbuilding Labor Adjustment Board (SLAB), 88–9
Silverberg, Helen, 191
Sklansky, Jeffrey, 158
Sklar, Kathryn Kish, 22, 183n8, 211
Sklar, Martin, 27–8, 80n1
SLAB (Shipbuilding Labor Adjustment board), 88–9
Slayden, James L., 266
Slichter, Sumner, 112, 116–17
Smith, Edwin E., 164–5
Social Control of Business (Clark), 100
social insurance, 102, 103
social justice feminism, 182
Social Science Research Council (SSRC): Advisory Committee on the American Negro, 260n21; immigration studies, 260–3; "Mexican problem" studies, 259–60; need for, 257; organizational structure of, 262n28; origin of, 125; purpose of, 251; Spero and, 269n48; studies of, 280–3

social sciences and scientists: activism of, 23–4; African American, 216, 218; institutions of, 22–3; *Origin of American Social Science*, 24; racist, 220–1; women, 191–3
Social Security Act, 116, 303
social wages: concept of, 126; decline in, 138; LBI on, 127; measurement of, 135; support for, 128–9
social workers, 21, 252
Soule, George: relations with AFL, 130; at LBI, 122, 123; on productivity and wages, 118; on Rockefeller, 66; on society, 1; on unions, 106; on wages, 132
Southern Workman, 236, 267–8
Spero, Sterling, 269–70
Spingarn, Joel E., 274
standard of living, 104–5, 106
Stanfield, John H., 221, 269n48
Stapleford, Thomas A., 89n28, 91n32
statist policies, 8, 29, 110, 301
Stecker, Margaret Loomis, 91
steel industry, 39, 47–51, 63. *See also* Colorado Fuel and Iron Company; U.S. Steel
Steinfeld, Marguerite, 122, 135, 139
stereotypes, racist, 221, 251, 263, 284–5
Stewart, Ethelbert, 58–9, 231
Stewart, Ira, 48
Stewart, Walter W., 138
stockholders, 31, 155, 159–60, 170
Stone, N.I., 66
strikes: BIIS on, 61; black workers in relation to, 277; rise in, 4; role in waste in industry, 47; by shipbuilders, 89; statistics on. *See* expertise and investigation, the use of; steel industry, 39; use of black women, 245
Stroughton, Bradley, 51–2, 53–4
The Structural Transformation of the Public Sphere (Habermas), 5n14
Studies in the Economics of Overhead Costs (Clark), 98
Survey Graphic: on 12-hour day, 54–5; on immigrants, 263; on Mexican problem, 290–1, 303; on Mexicans, 288; on segregation, 282; on unions, 277
Sweatt v. Painter, 262

Taylor, Frederick W., 45
Taylor, Paul S.: compared ethnic studies of, 280–2, 283; legacy of, 303; *Mexican Labor in the United States*, 281; significance of, 262–3, 266, 285, 289–90; in *Survey Graphic*, 290–1
Teague, Charles, 264
Terrell, Mary Church, 200
TFP (Total Factor Productivity), 11
The Origin of American Social Science (Ross), 24
Thomas, Norman, 167
Thompson, Sanford E., 45
Thorne, Florence, 120, 129n45
Thorp, William L., 70
Tichenor, Daniel J., 265
Total Factor Productivity (TFP), 11
trade associations, 28
transportation industries, 137
Trotter, Joe, 250n2
twelve-hour shift: attitudes toward, 49–50, 54–5; as public concern, 55–6; *The Twelve Hour Shift in Industry*, 52; at U.S. Steel, 49, 52, 60. See also workday issues
Twentieth Century Fund, 163
Typographical Journal, 125
Tyson, Francis D., 216, 225, 226, 227

underconsumption, 133–4
underwear industry, 62n88
unemployment, 10n22, 20, 68, 98–9
unions: benefits of, 300–1; BIIS on, 62–4; relations with black workers, 244–5, 250, 303; craft unions, 236, 276, 277; decline in, 76; as industry partners, 115; International Brotherhood of Electrical Workers, 244–5; ITU, 125; Machinists' Union, 244–5; management role of, 141–2; relations with NUL, 18; NUL studies on, 276–8; opposition to, 114; research departments of, 119; role in New Era, 41–2; role in wage policy, 106–7; role of, 11–12, 31, 112, 113–14; social function of, 117; UMW, 58, 172, 177f, 229n43; unemployment benefits of, 68; wage theory of, 114; in *Waste in Industry*, 45. See also American Federation of Labor (AFL); Labor Bureau Inc. (LBI)

United Mine Workers (UMW), 58, 172, 177f, 229n43
United States Employment Service (USES), 231, 232
upward mobility of workers, 201, 272, 284
U.S. Steel: 8-hour day at, 56; on 12-hour day, 49, 60; black and Mexican workers at, 254; in *The Twelve Hour Shift in Industry*, 52; workday issues, 50, 52

van Kleeck, Mary: on capitalism, 178–9; career of, 32, 155–6, 157; on Dutchess Bleachery, 167; on Filene plan, 171; on GPWB, 163–4; influence of, 193n36; relations with Johnson, 251n4; on labor standards, 211; legacy of, 294, 301; on "new capitalism," 154–5; on *Report on the Condition of Women and Child Wage-Earners*, 188; on Rockefeller plan, 175; role in Johnson study, 260n21; on RSF studies, 161; relations with Selekmans, 165n14; on stockholders, 159–60; at the WB, 187; on WB, 189–90; on women workers, 181. See also Women's Bureau research; Women's Bureau (WB)
Veblen, Thorstein, 42, 81
Vincent, Bird, 256
violence, racial: of 1947, 4; causes of, 234; riots, 33, 218, 227, 234, 274; studies of, 258; in the workplace, 3
voluntary corporatism: corporate liberalism in relation to, 27–8; Hawley in relation to, 9; under Hoover, 41; of NBER, 65; opposition to, 29; significance of, 36–7; wages and, 77; WB and, 214
voting rights, 255n12, 274, 275
Vrooman, David M., 145

wage determination: AFL on, 126; cost of living linked to, 126–7; economic stability linked to, 127–9, 132–3, 134; labor's policy, 125; labor's share studies and, 137–8; productivity linked to, 118; profits linked to, 139–40; as a public concern, 124; representation plans and, 173; theories of, 131–2

wages: AFL & LBI theories of, 115; attitudes toward, 74; BIIS on, 62–4; consumption in relation to, 10; at Dutchess Bleachery, 167; economists on, 84–5; fluctuations of, 139; gender and, 61; "high-wage doctrine," 77; inequality in, 11–12, 197–8; international aspects, 100–1; linked to productivity, 112, 113, 118, 300; measuring, 91–4; of Mexican workers, 288–90; Mills on, 71–2; Persons on, 92; policy reforms, 100–1, 102–3; as a public concern, 94–5, 97, 102, 109; real, 104–5, 151–2; rise in, 105–6; rise of, 79, 83; social, 126, 127, 128–9, 135, 138; social role of, 108; statist policies on, 110; statistics on, 85–8; unions and, 300–1; *Wages and the Family*, 100; women's, 205–6, 208–9
Wagner Act (1935), 19, 116, 303
Walsh, Carey, 259, 260n22
Washington Bee, 229
Washington, Forrest B., 231
waste in industry: definition of, 7; report on, 41–6; workers' role, 46–7
WB. *See* Women's Bureau (WB)
Weber, Max, 303
West Coast Hotel Co. v. Parrish, 214
white gangs, 4
white workers: attitudes of, 272, 273, 280; NUL on, 16; violence by, 3; wages for, 198
Wilcox, Clifford, 261
Williams, John H., 45
Williams, W.T. B., 226–7
Williard, Daniel, 144–5, 148
Wilson, Riley J., 265
Wilson, W. B., 224, 229, 236
Wilson, Woodrow, 38, 39
Winnipeg Lodge #122, 150
Winslow, Mary N., 196
Wissler, Clark, 260n22
Wolman, Leo, 68–9, 71, 73, 112, 147
Woman in Industry Service (WIS): Irvin at, 199; labor standards studies of, 207–9; origin and purpose of, 189; S. Haynes at, 201–2; significance of, 188; WB in relation to, 181n4

women workers: Committee on Women's Work, 156; demographics of, 196; Douglas on, 182; Evans on, 95; goals of, 196; occupations of, 195; perceptions of, 185. *See also* black women workers; labor standards for women
Women's Bureau research: on black women, 198–2, 203–4t; on discrimination, 197–8; historians use of, 184; *NYT* on, 184; in print media, 183–4; significance of, 211, 214–15; for states, 203–4, 207; on wages, 208–10; on workday issues, 213
Women's Bureau (WB): activism of, 15, 32, 183, 185; budget of, 194; challenges, 214; Children's Bureau compared to, 187; relation with DNE, 199; ERA and, 187; on facts, 180; historians in relation to, 185–6; origin and purpose of, 180–1, 188–90, 199–200; significance of, 187, 194–6, 200, 204–5, 252, 301; staff of, 191–3; relations with states, 205; success of, 17; support for, 190; supporters of, 182; on wages, 205–6; as Women's Division, 188
Women's Division, 188–9
Women's Trade Union League, 187, 245
Wood, L. Hollingsworth, 233, 267
Woofter, T.J., 222–3
Work, J.W., 248, 253
Work, Monroe, 268
workday issues: attitudes toward, 54–5; BIIS on, 60–4; FPHS study of, 49; Gary on, 50–1; as a public concern, 25, 37, 47–8; as public concern, 55–6; race and ethnic aspects of, 254; shift system report, 52–3; *The Twelve Hour Shift in Industry*, 52; WB on, 206; for women, 208–9
World War I era unrest, 2–6, 35–6, 82, 114, 117–18, 217
World War I postwar culture, 2–5
Wright, Carroll, 5, 83, 230

Young, Owen D., 160

Zieger, Robert, 44, 57

For EU product safety concerns, contact us at Calle de José Abascal, 56–1°, 28003 Madrid, Spain or eugpsr@cambridge.org.

www.ingramcontent.com/pod-product-compliance
Ingram Content Group UK Ltd.
Pitfield, Milton Keynes, MK11 3LW, UK
UKHW011324060825
461487UK00005B/314